D1544177

PARK RIDGE PUBLIC LIBRARY
20 S. PROSPECT
PARK RIDGE, IL 60068

THE
STRATEGIC
BOND
INVESTOR

THE STRATEGIC BOND INVESTOR

Strategies and Tools to Unlock the Power of the Bond Market

Second Edition

ANTHONY CRESCENZI

New York   Chicago   San Francisco   Lisbon
London   Madrid   Mexico City   Milan   New Delhi
San Juan   Seoul   Singapore   Sydney   Toronto

The McGraw·Hill Companies

Copyright © 2010 by The McGraw-Hill Companies, Inc. All rights reserved. Printed in the United States of America. Except as permitted under the United States Copyright Act of 1976, no part of this publication may be reproduced or distributed in any form or by any means, or stored in a database or retrieval system, without the prior written permission of the publisher.

2 3 4 5 6 7 8 9 0   DOC/DOC   1 8 7 6 5 4 3 2 1 0

ISBN 978-0-07-166731-9
MHID 0-07-166731-8

This publication is designed to provide accurate and authoritative information in regard to the subject matter covered. It is sold with the understanding that neither the author nor the publisher is engaged in rendering legal, accounting, futures/securities trading, or other professional service. If legal advice or other expert assistance is required, the services of a competent professional person should be sought.

—From a Declaration of Principles jointly adopted by a Committee of the American Bar Association and a Committee of Publishers

The views contained herein are the authors but not necessarily those of PIMCO. Such opinions are subject to change without notice. This publication has been distributed for educational purposes only and should not be considered as investment advice or a recommendation of any particular security, strategy, or investment product. Information contained herein has been obtained from sources believed to be reliable, but not guaranteed.

References to specific securities and their issuers are for illustrative purposes only and are not intended and should not be interpreted as recommendations to purchase or sell such securities. The author or PIMCO may or may not own or have owned the securities referenced, and if such securities are owned, no representation is being made that such securities will continue to be held.

Nothing contained herein is intended to constitute accounting, legal, tax, securities, or investment advice, nor an opinion regarding the appropriateness of any investment, nor a solicitation of any type. This publication contains a general discussion of the bond market; readers should be aware that all investments carry risk and may lose value. The information contained herein should not be acted upon without obtaining specific accounting, legal, tax, and investment advice from a licensed professional.

McGraw-Hill books are available at special quantity discounts to use as premiums and sales promotions, or for use in corporate training programs. To contact a representative, please e-mail us at bulksales@mcgraw-hill.com.

To my enchanting daughters, Brittany, Victoria, and Isabella.
Each of you adds immeasurable joy
and happiness to my life;
I will work all of my days with all of my might
to bring lots of smiles to your beautiful faces.
I love each of you so much.

To my nurturing parents, Anita and Joseph,
who gave me the freedom to
think creatively, explore, dream, and have fun—lots of it.
To my brother Joseph, and my sisters Theresa, Gina, and Nicole
(and Enrico!).
Gina, we love you so very much.
To all of my family and friends, to Jeffrey Miller and Jeffrey Tabak,
and to the great cities of New York and Newport Beach.

To all who, in one way or another, are survivors, and who,
despite the many
obstacles and challenges they face in their daily lives, each day find
the inner strength to endure and to excel.

To Tracey, whose beguiling eyes, vivacity, and love inspire me.

CONTENTS

Foreword by Mohamed El-Erian ix

1. The Importance of the Bond Market 1

2. The Composition and Characteristics of the Bond Market 27

3. Bond Basics: Building Blocks and Warning Labels 63

4. Types of Bonds 81

5. Risks Facing Today's Bond Investors: Asset Diversification Does Not Equal Risk Diversification 111

6. Don't Fight the Fed: The Powerful Role of the Federal Reserve 139

7. The Yield Curve: The Bond Market's Crystal Ball 175

8. Real Yields: Where Real Messages Can Be Found 197

9. The Five Tenets of Successful Interest Rate Forecasting 215

10. From Tulips to Treasuries: Tracking Market Sentiment to Forecast Market Behavior 251

11. Using the Futures Market to Gather Market Intelligence 275

12. Credit Ratings: An Essential Tool for Bond Investors 293

13. Bond Strategies 313

14. How Interest Rates Have Shaped the Political Landscape 323

15. Utilizing Economic Data to Improve Your Investment
Performance 341

Appendix. Handbook of Economic Data: Power
Tools for Investors 351

Endnotes 401

Index 403

FOREWORD

As public debt soars in many countries, the bond market is of even greater relevance to large segments of the global population. Governments are tapping the bond market in bigger and more frequent installments to cover their higher financing needs; households and corporations confront a confusing outlook for interest rates, be they borrowers or lenders; and investors are dealing with a changing configuration of risk and returns, within the bond market itself and relative to other markets.

In the midst of all this, more people are discovering a reality that has been known for years in the investment profession: the bond market is as far away from offering a single vanilla-flavor product as is a Baskin-Robbins ice cream store.

Like Baskin-Robbins, the bond market encompasses a wide—and at times bewildering—range of flavors: specifically, all types of creditors and debtors, of maturities, of structures, and of geographical jurisdictions. It blends different risk factors in interesting, and at times volatile, ways. It provides households and companies with an array of offerings, ranging from AAA bonds to highly speculative CCC junk bonds and distressed securities—domestically and internationally. And traditional fixed rate 10-year bonds coexist happily with a seemingly endless array of hybrid instruments that combine both fixed-income and equity characteristics.

Today's bond market is much more than a construct that brings together, and reconciles, a very wide range of participants with differing preferences, objectives, and risk tolerances. It is also more than a clearinghouse for a very broad range of financial instruments. More importantly and additionally, it is a significant source of forward-looking information that speaks directly to the outlook for global and national economies, sectors, companies, and households.

It is easy to be overwhelmed by all this; and it is tempting to fall hostage to the alluring attractiveness of oversimplifying the complexities of a $90 trillion global market. Don't! Such an option, while seemingly appealing, is full of peril. The world is changing rapidly in front of our eyes, and in a manner that is consequential for us and for our children and grandchildren.

My PIMCO colleague Tony Crescenzi is uniquely placed to help us all understand the twists and turns of the bond market, and what it can tell us about the outlook for the global economy. Indeed, Tony is a master when it comes to providing strategies and tools for understanding and navigating the complexities and fluidity of today's bond market.

For 20 years, Tony has been expertly dissecting daily market movements and insightfully relating them to what is happening in the world beyond bonds. In filtering through the inevitable flood of daily data releases and market chatter, Tony has shown an amazing ability to separate signals from noise. He knows what is important and what should be dismissed as irrelevant, if not misleading. As a result, he has gained enormous respect in the marketplace where he is also greatly admired for his ability to use the bond market as a forward-looking prism to shed greater visibility on the often-cloudy future of the economy and government policies.

Many of you have seen Tony on television, sharing his timely analyses and penetrating insights and opinions. He is frequently quoted in the press. Indeed, reporters repeatedly go to him for his ability to interpret data releases and relate them to the currents and crosscurrents influencing markets around the globe. And they just love his insights, as well as his time-tested ability to think outside the box.

Tony's high standing in the industry is not an accident. It has happened because of his deep expertise, outstanding credentials, and strong communication skills. No wonder my PIMCO colleagues and I feel so privileged to have daily access to Tony's brain and experience. This well-written book will illustrate to you why we, in the marketplace, all value Tony's insights so highly.

When it was first published in 2002, Tony's book was eagerly read by lots of people in the financial services industry. They went to it for remarkable insights into the role of the bond market and for valuable tools that would help them better understand developments and position portfolios. Readers recognized that Tony's book was different from other books written about the bond market, particularly because it was more comprehensive and it combined robust detailed analyses with insightful top-down perspectives.

In this new edition, Tony updates and expands the analysis that so many have already found of great value. Among the many updates, you will find a new chapter that discusses strategies that fixed-income professionals use when constructing portfolios. This supplements the many strategies and ideas that can be found throughout the book. Tony also discusses the new tools used by the Federal Reserve during the global financial crisis. Indeed, this new edition will also provide you with important perspectives on the crisis and how it will affect the economic and financial landscape going forward.

I am confident that you will find Tony's book of remarkable value to you in its ability to explain the bond market in all its complexities. I strongly believe that this updated and expanded edition is yet another important contribution in advancing our collective knowledge of the bond market; and it does so at an especially important time in the evolution of the market and its role in the global economy.

I hope that you will enjoy, and benefit from, this book as much as I have.

Mohamed El-Erian
CEO and co-CIO, PIMCO
Newport Beach, California
April 2010

1

THE IMPORTANCE OF
THE BOND MARKET

I opened the first edition of *The Strategic Bond Investor* by saying, "The bond market affects you more than you probably know." At the time, history and the facts had made this notion abundantly clear. Now, however, following an epic collapse in the financial markets rooted in the bond market, the notion has become even more compelling. Most people now understand that the bond market was the main instrument by which credit became superfluous and that this was the case for a lengthy period of time. The availability of credit made possible by the bond market enabled borrowers from all ends of the credit spectrum to finance spending levels that ultimately proved to be unsustainable relative to income trends. The results left broken economics models in nearly all sectors of the economy, including the household, corporate, and government sectors.

Spending levels are now reverting to a "new normal" that reflects income trends rather than credit availability. These lower levels of spending mean that many of the problems that have beset the U.S. economy are likely to prove structural rather than cyclical, resulting in major repercussions for both the economy as a whole and the financial markets in particular. It therefore behooves everyone to gain a better understanding of the bond market even if one is not a bond investor.

In many ways the bond market profoundly affects nearly everyone. Recent events have illustrated very clearly that the bond market's influence stretches well beyond the conventional wisdom in ways that most people are never aware of. In short, the bond market, where interest rates are set and where credit is formed, is little understood yet immensely important to the national standard of living.

Throughout this book I will highlight the many ways in which the bond market affects the economy, the financial markets, and most importantly your life. I am convinced that when you have finished reading it, you will be surprised and enlightened and you will look at the bond market in a new light. I will show you how you can unlock the power of the bond market either by investing in bonds or by gaining a greater understanding of how the bond market's behavior could be influencing economic and financial conditions in a way that directly impacts your life. At the same time you will gain valuable insights into how the bond market operates and the role that it will play in the new normal, both for investors and borrowers.

You will learn important insights that are absent in other books about the bond market. More often than not, those books are filled with information that is of little personal relevance to the reader—information that is important but often uninteresting and overly technical.

Of course, some technical content must be included in any book about bonds and the bond market, and there will be plenty here to please both the novice and the professional. But the central theme of this book will be to educate in a way that can be used in the real world, avoiding indulgence into wonky discussions that do nothing more than serve the interests of the writer. There are many excellent books about the stock market that are geared to the general reader and that rarely delve into the intricacies of equity investing. These books tend to stick to what is relevant to the reader personally while making it interesting. That is what I will do in this book, and I will do my utmost to keep the topics relevant every step of the way.

The Bond Market Is the Dog That Wags the Tail

Until the credit crisis erupted in 2007, most people viewed the bond market as an afterthought. This is mostly because bonds are not very sexy to the average investor, and the bond market is either too complex or too uninteresting for most individuals to consider paying it much attention. This is a by-product of a secular era of financial innovations gone amok, a secular bull market in the stock market, and a long period of economic prosperity spanning roughly a quarter century.

But this is where reality and perceptions clash: the bond market is really the dog that wags the tail. The bond market and, more specifically, the interest rate levels and credit conditions that are affected by the bond market significantly influence the performance of the financial markets and the economy much more so than the other way around. Since the financial markets and the economy affect everyone somehow, a great deal of every individual's financial well-being can be traced to the bond market.

Unfortunately, many individuals miss this point and therefore miss the many opportunities that the bond market presents, both in making investments and attaining credit. These opportunities can surface in a wide variety of places, particularly when investing in the stock market or attempting to achieve true risk diversification (as opposed to just asset diversification—we will discuss this in Chapter 5). They can also surface when seeking home mortgages or other forms of credit such as home equity loans, credit cards, personal loans, and car loans. Reduced availability of credit in the new normal resulting from changed conditions in the bond market mean that investors more than ever need to understand how the credit system works. This will be discussed in this book.

The Bond Market Is Where Interest Rates Are Set

As was mentioned previously, the bond market is where interest rates are set. The interest rate levels quoted on loans, credit cards, savings accounts, money market funds, and the like are all linked to the bond market. This is the case because rates for these instruments generally are correlated with an interest rate level set in the bond market. Most of these interest rate levels are linked to the U.S. Treasury market, which is where debt securities in the bond market are most actively traded. Mortgage rates, for example, are tightly correlated with the yield on the 10-year U.S. Treasury note.

Take a look at Figure 1.1. As you can see from the chart, the 10-year U.S. Treasury notes and the 30-year fixed rate mortgages basically move in lockstep with each other, with the 10-year T-note leading a bit. The exception was in 2008 at the height of the credit crisis when mortgage securities, which have a major bearing on mortgage rates, underperformed Treasuries, as did just about every other financial instrument. This changed toward the end of 2008 when on November 25 the Federal Reserve announced that it would purchase $500 billion of mortgage-backed securities, eventually expanding the amount to $1.25 trillion, rallying mortgage-backed securities and putting downward pressure on mortgage rates.

The tight correlation between mortgage rates and the performance of Treasury and mortgage-backed securities is one example of the bond market's influence on broader interest rate levels. It shows the importance of staying atop developments in the bond market, for example, when obtaining a home mortgage.

FIGURE 1.1 Mortgage Rates Track Treasury Yields Closely

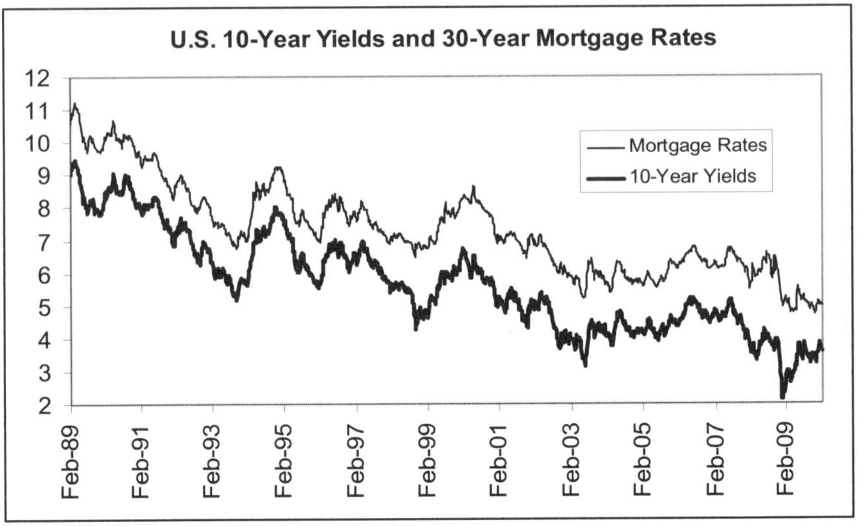

Source: Bloomberg and Freddie Mac.

The reason so many interest rate instruments are linked to the bond market is the fact that the bond market serves as a reference, or benchmark, for where the investing public believes interest rates should be. In addition, the Federal Reserve sets interest rate levels that are reflected in the bond market. Importantly, in the bond market's new normal, the Federal Reserve's impact on market interest rates has increased because by becoming an active buyer of securities, it has become a price setter—a player, if you will, rather than just a referee. This has important implications for investors. This will be discussed in greater detail in Chapter 6.

Because nearly all interest rate levels are dependent on the bond market in some way and since interest rates affect almost everyone in one way or another, gaining a better understanding of the bond market is a worthwhile endeavor.

Let's take a closer look at how the bond market affects many important facets of our daily lives. As you read on, think about the many ways in which your life has been touched by these powerful forces.

The Effects of Interest Rate Changes and Credit Availability on Personal Finances and Lifestyles

For most households, interest rates have a large impact on everyday finances. In the United States, where for decades households have used debt to finance many of their hopes and dreams, this impact is largely manifested in the household sector's monthly bills. Unfortunately for many, the repercussion of the accumulation of debt and the inability to either service or refinance the debt has had enormous consequences. Worst of all has been the eruption in home foreclosures in the recent past resulting from lax lending practices, insufficient regulatory oversight, and debt use that was too high relative to underlying income trends (see Figure 1.2).

The explosion in consumer debt over the past few decades was a cultural phenomenon, influenced by the factors mentioned above as well as demographics. The baby boomers—those born from 1946 to 1964—increased their use of debt to finance their well-documented love for consuming goods and services. And the binge did not stop until the financial crisis began in 2007 when the credit spigot began to close. In the new normal, consumption has been cut back and savings rates are moving higher, as shown in Figure 1.3. Deleveraging is now the mantra, not "Charge it!"

Whatever the cause of the debt explosion, the fact is that on average most households have significant amounts of debt outstanding in a variety of forms. Table 1.1 highlights the enormous amount of household debt outstanding. Take note of the decline that has occurred amid the deleveraging impulse.

As the table shows, the total amount of mortgage debt outstanding surpasses all other forms of debt. This clearly indicates that the biggest way in which interest rates affect a household's finances is through mortgage

FIGURE 1.2 Home Foreclosures as a Percentage of Total Mortgages

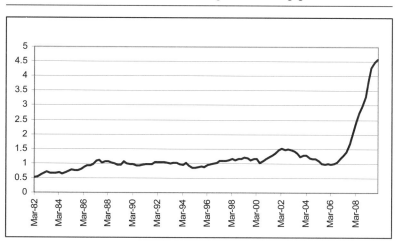

Source: Mortgage Bankers Association.

FIGURE 1.3 Today, "Charge It!" Is No Longer the Mantra

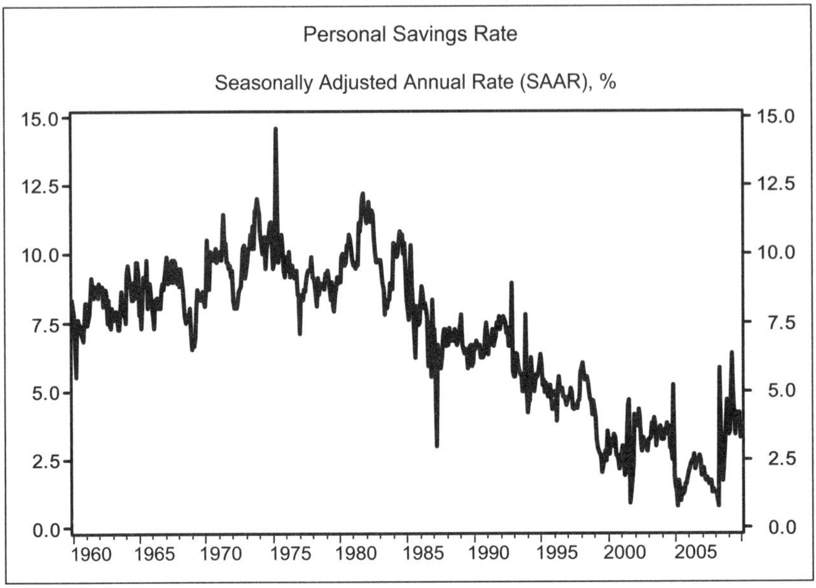

Personal Savings Rate

Seasonally Adjusted Annual Rate (SAAR), %

Source: Bureau of Economic Analysis and Haver Analytics.

rates. The mortgage rate directly affects every homeowner's monthly financial situation. I am sure that many of you can relate to this and are aware of the huge influence that the resetting of adjustable-rate mortgages had on a very large number of households in the United States. Many homeowners had been lured into taking mortgages at so-called teaser rates. These rates were eventually adjusted upward when the Fed began a series of interest rate increases in June 2004, which resulted in burdensome mortgage payments that were too high for many homeowners, as Figure 1.2 shows.

I learned firsthand the importance of tracking interest rates and understanding the factors causing them to rise and fall many years ago.

TABLE 1.1 Household Liabilities, as of December 2009, in Billions

Debt Category	Amount
Home mortgages	$10,262
Consumer credit	2,481
Bank loans	151
Other loans	134
Security credit	203

In 1989, the year before I began my career in the bond market, I purchased my first house, a town house. It was a special time, filled with excitement. I was elated to be realizing the American dream of owning one's own home.

While the home itself was a great source of pride and satisfaction, the financial side of the equation evolved in ways I did not envision at that time. I had taken out a mortgage at a whopping 11.25 percent, the prevailing rate at that time. I didn't give much thought to the interest rate level because I felt as others did in the early 2000s that the price of the home would rise, as home prices always had, and offset the interest costs. The mistake I made was the same that millions of others recently made.

My initial judgment was so wrong! As I came to understand, the Federal Reserve was in the middle of a campaign to slow the economy in an effort to stamp out inflation and a brewing price bubble in the real estate market. The Fed's rate increases therefore hit me with the same double-barreled whammy that hit millions of homeowners during the financial crisis: I was stuck with a high mortgage payment, and my home's price fell when the Fed burst the real estate bubble.

When the real estate bubble burst, the price of my town house fell 25 percent in short order. I tried to refinance for years, but no bank would consider it because my town house had negative equity. Therefore, I was stuck. For years I was saddled with high payments on an investment that had gone awry.

What do I know now that I didn't know then? For starters, I have learned that the interest rate I pay on debt matters—big time—and I therefore will be leery about accepting either a relatively high interest rate or one that could turn out to be high in relation to my income. Never again will I borrow money without giving strong consideration to interest rates. That means paying more attention to the bond market. Following the bond market has enabled me to make better financial decisions and plan better. New lessons from the recent financial crisis also have me leery about taking on debts that I could have difficulty refinancing if the credit spigot were to get cut off again.

I have also learned to respect the adage "Don't fight the Fed." The Federal Reserve has enormous influence on the economy and the financial markets, and hence, my financial well-being. I can't emphasize this point enough. We'll learn more about the importance of respecting the power of the Fed in Chapter 6.

So I eventually turned the tables, locking into a mortgage rate that was the low of the 2000s. Instead of having the highest interest rate of anyone I know, I now have one of the lowest. By staying in tune with the bond market,

I have learned to be opportunistic with interest rates when they fall. Moreover, by watching the Federal Reserve, I am more on top of the investment and economic climate.

Stay in tune with the bond market as I have and keep the graph in Figure 1.1 fresh in your mind. Let it always remind you that the bond market can have a great impact on your personal finances.

Credit Cards

Aside from home mortgages, interest rate levels have a great impact on the payments that most people make on their credit card balances. Some of you, I am sure, have obtained new credit cards with low introductory interest rate levels on balance transfers. Have you noticed the big difference that the interest rate level makes on the monthly interest charges? It can be staggering.

The attraction of credit cards with low introductory interest rates has been partly responsible for the sharp increase in consumer debt over the past 30 years. By developing various types of creative financing arrangements that entice consumers to take on more debt, opportunistic financial companies have capitalized on consumers' increased willingness to run up debt. And boy did they!

Americans hold hundreds of millions of credit cards and have debit balances of roughly $900 billion. That is well above the level in the mid-1990s, when there was about $500 billion outstanding.

The pervasive use of credit card debt can be used to illustrate the large impact that interest rates can have in an individual's personal finances.

Consider, for example, a consumer who has $8,000 of credit card debt outstanding carrying an annual financing rate of 18 percent. That consumer will incur roughly $1,363 in interest charges through the course of a year, assuming the consumer pays only the minimum payment of the standard 2.0 to 2.5 percent. (And the minimum payment, by the way, is on the way up because banks are trying to de-risk their balance sheets by reducing the amount of credit they extend.) If the consumer transfers that balance to a new credit card with a low introductory interest rate of 5.9 percent, the consumer will incur just $424 of interest charges over the course of a year. The difference is obviously significant.

Perhaps even more significant is the amount of time it would take for that consumer to eliminate the debt entirely, assuming the consumer pays the minimum monthly payment. If the debit balance is carried at the low introductory interest rate of 5.9 percent, the consumer would eliminate the debt in 16 years. But at 18 percent, the consumer would need 30 years. What

FIGURE 1.4 Consumers Are Cutting Up Their Credit Cards

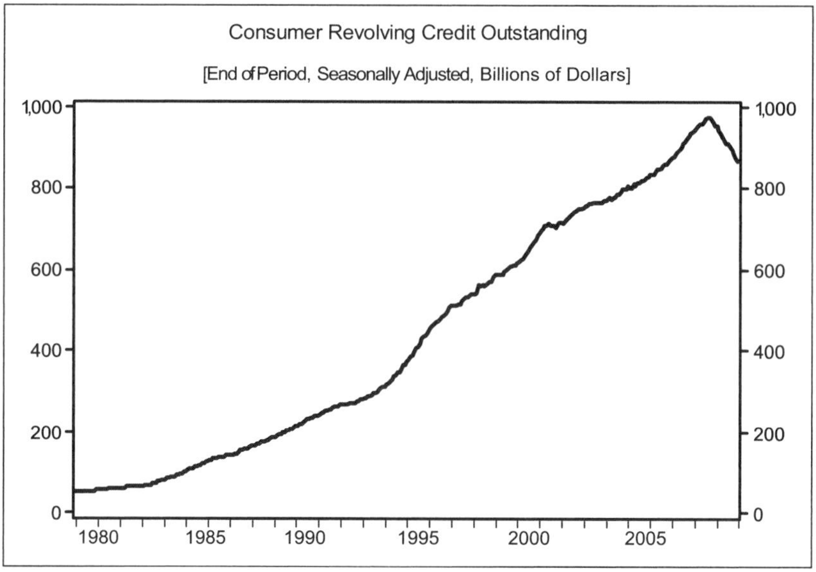

Consumer Revolving Credit Outstanding

[End of Period, Seasonally Adjusted, Billions of Dollars]

Source: Federal Reserve Board and Haver Analytics.

a difference! This realization, which has been long overdue, is one of the many reasons that households have been cutting back on their credit card use. This is evident in Figure 1.4, which shows an unprecedented decline in the use of revolving credit, which consists mostly of credit card debt.

The following sections in this chapter show additional ways that interest rates can affect people's personal finances and additional reasons people need to have a good understanding of the bond market.

The Profound Impact of Interest Rates on the Stock Market and Other Asset Classes

The impact of interest rates on your personal finances extends well beyond your debts. Interest rates can affect your equity portfolio too, as well as your holdings of other financial assets. Indeed, history has proven that interest rates can have a profound impact on the stock market. As a result, the stock market watches the bond market like a hawk. It's no wonder that one of the most famous adages in the stock market is "Don't fight the Fed." To wit, investors in 2009 took to heart the Federal Reserve's massive response to the financial crisis, which included the injection of more than $1 trillion of financial liquidity into the U.S. banking system, which rallied the S&P 500 to a gain of 23.5 percent.

By gaining a better understanding of the bond market, you can empower yourself with an improved ability to recognize the potential risks and opportunities that the gyrations of the bond market present to the stock market as well as other asset classes every day. For example, gains in the prices of corporate bonds, and in particular junk bonds, signaled increased appetite for risk taking early in 2009, which provided an important signal for equity investors to consider stepping back into the waters.

Your goal should be to become less of a casual observer of the goings-on in the bond market and more of a thinker with respect to how the bond market's fluctuations may affect the stocks you own and how the bond market's behavior can be integrated into your investment decisions. This does not mean that you have to become an investor in bonds; it merely means that you should weave your understanding of how the bond market affects the stock market into your investment decision-making process. I will discuss how you can do this throughout the book.

The behavior of the stock market over the years has made one simple fact of investing abundantly clear: the bond market is the dog that wags the tail. When the bond market flutters, the stock market quakes. This has been proven time and time again, as recent events have demonstrated so profoundly.

Interest Rates and the Bond Market as Both Crisis Catalysts and Crisis Tools

The financial crisis was caused by a plethora of factors, some of which date back decades. Identifying the specific cause of the crisis is a subjective exercise, and no two people are likely to agree on what happened. An area of fairly broad agreement is the idea that debt was used excessively as a means of financing consumption. Consumers in particular persistently increased their use of debt, as shown in Figure 1.5. At the same time, consumers let their savings rate decline (Figure 1.3). The combination ultimately proved lethal for the financial system, with consumers defaulting on their debts at the expense of financial institutions, which themselves had gone on their own leveraging binge.

Enabling the debt culture that brought down the financial system was the bond market. So, when interest rates in the early 2000s fell to levels not seen since the early 1960s, the leveraging mindset went into overdrive, driving up asset prices to levels that would prove unsustainable relative to in-

FIGURE 1.5 Ratio of Household Debt-Service Payments to Household Disposable Income

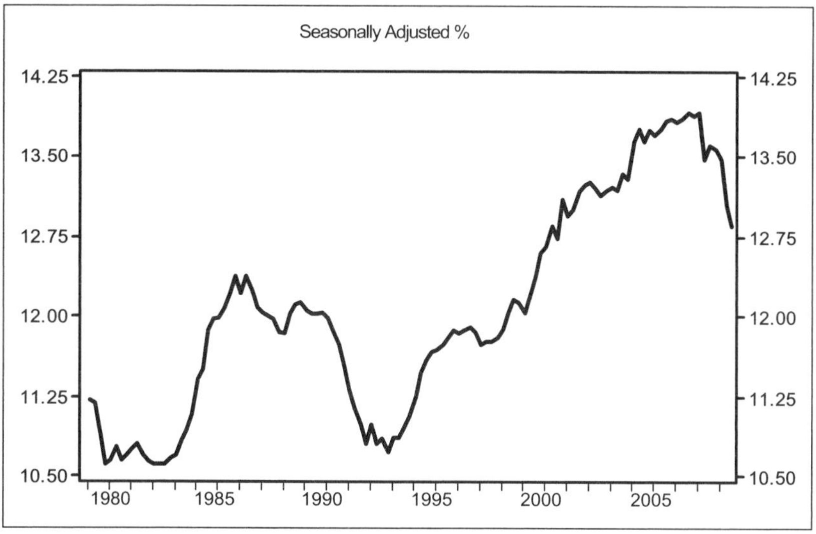

Source: Federal Reserve Board and Haver Analytics.

comes. The bond market enabled it all by acting as the main conduit for borrowers to finance their profligacy. The main culprit was the rapid expansion of *securitization*, the process by which creditors holding mortgage loans and credit card loans bundle them together as collateral for securities to be sold to investors in the capital markets. Securitization dates back to 1970 when the Government National Mortgage Association (Ginnie Mae) issued the first mortgage-backed security.

In a study conducted by the Federal Reserve Bank of Dallas, researchers quantified the sharply increased role that the securities market played from 1979 to 2008 in providing funding to a wide range of entities, noting that at the end of 1979, securities funded about 33 percent of household, nonfinancial corporate, and nonfarm business debt. By the third quarter of 2008, that figure had risen to around 64 percent.[1] The results are shown in Figure 1.6.

Securitization and other financial innovations put money more easily into the hands of borrowers that might not otherwise have been able to obtain money. Nadauld and Sherlund (2009) found evidence supporting the idea that in the height of the housing market frenzy of the early and mid-2000s, banks sought the purchase of loans having low credit quality, expecting that these "cheap" loans would be sought by underwriters of securitized

FIGURE 1.6 Funding of Nonfinancial Sector Debt

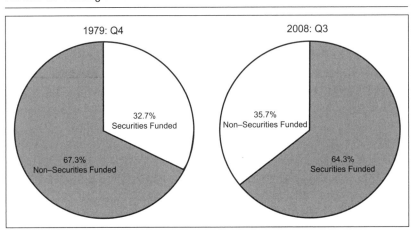

Note: From 1979 to 2008, households increasingly depended on the securities markets to finance consumption.

Source: Federal Reserve Bank of Dallas.

loans, which themselves were looking for cheap loans having the potential to appreciate because of rising home prices.[2] The researchers found that in 2005, on average, a 10 percent increase (close to one standard deviation) in the percentage of originated subprime loans being sold in the secondary market resulted in the origination of an additional four subprime loans per 100 housing units (over one-half of a standard deviation). In this way, the bond market acted as a catalyst to the financial crisis.

The bond market was also a crisis tool, chiefly through the auspices of the Federal Reserve, which used all its available tools to revive the financial system. This included becoming an active participant in the bond market (through its securities purchase program) and lowering the federal funds rate, the rate the Fed controls, to close to zero. We will discuss this further in Chapter 6.

The Role of Interest Rates and the Bond Market in Crises Generally

Think back to 1998, when the world was gripped in a wretched series of financial crises that began in Asia and spread throughout the rest of the world, including the United States. The crisis had its roots in the excessive use of external debts by nations such as Thailand, brought about in part by the increased availability of credit made possible by the bond market. The crisis taught Asia lessons that served it well in the 2000s—lessons that developing nations are now learning. Consequently, Asia and other developing regions were, before the financial crisis erupted, in an enviable position and in much better fiscal condition than were most of the developed nations.

In 1998, the financial contagion that spread from Asia caused markets to swoon lower worldwide, and foreign currency and debt markets began to seize up. A liquidity crisis developed as investors shunned foreign markets and avoided financial securities that were not actively traded. U.S. Treasuries, for example, considered the safest financial securities in the world, were partly shunned as older, less active maturities (called *off-the-runs*) performed poorly compared with actively traded maturities. For the U.S. Treasuries market to have experienced price anomalies was an extraordinary event that highlighted the state of crisis the markets were in at the time.

Enter the Federal Reserve. On September 29, 1998, the Fed responded to the crisis with the first of three rate cuts that year.

In the policy statement that accompanied that first cut, the Fed explained that it decided to lower interest rates "to cushion the effects on prospective economic growth in the United States of increasing weakness in foreign economies and of less accommodative financial conditions domestically." The Fed clearly recognized the deleterious impact that dysfunctional financial markets could ultimately have on the U.S. economy. In addition, the Fed knew that it could use the power of interest rates to help restore investor confidence, which had been shattered throughout the world.

The Fed's interest rate tonic worked its usual magic as the global markets staged a substantial recovery. The Dow Jones Industrial Average, for example, which had fallen from an all-time high of 9,367.84 just two months before the Fed's rate cut to a low of 7,400.03 on September 1, roared back to a new all-time high two months after the rate cut. That recovery illustrated the powerful impact of interest rates.

While there's no question that the Fed's rate cuts were needed to help restore stability to the financial markets in 1998, the rate cuts arguably sowed the seeds for one of the most explosive and ultimately harrowing periods in economic and financial history.

The problem was that the rate cuts became a classic case of too much of a good thing, a double-edged sword, if you will, just as they became in the early 2000s. Arguably, the rate cuts were meant to address a market problem, not an economic one, and so the Fed should have reversed its rate cuts once the crisis was over. It didn't. What followed in 1999 was a bubble in both the economy and the stock market. The Fed tried to arrest the bubble in June 1999 with the first of six interest rate increases, but it responded slowly and the bubble grew.

You might recall that the Federal Reserve began raising interest rates in June 1999. The stock market, however, was caught in a euphoric mood—a mania, in fact—and it turned a blind eye to the Fed. The stock market also turned its back on a critical development in the bond market: an inversion of the yield curve (to be discussed further in Chapter 7), which is a development normally considered an ominous signal for both the economy and the stock market.

However, the equity market continued to plow ahead and chose to ignore historical precedent. For many investors that would turn out to be a disastrous mistake.

When 2000 began, it was the same old story. The Fed was still raising interest rates, while the equity market was caught in the dot-com mania. It was a bubble that was about to burst, and it was the Fed and the bond market that would burst it.

The Fed continued raising interest rates until May 16, 2000, when it decided to increase the size of the rate hikes from a quarter of a percentage point at a time to a half point. The Fed did this to ensure that the stock market, which had started to slip, would stay down for the count. It did. As in many earlier eras, the stock market succumbed to the powerful influence of interest rates. And so did the economy.

By the end of 2000 signs of an economic slowdown and talk of recession abounded. The exuberant free-spending consumer gave way to a more cautious, tepid one. Spending during the 2000 holiday season, in fact, was dreadfully weak and the worst since the last recession back in 1990 to 1991. Businesses responded to the weakness in the economy by cutting production and shedding workers. Businesses also began to curtail capital spending by lowering spending on new plants and equipment, for example, and by cutting back heavily on technology spending. This contributed to the battering of the technology-laden Nasdaq index.

September 11, 2001

In 2001, the Federal Reserve faced virtually unprecedented challenges, having to battle not only the busted financial bubble and the ensuing economic recession that began in March but also the economic effects of the tragic events of September 11. As Federal Reserve Chairman Alan Greenspan put it in February 2002 in testimony before Congress, "If ever a situation existed in which the fabric of business and consumer confidence, both here and abroad, was vulnerable to being torn, the shock of September 11 was surely it."

Led by Chairman Greenspan, the Fed met the unprecedented challenges of 2001 by aggressively lowering interest rates, cutting the federal funds rate 11 times to a 40-year low of 1.75 percent at year's end from

6.50 percent at the start of the year. The Fed's interest rate cuts helped to lift key interest-sensitive sectors of the economy, chiefly the housing and automobile sectors, which both grew strongly at the end of 2001. In addition, the Fed's rate cuts spurred a massive wave of mortgage refinancing activity, with nearly $1 trillion of mortgages refinanced, thereby helping to reduce mortgage payments for millions of households. In these and other ways, the Fed's rate cuts helped the economy to recover in short order. While the indomitable spirit of Americans was no doubt as good a reason as any for the economic rebound, the Federal Reserve's interest rate reductions played an immense role. Unknown at the time was that the rate cuts, which by June 2003 had brought the federal funds rate down to 1 percent—its lowest since 1958—would sow the seeds to a vastly greater financial crisis years later.

These recent episodes in the financial markets should help convince you that when it comes to investing, the bond market is a power to be reckoned with. If you can learn to read the bond market's signals, and I will show you ways to do that throughout this book, you can improve your investment performance sharply as well as increase your awareness of developments in the economy. You will learn, for example, how to know when to increase or decrease your risk taking and where you should put your money during the different stages of the economic cycle, in both the financial markets and the economy.

Equity Risks Are Everywhere—Including Bonds

A major lesson to be taken from the financial crisis is the idea that asset diversification does not equal risk diversification. In other words, simply because an investment portfolio consists of a variety of assets does not ensure that it will be immune to losses that are any less than the losses in the equity market itself.

Look at Figure 1.7. It shows two very different portfolios, both viewed by large numbers of investors as diversified portfolios. The one on the left is the classic 60/40 mix of stocks and bonds. The one on the right is the more modern endowment style model, which consists of a much larger number of asset classes. Now take a look at Figure 1.8. Contrary to common belief, neither portfolio shielded investors from the equity risk factor; instead, the portfolios exposed investors to losses nearly equal to having invested in the equity market alone. Why did this happen? It happened because there are commonalities between the risk factors in each of the asset classes. For

FIGURE 1.7 Two Types of "Diversified" Portfolios

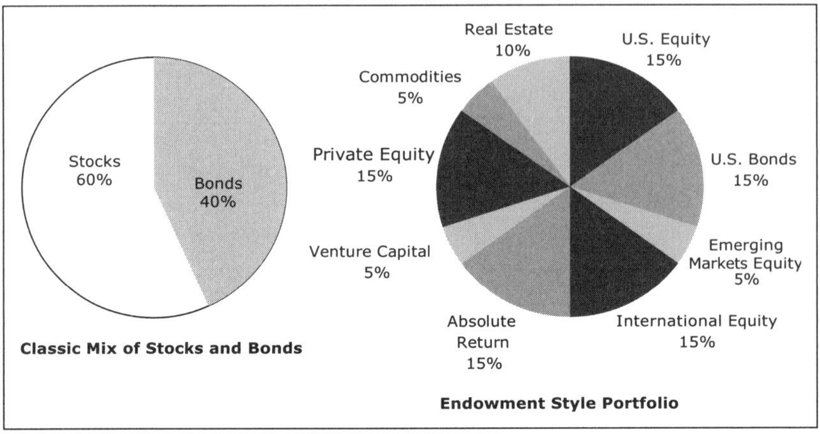

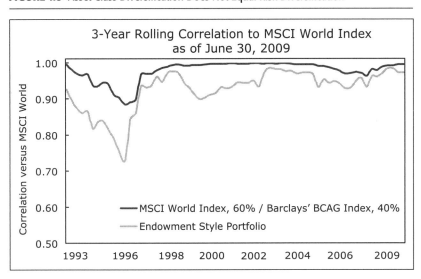

Source: Morgan Stanley, Bloomberg, Cambridge Associates, and Hedge Fund Research.

example, there is equity risk in a bond, and interest rate risk in a stock. There's also equity risk and interest rate risk in real estate.

When investing in the postcrisis world, it behooves investors to identify the commonalities that exist in the risk factors embedded in the assets they own. The objective is to neutralize the equity risk factor, the biggest risk

FIGURE 1.8 Asset Class Diversification Does Not Equal Risk Diversification

Source: Morgan Stanley, Bloomberg, Cambridge Associates, and Hedge Fund Research.

factor that investors face. The goal is to reduce the correlation between the portfolio to the equity market—to levels well below that shown in Figure 1.6. This means that in addition to interest rate risk and equity risk, investors must look for other commonalities such as currency risks (a "diversified" portfolio of international stocks and bonds would carry the same currency risk for both asset classes); liquidity risks (certain stocks and bonds could together be a bad mix if liquidity affects both similarly when liquidity dries up); and volatility risks. Risk diversification is the new wave of investing, and investors therefore must look at the bonds they own differently than they have in the past and use all of the tools available in the bond market. We will discuss this in greater detail in Chapter 5.

The Bond Market's Impact on the Economy

The biggest reason the financial markets react so strongly to developments in the bond market is the fact that investors recognize the major role that interest rates play in shaping the health of the economy. They also recognize that the health of the economy has a direct bearing on corporate profits and, hence, stock prices and performance of other so-called risk assets, such as including corporate bonds. Investors during the financial crisis of the late 2000s also discovered the very important role that the bond market has played in financing economic activity.

The primary way in which the bond market affects the economy can be expressed as a fairly straightforward relationship. The rule of thumb is that rising interest rates tend to weaken the economy while falling interest rates tend to strengthen it. High interest rates tend to discourage borrowing while low interest rates encourage it. This relationship can break down in periods during which both lenders and borrowers shun debt, but it tends to hold over time.

Interest rates generally rise or fall, of course, mainly as a result of actions taken by the Federal Reserve. The Fed adjusts the level of interest rates to regulate the health of the economy. It does this by raising or lowering the federal funds rate, which is the interest rate banks charge each other for overnight loans. The federal funds rate is considered the anchor for all short-term interest rates. It is therefore one of the most important interest rates. This is discussed in greater detail in Chapters 6 and 7.

Although the Fed controls short-term interest rates, it has limited control over long-term interest rates. As a result, the interest rate levels on a wide variety of long-term financial vehicles, such as home mortgages, are anchored against interest rates that are set in the bond market. We showed this in Figure 1.1.

Credit availability is the other means by which the bond market affects the economy. We showed the increased role that the bond market has played in providing funding to the economy in Figure 1.6.

These are the things that make the bond market so important to the economy. Its daily fluctuations have a direct bearing on the interest rate instruments that directly affect the economy, and it serves as a conduit for borrowers. It is what puts the bond market as much in control of the economy as the Federal Reserve is.

The Bond Market's Impact on the Interest Rate–Sensitive Sectors of the Economy

As we will discuss further in Chapter 6, there are three interest rate–sensitive sectors of the economy that can be greatly affected by developments in the bond market: housing, automobiles, and capital spending. Each sector by itself can have a very big effect on the economy—the housing market's influence has been huge. Collectively, their impact can be enormous. This is why these sectors are the first places you should look to see impacts from interest rate fluctuations. When these sectors start to respond to a change in interest rates, look out. At that point many other areas of the economy will be affected through so-called multiplier effects, resulting in a host of economic and investment implications.

Take the automobile sector, for example, a sector that accounts for roughly 7 percent of all industrial production in the United States, but with multiplier effects that can magnify its impact greatly.

If, for example, as a result of lower interest rates, automobile sales strengthened, the benefits of that sales increase would ripple through the economy in a variety of ways. Car salespersons, for example, would see their commission income increase. In turn, they probably would use their extra income to buy a variety of goods unrelated to the automobile industry—from clothing to furniture to chewing gum—and thus have a positive impact on the economy. Moreover, factory workers would also see their incomes rise as they worked extra overtime and longer workweeks to build new cars to meet the strong demand. This extra income would find its way into the economy too, of course. The impact would extend further to workers in the automobile parts supply industry, and the effect on the economy could be significant. Indeed, in the United States there are more people working in the automobile parts supply industry than there are working in the manufacture of automobiles.

A dilemma for the automobile industry in 2009 and 2010 was that interest rate changes alone couldn't solve what was ailing it. Consumers were less interested in levering up to purchase a car, and the money previously raised through the bond market had dried up and looked unlikely to return any time soon. Sales in the United States therefore appeared unlikely to reach the roughly 16 million or so annual rate that had existed before the financial crisis, leaving the industry structurally impaired and in need of shrinking. Interest rate changes can help, but they can't solve the industry's structural problems, which include the reduced availability of credit once made available in the bond market. Going forward, the impact of interest rates on the automobile sector will continue, but the cyclical effects will be smaller and more dependent on underlying trends in employment (because the debt market for automobile loans—the asset-backed securities market—is itself impaired).

In the housing sector, where multiplier effects are greater than they are in any other sector of the economy, interest rate changes play a large role in its performance, and the health of the housing sector can vastly influence the broader economy. This influence during the financial crisis was manifested mostly through the financial system, but there were also very large direct influences from changes in housing market activity. For example, the National Association of Home Builders (NAHB) has estimated that the construction of a single-family home generates 3.05 jobs and produces $89,216 in government revenue. Moreover, studies have shown that new homeowners tend to spend more of their income than do nonmovers.

The level of interest rates has long affected capital spending, which is business spending on new plants, machinery, equipment, and technology products. Interest rates affect capital spending in two ways.

First, businesses are apt to increase capital spending when the cost of doing so is lower. This occurs because capital spending projects are often costly—a new factory, after all, can be quite expensive—and many companies often finance their capital spending projects with borrowed money. The interest rate level can make or break the decision to engage in new capital spending projects.

Second, businesses are more apt to increase capital spending when they believe the interest rate environment will promote economic growth. When businesses feel that interest rates are low enough to spark economic growth, they generally feel compelled to expand their production capacity so that they can meet expected increases in the demand for their goods and services.

A constraint in the current environment is the very large amount of unused capacity, which reduces the motivation to purchase capital equipment. Nevertheless, the low interest rate helps facilitate the modernization of plants and equipment, and the purchase of new equipment and software can boost productivity, which is a desirable outcome in any economic situation and arguably one that is even more pressing in a downturn.

Three Ways the Economy's Performance Affects Nearly Everyone

As discussed in the preceding section, you can see by looking at the impact interest rate changes have on the housing, automobile, and capital spending sectors of the economy that there are a number of ways in which the bond market affects the economy. Three of the main impacts are discussed below.

First, the economy's performance directly affects job creation. Job creation has historically been linked directly to the economy's performance. A strong economy, for example, generally will result in the creation of about 200,000 jobs per month. A weak economy, in comparison, could spell job losses, and when the economy contracts, job losses usually total about 200,000 per month. Job losses were severe in the recent financial crisis, reaching a maximum of 779,000 in January 2009 and averaging 374,000 per month between December 2007 and June 2009.

Second, the economy's performance affects income growth. Wages tend to rise more rapidly when the economy is prospering, as workers share in growing corporate profits by demanding higher wages and working longer hours. In addition, individuals who derive some or all of their income from commissions see their earnings rise too. When the economy weakens, however, income growth slows as the workweek shrinks and individuals work fewer overtime hours and trade wage gains for job security.

Third, the national standard of living is tied directly to the economy's performance not only through job and income growth but also through the innovations companies develop in the products and services that consumers use. Companies innovate more when they are flush with cash than they do when they are strapped for cash. This means that the quality of the products and services that we buy, from cars to electronics to medical services, will vary with the economy's performance.

There are many other ways that the economy's performance affects us, as we will see in the Appendix at the end of the book, but these are some of the most prominent. In each case the bond market's role is unmistakable.

The Bond Market's Impact on the Formation of Capital

One big way in which the bond market affects the economy is through capital formation. We've seen from the financial crisis that without capital, the economy crumbles. Basically, capital is to the economy as gasoline is to a car. Money makes the world go round, as they say, and this is particularly true of the economy.

Corporations, municipalities, the U.S. government, and government agencies raise enormous amounts of capital in the bond market every year for a variety of purposes. Table 1.2 shows the total amount of money raised in the bond market from 1996 through the fourth quarter of 2009. Take special note of the surge in issuance of mortgage-backed securities in 2003 and its abrupt decline in 2008, as well as the sharp decline in overall issuance in 2008. The table helps tell the tale of the economy, as bond issuance is bound to impact the economy in one way or another, sometimes with a lag. For example, a corporation that raises money in the bond market and plans to use it to build a new factory will take time to draw up the plans to build, and then it will need still more time to actually build the factory. But it eventually will build the factory, of course.

Given that money borrowed in the bond market eventually finds its way into the economy, one might say that changes in the level of bond issuance are good leading indicators for the economy, meaning that those changes tend to foreshadow future economic activity. This is an indicator I recommend you follow closely.

Follow the money!

The Bond Market and Politics

The powerful influence of interest rates and the bond market goes well beyond conventional thinking. As I will argue in Chapter 14, the influence extends to the political arena too. While there's no doubt that many issues can shape the outcome of an election, the impacts of interest rates and the bond market activity historically have been quite palpable. This is a relatively new phenomenon, but the evidence is compelling.

President Jimmy Carter, for instance, was saddled with high interest rates throughout much of his administration in the late 1970s. Interest rates were high because of rampant inflation rates. Republicans, led by Ronald Reagan, seized on interest rates as a campaign issue, and in 1980 Carter lost his reelection bid partly because of the public's discontent with soaring interest rate levels.

Reagan benefited from the steady decline in interest rates that occurred during his administration. That decline contributed to perceptions that Reagan had restored and revitalized the nation, a perception that continues

TABLE 1.2 Issuance in the U.S. Bond Markets, in Billions of Dollars

	Municipal	Treasury*	Mortgage Related†	Corporate Debt‡	Federal Agency Securities	Asset Backed	Total
1996	185.2	612.4	492.6	343.7	277.9	168.4	2,080.2
1997	220.7	540.0	604.4	466.0	323.1	223.1	2,377.3
1998	286.8	438.4	1,143.9	610.7	596.4	286.6	3,362.7
1999	227.5	364.6	1,025.4	629.2	548.0	287.1	3,081.8
2000	200.8	312.4	684.4	587.5	446.6	281.5	2,513.2
2001	287.7	380.7	1,671.3	776.1	941.0	326.2	4,383.0
2002	357.5	571.6	2,249.2	636.7	1,041.5	373.9	5,230.4
2003	382.7	745.2	3,071.1	775.8	1,267.5	461.5	6,703.8
2004	359.8	853.3	1,779.0	780.7	881.8¶	651.5	4,424.3
2005	408.2	746.2	1,966.7	752.8	669.0	753.5	5,296.4
2006	386.5	788.5	1,987.8	1,058.9	747.3	753.9	5,722.9
2007	429.3	752.3	2,050.3	1,127.5	941.8	509.7	5,810.9
2008	389.5	1,037.3	1,344.1	707.2	984.5	139.5	4,602.1
2009	409.6	2,097.7	1,949.1	874.9	1,117.0	146.2	6,594.5
2008							
Q1	85.0	203.8	389.9	214.1	423.3	52.9	1,369.0
Q2	146.3	219.8	445.9	335.8	321.0	63.0	1,531.8
Q3	89.8	244.8	286.6	83.9	139.5	20.1	864.7
Q4	68.4	368.9	221.7	73.4	100.7	3.5	836.6
2009							
Q1	85.4	376.7	365.5	225.0	429.5	16.3	1,498.4
Q2	111.3	533.5	651.9	243.1	313.8	50.1	1,903.7
Q3	92.3	574.5	533.8	211.1	164.7	51.1	1,627.5
Q4	120.6	613.0	397.9	195.7	209.0	28.7	1,564.9
YTD 2008	389.5	1,037.3	1,344.1	707.2	984.5	139.5	4,602.1
YTD 2009	409.6	2,097.7	1,949.1	874.9	1,117.0	146.2	6,594.5
% Charge	5.2%	102.2%	45.0%	23.7%	13.5%	4.8%	43.3%

* Interest-bearing marketable coupon public debt.
† Includes GNMA, FNMA, and FHLMC mortgage-backed securities and CMOs and private-label MBS/CMOs.
‡ Includes all nonconvertible debt, MTNs, and Yankee bonds, but excludes CDs and federal agency debt.
¶ Beginning with 2004, Sallie Mae has been excluded due to privatization.

Source: U.S. Department of Treasury, federal agencies, Thomson Reuters.

to this day. In fact, many people agree that the bull market witnessed in the late 1990s actually got its start in 1982 under Reagan's watch.

Similar to Carter, President George H. W. Bush's bid for reelection was stymied by high interest rates. Early in Bush's term the Fed had raised interest rates in an effort to slow the economy and reduce inflation. The Fed's rate hikes eventually slowed the economy significantly and, combined with other factors, led to the recession of 1990 to 1991. To Bush's dismay, the Fed was slow to respond to the recession and lowered interest rates slowly and in small increments. The poor state of the economy became a campaign issue for the Democrats and helped sweep Bill Clinton into the presidency in 1992.

Bill Clinton, for his part, masterfully used the powerful influence of interest rates as the centerpiece of his economic strategy. He accomplished this by adopting strategies on fiscal policy developed by his Treasury secretary, Robert Rubin, which encouraged low market interest rates, hence promoting economic activity. The result was a historic shift in the government's yearly fiscal balance from deficit to surplus. What followed was an extraordinary drop in interest rates and a virtually unprecedented period of economic prosperity. The economy's strength helped Clinton weather a number of major personal and political challenges.

President George W. Bush initially benefited from the extraordinary rate cuts implemented by the Federal Reserve from 2001 to 2003, with the U.S. economy expanding at a healthy clip and producing job growth strong enough to push the U.S. unemployment rate to as low as 4.4 percent by October 2006. The Iraq War and other issues hurt Bush during his tenure, and when the bubble-enhancing elements of the Federal Reserve's rate cuts began to rear their head, the effects were potent. Bush's approval rate fell to extraordinarily low levels, and the approval rate never recovered.

President Obama entered office at a time when the Federal Reserve's policies were kicking into high gear, with the Fed having cut the federal funds rate to zero the month before Obama's inauguration. The Fed was also kicking into high gear an expansion of its balance sheet, which was accomplished mostly through the asset purchase program the Fed announced in November 2008—the program whereby the Federal Reserve over the course of about 16 months purchased $1.75 trillion of Treasury, agency, and agency mortgage-backed securities. Like Bush, benefits to the Obama administration—a stabilization of economic and financial conditions—were what accrued first from the Federal Reserve's monetary policies. Whether there will be a downside, as there was during the Bush administration, remains to be seen. The main worry, expressed in the financial markets in the context of the recent decline in the value of the U.S. dollar and the increase in the value of gold, is that the Federal Reserve's printing of money will result in accelerated inflation once the financial and economic situation "normalizes."

Stay tuned.

It is unconventional to think about the impact of interest rates on politics. However, the evidence clearly suggests that the bond market can play a major role in shaping the political landscape.

The Question of Our Age

If the United States is backing its financial system, who is backing the United States? This is the question of our age. The question is critically important because the United States needs massive amounts of money to finance its efforts to restore stability to its economy and its financial system. If support from the global investment community exists, the effort will work. If not, there will be financial and economic Armageddon. Thus far, the support has been substantial, as evidenced by the low level of U.S. Treasury yields; the very high bid/cover ratios (this is the dollar amount of bids submitted versus the dollar amount sold) for U.S. Treasury auctions; gains in the prices of risk assets such as equities, corporate bonds, and mortgage-backed securities; stability in the U.S. and global money markets; and little change in the value of the U.S. dollar.

In essence, what has happened is that the United States, as well as other developed nations, has had to use its balance sheet to repair the balance sheets of financial entities that were weakened by the battered housing sector as well as by proprietary trading activities. It can be said that the balance sheet problems of financial firms and the household sector have been transferred to the government sector. Now it is the government sector that is seeing its balance sheet weaken, as measured by its debt-to-gross domestic product (GDP) ratio, shown in Figure 1.9. This is expected to continue for a number of years.

Sovereign risk is therefore the new risk factor that investors must consider when deciding whether to own government debt. At a minimum, the worsened fiscal situation of developed nations probably means that the debt securities of developed nations will probably underperform those of developing nations, where in this upside-down world they have become creditor nations—Brazil and China are two among them.

How it ends depends a great deal on the fiscal prudence demonstrated by the government sector. The United States has a great deal of goodwill

FIGURE 1.9 Federal Debt Held by the Public as a Percentage of GDP

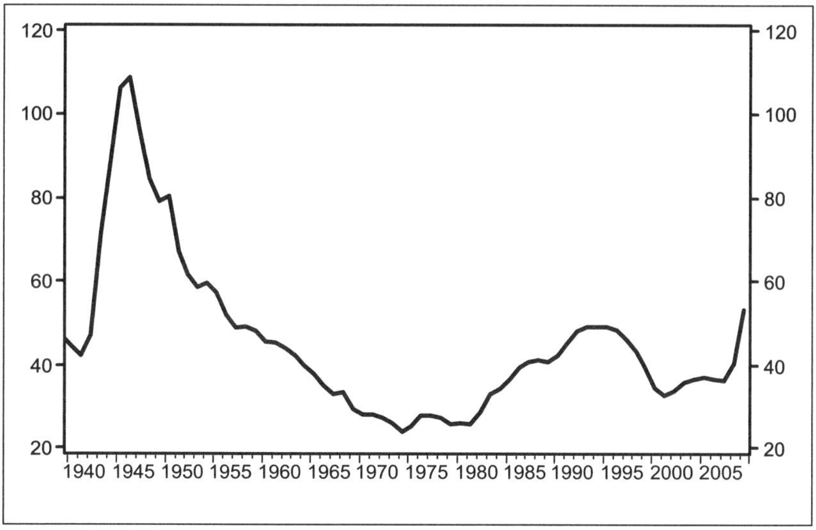

Source: U.S. Office of Management and Budget and Haver Analytics.

built up over decades, but we can't know the limits—and the United States certainly should not try to test those limits—of tolerance that foreign investors have for U.S. fiscal profligacy.

If the United States can get its fiscal house in order, it will retain its role as the world's reserve currency, chiefly because the United States remains the world's preeminent power economically, politically, and militarily. Moreover, the currencies of rising powers such as China are not yet ready to absorb the nearly $8 trillion in reserve assets the world holds, particularly because their bond markets are immature and can't house reserves as U.S. markets can. (When foreign nations such as China have trade surpluses, they build "reserves," which essentially amount to money in the bank, which they typically invest in government securities such as U.S. Treasuries.)

The idea that the United States and other developed nations are using debt to exit a debt problem is a rational reason for investors to be cautious and think differently than they did in the old normal. This has been a transformational downturn.

Summary

What happens in the bond market affects many aspects of our everyday life. Its impact is felt in home mortgages, investments, jobs, the economy, and politics. Throughout this book I will illustrate the powerful role the bond market plays in our lives and show you ways to use the bond market to your advantage.

If you're a bond investor, this book will help you understand the most essential elements of intelligent bond investing. You'll find strategies and tools that will give you a new perspective on investing and that you can use to help improve your investment performance.

But you needn't be a bond investor to benefit from this book. By simply gaining a greater understanding of the many ways the bond market can affect you and utilizing the tools in this book to your advantage, you'll be on your way toward unlocking the power of the bond market. So read on. Delve into the chapters and subjects you believe will help you the most. Find the tools you will need to meet your objectives, whatever they might be. If you keep an open mind and look at the bond market in ways you haven't before, you may be surprised at what you'll find.

Let's get started.

2

THE COMPOSITION AND CHARACTERISTICS OF THE BOND MARKET

One of this nation's greatest assets is its entrepreneurial spirit. In our storied history, we have had remarkable periods of economic prosperity spurred by the innovations and inventions of our citizens. From one generation to the next, entrepreneurs have opportunistically set their sails to the shifting winds of the American consumer, creating products and services that have boosted the national standard of living significantly. Scores of innovators, including now legendary greats such as Benjamin Franklin, Thomas Edison, the Wright Brothers, J. P. Morgan, Steve Jobs, and Bill Gates, have helped shape the way we live and usher in new eras.

As important as these and other entrepreneurs have been to the American society over the years, their innovations and inventions would not have had the impact that they had without a plentiful supply of capital. Innovations and inventions by themselves, of course, cannot lift a nation's standard of living; they eventually must be integrated into society on a national scale. For this to happen, mass production is necessary, which is an endeavor requiring large amounts of capital.

This is where the bond market comes in. In the bond market, vast amounts of capital are raised every day by numerous entities to meet the funding requirements for a variety of needs. Typical borrowers include the federal government, government agencies, local and state governments, and foreign and domestic corporations. The money these entities raise in the bond market is put toward a wide array of spending initiatives. A few examples are consumer products, U.S. Navy ships, local water supplies, and home mortgages. Without the bond market, the national standard of living would be far different from what it is today, as recent events have thoroughly demonstrated. Bonds, which in their simplest form are interest bearing documents issued or sold by either a government body or a corporation for the purpose of raising capital to meet a financial need, provide these entities with the capital they need to finance numerous endeavors.

Bonds That Helped Save the World

An extraordinary example of the powerful role bonds have historically played in this society is the war bond program established during World War II to help finance the war effort. On May 1, 1941, President Franklin D. Roosevelt bought the first of the so-called war bonds, also known as "victory bonds." A massive effort was undertaken to sell substantial amounts of those bonds, and the results were astounding. By the time the program ended and the last proceeds from the sale were deposited into the U.S. Treasury on January 3, 1946, $185.7 billion of war bonds had been sold and over 85 million Americans had invested in them. It is astonishing to consider that 85 million people had invested in war bonds, and the number is even more staggering when one considers that the population was just 130 million at the time. In contrast, today less than 20 percent of the population owns U.S. savings bonds.

War bonds were crucial not only for the role they played in financing the war but in the way they helped unify the nation. The sale of war bonds became a rallying cry, uniting Americans in a common cause and giving those who invested in the bonds a way to express their patriotism. The effort to raise money reached nearly every nook and cranny of the country, and it seemed that almost everyone was involved. The entertainment industry played an active role, with the nation's best-known and most-beloved entertainers using their star status to help the common cause.

It's fair to say that bonds have never played a more vital role than they did during World War II. The lives of our soldiers, the welfare of their families, and both the nation and the world were helped immensely by our ability to fight a well-financed campaign. Bonds have never shined more.

Today's Bond Market

The immense success of the war bond program helped elevate bonds as financing vehicles and paved the way for substantial growth in the bond market. Through the years, the bond market has grown rapidly, and financial innovations have led to the creation of many different types of bonds. The bond market has become so large that its dollar value now exceeds that of the stock market. Moreover, as we showed in Figure 1.6, the bond market and the securities market more generally have become a bigger source of capital than the banking system.

Despite the bond market's explosive growth and enormous size, it remains elusive, and many people do not have a clue about what "the bond market" really is. It is now apparent that in the most recent financial crisis of early and mid-2000, market participants themselves did not have a clue either, investing and promoting as they did in securities that were so complex that they did not fully understand the risks until the financial crisis erupted.

There are many reasons why the bond market seems so elusive. For one thing, there is no centralized marketplace for bond trading. This is the complete opposite of the equity market, where most trading takes place in centralized exchanges such as the New York Stock Exchange.

Specialization in the Bond Market

In the bond market there are presently no physical places, like stock exchanges, in which bonds are exchanged. However, the recent financial crisis is prompting calls for change—for example, some people are asking that there be established a centralized place in which to trade and clear transactions in the giant interest rate swaps market, where investors exchange rights to pay or receive a specified interest rate over a specified time, but no trading exchange appears to be around the bend. Instead, trading continues to take place over the counter or within a network of thousands of broker-dealers and the investing public. *Broker-dealers* are so named because they can act as either brokers, buying and selling securities on behalf of their customers, or dealers, buying and selling securities for their own accounts.

Usually these broker-dealers act as dealers, and they carry inventories of fixed-income securities that they resell to their clients. The inventories that broker-dealers hold vary widely, as these firms often specialize in trading specific types of fixed-income securities. Some firms, for example, specialize in trading corporate bonds, while others specialize in trading municipal securities. Larger firms tend to have specialist desks in all of the major segments of the bond market.

This specialization has advantages and disadvantages. A key advantage is that individual broker-dealers may have special expertise in the securities they trade. A firm that specializes in municipal securities, for example, is likely to know the ins and outs of the municipal bond market and generally will have more research and other tools available to help the investing public than do firms that don't specialize in trading those securities.

Going to a firm that specializes in trading specific types of fixed-income securities is akin to choosing to shop for automotive supplies in a store that specializes in automobile parts instead of going to a grocery store or supermarket that does not specialize in them.

Perhaps the main disadvantage of specialization in the bond market is the impact it has on the visibility of a bond's price and availability. This is certainly very different from the stock market, where prices are readily available and can be quoted literally to the penny. Not so in the bond market, where there are well over a million different bonds outstanding, and some of those bonds "trade by appointment." In other words, they trade so infrequently that they can be difficult to price, value, find, and sell. This lack of visibility is probably the main reason that the bond market seems so elusive to people. People probably would be more comfortable with the bond market if they could track it better. Luckily, new electronic systems and the Internet are making this increasingly possible.

Primary Dealers Facilitate Efficiency in the Bond Market

Despite some important disadvantages of the decentralized nature of the bond market, it is a robust market with vast liquidity. Playing a crucial role in supplying that liquidity are primary dealers. *Primary dealers* are banks and securities broker-dealers that trade in U.S. government securities with the Federal Reserve System. Collectively, primary dealers trade an average of approximately $400 billion in U.S. government securities every business day.

Primary dealers play an important role in the implementation of the Fed's monetary policy. They do this by buying and selling securities from the Fed in the open market. The purchase and sale of securities in the open market adds or removes money from the banking system, and this pushes interest rates to the Fed's desired levels. This process will be discussed in greater detail in Chapter 6.

The Federal Reserve Bank of New York established the primary dealer system in 1960. Many elite banks and broker-dealers have held the respected primary dealer designation since then; there were 18 in 1960 and the number peaked at 46 in 1988. The number of primary dealers has fallen over the years, owing mostly to consolidation in the industry, as government securities dealers have either merged or changed the focus of their business.

Currently there are 18 primary dealers, down from 22 in 2002, and the list includes many household names, as shown in sidebar "Primary Dealer List as of February 2010." Three notable firms were deleted during the financial crisis: Countrywide Securities in July 2008, Lehman Brothers in September 2008, and Bear Stearns in October 2008. Merrill Lynch's name was also removed in February 2009 as a result of its acquisition by Bank of America.

Primary Dealer List as of February 2010

Banc of America Securities LLC (a subsidiary of Bank of America)
Barclays Capital Inc.
BNP Paribas Securities Corp.
Cantor Fitzgerald & Co.
Citigroup Global Markets, Inc.
Credit Suisse Securities (USA) LLC
Daiwa Securities America, Inc.
Deutsche Bank Securities, Inc.
Goldman Sachs & Co.
HSBC Securities (USA), Inc.
Jefferies & Company, Inc.
J.P. Morgan Securities, Inc.
Mizuho Securities USA, Inc.
Morgan Stanley & Co., Incorporated
Nomura Securities International, Inc.
RBC Capital Markets Corporation
RBS Securities, Inc.
UBS Securities LLC

Source: Federal Reserve Bank of New York.

Becoming a primary dealer is not easy. Recognizing the critical role primary dealers play in the implementation of monetary policy, the Federal Reserve has established very stringent requirements for obtaining the primary dealer designation. For starters, primary dealers must be either a commercial bank subject to supervision by U.S. Federal Reserve Bank supervisors or broker-dealers registered with the Securities and Exchange Commission (SEC). There are no restrictions against foreign-owned banks or broker-dealers becoming primary dealers.

There are also very stringent capital requirements for becoming a primary dealer. According to the New York Fed's current criteria, bank-related primary dealers must be in compliance with Tier I and Tier II capital standards under the Basel Capital Accord, with at least $150 million in Tier I capital, an amount that represents a $50 million increase (announced by the Fed in January 2010) over levels that had been in place since the 1990s. Registered broker-dealers must have at least $50 million in Tier II capital and total capital in excess of the regulatory "warning levels" for capital set by the Securities and Exchange Commission and the U.S. Treasury, the two regulatory bodies that oversee nonbank securities trading organizations. A registered broker-dealer must have at least $150 in regulatory net capital (up from $50 million) as computed in accordance with the SEC's net capital rule. The broker-dealer must otherwise be in compliance with all capital and other regulatory requirements imposed by the SEC or its self-regulatory organization (SRO).

Tier I capital and Tier II capital are names for the types of capital that firms must obtain in order to be designated as primary dealers. Tier I capital includes common stockholders' equity, qualifying noncumulative perpetual preferred stock, and a minority interest in the equity accounts of consolidated subsidiaries. Tier I capital normally is defined as the sum of core capital elements minus goodwill and other intangible assets. The Tier II component of a firm's qualifying total capital may consist of supplementary capital elements such as allowance for loan and lease losses, perpetual preferred stock and a related surplus, hybrid capital instruments and mandatory convertible debt securities, and term-subordinated debt and intermediate-term preferred stock.

These stringent capital requirements are designed to help ensure that primary dealers are able to enter into transactions with the Fed in sufficient size to maintain the efficiency of their trading desk operations. The financial crisis is sure to result in more scrutiny over dealer balance sheets given the failings to either detect or reign in the risk taking that several doomed dealers engaged in during the crisis.

Primary dealers assist the Fed not only by facilitating the implementation of its directives on monetary policy but also by giving the Fed valuable information. For one thing, the Fed requires primary dealers to make reasonably good markets in their trading relationships with the Fed's trading desk.

In addition, primary dealers must participate meaningfully in auctions of U.S. Treasuries held by the U.S. Treasury Department. Interestingly, primary dealers also must offer market information and analysis to the Fed's trading desk, which the Fed uses in the formulation and implementation of monetary policy. Primary dealers also must report weekly on their trading activities, cash, futures, and financing market positions in Treasury and other securities.

Primary dealers tend to carry larger inventories of fixed-income securities and carry a greater variety of them. They also tend to have a greater ability to participate in offerings of new fixed-income securities. The willingness to hold securities has shrunk in the aftermath of the crisis, with several dealers, including Goldman Sachs, Morgan Stanley, and Merrill Lynch, converting their franchises to banks, which are required to have balance sheets that are typically far less leveraged than those of the dealer community. This de-risking, de-leveraging mindset is illustrated in Figure 2.1, which shows the aggregate amount of positions held by primary dealers in Treasury, agency, mortgage-backed, and corporate securities. This de-leveraging is having an impact on the depth of bid-ask spreads in the bond market, with dealers being less willing to bid or offer on positions they are now reluctant to hold, be it for the long or short term.

As you can see, primary dealers have a very big presence in the bond market in terms of both their daily trading volumes and their relationship with the Fed. Dealers therefore play a critical role in the functioning of the bond market, providing the substantial amounts of liquidity needed to keep the bond market running efficiently.

FIGURE 2.1 Dealers Have Reduced Positions in Riskier Assets

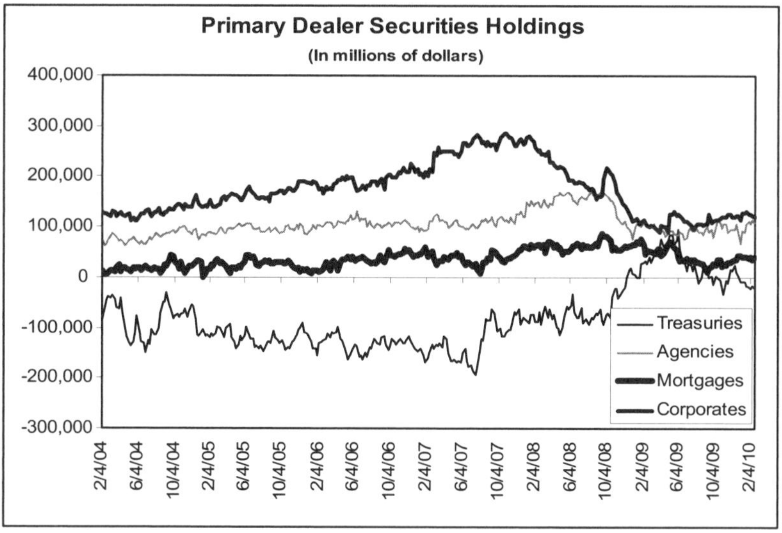

Source: Federal Reserve Bank of New York.

The Bond Market's Size, from Head to Toe

It might surprise you, because so much more attention is paid to the stock market than to the bond market, to hear that the bond market is far larger and far more active than the stock market, but it is. In many venues the stock market grabs the lion's share of media attention, and it is the subject of most conversations about investing. Similarly, investment-oriented firms such as brokerage firms and mutual fund companies spend far more of their time and money trying to lure individuals who are interested in stocks than they do trying to attract individuals interested in bonds.

This all seems rational, of course, since individuals frequently trade in and out of stocks but make relatively fewer changes to their bond holdings. Most people who buy bonds buy them with the intention of holding on to them for a while, and many people are leery about investing in bonds that seem too complex.

The relatively low level of attention paid to the bond market has contributed to the public's misconceptions about it, and it is one reason why the public knows so little about the bond market.

What is the bond market, and who are its participants? This chapter will help answer these questions.

There's No Bigger Market

The U.S. bond market is the biggest securities market in the world. At $34.644 trillion at the end of the third quarter of 2009, the bond market was more than double the size of the U.S. economy and much larger than the U.S. equity market, which had a market capitalization of about $19.5 trillion.[1] The bond market's growth accelerated in the 2000s, roughly doubling in size and growing faster than the growth rate of the U.S. economy. This sowed the seeds for the financial crisis.

There are many reasons for the bond market's rapid growth, although the composition of that growth has changed vastly in the aftermath of the financial crisis. First, as the economy grows, demand for credit grows too because companies need to borrow additional capital to finance their growth. They get this capital by issuing more bonds. Additionally, in an expanding economy, new companies are formed, and this increases the universe of companies that tap the bond market for money. Borrowing needs of both the federal and municipal sector also increase as the economy grows.

A second reason for the bond market's rapid growth has been the globalization of the financial markets. New technologies and reduced trade barriers have allowed global investors to move money across borders with relative ease, resulting in an increase in both the issuance of foreign bonds and the purchase of U.S. bonds by foreign investors. Figure 2.2 shows the net amount of foreign purchases of U.S. corporate bonds and U.S. Treasuries. The audience for bonds has become far vaster than it was not too long ago, and debt issuers across the gamut have taken advantage of the growing audience by issuing more bonds.

A third contributing factor to the bond market's rapid growth has been a sharp increase in the introduction of new financial products. One example is the market for so-called asset-backed securities, which are basically a repackaging of loans such as credit card loans, student loans, and car loans. The asset-backed securities market has grown sharply in recent years, more than tripling in size to nearly $2.9 trillion in the middle of 2008 compared to the start of the decade (although it had shrunk to about $2.5 trillion as of the end of the third quarter of 2009). Financial innovations such as asset-backed securities have been a big factor in the growth of the markets for many other types of fixed-income securities.

There are other reasons why the bond market has grown, of course, but the factors just listed are the most prominent. The composition of the

FIGURE 2.2 Net Foreign Purchases of Treasuries and Corporates, Monthly, in Billions of Dollars

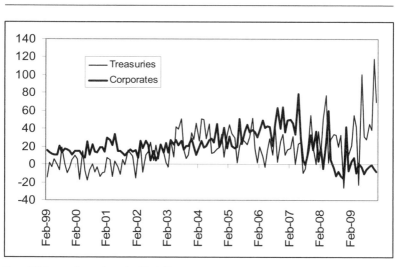

Source: U.S. Treasury, Treasury International Capital System.

growth has shifted dramatically in the aftermath of the financial crisis, with the government sector now accounting for the vast majority of the growth as a result of large budget deficits and the private sector's de-leveraging.

These forces appear likely to continue to influence the growth of the bond market for quite some time or at least until the government sector is able to pass the baton to the private sector in more normalized financial and economic circumstances.

Sizing Up the Market

The bond market consists of many different types of fixed-income securities. The most prominent of these securities are, from the largest segments to the smallest, as follows:

- Mortgage-related securities
- U.S. Treasuries
- Corporate bonds
- Money market securities
- Federal agency securities
- Municipal bonds
- Asset-backed securities

These securities account for all of the bond market's $34.6 trillion, and the market for each of these securities is $2.5 trillion or more—large enough to facilitate the needs of investors both large and small.

Knowing the size of each segment of the bond market can give you perspective on each segment's relative importance and put you well on the road to having a well-rounded knowledge of the bond market. This is becoming increasingly important from a tactical standpoint because the growth of the public sector poses increased risks to investors in that sphere, at least on a relative basis compared to other segments of the bond market, including versus that of other government securities markets.

To get started, take a look at Table 2.1.

As you can see in the table, the largest segment of the bond market is the mortgage securities market. Only recently has attention on the mortgage market matched its size. The mortgage securities market doesn't exactly make the front page of the business news every day, nor is it usually the focus of financial advertising and literature. Yet it is a market of immense importance, as we will discuss later.

TABLE 2.1 U.S. Bond Market Debt Outstanding

	Municipal	Treasury*	Mortgage Related†	Corporate Debt	Federal Agency Securities	Money Markets‡	Asset Backed¶	Total
1996	1,261.6	3,666.7	2,486.1	2,126.5	925.8	1,393.9	404.4	12,265.0
1997	1,318.7	3,659.5	2,680.2	2,359.0	1,021.8	1,692.8	535.8	13,267.8
1998	1,402.7	3,542.8	2,955.2	2,708.5	1,302.1	1,977.8	731.5	14,620.6
1999	1,457.1	3,529.5	3,334.3	3,046.5	1,620.0	2,338.8	900.8	16,227.0
2000	1,480.5	3,210.0	3,565.8	3,358.4	1,853.7	2,662.6	1,071.8	17,202.8
2001	1,603.6	3,196.6	4,127.4	3,836.4	2,157.4	2,587.2	1,281.2	18,789.8
2002	1,763.0	3,469.2	4,686.4	4,132.8	2,377.7	2,545.7	1,543.2	20,518.0
2003	1,876.8	3,967.8	5,238.6	4,486.4	2,626.2	2,519.9	1,693.7	22,409.4
2004	2,000.2	4,407.4	5,930.5	4,801.3	2,700.6	2,904.2	1,827.8	24,572.0
2005	2,192.1	4,714.8	7,212.3	4,965.7	2,616.0	3,433.7	1,955.2	27,089.8
2006	2,363.5	4,872.3	8,635.4	5,344.6	2,651.3	4,008.8	2,130.4	30,006.3
2007	2,568.1	5,081.5	9,142.7	5,946.8	2,933.3	4,170.8	2,472.4	32,315.6
2008	2,637.5	6,082.3	9,099.8	6,201.6	3,205.2	3,790.9	2,671.8	33,689.1
2008								
Q1	2,590.0	5,235.9	9,197.8	6,042.8	2,961.6	4,245.8	2,480.3	32,754.2
Q2	2,609.2	5,269.9	9,129.8	6,181.2	3,125.6	4,166.9	2,881.5	33,364.1
Q3	2,639.1	5,715.8	9,121.4	6,135.0	3,175.8	3,942.4	2,794.3	33,523.8
Q4	2,637.5	6,082.3	9,099.8	6,201.6	3,205.2	3,790.9	2,671.8	33,689.1
2009								
Q1	2,670.3	6,617.6	9,060.1	6,721.7	3,140.8	3,578.4	2,598.6	34,387.5
Q2	2,700.1	6,924.5	9,151.8	6,777.3	2,970.4	3,429.8	2,533.6	34,487.5
Q3	2,713.5	7,358.4	9,213.7	6,856.5	2,823.7	3,193.9	2,484.3	34,644.0
Q4								

* Interest-bearing marketable public debt.
† Includes GNMA, FNMA, and FHLMC mortgage-backed securities and CMOs, and CMBS, and private-label MBS/CMOs.
‡ Includes commercial paper, banker's acceptances, and large time deposits.
¶ Includes auto, credit card, home equity, manufacturing, student, and other loans. CDOs of ABS are included.

Source: U.S. Department of Treasury, Federal Reserve System, federal agencies, Dealogic, Thomson Financial, Bloomberg, Loan Performance, and the Securities Industry and Financial Markets Association (SIFMA).

Aside from the perspective you'll get from knowing the sizes of the various segments of the bond market, there are several other reasons to track its size. First, your tracking changes in the bond market's size can help you discern economic and financial trends. For example, an increase in the size of the corporate bond market could be taken as a sign that U.S. corporations are optimistic about the economic outlook or at the very least are obtaining the funding they need to expand; they borrow money, after all, to expand their businesses. In some cases, however, a surge in the growth of corporate debt may raise a red flag by hinting that corporations are accumulating an excessive amount of debt relative to their income prospects. Nimble U.S. companies have avoided this problem for quite some time and arguably were in better shape than households, financial institutions, and government at the start of the financial crisis. In hindsight a glaring signal about the excessive use of debt was the mortgage market's explosive growth in the early and mid-2000s.

A second reason to learn more about the bond market's size is to gain an improved perspective on the impact that developments in each of the market segments may have on the economy and the financial markets. If, for example, a dislocation in the municipal bond market were to surface after a municipality's failure to repay its debt obligations, it would be helpful to have a perspective on how large the default was relative to the size of the market. This could help you make a judgment about whether the dislocation was presenting a risk or an opportunity for investments in that market.

A third benefit of tracking the bond market's size is the perspective it provides on both the quote depth and the liquidity of each market segment. Quote depth refers to the size of the bids and offers for individual securities. The size of the markets has an important bearing on the market's liquidity and quote depth, and this can influence when and at what prices you buy and sell securities. Basically, the bigger the market is, the more liquid it is likely to be. This should translate into greater quote depth, better visibility on market prices, and prices that are indicative of each security's fair value.

For forecasters and academicians, tracking changes in the sizes of the various segments of the fixed-income market helps provide documentation of the flow of funds between different types of financial assets. This helps them study trends in personal savings, for example. In the years ahead, it will provide a gauge of the degree to which the financial system is healing and how it is changing. One expectation is that the mortgage- and asset-backed markets will shrink as a share of the overall market while the government and corporate sectors expand.

The Federal Reserve tracks the flow of funds not only between the different segments of the fixed-income market but across other financial assets as well. This helps the Fed quantify the effects that changes in financial conditions may have on real activity. The data on the flow of funds, which are produced quarterly by the Fed, helps the Fed develop forecasts on the economy because changes in balance sheets and financial conditions can be important factors that affect the spending decisions of households, businesses, and governments.

Given the value of having a good understanding of the various segments of the bond market, let's take a look at each of the segments and size them up.

U.S. Treasury Securities

For most people the "bond market" and "U.S. Treasuries" are synonymous. Public awareness of the Treasury market easily exceeds that of all the other segments of the bond market. You can understand why when you look at its mammoth size and daily trading volume. Although the mortgage market is the biggest segment of the bond market, Treasuries, which are issued by the U.S. Treasury, are by far the most active segment, and the Treasury is the single largest issuer of debt in the world. In fact, Treasuries are the most actively traded securities in the world.

U.S. Treasury securities are so prominent that their interest rates are used as a benchmark for rate markets throughout the world, including the swaps market, as well as markets throughout the world. This will be discussed in greater detail later in this chapter, and a definitional guide to Treasuries and other types of bonds will be presented in Chapter 4.

As you saw in Table 2.1, there were $7.358 trillion of Treasuries outstanding at the end of the third quarter of 2009, and by early in the first quarter of 2010, the figure had ballooned to close to $7.8 trillion. While high, many people expect the figure to be even higher because the U.S. government is often quoted as having even more debt. Indeed, on February 13, 2010, the U.S. had $12.35 trillion of debt outstanding, equal to about 85 percent of its gross domestic product. There are two reasons for the $4.5 trillion difference between the amount of publicly traded debt and the total amount of debt outstanding. First, there are approximately $4.5 trillion in nonmarketable securities held in a trust fund for various programs, particularly the Social Security program. These trust funds are essentially IOUs. Currently, approximately $2.5 trillion is owed to the Social Security trust fund (called the Federal Old-Age and Survivors Insurance Trust Fund) by the Treasury Department. These IOUs began accumulating in the 1980s as the U.S. government essentially dipped into the trust fund's yearly surpluses.

The trust fund has been running surpluses for a number of years, as the population of people paying Social Security taxes has exceeded the population of people receiving Social Security benefits. The main reason for this involves favorable demographics: a baby boom took place between 1946 and

1964, resulting in a large pool of taxpayers. The increase in the number of taxpayers has greatly exceeded the increase in the number of Social Security recipients, resulting in large surpluses. (Of course, as baby boomers retire, this dynamic will work in the opposite direction, carrying with it a bundle of economic, financial, and political ramifications.) Through creative accounting and political will, the surpluses have been included in the yearly readings on the U.S. fiscal balance. This has produced smaller reported deficits and larger surpluses than have actually been the case, but the debts owed to the Social Security trust fund and other funds have been kept out of the public eye.

A second reason why the total amount of publicly traded Treasuries differs from the U.S. government's total debt relates to the Federal Reserve. The Fed holds roughly $780 billion in Treasuries for its own account. As will be discussed in Chapter 6, the Fed has been accumulating Treasuries for many years to help it implement monetary policy, and the purchase of $300 billion of Treasury securities was included in the asset purchase program it began in November 2008. Thus, while the Fed's holdings are not included in the $3 trillion tally of publicly traded Treasuries, they are nonetheless part of Uncle Sam's total debt outstanding.

Now more than ever it is important to monitor the total amount of publicly traded U.S. Treasuries outstanding and the total amount of U.S. debt outstanding. With respect to the former, investors need to constantly assess the world's appetite for U.S. Treasuries because increases in the amount of Treasuries outstanding are a technical burden for the Treasuries market—the laws of supply and demand have not been repealed. As for the latter, the more investors perceive there to be burdens on the U.S. fiscal situation, the more difficult it could become for the United States to sell its Treasury securities.

A very important technical element in the U.S. Treasuries supply picture is the U.S. Treasury Department's stated goal of increasing the average maturity on the U.S. Treasury debt outstanding from the 26-year low of 48 months it reached at the end of 2008, to at least 66 months and possibly as high as 84 months sometime over a period of 5 or 6 years (see Figure 2.3). An increase to around 60 months was expected by the end of 2010. This is important because long-dated maturities move more in price than do short-dated maturities for an equal shift in yield. (This idea is based on the concept of duration, will be discussed further in Chapter 3.)

There is limited scope for investors to absorb the increased supply of longer maturities compared to the ability to absorb an equal amount of shorter maturities because there is more interest rate risk (we discuss interest rate risk in Chapter 5) in long-dated maturities than there is for short-

FIGURE 2.3 Average Maturity of the Treasury Debt

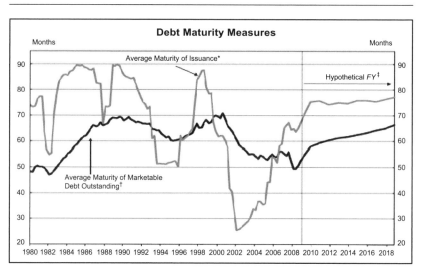

* Quarterly data are actuals through September 30, 2009. Actuals and fiscal year projections use a four-quarter average.
† Quarterly data are actuals through September 30, 2009. Fiscal year projections are yearly data.
‡ Net financing projections for fiscal year 2010 through fiscal year 2019 are based on the Office of Management and Budget's 2010 MSR Budget estimates released in August 2009. Future residual financing needs are spread proportionally across auctioned securities and are derived from hypothetical auction sizes. Initial sizes are based on announced coupon amounts as of October 23, 2009, and they assume the outstanding level of bills on September 30, 2009. All projections exclude cash management bill (CMB) issuance and maturing amounts.

Source: U.S. Treasury.

dated maturities. This is true because portfolio managers tend to keep the average maturity of their portfolios fairly close to the average maturities of indexes produced by organizations such as Barclays Capital. In other words, the Treasury Department is essentially asking investors to take on more risk, but there is limited scope for it. One possible result could be an increase in Treasury yields on an outright basis (because investors would demand a higher yield in order to be enticed to purchase the longer maturities and increase their risk). Or there could be an increase on a relative basis compared to government securities for other nations, particularly those with more stable debt-to-GDP ratios. An end to the Federal Reserve's asset purchase program adds to the supply burden because a great deal of "duration" was absorbed by the Fed while it purchased fixed-income assets.

Volume in Treasury Securities

As was mentioned earlier, U.S. Treasuries are the most actively traded securities in the world. This makes the Treasury market the most liquid financial market in the world. Treasuries trade literally around the clock and around the globe.

Investors are drawn to the Treasury market for its safety element. As obligations of the U.S. government, Treasuries are backed by the full faith and credit of the U.S. government, and, notwithstanding recent events, they are therefore considered risk free. Investors also are drawn to the Treasuries market because of its deep liquidity and quote depth; large transactions of up to $1 billion or more are commonplace in the Treasury market.

As is shown in Figure 2.4, the daily average trading volume by primary dealers for all Treasuries was $410 billion in 2009, which was well below levels seen in prior years. Volume figures have declined in the aftermath of the financial crisis because dealers have been de-risking their balance sheets by reducing their holdings of fixed-income securities, resulting in reduced trading volumes.

Three major determinants of trading volume in Treasuries are the state of the economy, the Federal Reserve's actions, and the global economic and financial conditions. Also impacting trading volume is activity in other segments of the bond market. For example, the issuance calendar for corporate securities can spur hedging activity involving Treasuries (issuers might sell Treasuries to hedge against yield increases that might occur before the actual issuance of their debt securities). The mortgage market can also spur activity by market participants that use Treasuries to hedge their exposures to mortgage securities. The swaps market also spurs activity in the Treasury market.

FIGURE 2.4 Daily Volume of Treasuries Traded by Primary Dealers, in Billions of Dollars

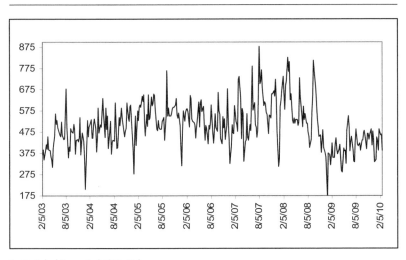

Source: Federal Reserve Bank of New York.

Municipal Securities

The municipal bond market may not be the biggest segment of the bond market in terms of total dollar size, but it is easily the biggest in terms of the total number of bonds outstanding. It's easy to understand why there are so many municipal bonds outstanding when one considers the large number of state and local government entities in the United States: there are over 50,000 government entities that have issued municipal bonds.[2] In all, a whopping 1.5 million separate bond issues are outstanding. That stands in stark contrast to the other segments of the bond market, where far fewer securities have been issued. The market for U.S. Treasuries, for example, consists of only about 170 separate securities, not including U.S. Treasury bills.

One might think the large number of municipal bonds outstanding would translate into a market bustling with activity, but it doesn't. Daily volume in the municipal bond market is actually quite low. In fact, many municipal bonds "trade by appointment." In other words, they rarely trade.

The municipal bond market at the end of the third quarter of 2009 was roughly $2.7 trillion in size. As with other debt markets, it grew sharply over the past decade, by about 7 percent per year, up from a 5 percent growth rate in the late 1990s.

Individual investors historically have shown the greatest amount of interest in the municipal bond market, and their continued interest has helped the municipal bond market continue its steady growth. Individuals, in fact, are by far the largest holders of municipal securities, holding about 70 percent of all outstanding issues, down from 75 percent in 2001. The decrease reflects the birth of the market for Build America Bonds (BABs), which were created in 2009. Build America Bonds are taxable municipal bonds subsidized by the U.S. government in order to market them to a broader group of investors, particularly those that traditionally invest in the corporate bond market.

The municipal bond market is the only segment of the bond market whose securities are held primarily by individuals rather than institutions. Over 5.1 million households hold municipals in one form or another, either directly or indirectly, through mutual funds and the like.

Individuals are drawn to municipal bonds for their tax advantages: the interest paid on most municipal bonds is exempt from federal taxes. This makes municipal securities most attractive to individuals in high income tax brackets. We will discuss the special tax-exempt status of municipal securities in greater detail in Chapter 4.

The municipal bond market is likely to continue to grow for quite some time unless the federal government cuts income tax rates to zero (in the next millennium perhaps). Individuals therefore are likely to remain attracted to municipal bonds for the foreseeable future.

Large borrowing needs will keep municipal bond issuers active in the debt markets. The National Governors Association in November 2009 estimated that states faced $250 billion in annual budget gaps for the fiscal years 2009 through 2011.

One major factor that in theory could slow the growth of borrowing relates to the decline in the housing market, which by itself has hurt the fiscal situations of municipalities. Borrowing needs can be slowed in theory by a decline in so-called urban sprawl. *Urban sprawl* is basically what the name implies: it is the spreading of communities' built environments from their urban areas to their surrounding rural areas. If fewer homes are built, there will be a relative decline in the need for new roads, sewers, and other infrastructure associated with the construction of new neighborhoods. The aging of the nation's infrastructure will serve as an offset, as will the political impetus to push spending dollars toward infrastructure.

Volume in Municipal Securities

Despite the popularity of municipal bonds among individual investors and the massive number of municipal securities outstanding, the municipal bond market is an illiquid market. The average daily trading volume of municipal securities was just $12.3 billion per day in the first nine months of 2009, about 3 percent of the daily trading volume in U.S. Treasuries.[3]

Daily trading volume in the municipal bond market is low largely because individuals do not buy and sell municipal securities in the same way they buy and sell stocks. Municipal securities are not trading vehicles, and therefore they are rarely used for speculative purposes. Individuals generally buy municipals with the intention of holding on to them for a while, often until the bonds mature. As a result, individual investors are apt to be only occasional participants in the municipal bond market.

Trading volume in the municipal bond market can be influenced by a number of factors. For example, individual investors tend to vary in their preference for municipals depending on interest rate levels. Individuals tend to shy away from municipals when interest rates fall and flock to them when interest rates rise. They are apparently very sensitive to the impact that interest rate levels can have on their interest income and, hence, their tax liabilities.

An exception to the notion that individuals shy away from municipals when interest rates decline is the way they behave when the decline is due partly to weakening in the stock market. In such cases, rather than move out of interest bearing assets, individual investors often shift money out of stocks into high-quality bonds such as Treasuries, as well as high-quality municipal securities (not all municipal securities are considered high quality). They do this because bonds tend to perform well when the equity market falters.

Another way in which the interest rate environment influences trading volume in municipals is through activity associated with refunded bonds. *Refunded bonds* are previously issued bonds that essentially are refinanced with new bonds at a lower interest rate. In a refunding, an issuer sells new bonds to raise the money needed to eventually "refund," or prepay, the older bonds on their first call date (see Chapter 3 for more on call dates and call-able bonds). The issuance of new bonds leads to an increase in volume by spurring investors to participate in the market through purchases of the new bonds. In some cases the buyers of the new bonds sell or swap out of their existing holdings of municipal bonds to pay for their purchases of the new bonds. This boosts volume further.

A downside of refunding issuance is that the investors in bonds that are refunded have to find new investments to replace their prepaid bonds. This usually means that they wind up reinvesting the money they receive from the refunded bonds into new bonds that have a lower interest rate than the refunded bonds. This reduces the rate of return on their money.

Refunding issuance often can account for a meaningful percentage of the total issuance of new municipal bonds. In 2009, for example, refunding issuance accounted for 25 percent of the total issuance of municipal bonds, and it was expected to account for a similar percentage in 2010, according to the Securities Industry and Financial Markets Association (SIFMA).

It is important to bear in mind that interest rate levels affect activity in the municipal bond market and hence key investment considerations such as market liquidity, quote depth, and refunding risk.

Corporate Bonds

At $6.202 trillion, the corporate bond market is the second largest segment of the bond market. Corporate bonds are widely held, with most of them in the hands of large institutions such as insurance companies, pension funds, and foreign entities. Households are also large holders of corporate bonds, owning more of them ($2.7 trillion) than of any other type of bond.

As with the municipal bond market, investors in the corporate bond market are also buy-and-hold investors, and speculators don't dabble in cor-porate bonds much. This keeps volume levels relatively low. In 2009, data from the Financial Industry Regulatory Authority (FINRA) indicated that the average daily trading volume for investment-grade corporate bonds was around $12.0 billion, and for high-yield bonds it was around $5.5 billion.

The corporate bond market consists of many names that are familiar to most people. As we have learned, these are generally large corporations that frequently issue new debt to finance their expansion, and this contributes to the growth of the corporate bond market.

Almost daily, corporations issue new bonds to what has tended to be a receptive audience of investors. The exception was in the final months of 2008 following the collapse of Lehman Brothers when daily issuance was near nil for almost two months. For all of 2008, corporate bond issuance was around $800 billion, well below the previous year's record of about $1.2 trillion, although a rebound in issuance was posted in 2009 (see Figure 2.5).

Numerous factors affect the issuance of corporate bonds. Monetary policy certainly plays a role, with interest rate cuts typically producing economic and financial conditions that are conducive to issuance, and rate hikes producing the opposite. When the Fed lowers rates, yields on corporate bonds tend to fall faster than Treasury yields because investors become more willing to take risk and because they expect the rate cuts to promote economic growth. In this case, corporate bond prices rise faster too, since bond prices and yields move inversely with each other. This outperformance means that investors can gain from a two-pronged drop in interest rates on corporate bonds—that is, the decline associated with the general decline

FIGURE 2.5 Corporate Bond Issuance, 2001 through 2009, Third Quarter, in Billions of Dollars

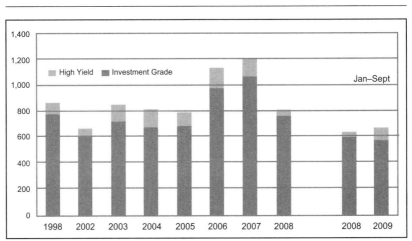

Note: Includes all nonconvertible debt, medium-term notes (MTNs), Yankee bonds, and Temporary Liquidity Government Program (TLGP) debt, but excludes all issues with maturities of one year or less, certificates of deposit (CDs), and federal agency debt.

Source: Thomson Reuters.

in interest rates and the decline associated with the yield spread that exists between corporate bonds and Treasuries. A yield spread exists because of the difference in credit quality. When companies issue new bonds to take advantage of declines in interest rates, this is referred to as *opportunistic issuance.* It is one of the most important factors affecting the issuance of corporate bonds.

Another factor that affects issuance is the condition of the U.S. equity market, which is correlated with the corporate bond market because it is also dependent upon the outlook for corporate cash flows and investor sentiment. Companies that investors purchase in the equity market could be the same as those they purchase in the corporate bond market, and which of the two securities investors decide to invest in depends upon where investors would like to be in the capital structure. A high priority for investors in the aftermath of the financial crisis was to be as high up in the capital structure as possible because default risks had increased. Bond investors have priority over equity investors in the case of a company's failure.

Another factor that influences issuance is the degree to which there is any switching to or from the use of short-term financing. For example, when interest rates are low, issuers seek to "term out" their debts by locking in low rates for longer. The opposite occurs when rates are high. This is akin to a homeowner's refinancing an adjustable-rate mortgage by converting it to a fixed-rate loan of, say, 15 or 30 years. In doing so, the homeowner removes uncertainties about the monthly payments and locks in a low long-term interest rate. Companies refinance their debt in the same way, hoping to remove uncertainties about near-term debt servicing while simultaneously locking in low long-term interest costs. This has become a new priority for companies worried in the aftermath of the financial crisis about the availability of credit. Companies with short-term liabilities are more fearful than before about having to repeatedly access the capital markets for funding.

As you can see, the size of the corporate bond market is influenced by a variety of factors. At the core, the Fed, the interest rate environment, risk attitudes, and the economy are the most critical factors in shaping demand for corporate bonds. This becomes even more obvious when one takes a closer look at their impact on the various industries within the corporate bond market. We'll do that in Chapter 4.

Volume in Corporate Bonds

Volume in the corporate bond market has become easier to quantify than it once was. In the 1990s, the bean counters that tallied the daily volume in Treasuries and municipals could not as easily quantify the volume of bonds that traded in the corporate bond market. There were many reasons for this, but the primary reason related to the fact that corporate bond trades were not recorded in ways that could be captured easily. Transactions in Treasuries, for example, could be tracked through government brokers: intermediaries that facilitate trading between primary dealers and, to a lesser degree, between broker-dealers. Moreover, the Federal Reserve collects data on volume from dealers. The transactions are therefore easily tabulated. No such network exists in the corporate bond market. While some corporate bond transactions are handled through brokers, the preponderance of trades take place over the counter, essentially invisible to the public.

Recognizing the lack of transparency that existed in the corporate bond market, regulators sought change. In July 2002, the National Association of Securities Dealers (NASD) launched a regulatory system designed to capture the reporting and dissemination of eligible corporate bond transactions in investment-grade and high-yield debt, medium-term notes, and convertible bonds. The system was called the Trade Reporting and Compliance Engine (TRACE). It is a mandatory system. All brokerage firms in the United States are required to report eligible secondary market activity and over-the-counter transactions to TRACE under rules approved by the Securities and Exchange Commission (SEC). The NASD in July 2007 was consolidated with the member regulation, enforcement, and arbitration functions of the New York Stock Exchange to form the Financial Industry Regulatory Authority (FINRA), which now controls the TRACE system.

As mentioned earlier, volume in corporate bonds averaged around $12 billion per day in 2009. Volume in high-yield bonds averaged around $5.5 billion per day.

There is another source of data on daily trading volume in corporate bonds, and it comes from an unusual source: the New York Stock Exchange (NYSE) Euronext. A large number of bonds are listed on the NYSE Euronext: about 29,000 bonds issued by 4,000 entities in 100 countries, a multiple of the number of equity listings there, although volume is scarce by comparison to the over-the-counter market. The vast majority of NYSE Euronext volume in bonds is in corporate bonds: 94 percent of the volume consists of straight corporate bonds and the rest consists of convertible bonds.

Agency Securities

At $2.8 trillion, the government agency securities market is a large and active market. It is also a market that has undergone substantial change as a result of the financial crisis. The biggest occurred on September 7, 2008, when the Federal Housing Finance Agency (FHFA), which was created by an act of Congress from the Housing and Economic Recovery Act of 2008 on July 30, 2008, put Fannie Mae and Freddie Mac, the giant federal agencies whose public mission is to provide stability and liquidity to the housing market, into conservatorship. Through the legal process of conservatorship, an entity is appointed to establish control and oversight of a company to put it into a sound and solvent condition. The conservator in this case was the FHFA, and it now controls and directs the operations of the two companies. We will discuss Fannie and Freddie in greater detail in Chapter 4.

The agency securities market consists largely of debt issued by eight separate government securities agencies commonly referred to as *government-sponsored enterprises* (GSEs). These agencies are discussed in greater detail in Chapter 4. With the exception of one of the eight government-sponsored enterprises, the GSEs are not explicitly backed by the full faith and credit of the U.S. government.

Importantly, this means that they carry an element of credit risk. Nevertheless, since they are government-sponsored agencies, many investors believe that the GSEs have an implicit guarantee. On December 24, 2009, these sentiments were reinforced when the Treasury Department said that it was removing the $400 billion cap ($200 billion for each company) that the Treasury previously said it would be willing to provide to sustain the companies, saying that it would allow the cap to increase "as necessary to accommodate any cumulative reduction in net worth over the next three years."[4]

These are the extraordinary measures that investors for years felt that the U.S. government probably would take to help the agencies if they encountered financial difficulties.

It's easy to understand why investors would feel this way even if it were not entirely technically correct. Consider the biggest of the GSEs, Fannie Mae, which is short for the Federal National Mortgage Association. Over the years since Fannie Mae began its operations in 1938, it has helped millions of Americans buy their own homes. Over the last 40 years alone, Fannie Mae has helped over 40 million families buy their own homes. In 2008, Fannie Mae, in combination with Freddie Mac, which is short for Federal Home Loan Mortgage Corporation, had $5.4 trillion of guaranteed mortgage-backed securities (MBS) and debt outstanding, equal at that time to the amount of publicly held debt of the United States. In addition, the market share of all new mortgages was as high as 80 percent in 2008, owing in no small part to the collapse of the private MBS market. With numbers like these, it is evident why many investors believe that the government would do its utmost to ensure that Fannie Mae and Freddie Mac and the other GSEs stay in business, even if still technically incorrect since there is no explicit guarantee other than the one that looks obvious.

Led by the GSEs, the agency securities market grew rapidly in the late 1990s and 2000s, reflecting the strength of the housing market. After doubling in size between 1996 and 2000, the total amount of federal agency debt outstanding slowed but continued to grow fast, as previously shown in Figure 2.3.

The sharp growth in the agency securities market during the late 1990s was fueled by a sharp increase in the homeownership rate in the United States, which continued to climb in the 2000s, reaching a record 69.3 percent in June 2004, as shown in Figure 2.6. The increase was fueled by government policies designed to expand homeownership, as well as an expanding economy and low interest rates. As homeownership expanded, so did the need for financing since most homeowners take out a mortgage to buy a home. Government agencies such as Fannie Mae play an integral role in providing this financing by issuing debt securities and using the money to purchase pools of mortgage loans and by guaranteeing others.

Another factor that spurred housing activity was favorable demographics. The aging of baby boomers—individuals born between 1946 and 1964—led to an increase in home buying as baby boomers used the wealth they had accumulated to buy larger homes and second homes. Another positive demographic factor for the housing market, and hence the growth of the agency securities market, was the rise in the number of single-person households and in immigration.

FIGURE 2.6 Homeownership Rate, United States, Seasonally Adjusted, Percentage

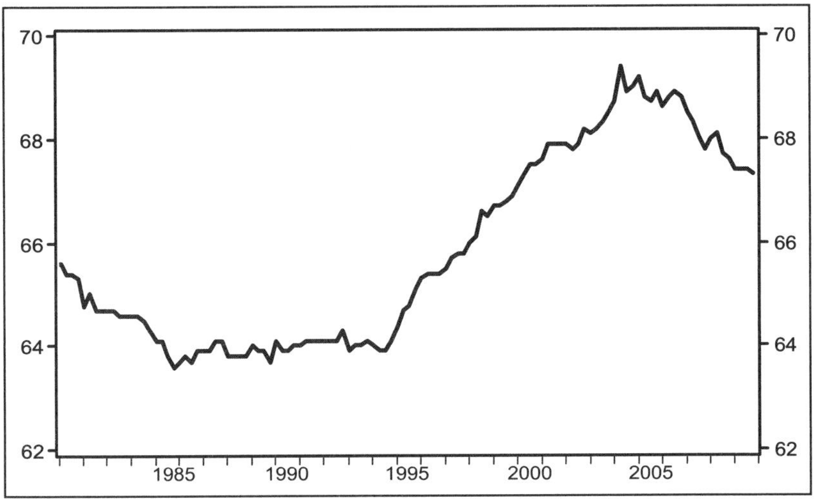

Source: U.S. Census Bureau and Haver Analytics.

When confidence and economic vitality return to the United States, demographics are likely to buoy housing and further reduce the excess amount of unsold homes, stabilizing prices. Birth statistics indicate that household formation should average as much as 1.2 million per year in normal economic times. The growth rate drops during a recession as people delay the formation of new homes—the number of people per household increases. Even assuming a decline to around 800,000 or so in the recession, housing starts at 500,000 suggest inventory levels will drop. (As much as 150,000 of the starts figure could even represent "restarts," or the reconstruction of damaged or unwanted homes, which means that the addition to the housing stock is less than the level of home construction.) Even if home buying is weak, people need shelter, and they will rent a home if they have to. People are essentially born short a roof over their heads and need to cover their short at some point.

Thus, three critical factors that have influenced the growth of the agency securities market are the economic climate, the interest rate environment, and demographics. These forces appear likely to influence the growth of the agency securities market positively in the years to come, but cyclical forces almost certainly will interrupt the positive trend occasionally. The big wild card is GSE reform, which was expected to get into high gear in 2010 and 2011. GSE reform will affect the way that GSEs are run and therefore their wherewithal to extend credit to prospective homeowners.

Volume in Agency Securities

Trading volume in agency securities grew fairly strongly in the late 1990s, but it did not change all that much in the 2000s even as the agency market continued to grow. Volume growth hence lagged that of Treasuries and mortgage-backed securities, as shown in Table 2.2. A top reason is because the ownership of agency securities is concentrated in the hands of investors more likely to buy and hold the securities, including the top two holders of agency securities: commercial banks and foreign investors.

Trading volume in agencies has decreased in recent times on a par with Treasuries, but a revival in volume is not likely given that the political impulse is to shrink the agencies over time. Despite the decrease in volume, the agency securities market is still active enough to be considered a relatively deep and liquid market suitable for most investors, although not as much as it was in past years. Liquidity, or the ease with which investors can trade in and out of securities holdings in the secondary market, is likely to diminish in the agency market as it did in the immediate aftermath of the FHFA's decision to put Fannie and Freddie into conservatorship.

TABLE 2.2 Average Daily Trading Volume in the U.S. Bond Markets, in Billions of Dollars

	Municipal	Treasury*	Agency MBS*	Corporate Debt†	Federal Agency Securities*	Total‡
1996	1.1	203.7	38.1	–	31.1	274.0
1997	1.1	212.1	47.1	–	40.2	300.5
1998	3.3	226.6	70.9	–	47.6	348.5
1999	8.3	186.5	67.1	–	54.5	316.5
2000	8.8	206.5	69.5	–	72.8	357.6
2001	8.8	297.9	112.0	–	90.2	508.9
2002	10.7	366.4	154.5	16.3	81.8	629.7
2003	12.6	433.5	206.0	18.0	81.7	751.8
2004	14.8	499.0	207.4	18.8	78.8	818.9
2005	16.9	554.5	251.8	16.7	78.8	918.7
2006	22.5	524.7	254.6	16.9	74.4	893.1
2007	25.0	570.2	320.1	16.4	83.0	1,014.7
2008	19.2	553.1	344.9	11.8	104.5	1,033.4
2009	12.3	407.9	299.9	16.8	77.7	814.5
2008						
Jan	24.9	594.7	439.7	13.8	121.1	1,194.1
Feb	29.2	662.3	411.1	12.7	119.4	1,234.8
March	25.8	756.2	405.1	11.8	122.8	1,321.7
April	22.0	551.8	306.5	13.1	121.2	1,014.7
May	17.0	521.5	315.9	13.4	106.3	974.1
June	19.3	604.1	312.1	11.3	108.5	1,055.4
July	15.4	533.1	312.8	9.8	101.9	973.0
Aug	13.7	443.3	258.9	8.3	94.0	818.1
Sept	20.4	694.5	359.0	12.2	116.6	1,202.7
Oct	17.1	524.2	371.3	12.5	85.3	1,010.5
Nov	12.4	439.7	357.2	11.4	76.6	897.3
Dec	12.7	311.3	289.5	11.6	79.8	704.8
2009						
Jan	12.1	358.0	363.6	16.1	75.0	824.8
Feb	11.6	387.0	331.6	15.6	85.1	830.9
March	10.9	402.1	337.7	15.5	89.4	855.6
April	12.6	350.9	291.6	17.1	85.2	757.4

TABLE 2.2 (Continued)

	Municipal	Treasury*	Agency MBS*	Corporate Debt†	Federal Agency Securities*	Total‡
May	11.9	396.3	277.6	19.7	85.2	790.7
June	12.9	466.5	325.3	19.3	84.6	908.5
July	11.8	353.4	256.0	17.1	74.1	712.5
Aug	11.9	433.3	270.5	15.7	73.1	804.4
Sept	14.4	432.0	276.1	17.9	76.3	816.6
Oct	12.7	450.4	318.6	17.7	74.5	873.8
Nov	12.3	463.7	305.9	16.1	67.8	865.8
Dec	12.5	401.4	243.8	13.3	61.8	732.7
2010						
Jan	13.6	439.8	312.1	19.7	67.8	853.0
YTD 2009	12.1	358.0	363.6	16.1	75.0	824.8
YTD 2010	13.6	439.8	312.1	19.7	67.8	853.0
% Change	12.4%	22.9%	-14.2%	21.9%	-9.6%	3.4%

* Primary dealer activity.
† Excludes all issues with maturities of one year or less and convertible securities.
‡ Totals may not add due to rounding.

Source: Federal Reserve Bank of New York, Municipal Securities Rulemaking Board, and the Financial Industry Regulatory Authority (FINRA).

Mortgage-Backed Securities

When most people think of debt, they think of mortgage debt because a home mortgage is their biggest debt and it is usually the biggest debt they will ever incur. When one considers that millions of Americans have mortgages on their homes, one begins to realize that the total amount of mortgages outstanding is quite large. That is indeed the case. Americans owe approximately $10.3 trillion on their home mortgages, up from $4.8 trillion in 2000, and mortgage debt accounted for about 75 percent of all household debt outstanding in the third quarter of 2009, up from 65 percent in 2000.

Given the staggering amount of mortgage debt outstanding and the proliferation of mortgage-related financial instruments that has occurred over the years, it should not be surprising that the largest segment of the bond market is the market for mortgage-backed securities. At $9.2 trillion, the mortgage-backed securities market is the largest debt market in the world and larger than the U.S. Treasury securities market. The mortgage-backed securities market is also an active market, with average daily trading volume second only to that of U.S. Treasuries.

The mortgage-backed securities market doubled in size in the 1990s and grew about 275 percent in the 2000s through the end of 2008. Its growth was fueled by many of the same forces that fueled the rapid growth of the agency securities market. The main driver of growth in both markets was the sharp growth in the number of mortgage originations resulting from the surge in home buying during the housing boom. The sharp increase in the number of mortgages outstanding created a vast pool of mortgages that could be securitized into mortgage-backed securities.

Most mortgage-backed securities are issued by three U.S. government agencies: the Federal National Mortgage Association (Fannie Mae), the Federal Home Loan Mortgage Corporation (Freddie Mac), and the Government National Mortgage Association (Ginnie Mae, or GNMA). The biggest issuer of mortgage-backed securities is Fannie Mae, followed by Freddie Mac and then GNMA, whose issuance has grown at a faster-than-historical pace because of increased government involvement in the mortgage market. Data from the Securities Industry and Financial Markets Association have indicated that in the first nine months of 2009, the amount of Ginnie Mae securities outstanding had increased about 30 percent to $803 billion and was on track to reach $1 trillion in 2010, a much faster growth rate than that of Fannie Mae and Freddie Mac, where MBSs outstanding hadn't changed much.

The financial crisis purged many nonagency, or private-label, issuers from the mortgage-backed securities market. For example, in the first nine months of 2009, only $3.4 billion of private-label residential mortgage-backed securities were issued. The decline suggests that the model for mortgage financing has been broken. Figure 2.7 shows the collapse of private-label mortgage finance.

The growth of the mortgage-backed securities market will depend largely on the same factors that influence the growth of the agency securities market, not the least of which will be the way that the United States goes about its financial regulatory reform, particularly for the GSEs.

Volume in Mortgage-Backed Securities

Although the mortgage-backed securities market is the largest debt securities market in the world, it is not the most active; the Treasury market is. Average daily trading volume in mortgage-backed securities in 2008 was about $350 billion.

FIGURE 2.7 The Collapse of the Issuance of Private-Label Mortgages, First Quarter 2001 through Third Quarter 2009

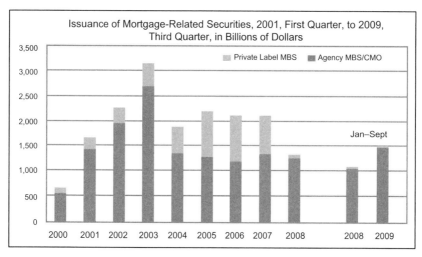

Source: Federal agencies and Thomson Reuters.

The disparity in daily trading volume between Treasuries and all the other segments of the bond market is so large that Treasuries should not be used as a yardstick to assess the extent to which the other segments of the bond market are active. A comparison would no doubt lead to the incorrect conclusion that other segments of the bond market are "inactive" by comparison. While this is true of some sectors and of specific bonds and in particular municipal and corporate bonds, it certainly is not true of the mortgage-backed securities market, which trades a great deal more than the U.S. equity market on a daily basis, at least in terms of dollar value, although not in terms of the number of transactions. One would never know this by reading the daily financial newspapers, where except for stories surrounding the financial crisis and the role that the mortgage market played in it, there is hardly a mention of daily activity in the MBS market.

Liquidity: A Measure of the Vibrancy, Depth, and Efficiency of Markets

The financial crisis showed that liquidity is vital for the normal and optimal functioning of markets. When it dried up, the highly leveraged U.S. financial system split at the seams, and debtors suddenly were unable to obtain financing, forcing the collapse of major financial institutions and severe strain for households and the U.S. economy. Liquidity is not the same as solvency, but without it insolvency is hastened.

Liquidity can be defined as the ease or difficulty with which buyers and sellers can transact in small and large quantities at prices that are considered representative of the true market value. A highly liquid market ensures that observed prices are close to the market consensus on where prices should be and that changes in prices reflect revisions in the market consensus rather than dislocations associated with illiquidity.

Liquidity enhances the efficiency of markets, encouraging broader market participation. In turn, this increases the availability of credit at lowered costs, encouraging the use of credit and spurring economic growth.

In the United States, where the financial markets are both vast and mature, liquidity has historically been quite good. This is one of the biggest reasons why the U.S. economy has performed so well for so long. Capitalist societies such as the United States simply cannot thrive without liquid markets. This is why the Federal Reserve injected more than $1 trillion of financial liquidity into the U.S. financial system during the financial crisis, seeking to restore "normal" functionality of the markets and make them conducive toward promoting economic growth.

How to Measure Market Liquidity: Bid-Ask Spread, Market Depth, and Price Transparency

Market liquidity is an important risk factor that investors are behooved to consider when constructing their investment portfolios. The financial crisis helped make this abundantly clear. Portfolios should be designed in a way that takes into account how the portfolios will react in the event that market liquidity diminishes. It is therefore important to gain an understanding of the tools available for measuring market liquidity. Following are a few of these tools.

Bid-Ask Spread

There are several ways to measure market liquidity, and those methods can be applied to almost any market, including the bond market. One measure of market liquidity is the bid-ask spread on individual securities. The narrower the bid-ask spread, the more liquid the market; the wider the spread, the less liquid the market. The reason for this is fairly simple: The closer buyers and sellers are in agreement on the price of what they are trying to buy or sell, the more likely it is that they will actually transact with each other. Of course, a wider bid-ask spread indicates that buyers and sellers are in disagreement on the fair market price, and this decreases the likelihood that a transaction will take place.

In the bond market the bid-ask spread varies with the type of fixed-income security and its maturity. In U.S. Treasuries, for example, Fleming and Mizrach (2009) have indicated that the bid-ask spread on 2-year notes is typically about 2/256ths of 1 percent of par; for 10-year notes the spread is typically 3.8/256ths of 1 percent of par.[5] Typical spreads with some historical context are shown in Table 2.3. Shorter Treasury maturities such as 2-year notes generally trade at a smaller spread because of their lower level of volatility compared with that of longer maturities and because price changes in short maturities have a greater impact on their yield-to-maturity than do price changes on longer maturities. The impact of price changes on a bond's yield will be discussed in greater detail in Chapter 3.

Outside of U.S. Treasury securities, the bid-ask spreads on other types of fixed-income securities are generally wider, in some cases much wider. This means that they are much less liquid than Treasuries are. The bid-ask spread on corporate bonds, for example, varies greatly, depending on issue-specific factors, with credit risk being one of the main determinants of the bid-ask spread.

Junk bonds, for example, which are bonds that carry a low credit rating and are considered at risk of default (see Chapter 3), generally will have a much wider bid-ask spread than Treasuries do, although less so than a decade ago when a spread of a full point (1 percent of the par value) or more was possible. In those days, Wall Street traders would often quip that they could ride a truck through the bid-ask spreads of some junk bonds.

TABLE 2.3 Inside Bid-Ask Spreads and Depth

		Visible				Hidden			
Maturity	Spread	Bid Depth	Ask Depth	No. Bids	No. Asks	Bid Depth	Ask Depth	No. Bids	No. Asks
2 years	1.9956	231.45	219.33	23.84	23.64	10.53	8.42	0.12	0.09
3 years	2.2389	59.58	59.75	14.08	14.29	3.24	1.88	0.06	0.04
5 years	2.0033	47.15	47.61	12.89	13.02	1.81	1.91	0.05	0.04
10 years	3.8089	47.89	47.43	15.15	15.10	1.53	1.88	0.06	0.05
30 years	7.5770	5.93	5.95	3.90	3.95	0.26	0.28	0.03	0.02

Notes: The table reports average inside bid-ask spreads and depth on BrokerTec for the hours 07:00 to 17:30 from January 3, 2005, to February 3, 2006. Inside spreads are reported in 256ths of 1 percent of par, and depth is reported in millions of dollars.

Source: Michael Fleming and Bruce Mizrach, The Microstructure of a U.S. Treasury ECN: The BrokerTec Platform, Federal Reserve Bank of New York Staff Reports, July 2009.

AAA-rated bonds, in contrast, which are bonds that carry an exemplary credit rating, tend to have a relatively narrow bid-ask spread and are much more liquid. Corporate bond investors have benefited over the past decade from the requirement imposed by FINRA to have secondary market prices posted on TRACE, which we discussed earlier in the chapter.

Numerous studies have documented the idea that in the aggregate the average bid-ask spread on corporate bonds is as much as several times larger than that for U.S. Treasuries. This means that it is usually more difficult to enter into and exit from corporate bonds and to obtain accurate price information on individual securities.

In the municipal bond market, liquidity can also vary greatly, depending on issue-specific characteristics and the maturity length of the issues that are trading. In the aggregate the average bid-ask spread for municipals is wider than it is for corporates. A major influence on the liquidity of municipal securities is the large amount of municipal securities outstanding. Indeed, there are well over 1 million municipal bonds outstanding. Many of these bonds are small, issued by small local governments, and therefore they are held by a relatively low number of investors. This means that a large number of municipal securities are extremely illiquid and rarely trade. Luckily for municipal bond investors, municipal securities usually are bought with the intention of holding them until maturity, and so those investors do not have to be overly concerned about their ability to resell them if they so choose. If they do choose to sell before maturity, there is a risk that they will not be able to do so at the fair market price. In this case investors should take pains to ensure that they are getting a price that is as close to the fair market price as possible.

The bid-ask spread on other types of fixed-income securities differs, but it is affected by many of the principles that dictate the bid-ask spreads on Treasuries, corporate bonds, and municipal bonds. That is, the bid-ask spread is largely influenced by credit risk, maturity length, trading volume, and issuer-specific characteristics.

Market Depth

Another measure of market liquidity is market depth. *Market depth* refers to the quantity of securities that broker-dealers are willing to buy and sell at various prices. This means that bonds that have larger bids and offers have greater market depth and liquidity than do bonds that have smaller average bids and offers. For example, a bond that averages $5 million in both bids and offers is much more liquid than is a bond that averages just $1 million in bids and offers. Transaction size can be misleading as to market depth because the quantity traded is often less than the amount that could have traded at the traded price.

When a bond has a large amount of market depth, it is easier for investors to find willing buyers and sellers under a variety of market circumstances. Conversely, bonds with shallow market depth are more difficult to buy and sell, especially when market conditions are adverse.

Market depth is extremely important to institutional investors, who can buy or sell up to $1 billion or more of bonds in a single trade. These institutions sometimes need to buy and sell securities on days when the market is volatile, and they therefore depend on deep quote depths to execute their trades. Luckily, there are usually plenty of institutions on both sides of the market in such situations, and these investors are able to execute most of their trades without a hitch.

It takes great skill on the part of the traders involved in large trade executions to get them done at a price that is indicative of the fair market price. The skill involved in executing large orders is considered valuable on Wall Street, which is one reason why traders are paid a lot. These skills are sometimes innate and sometimes learned, but in either case, they are no doubt a valuable commodity to Wall Street firms and their clients in volatile times.

Oddly, deep market depth does not always help the individual investor because the bond market is largely an institutional market. In essence, the market is bifurcated, with quote depth differing for institutions and individuals. This means, for example, that on any given day 10-year Treasury notes could have total bids of $5 million yet there could be very few offers for smaller lots of, say, $10,000. This means that the institution may be able to get a better price on the notes than the individual investor can.

The quote depth of the bond market therefore is broken into two parts: separate markets for odd lots and round lots. In the bond market, trades of under $1 million are considered *odd lots*, and trades of $1 million or more are considered *round lots*. This is in stark contrast to the equity market, where trades of fewer than 100 shares of stock are considered odd lots and trades of 100 shares or more are considered round lots. The inherent message is that institutions dominate the bond market while individuals dominate the stock market. Individual investors therefore should avoid being lulled into thinking that they can obtain good quote depth levels simply because there's a high level of quote depth on an institutional level. In other words, caveat emptor (buyer beware).

Price Transparency

These days, obtaining a price on a stock is extremely simple, and there are numerous ways to do it. Prices can be retrieved easily from the Internet, newspapers, and financial programs on television, for example. In the bond market, prices are much more difficult to obtain except on a handful of securities, such as the most actively traded U.S. Treasuries. This lack of transparency poses challenges to fixed-income investors and for anyone trying to track the bond market. It is a challenge that must be constantly overcome.

The reason the bond market lacks transparency is related largely to the fact that there is no centralized location for trading and no centralized location reporting quotes and trade prices. Instead, prices are obtained through phone calls between broker-dealers and by quotes posted on a number of electronic trading systems that are not available to the general public. This lack of price transparency impedes market liquidity and serves as a reminder to investors to be cautious about the quotes and prices they obtain on bonds. TRACE has nonetheless helped improve transparency a great deal.

The lack of transparency in the bond market probably has affected the degree to which individual investors have been attracted to the bond market. In other words, individual investors probably would be more attracted to the bond market if it had greater transparency. The lack of transparency was a very big negative during the financial crisis, as it bred uncertainty. To investors, uncertainties are risks that can't be measured—there is a big difference between these risks and those that can be measured. Investors will, as they did during the financial crisis, value assets lower when they can't measure the risks they are taking.

The Financial Crisis of 1998: A Case Study of the Impact of Changes in Market Liquidity

In the fall of 1998 financial problems beset Asia and reverberated throughout the rest of the world. A series of escalating financial crises led to what at that time was unprecedented turmoil in the global financial markets, spurring investors to seek the safety of U.S. Treasury securities.

Surging demand for Treasuries pushed prices to extraordinary heights, and yields plunged (prices move inversely with yields). This so-called flight to quality caused Treasuries to significantly outperform other fixed-income securities as investors shunned riskier assets for the risk-free feature of Treasuries.

While a divergence in the performance of Treasuries and that of other fixed-income securities is not unusual during times when markets are in crisis or when the economy is weak, it would be unusual for two Treasury securities with almost identical characteristics to diverge in performance. Yet in 1998 there was a sharp divergence in the performance of *on-the-run Treasuries* (the most actively traded Treasuries) and *off-the-run Treasuries* (the less actively traded Treasuries). This was unusual because both on-the-run and off-the-run Treasuries carry no risk of default, and so there should be little or no variation in their performance, especially if they have other characteristics that are similar, such as their coupon and maturity dates. Assuming all the characteristics of two separate Treasuries are roughly the same, the only factor that could explain the differences in their price performance is liquidity or small changes due to changes in the shape of the yield curve.

The sharp divergence in performance that occurred in 1998 highlights the impact that market liquidity can have on a security.

The bid-ask spread on 10-year Treasury notes, for example, increased from its typical 1/64 to 1/32 spread to roughly a 3/32 average spread in the heat of the crisis on October 9, 1998. In addition, market depth was impacted, with the quote depth on the on-the-run 10-year notes falling from about $10 million in the months leading up to the crisis to roughly $6 million in October 1998.

The impact that the financial crisis of 1998 had on U.S. Treasuries endures as a classic case study in which the effects of changes in market liquidity can be isolated and clearly identified. The episode highlights the important role that liquidity plays in the proper functioning of the markets, a lesson learned in large scale during the financial crisis of the late 2000s.

Summary

- The bond market plays a vital role in our economy and our nation. It is the spigot that helps supply capital to the nation's dreamers and entrepreneurs. The bond market helps ensure that there is plenty of capital available to mass-produce the innovative products and services dreamed by American citizens that raise the national standard of living. The bond market also supports the vitality of nations abroad.
- Bonds probably never played a more vital role than they did when they were used to help finance the war effort in World War II. Over 85 million people bought war bonds and helped lift the nation to victory. For bonds, it was their finest hour.
- The bond market is vast at about $34.6 trillion, and it is composed of a variety of different segments. The best-known segment of the bond market is the U.S. Treasury market. While it is not the largest segment—the mortgage-backed securities market is—it is easily the most active, the most liquid, and the most transparent.
- Nevertheless, other segments are also quite active as well as liquid, including the agency securities market and the MBS market.

- Primary dealers play an important role in facilitating the roughly $1 trillion in trading volume that passes through the bond market every day. Their role is especially vital given the minuscule volume traded on central exchanges every day.
- The bond market is likely to continue growing in the coming years even if cyclical forces slow it down at times, although more of its growth is now likely to come from the government sector rather than the private sector. This is because of continuing efforts to stabilize economic and financial conditions as well as the de-leveraging process.
- Innovation, securitization, and continued widespread use of bonds for funding purposes are a few reasons to expect continued growth of the bond market.
- Market depth, liquidity, and price transparency are three important risk factors investors must consider when investing in bonds.
- As important as the bond market has always been to the American way of life, few people ever suspected its influence and importance until the financial crisis made it abundantly clear. When the bond market is functioning normally, it is a very positive force in improving the nation's standard of living.

3

BOND BASICS
Building Blocks and Warning Labels

John Adams once said, "Facts are stubborn things," referring to our inability to change facts no matter what our wishes or inclinations may be. Since we cannot change facts, we must work with them, around them, and in spite of them. Facts sometimes are misunderstood, however, and often are taken out of context, overblown, or overemphasized, misleading individuals about the subject matter.

That is how it is in the bond market, where investors often are intimidated by the market's apparent array of complexities. Faced with what appear to be numerous hindrances, many investors would rather avoid the bond market altogether than attempt to climb the mountainous learning curve they feel must be surmounted to be successful at bond investing. They feel there is no way around immersing themselves in the numerous facts involved in bond investing, and so they choose to disengage instead.

These investors are missing the forest for the trees, however, and focusing too much on the wrong set of facts. Instead of concentrating on the most critical aspects of bond investing, they let themselves get tangled in the bond market's apparent complexities. They forget that the single most important element of successful bond investing is making an accurate assessment of the major fundamental factors that affect the direction of interest rates, the shape of the yield curve, and the level of real interest rates. The factors that affect these key fundamental forces and with which investors should be more concerned include the pace of economic growth, inflation, and the Fed. These are the same macro variables that investors consider when investing in other asset classes, including equities and commodities, among others, so in a way investors are already doing the homework they need do in order to be successful bond investors.

It is easy to see how the bond market can intimidate investors. There does seem to be a bit more math involved in buying bonds than there is in buying stocks. Bonds in general also seem to have a plethora of unusual characteristics, and those characteristics seem to differ from one segment of the bond market to the next as well as between bonds within each segment. And then there are all those surprise elements that sometimes land at bond investors' proverbial doorsteps when their bonds are called away from them out of the blue. There's also the legal mumbo jumbo that can make it seem that only lawyers can be bond investors. In light of these intimidating factors, some investors see more risk in investing in bonds than in investing in stocks despite the fact that the opposite is generally the case.

Investors should recognize that investing successfully in both stocks and bonds requires a lot of knowledge and that the set of knowledge needed for each type of investment in many respects is not materially different from the other. Equity investors who are intimidated by the set of knowledge needed to invest in bonds should look in the mirror and ask themselves whether they have made similar efforts to learn all that is needed to invest successfully in the stock market too. (Unfortunately, many equity investors do not do this and appear to believe that the main prerequisites for investing in stocks are knowing how to open a trading account and knowing how to place an order.) The fact is that regardless of the financial instrument, some degree of legwork is needed for an investor to be successful.

In this book I emphasize those elements of bond investing that are most critical for achieving the highest possible total rate of return. A grasp of critical factors such as the Federal Reserve, inflation, and the economy, and their impact on the yield curve, nominal and real interest rates, and the various segments of the bond market generally will have a far more substantial impact on your total investment returns than will knowledge of what I call *hygienes,* or factors that are essential but are not nearly as important as the major factors just mentioned. Some of these hygienes are a bond's indenture, its yield-to-call, and its yield-to-worst. These are important, but the lion's share of the total return of a bond portfolio is going to be driven by consideration toward big-picture, top-down variables. The way to think about the other considerations is that they are important because careful consideration toward them can augment the total return of a bond portfolio 1 basis point at a time.

As important as some of these hygienes can be, investors tend to place too much emphasis on them and are intimidated by them. Nevertheless, it is important for investors to be knowledgeable about them, and they are covered in this book. We will go beyond the basics, however, to give you insights about the bond market that you won't find in other books about the bond market. We will blend the bond basics with insights you can use.

One way to look at these so-called hygienes is to think of them as warning labels similar to those that accompany medical prescriptions. Reading those warning labels is a must, of course, but knowing all the details of the science behind the warnings serves little purpose for the average consumer. Similarly, individuals need not know everything about the medication they take; they simply need to know how it fits their needs and how to make it work for them. Individuals need only heed the warnings on the label to avoid unexpected complications.

Many bonds have their own warning labels, and those labels should be heeded before one purchases a bond. In this chapter we'll take a look at the most essential elements of a few of them. All the while, keep in mind that your main objective should be to learn about the major influences on the bond market. In other words, don't sweat the small stuff.

Also included in this chapter are definitions of many of the important basics of bond investing. These basics are probably the most frequently cited ones in the literature written about the bond market. Let's start with the simple ones and work our way to some of the more complex topics.

What Is a Bond?

In its simplest form, a *bond* is an interest bearing document issued or sold by either a government body or a corporation for the purpose of raising capital to meet a financial need. The three largest groups of issuers of bonds are corporations, municipal governments, and the federal government and its agencies. Bonds often are looked at as loans or IOUs because the borrower promises to repay money to investors on a specific maturity date, or term-to-maturity date, which is the date on which the borrower will repay the face value, or principal value, of the bond. The principal value of the bond is merely its dollar value at maturity, usually $1,000. Most bonds trade in minimum denominations of a single bond with a principal value of $1,000, although many trade in minimum denominations of five bonds with a principal value of $5,000 together. The term-to-maturity can span anywhere from one day to 30 years, and in some cases it can be as long as 100 years, although only rarely. When the principal on a bond is repaid, the issuer of the bond has no further obligations from the debt.

An issuer's failure to meet the payment obligations on its debt when the payments are due is a breach of the issuer's contractual obligations and is considered a default. In such an instance, bondholders can undertake legal actions to enforce the terms of the contract set out in the indenture, which is defined below. For credit default swaps, the technical definition of default varies, and it is important to know because it determines whether the buyer of credit protection can make a claim on the protection seller.

Unlike most loans, bonds are securities because they can be bought and sold in the open market—the bond market! The bond market is not a marketplace in the literal sense. Most bonds do not trade on an exchange but are bought and sold over the counter, with transactions taking place between broker-dealers and between broker-dealers and the investing public.

In the bond market, the term *bonds* is synonymous with most types of fixed-income securities, even though different names are used to distinguish between bonds of varying maturities. For instance, *Treasury bills* and *agency discount notes* are fixed-income securities with maturities of 12 months or less. Fixed-income securities with maturities of 1 to 12 years are known as *notes,* and fixed-income securities with maturities of 12 years or more are known as *bonds,* although in the Treasury market, securities with a maturity over 10 years usually are considered bonds, not notes. Because Treasuries are considered the benchmarks for pricing and quoting most bonds in the bond market, the term *bond market* often is used interchangeably with *Treasuries* since the behavior of most bonds tends to mirror the behavior of bonds in the Treasury market. When the media discuss how the bond market faired on a given day, they usually cite the Treasury market.

As far as what constitutes a short-, intermediate-, or long-term maturity: maturities between 1 and 5 years are considered short term, maturities between 5 and 12 years are considered intermediate, and maturities greater than 12 years are considered long term. Maturities under 12 months generally are considered money market instruments.

As shown later in this chapter, there are many different types of bonds representing the three major issuers cited above. Moreover, not all bonds are alike even when they are issued by the same entity. That's why it is particularly important to look closely at the specifics of every bond: their differences make them a bit like fingerprints and DNA at times, and their characteristics can therefore differ materially from one bond to the next. One must look closely for differences the same way one should look closely at every warning label on medical prescriptions. It makes no sense to take chances. This is especially true in today's environment because investors are paying closer attention than they did before the financial crisis. For example, corporate bond investors are more interested than ever in knowing where their bonds sit in the capital structure of the company bonds they own because the position will determine their place in line for the money that remains in the event that a company defaults on its obligations and is liquidated. This can be found in the indenture, described below.

The Indenture: The Contract between the Bond Issuer and the Bondholder

The *indenture* is an important legal document that sets forth the terms of agreement between the issuer of a bond and the buyers of the issuer's bond. The indenture is legally binding on the issuer until the principal value of the bond is repaid, usually on the maturity date but not always, as you will see later. The indenture contains a significant amount of detailed information that spells out the key characteristics of a particular bond. Some of these features, which will be covered later in this chapter, include the promised interest payment on the debt; the maturity date; the call and refunding provisions, and the period of call protection; the put provisions; the number of bonds sold; the collateral put up against the bonds; and sinking fund provisions.

The indenture contains a great deal of legal mumbo jumbo that can confuse the average investor. Luckily, the indenture is made out to a corporate trustee who acts as a third party to the indenture contract and acts in a fiduciary capacity on behalf of the bondholders. The corporate trustee monitors whether the bond issuer is complying with the covenants set forth in the indenture, and the trustee may take action to protect the rights of bondholders, although action on breaches of some covenants in the indenture is not always assured or legally mandated. The indenture provisions are summarized in a document known as a *prospectus*, which is a legally required preliminary statement describing the entity issuing the bond as well as the characteristics of the security. The prospectus is issued to prospective buyers before the sale of the bond. The prospectus spells out some of the legal terms contained in the indenture, and it is relatively easier reading. It can be obtained from broker-dealers involved in the underwriting of a bond, or, once the bond has been issued, it is often available on the Internet. These days the crux of the indenture—the coupon rate, the maturity date, the call provisions, and the like—are available in many places, including the Internet, and from financial information providers such as Bloomberg.

When you buy a bond, you have to think of yourself as a banker and remember that a good banker is always diligent about setting terms that protect the bank's capital. You must do the same thing. Read the indenture or at least find a summary of the terms of the indenture so that you can protect your capital. It's the prudent thing to do.

Coupon Rate: Not for Clipping Anymore

The *coupon rate* is a term from the days when most bonds were sold in so-called bearer form. A *bearer bond* is a bond that pays interest to the *bearer*—that is, the presenter of the coupons physically attached to the bond. In the United States the issuance of bonds in bearer form was disallowed in 1982, as it was felt that bearer bonds could be used as payment for illegal activities, could be used for money laundering, and could be easily stolen and converted into cash without the need to prove ownership. Attached to bearer bond certificates issued before 1982 were a series of coupons, one for each coupon payment date stipulated in the bond's indenture. At each coupon payment date, the bondholder would clip the appropriate coupon and present it to the trustee for payment, either by mail or in person. This is the reason these issues were known as *coupon* or *bearer bonds.* Today almost all bonds are offered in book-entry registered form, with an increasingly large percentage offered in book-entry form only. In other words, bonds are now held in electronic rather than paper form.

These days the *coupon rate* refers to the stated interest rate that a bond issuer agrees to pay on a bond to holders of that bond throughout the bond's life. The coupon rate is quoted as a percentage of the bond's principal, or *par value.* For example, if XYZ Corporation issues a bond with a coupon rate of 6 percent and the bond's principal value is $1,000, the issuer has stipulated that it will pay $60 per year to the holder of the bond. Most coupons are paid semiannually, with the semiannual date usually coinciding with the one-year period that follows the original issuance date of the bond.

Call and Refunding Provisions: A Call That Bond Investors Would Rather Not Take

For some bonds there's a provision in the indenture that allows the issuer to *call,* or redeem, the bond before its maturity date. These bonds are known as *callable bonds.* Callable bonds can be redeemed by the issuer either in whole or in part on or after a specific date at a specific price, generally above par (this is known as the *call premium*). Issuers benefit from the call feature on a bond when a borrower can issue new bonds at an interest rate level that is below the interest rate level of the callable bond. This is detrimental to the holder of the callable bond, however, because it exposes the investor to reinvestment risk. As will be described in Chapter 5, *reinvestment risk* is basically the risk of having to reinvest cash flows at lower and lower interest rate levels. Thus, when a bond is called, the holders of the callable bond will receive cash for their bonds and therefore will have to reinvest that cash at reduced interest rate levels. This was something that many investors experienced both in the early 2000s and then again in the aftermath of the financial crisis.

Call features are prevalent on corporate and municipal bonds and on older Treasuries (the Treasury last issued callable bonds in the early 1980s). Most entities issue bonds with a call date that assures investors that the bonds will not be called for at least several years. This does not mean, however, that the investor is completely protected. Indeed, this call protection is not the same as protection against a bond's possible refunding, or early redemption, which can happen well before the call date under conditions specified in the indenture. Read the indenture closely (see Chapter 5 for added risks and strategies related to callable bonds).

Yield-to-Call and Yield-to-Worst: Important Footnotes

The *yield-to-worst* on a bond is simply the lowest possible yield an investor would earn if the bond were redeemed for any reason specified in the bond's indenture, including its call and refunding provisions. The *yield-to-call* is the yield an investor would earn on a bond if it is held to and redeemed at the call date for that bond.

When some investors buy a bond, they make the mistake of looking exclusively at its yield-to-maturity (to be explained later) when they should be looking at both the yield-to-call and the yield-to-worst (which are sometimes the same). This is a mistake because both the yield-to-call and the yield-to-worst may be the actual yield the investor receives when he or she redeems it. Yield-to-call is computed in the same manner as yield-to-maturity except that the maturity date is replaced by the call date and the principal value at maturity is replaced by the call price.

Just as with the yield-to-maturity, the yield-to-call assumes that the investor will reinvest the cash flows from the bond at the computed yield-to-call. In addition, it is assumed that the investor will hold the bond until its call date.

Another mistake investors sometimes make with callable bonds is to compare the yield-to-call on one bond with the yield-to-maturity on another bond that has the same maturity date but no call feature. Investors who do this run the risk of mistakenly believing that the callable bond is the more attractive of the two because of its desirable yield-to-call. These investors sometimes ignore the callable bond's reinvestment risks that could actually make the callable bond the worst choice in terms of achieving the highest possible yield-to-maturity over a given time period.

The yield-to-call and the yield-to-worst are like footnotes on the yield-to-maturity, and they are a must-know when one is buying a bond with provisions for early redemption.

Put Provision

A bond that contains a *put provision* gives the bondholder the right to redeem the bond, or "put" it, by selling it back to the issuer at par on dates specified in the indenture. This has both advantages and disadvantages for the bondholder. The main advantage is that the bondholder can redeem the bond at par when interest rates are rising and therefore avoid the price declines that occur with bonds when interest rates rise. A second advantage is the ability to reinvest the proceeds from the redemption at a more attractive interest rate. The major disadvantage is that bonds with put provisions tend to have a lower yield-to-maturity than do other bonds.

Current Yield

The *current yield* is a very simple but flawed calculation that gives investors an immediate sense of the rate of return they will achieve on their invested capital. This method is useful for investors who plan to spend the interest they receive on their bonds. It is calculated by dividing the annual coupon on a bond by its price:

$$\text{Current yield} = \frac{\text{annual coupon rate}}{\text{price}}$$

The main flaws in this calculation are twofold: it does not consider the interest on interest that could be received on the reinvested interest payments, and it does not consider the difference between the purchase price and the redemption value, completely ignoring the capital gains and losses that could materially affect a bond's total rate of return. Thus, current yield fails to capture two of the most important elements of a bond's total rate of return.

Yield-to-Maturity: Not Necessarily

Yield-to-maturity traditionally has been defined as the total rate of return that will be achieved on a bond from the date of purchase until the time the bond matures. The yield-to-maturity takes into account all of the bond's cash flows, including its coupon income; gains or losses from the difference between an investor's purchase price and the bond's redemption value; interest earned on interest; and the timing of each cash flow. Put simply, the yield-to-maturity represents all possible income as well as the gains or losses that will be realized from the settlement date to the maturity date. On Wall Street, the terms *yield-to-maturity* and *yield* are generally synonymous.

Here's a critical point to remember: A bond's stated yield-to-maturity will be achieved only if the bond's coupon payments are reinvested at a rate equal to its yield-to-maturity and if the bond is held until its maturity date. Investors often misunderstand this point and incur sharp reductions in the returns on their portfolios. It is critical to remember that one of the most important factors affecting the total return on a bond is the return that stems from interest on interest. Indeed, interest on interest can account for as much as or more than half of a bond's total rate of return, depending on interest rate levels and the bond's maturity length.

Here's an illustration. Assume that an investor has purchased a bond in XYZ Corporation maturing in 10 years and paying a semiannual coupon of 4 percent ($40 every six months). Assume that the investor paid $1,000 (par) for the bond for a yield-to-maturity of 8 percent. This investor therefore will receive $80 per year in annual coupon payments for a total of $800 over the 10-year period. In addition, assuming the principal value of the bond is $1,000, at the maturity date the investor will realize neither a capital gain nor a capital loss. The cash flows received on this bond therefore will have totaled $800 over 10 years. Let's make an additional assumption. Let's say that this investor spent the coupon payments rather than reinvesting them. It may still seem, however, that having received a coupon return of 8 percent per year for 10 years, the yield-to-maturity was still 8 percent. However, the yield-to-maturity on this bond was actually 5.79 percent. If the 8 percent coupon had been reinvested semiannually at an interest rate of 8 percent, the total cash flows would have been $22,787. That's significantly more than the $18,400 in total cash flows that would be received if the coupon payments were spent. Importantly, 52 percent of the return related to interest income stemmed from interest on interest.

Let this example serve as a reminder of the importance of interest on interest and the fallacy of the stated yield-to-maturity calculation, which makes the assumption that the interest payments will be reinvested at an interest rate equal to the yield-to-maturity.

The math behind the yield-to-maturity on a bond can get a bit complicated as it involves calculating the present value of all the bond's cash flows. *Present value* is the amount of money that must be invested today to realize a specified value in the future. Applying this to the example above, the yield-to-maturity basically reflects the interest rate level at which the interest payments must be reinvested to result in the cash flow of $22,787. Put another way, the yield-to-maturity is essentially the discount rate at which the present value of future payments (the coupon payments and the redemption value at maturity) equals the price paid for the security.

It is not necessary or efficient to do the math for a bond's yield-to-maturity by hand; there are a variety of modern means of doing the calculations. These days most investors use financial calculators, many of which contain functions that are specifically designed to do a variety of bond calculations. Investors also can utilize calculators available on financial information providers such as Bloomberg and Reuters. Most brokers and investors have access to these tools. In addition, there are a number of Web sites that enable investors to conduct bond calculations on their own.

No matter how you obtain the yield-to-maturity on a bond, the main point to remember is that the yield-to-maturity can be achieved *only* if the interest payments are reinvested at the yield-to-maturity *and* if the bond is held to maturity!

Par Value

The *par value* of a bond is its principal, or face value, at maturity. In other words, it is the amount of money that an investor will receive at the maturity date, as stated by the obligor, or borrowing entity. The par value is the dollar value on which interest payments are computed. The par value is not necessarily equal to its market value, which fluctuates.

A bond that trades below its par value is said to be trading at a discount to its par value, and a bond that trades above its par value is said to be trading at a premium to its par value. Bond prices are quoted as a percentage of their par value. Most bonds have a par value of $1,000. A bond with a par value of $1,000 that trades at a price of 95.0 has a market value of $950.00. Take special note of the fact that the par value of U.S. Treasury inflation-protected securities (TIPS) changes along with the rate of inflation. In other words, if inflation increases by 3.0 percent in the first year of the life of an inflation-protected Treasury security, its par value will be $1,030 because of the inflation accrual, which accretes to the par value and is not paid out. We will discuss this further in Chapter 4.

Accrued Interest

In between the actual coupon payments paid on a bond, bondholders earn what is known as *accrued interest*. Accrued interest is an important part of most bond transactions, and investors should make sure that the accrued interest they either pay (when buying a bond) or receive (when selling a bond) is correct. Accrued interest is paid to the holder of a bond on the settlement date regardless of who has owned the bond throughout the period since the last interest payment. The calculation for accrued interest is simple:

$$\text{Accrued interest} = \frac{\text{annual interest} \times \text{days in holding period}}{360 \text{ days}}$$

Basis Points: Bond Lingo

A *basis point* is equal to one-hundredth of a percentage point, and it is a term used frequently in the bond market. It is the smallest measure used to quote yields. A basis point is the distance, say, between a bond that yields 4.75 percent and one that yields 4.74 percent. On Wall Street the yield differences between securities are almost always quoted in basis points, particularly relative to Treasuries and/or securities with similar characteristics. In tracking bonds with different maturities, it's best to look at the basis point changes rather than the price changes. This is the case because even if two bonds with different maturity dates have experienced the same price change, their basis point changes could be much different. Looking at the basis point changes between bonds is the best way to track their relative performance; look at price differences only if you want to gauge a bond's outright performance in terms of price. Moreover, the Federal Reserve's interest rate changes are announced in basis points. This is a very fungible term that is applicable to a variety of fixed-income instruments.

Price Value of a Basis Point (PVBP), or Basis Point Value (BPV)

The *price value of a basis point* (PVBP)—also known as the *basis point value* (BPV) or the *dollar value of a 01* (DV01, where 01 is equal to 1 basis point)—is the price change that will occur in a bond if its yield changes by 1 basis point. The price value of a basis point is a useful tool to determine a bond's volatility. Although this is best measured by a bond's duration (discussed in the following section), the price value of a basis point can help an investor convert a bond's yield changes into dollars. For example, if the PVBP of a bond is $1 and the bond's price is $985, a yield decrease of 10 basis points will cause the price of the bond to increase to $995. (Prices move inversely with yields, of course.) Using this method, it is far easier to assess potential risks and opportunities. Both the dollar and price value of a basis point are used extensively in hedging one security versus another. For the PVBP, the quantity of the hedge is calibrated to equal the basis point value of the security being hedged. This way, equal basis point changes will cause equal dollar changes in the value of the two bonds. Market participants go through the same exercise when swapping out of one security for another. One can obtain the price value of a basis point on a financial calculator or by observing the price change that occurs in a bond for every basis point change.

Duration Dollars

Another way of expressing or comparing the price sensitivity of one bond versus another is to do so in *duration dollars*. Portfolio managers in particular are apt to do this, and the phrase is uttered with frequency in the trading rooms of portfolio management firms.

Duration dollars are calculated as follows:

$$\text{Duration dollars} = \text{market value} \times \text{duration}$$

Here's an example: Say you want to sell $10 million of a fixed-income security with a duration of 8 years and purchase another fixed-income security with a duration of 2 years. Your objective is to make the transaction *duration neutral*, which is to say that you want the price sensitivity for each basis point change to be equal. You want the dollar value of change for each bond to be equal for each basis point change that occurs. Assume in this example that the $10 million security has both a face and market value of $10 million. To calculate the amount of securities to purchase, first find the amount of duration dollars for the security you are selling:

$$
\begin{aligned}
\text{Duration dollars} &= \$10,000,000 \times 8.0 \\
&= \$80,000,000
\end{aligned}
$$

Now, using an algebraic twist of the above formula, take the 80 million of duration dollars and divide it by the duration of the security:

$$\frac{\$80,000,000}{2} = \$40,000,000$$

The $40 million represents the amount of securities that need be purchased in order to approximate the dollar change of the swapped security to that of the new security for an equal change in interest rates. In other words, if the yield on each security were to move by, say, 15 basis points, the impact on the investor in terms of dollars would be the same whether the portfolio owned $10 million of the swapped security or $40 million of the security swapped into.

Duration: A Key Gauge of a Bond's Price Sensitivity to Interest Rate Changes

Duration is a measure of a bond's price sensitivity to changes in interest rates. It can be used to gauge the volatility of one bond compared with another and for the purpose of hedging securities. A complex mathematical formula is used to compute duration, and so it is generally best not to compute it by hand. Let's take a look at a simple example before discussing it further.

Assume that the duration on a bond is 5.0. In this case, if the yield on the bond were to change by 100 basis points, the price on the bond would change by approximately 5 percent. That sounds simple enough. There is actually a whole lot more to it, but I want to impress upon you the importance of remembering this simple example before the detailed explanation begins to cloud the main message. If you remember nothing more about duration than the notion that duration is an approximation of a bond's percentage price change for a given change in interest rates, you will have learned enough to help you with most bond investments.

There are, however, a number of important details, so let's get into the nitty-gritty and look at some of the more important elements of the concept of duration.

1. Duration is not an exact measure of a bond's price sensitivity to changes in interest rates, but it is generally a very close approximation if the interest rate changes are small. The measurement that estimates the price change in a security or a portfolio when interest rate changes are fairly small is the *effective duration*. When interest

rate changes are large, the concept of convexity must be introduced. *Convexity* is known in mathematical circles as the second derivative of a bond's price change for given changes in yield. Convexity basically measures the percentage change in a bond's price change for a given change in yield that cannot be explained by duration. In other words, if the duration on a bond is 5.0 and its yield changes by 100 basis points but the price of the bond changes by just 4.9 percent instead of the 5 percent change that should be expected based on the bond's duration, the difference can be explained by the bond's convexity. Convexity generally is used to assist in the approximation of large yield changes in a bond, and it is a very important concept in today's environment because it is a risk factor that investors must weigh in order to be prepared for *tail events*—that is, events that by mathematical estimation appear to have a low probability of occurrence but which appear to occur far more often than investors are prepared for.

2. Duration increases with maturity length (assuming all other characteristics are the same). The degree to which it increases depends on many other factors such as the coupon rate, as mentioned below.

3. Bonds with high coupon rates have lower duration than do bonds with low coupon rates (assuming all other characteristics are the same). This is because an investor's initial investment is returned faster.

4. The duration on a zero coupon bond is always equal to its term-to-maturity. Thus, a zero coupon bond that matures in 10 years will have a duration of 10.0. This principle indicates that zero coupon bonds are very volatile instruments compared with conventional coupon bonds. That is why aggressive investors such as hedge funds often purchase zero coupon bonds when they sense that interest rates are about to decline. Those investors recognize that zero coupon bonds will appreciate faster in price than will conventional bonds (of the same maturity) for a given change in interest rates, and thus they can maximize capital gains opportunities. Zero coupon bonds are favored by entities with long-term liabilities, such as insurance companies and pension funds. These entities favor zero coupon bonds for their long duration because it enables them to more closely match their assets to their liabilities.

5. There are two popular formulas for duration. *Macaulay's duration*, developed in 1983 by Frederick Macaulay, is defined as the weighted average term-to-maturity of a security's cash flows. It basically takes

the present value of all the cash flows and then adjusts them by weight based on when they are received. The result is stated as the weighted average of the life of the bond in years. As such, it is a good measure for ranking different bonds in regard to their price sensitivity and for constructing portfolios that will fully defease, or immunize, a future series of cash flows against market risk (see Chapter 5 for a discussion of market risk). *Modified duration* basically is defined as it was defined above; that is, it is a measure of a bond's price sensitivity to changes in the interest rate.

6. Duration fails to capture the risks associated with bonds of varied credit quality. For example, a AAA-rated company with a duration of 5.0 is likely to be subject to less volatility than is a CCC-rated company with the same duration. The poor creditworthiness of the CCC-rated company tends to make that company's bonds subject to greater yield (and price) volatility owing to both macro and micro risks. Thus, duration should not be taken on its own to mean that one company will be more or less volatile than another.

7. Duration increases when a bond's yield decreases and decreases when its yield increases. The exception to this is callable and puttable bonds. On callable bonds, duration decreases when yields fall because the call feature reduces the price appreciation and thus the duration. Similarly, on puttable bonds, duration increases as yields increase because the put feature increases the value of the bond (because an investor can sell the bond back to the issuer and reinvest the proceeds at higher market interest rates).

8. A portfolio's aggregate price sensitivity to changes in interest rates cannot be determined easily by using its average duration. This is the case because individual bonds can and do have varying degrees of yield fluctuations on a day-to-day basis. Therefore, there is no specific yield change on which the duration level can be used to estimate the aggregate price change in a portfolio. In other words, since the yield changes on each of the portfolio's securities generally will vary, so will the price changes. This will be especially apparent when the yield curve shifts and results in sharply varying performances of short- and long-term maturities. This is why portfolio managers are interested in approximating so-called curve duration, described next.

9. A portfolio's *curve duration* is a measurement of a portfolio's price sensitivity to changes in the shape of the yield curve (that is, steepening or flattening). A portfolio's curve duration is considered positive if it has more exposure to the 2- to 10-year part of the curve. A

portfolio with positive curve duration will perform well as the yield curve steepens, but it will perform poorly as the yield curve flattens. A portfolio with negative curve duration has greater exposure to the 10- to 30-year portion of the curve. It will be a poor performer as the yield curve steepens and a strong performer as the yield curve flattens.

10. A portfolio's *spread duration is a* measurement that estimates the price sensitivity of a specific sector or asset class to a 100-basis-point movement (either widening or narrowing) in its spread relative to Treasuries. For example, corporate spread duration applies primarily to the widening or narrowing of the spread over the LIBOR (London Interbank Offered Rate) in floating-rate notes. The spread duration for fixed-rate corporates is the same as the standard duration. In addition, mortgage spread duration applies to the widening or narrowing of the option-adjusted spread (OAS) that takes into account the prepayment risk associated with mortgage-backed securities.

11. The average duration of the universe of fixed-income investment portfolios can be used to track market sentiment because it captures the way that portfolios are positioned. This topic is covered in Chapter 10.

As you can see, there are many important elements of the concept of duration. Although there are shortcomings, duration can be an extremely useful tool for gauging market risks in individual bonds and portfolios as well as for gauging market sentiment. For most investors, duration is best used in its simplest form as a gauge of a bond's price sensitivity to changes in interest rates. Portfolio managers need to measure duration from a broader perspective, knowing well in particular the concepts of convexity, curve duration, and spread duration. Don't let the complicated details cloud the concept of duration in its simplest form.

Summary

- As with many other investments, it behooves investors to obtain a certain degree of knowledge before they consider investing in bonds. Investors often are intimidated, however, about the knowledge set they feel is needed to be successful at investing in the bond market, leading them to shy away from that market.

- However, the degree of knowledge actually necessary for investors to be successful in the bond market is not materially different from that needed for other markets.
- While endeavoring to learn as much as possible about bonds, bond investors should be mindful of the factors that are most likely to affect their investment performance. Factors such as the Federal Reserve's actions, the economy, and inflation can have a far more significant impact on a bond investment than do other factors. That is why I have placed a great deal of emphasis on these factors throughout this book.
- Once you've reviewed the "warning labels" that come with each bond, don't sweat the small stuff and keep your focus on the big picture.
- Duration is an extremely important concept that helps investors to understand a bond's price sensitivity to changes in interest rates. Fixed-income portfolio managers actively utilize the concept when constructing and managing their portfolios, looking closely at broader concepts such as curve duration and spread duration.

4

TYPES OF BONDS

It is much easier to generalize about the types of bonds that exist in the bond market than it is to describe their many differences because unlike stocks, the characteristics of bonds can differ sharply from one bond to the next. Moreover, the performance of each type of bond can differ sharply from one bond to the next regardless of the general direction of interest rates. It is therefore important for investors to understand the types of bonds and their differing degrees of performance before considering the purchase of a bond.

This chapter will provide an overview of the largest segments of the bond market, concentrating on their most important elements. The types of bonds that will be covered are these:

- U.S. Treasuries
- Corporate bonds
- Government agency securities
- Mortgage-backed securities
- Municipal bonds

These segments account for the bulk of the bond market's $34.6 trillion in total size. Although the list is short, there are considerable differences between these types of bond, and there are differences within each segment. Most of these differences relate to creditworthiness, taxation, cash flows, maturity dates, call and refunding provisions, and collateralization (these topics are covered in Chapter 3). One can't judge a bond by its cover, so look closely at the various features of every bond before considering a purchase.

U.S. Treasuries

We showed in Chapter 2 that the U.S. Treasury market is the most active and liquid market in the world. Treasury securities are issued by the U.S. Treasury Department to meet the funding requirements of the U.S. government, and they are backed by the full faith and credit of the U.S. government. Treasuries therefore historically have been perceived to be free of the risk of default, although worries have grown recently over the high and persistent budget deficits in the United States. The deep liquidity of the Treasury market and its risk-free characteristics attract investors to use Treasuries as benchmarks for quoting and pricing other fixed-income securities.

The Treasury's Issuance Credo: Regular and Predictable

The most important principle guiding Treasury issuance since the 1970s has been to maintain a regular and predictable schedule of issuance. This pattern began in particular in 1975 when the U.S. budget deficit grew fivefold and Treasury issuance soared (Figure 4.1). A catalyst to the change occurred in March 1975 when the Treasury announced it would auction $1.25 billion of 15-year bonds at the same time that General Motors brought what was then the largest-ever industrial-debt offering. The impact of the joint offerings was described by a dealer quoted in the *New York Times* as a "disaster," and others said the market was in a "shambles" and in "chaos." Political pressure was brought to bear when Senator Hubert Humphrey, who was the chairman of the Joint Economic Committee, said that Treasury debt management was "being conducted in an inexplicable and seemingly highly inappropriate fashion." There were several events that played a role in leading the Treasury to abandon tactical issuance in favor of regular and predictable issuance, as shown in Figure 4.1, but the joint offerings of March 1975 was one of the most important.

The benefits of the "regularization" of Treasury issuance have been well documented, and it is widely believed that regular and predictable debt issuance removes a potentially major source of market uncertainty that if in play would lead to higher funding costs for the U.S. government. Research by the New York Fed's Kenneth Garbade validates this idea and documents the benefits of regularization in an environment of large budget deficits.[1] Regularization is apt to remain a dominant influence in any change to the issuance calendar in the times ahead.

The Treasury Department issues three different categories of Treasury securities: discount, coupon, and inflation linked. Although the issuance

FIGURE 4.1 After 1975, Treasury Debt Management Shifted from Tactical Issuance to Regular and Predictable Issuance

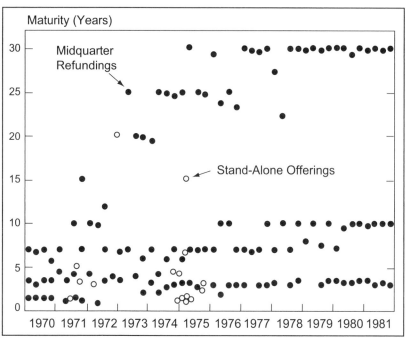

Source: Federal Reserve Bank of New York circulars, 1970 through 1981.

calendar changes, the Treasury Department endeavors to the greatest extent possible to maintain its "regular and predictable" credo.

Discount Securities

Discount securities are securities that are sold at a discount to their maturity (face) value and are paid at their par, or face, value. In the Treasury market, these securities are known as *Treasury bills*. Treasury bills are issued regularly in four maturities: 4 weeks, 13 weeks (commonly known as *three-month bills*), 26 weeks (*six-month bills*), and 52 weeks (*year bills*). Occasionally, the Treasury issues bills that mature in different (*oddball*) numbers of days or weeks. These bills are sold to meet short-term funding needs, particularly before April, when the Treasury rakes in tens of billions of dollars in tax payments from individuals. These bills are called *cash management bills* and have the same characteristics as regularly issued Treasury bills.

Auctions for 4-, 13-, and 26-week Treasury bills take place every Monday and settle on Thursday. Auctions for 52-week bills take place once per month, on a Tuesday, generally around midmonth, settling two days later. Cash management bills are auctioned only as Treasury financing needs require. Each of the Treasury bills actually begins trading on a when-issued basis, when they are announced. For 4-week bills, this occurs the day before each auction. For 13-, and 26-, and 52-week bills, announcements are made on the Thursday prior to the auctions.

Bids for Treasury bills may be submitted in minimum denominations of $100 (face value) to any Federal Reserve bank, to the Treasury's Bureau of the Public Debt in Washington, D.C., or over the Internet using Treasury Direct (www.treasurydirect.gov/tdhome.htm), a highly popular program run by the Treasury Department. Of course, an investor can always submit bids through a conduit such as a broker-dealer.

Once issued, Treasury bills are quoted at their discounted value in basis points rather than at the price that corresponds to the discounted rate. The purchase price for the auction is expressed as a price per hundred dollars.

Coupon Securities

The preponderance of Treasury issuance is in *coupon securities*, which are securities that pay interest periodically (usually every six months) and pay their principal at maturity. Of the roughly $7.3 trillion in Treasuries outstanding at the end of the September 2009, about $5.0 trillion of that issuance was in coupon securities. The $5.0 trillion consisted of $3.772 trillion of notes, $677 billion of bonds, and $551 billion of inflation-protected securities.

The Treasury Department in 2009 embarked on an effort to increase the average maturity of the Treasury debt, which in 2008 had fallen to a 26-year low of 48 months (see Figure 4.2). The sense at this writing, in January 2010, was that the Treasury would extend its average maturity to around 60 months by the end of 2010, and eventually to around 72 months and possibly to as high as 84 months over the next 5 to 7 years. The reasoning for doing this is simple: as a result of the very large and protracted U.S. budget deficit, the United States must issue large amounts of Treasury securities. Increasing the average maturity of the debt helps the United States to reduce its reliance upon the issuance of short-term debt and hence avoid the pitfalls associated with doing so, not the least of which is the need to continuously tap investors for money.

Because of the U.S. government's heavy borrowing needs, Treasury coupon issuance is as frequent as it has ever been. For example, whereas the issuance of 30-year bonds was once a quarterly affair—and between

FIGURE 4.2 Average Maturity of the Treasury Debt

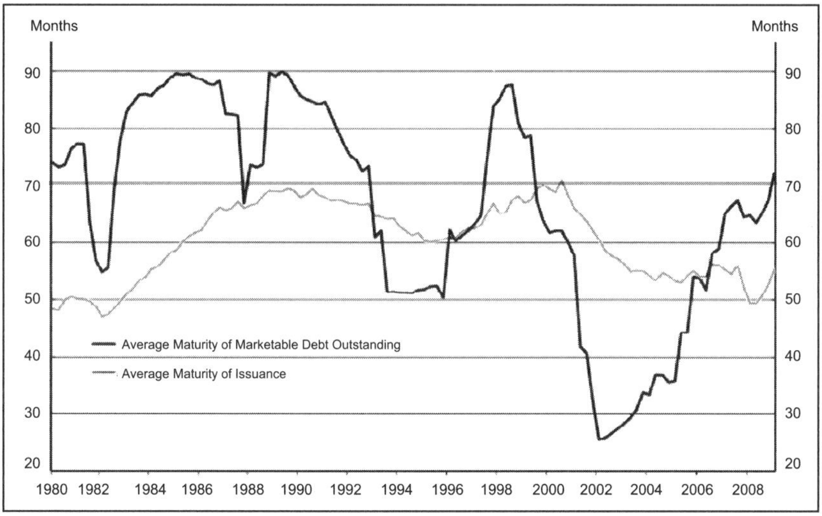

Note: Data through December 31, 2009. Average maturity of issuance uses a four-quarter average.

Source: U.S. Treasury.

August 2001 and February 2006, the Treasury did not issue any 30-year bonds at all—30-year bonds are now issued every month. All 30-year bonds are generally auctioned during the second week of each month, settling on the fifteenth of the same month, unless the fifteenth falls on a Saturday, Sunday, or federal holiday. In this case, the newly issued securities settle on the next business day. The 30-year auctions in months other than the Treasury's quarterly refundings held in February, May, August, and November are re-openings of the most recently auctioned issue. This means that they have the same maturity date, coupon interest rate, and interest payment dates as the original security. The 10-year notes are also reopened in the same months as the 30-year bonds. No other Treasury securities are reopened. The minimum purchase amount for all Treasury coupon issues is $100, and securities can be purchased in increments of $100.

Table 4.1 shows the issuance calendar as it stood on January 19, 2010.

Treasury auctions are conducted on a competitive and a noncompetitive basis. That is, competitive bidders submit bids at yields they would like to receive, and noncompetitive bidders submit bids for yields that will be determined at the auctions.

Noncompetitive bidders are guaranteed to receive the full amount of the security they bid for at a rate or yield that is equal to the highest accepted

TABLE 4.1 Treasury Auction Calendar as of January 19, 2010

Security Type	Frequency of Auctions	Announcement Dates	Auction Dates	Settlement Dates
4-, 13-, and 26-week bills	Weekly	Monday	Tuesday	Thursday
52-week bills	Weekly	Thursday	Tuesday following the announcement	Thursday
2-year notes	Monthly	Second half of the month, generally a Thursday	Tuesday following the announcement	Final day of auction month
3-year notes	Monthly	First half of the month, generally a Thursday	Tuesday following the announcement	15th of the month
5-year notes	Monthly	Second half of the month, generally a Thursday	Tuesday following the announcement	Final day of auction month
7-year notes	Monthly	Second half of the month, generally a Thursday	One week following the announcement	Final day of auction month
10-year notes	Monthly	First half of the month, generally a Thursday	Wednesday following the announcement	15th of the month
30-year bonds	Monthly	First half of the month, generally a Thursday	Thursday following the announcement	15th of the month
5-year TIPS	Twice per year	Second half of April and October	Last week of April and October	Final day of auction month
10-year TIPS	Four times per year	First half of January, April, July, and October	Second week of January, April, July, and October	15th of the month
30-year TIPS	Twice per year	Second half of February and August	Last week of February and August	Final day of auction month

bid. Competitive bidders compete in a Dutch, or single-price, auction, and all bidders receive the same yield regardless of the bid submitted (unless the bidders bid at a yield that is above the stop-out yield—the highest yield needed to clear all the securities being sold at the auction). Therein lies the risk of submitting a competitive bid: a competitive bidder that places a bid at a yield that is above the stop-out yield will not be awarded any securities at the auction. This is the advantage of submitting a noncompetitive bid. However, noncompetitive bids cannot be larger than $5 million for auctions of bills, notes, bonds, and TIPS. That's why most institutional investors submit competitive bids. Limits apply to competitive bids, at 35 percent of the issue amount for each bidder.

The difference between the stop-out yield and the yield prevailing on an issue being auctioned at the time of the auction deadline (for coupon issues this is generally at 1 p.m. ET) is known as the *tail*. The tail is used as a gauge of the success of an auction. A large tail indicates that the Treasury had to sell securities to low bidders in order to sell all the securities being auctioned; it is therefore an indication of a weak auction. A small tail, by comparison, occurs when there is a plentiful supply of aggressive bidders. When a stop-out yield is "through" the auction-deadline yield, it indicates even greater intensity among bidders because it shows they were willing to pay a higher price (receive a lower yield) in order to be sure they would purchase the amount they desired. Large institutional investors would do this if they felt that an auction were likely to draw strong demand, and also if they wanted to use the auction as a *liquidity event*, which is to say as a means of purchasing a large amount of the auction security that would not be as easy to replicate in the secondary market without affecting its price.

Newly auctioned Treasuries are known as *on-the-run issues*, and previously auctioned Treasuries are known as *off-the-run issues*. On-the-run issues are far more actively traded than are off-the-run issues, and therefore they tend to be much more liquid, as shown by their bid-ask spreads and quote depths. This is why off-the-run issues often offer value (more relative yield after considering the shape of the yield curve and other factors) compared to on-the-run issues, which trade *rich* relative to off-the-run issues, reflecting a *liquidity premium*, which is the price premium that investors pay in order to own the most liquid issue.

Whereas the 30-year Treasury bond was once considered the benchmark maturity with which to gauge daily price movements in the bond market, the Treasury's 10-year maturity is now the benchmark. There nonetheless remains a considerable amount of longer-dated maturities outstanding beyond 10 years, and the tally will be rising in the years ahead owing to more frequent issuance of 30-year bonds. The introduction in January 2010 of a new *ultra* Treasury bond future, whose underlying unit is a Treasury bond with a remaining term-to-maturity of not less than 25 years, is expected to increase the attention of the bond market on the long end of the yield curve. For these and other reasons, long-dated maturities are therefore worthy of attention both from an investment perspective and as a gauge of market sentiment on a variety of fronts. Moreover, as is discussed in Chapter 10, there are other maturities along the yield curve that are extremely useful gauges of market sentiment.

Inflation-Linked Securities

In January 1997 the Treasury began issuing bonds that provided investors with protection against inflation. These bonds are commonly known as *Treasury inflation-protected securities*, or *TIPS*. They are also known as *inflation-indexed* or *inflation-linked bonds*. TIPS provide protection against inflation by indexing interest and principal payments to the inflation rate. Thus, the cash flows on TIPS increase along with the inflation rate. With TIPS, an investor is protected against inflation risk (discussed in Chapter 5), which is one of the biggest risks facing bond investors.

TIPS are indexed to the Consumer Price Index for All Urban Consumers (CPI-U), a monthly index released by the Bureau of Labor Statistics with its widely followed CPI statistics. As the CPI-U increases, the face value of TIPS increases. For example, if you purchased an inflation-indexed security on its issuance date at a face value of $1,000 and the CPI-U increased 3 percent over the subsequent year, the face value of that security would increase to $1,030. Assuming the security paid a coupon rate of 3 percent (it stays fixed throughout the life of the bond), your interest income would rise from $30 per year ($1,000 times 3 percent), to $30.90 ($1,030 times 3 percent). Each year the face value would increase along with the inflation rate, resulting in an increase in coupon payments. At maturity, the security would be redeemed at the inflation-adjusted face value or the face value at issuance, whichever was greater. This assures that even if the CPI-U declines as a result of deflation, the maturity value of inflation-indexed bonds on their maturity date will be no less than the initial face value, an important consideration for investors worried that the financial and economic crisis will lead to deflation.

It is important to keep in mind that at any point before the maturity date on an inflation-indexed bond, the inflation-adjusted principal value of the bond could fall below the initial face value. This should not concern investors who plan to hold TIPS until their maturity dates because the Treasury Department will implement its "minimum guarantee" if deflation persists long enough. The Treasury will never repay less than the bond's initial face value ($1,000).

Inflation-indexed bonds have a distinct advantage over conventional Treasuries because of their indexation to the inflation rate, at least as long as the inflation rate increases more than market participants expect. The principal value of conventional Treasuries, by contrast, will not change; it will stay at $1,000 throughout the life of the bond.

Figure 4.3 provides an illustration of the differing cash flows that the two types of bonds would experience over a 10-year horizon. Note that even

FIGURE 4.3 Differing Cash Flows for Conventional and Indexed Bonds over a 10-Year Period

Example of Payments on Nominal and Indexed Bonds

Consider a 10-year conventional nominal bond and a 10-year inflation-indexed bond. Each bond is purchased at its face, or principal, value of $1000. Although Treasury notes and bonds provide semiannual payments, the bonds in this example are assumed to provide annual coupon payments. Each coupon payment on a conventional bond is the coupon rate stated on the bond times the principal. Each coupon payment on an indexed bond is the coupon rate times the indexed principal. The indexed principal is simply the beginning principal of $1000 scaled up through time at the rate of inflation. We'll assume that the coupon rate on the indexed bond is 3 percent and that actual inflation over the 10-year horizon turns out to be a steady 2 percent, equal to expected inflation, and that the coupon rate on the conventional bond is 5.06 percent so that its expected real rate of return equals the coupon rate on the indexed bond.

A schedule of nominal and real values of payments on the bonds is given below. The real values give the purchasing power of the nominal payments. For example, suppose a given item today cost $1. With 2 percent inflation, at the end of the year the same item will cost $1.02, and $1 will purchase .98 (1/1.02) units of the item. So, $50.60 received at the end of year 1 from the nominal bond will purchase 49.61 units.

As the schedule of payments shows, the nominal value of the conventional bond's principal stays fixed. The real value is eroding through time because of inflation. When received at maturity, the $1000 principal can purchase 820.35 units of the good. In contrast, when the bond was first purchased, that $1000 could buy 1000 units. The payment schedule also shows how the fixed nominal payment of $50.60 per year on the nominal bond has a smaller real value over time because of inflation. Note that for the indexed bond, the real values of the principal and interest payments are preserved for the life of the bond. The nominal principal gets scaled up year by year according to inflation. As the principal gets scaled up, so too does the nominal coupon payment to preserve the real return of 3 percent. The indexed bond pays less interest than the nominal bond each year, but that is offset by its larger payment of principal at maturity.

Schedule of Payments

Year	Conventional Bond				Index Bond			
	Nominal Value of Principal	Real Value of Principal	Nominal Interest Payment	Real Value of Interest Payment	Nominal Value of Principal	Real Value of Principal	Nominal Interest Payment	Real Value
1	$1000	980.39	$50.60	49.61	$1020.00	1000	$30.60	30
2	$1000	961.17	$50.60	48.64	$1040.40	1000	$31.21	30
3	$1000	942.32	$50.60	47.68	$1061.21	1000	$31.84	30
4	$1000	923.85	$50.60	46.75	$1082.43	1000	$32.47	30
5	$1000	905.73	$50.60	45.83	$1104.08	1000	$33.12	30
6	$1000	887.97	$50.60	44.93	$1126.16	1000	$33.78	30
7	$1000	870.56	$50.60	44.05	$1148.69	1000	$34.46	30
8	$1000	853.49	$50.60	43.19	$1171.66	1000	$35.15	30
9	$1000	836.75	$50.60	42.34	$1195.09	1000	$35.85	30
10	$1000	820.35	$50.60	41.51	$1218.99	1000	$36.60	30

Total nominal receipts: $1506	Total nominal receipts: $1554.07
Real value of principal at maturity: $820.35	Real value of index principal at maturity: $1000

Source: Federal Reserve.

though the inflation-indexed bond receives a smaller interest payment during the 10 years, the purchasing power of the money received at maturity is higher for the inflation-indexed bond.

When deciding whether to purchase an inflation-indexed bond, one of the first things to look at is the breakeven rate. The *breakeven rate* can be defined as the inflation rate that would make the rate of return on an inflation-indexed Treasury equal to the rate of return on a conventional Treasury if the two securities had the same maturity dates and both were held to maturity. An inflation rate higher than the breakeven rate would make the purchase of the TIPS superior in terms of its rate of return compared to a conventional Treasury. Similarly, if the inflation rate averaged less than the breakeven rate until the bonds matured, the rate of return on the TIPS would be less than that on the conventional Treasury.

This may seem a bit tricky, but it is actually quite simple. A key principle in the analysis is that the yield-to-maturity on most conventional bonds consists of four main components:

- A real rate of return
- Compensation for inflation
- A term premium
- Compensation for credit risk

On a conventional Treasury the yield consists of just the first three components, since Treasuries are considered free of the risk of default. This makes the analysis even simpler. Working with this premise, since the yield on a conventional Treasury consists of a real rate of return, compensation for inflation, and a *term premium* (the excess yield that investors demand for holding long-term maturities instead of a series of short-term maturities), we need only determine either the real rate of return or the amount of inflation expectations to find one or the other or both. The term premium isn't as important in this analysis because it will be roughly equal for both a conventional Treasury and an inflation-indexed security of equal maturity.

This is where TIPS come in. TIPS can help us find both the real yield and the amount of inflation expectations embedded in the convention security because its yield-to-maturity consists of a real rate of return plus compensation for inflation. In fact, on an inflation-indexed bond, the *stated* yield-to-maturity is the real rate of return (the *actual* yield-to-maturity cannot be known in advance because it depends on the inflation rate that presides over the life of the security). The key here is that unlike conventional Treasuries, you know what the real rate of return is. The rest of the return consists of an unknown inflation rate. You can use this real rate of return to find the inflation expectations embedded in the conventional Treasury.

With the real rate of return in hand, simply subtract it from the nominal, or stated, yield-to-maturity on the conventional Treasury. The difference represents the market's inflation expectations over the life of the bond. How do we know this? There is no reason to think that investors in TIPS have views of inflation that are different from those of investors in conventional Treasuries. However, both investments have nearly equal real rates of return, the difference between their nominal, or stated, yields must be the market's inflation expectations.

There are caveats to this analysis, however, as the yield differences may reflect more than the market's inflation expectations. For example, TIPS are notoriously illiquid compared with conventional Treasuries. This reflects the fact that at $550 billion (as of February 2010) the market for TIPS is much smaller than for conventional Treasuries. Moreover, TIPS are not used as hedging or trading vehicles in the same way that conventional Treasuries are, reducing their liquidity. Thus, during periods when investors express a preference for liquid securities, the yield on TIPS could be kept artificially high in compensation for the illiquidity, lowering the breakeven rate.

Second, TIPS are subject to a so-called *indexation lag*. That is, since the principal value of an inflation-indexed bond is based on an inflation rate set as much as three months before the semiannual coupon payment, there is a risk that the holder of an inflation-indexed bond will not be fully compensated for the actual inflation of the prior three months. For example, if you buy an inflation-indexed bond in July, the interest payment that you receive from July through October will be based on the semiannual adjustment made to the price of the bond in October based on the CPI-U from January through June. Therein lies the risk. From July through October you will be paid interest based on an inflation rate in the past (January through June). If inflation were to rise sharply in those three months, your October interest payment would not reflect the rise.

A third reason to be wary of a strict interpretation of the amount of inflation expectations derived using TIPS is the differences in the tax implications for the cash flows. Because a TIPS investor is compensated for inflation, when inflation accelerates, so does the cash flow on the bonds. In turn, so does the tax liability. Therefore, the TIPS investor is not fully insulated from the effects of inflation.

Finally, investors in TIPS may be naturally more averse to inflation risks than are investors in conventional Treasuries. This means that they may be more willing to accept a lower real rate of return. Therefore, the difference between yields on TIPS and those on conventional Treasuries may overstate the market's true inflation expectations.

Corporate Bonds

Just a few steps past the comfortable realm of the Treasury market lies a very different bond market. The corporate bond market, which at first blush seems fairly simple to understand, is full of intricacies. Corporate bonds are more than just the bond market's version of familiar stocks. There's a multitude of differences between corporate bonds and Treasuries and between individual corporate bonds. Indeed, there is much that investors must be aware of before they consider investing in corporate bonds.

Corporate bonds are bonds issued by corporate entities to raise capital for a variety of purposes. Those entities turn to the corporate bond market for long-term funding as an alternative to borrowing money from financial institutions and raising capital via other means such as issuing stock. Borrowing large amounts of capital from banks for long periods is generally not possible and can be costly, especially with today's tight credit conditions, and selling stock can dilute the equity of existing shareholders. The bond market is therefore a superior source of funding for many major companies.

There are many types of issuers in the corporate bond market reflecting the major sectors of the economy. The following are some of the issuer types:

- Industrials
- Banks
- Finance companies
- Broker-dealers
- Transportation companies
- Utilities
- Pipelines

Within each type of issuer there are many subgroups. Within the transportation group, for example, issuers include air, rail, and trucking companies. Importantly, each of the major groups and each of their subgroups have a different level of sensitivity to the economic and financial climate. As with stocks, the investment performance of individual corporate bonds can depend greatly on the group or subgroup of which they are a part. To be sure, company-specific factors are critically important to the performance of a particular corporate bond, but industrywide factors can play a substantial role too and can also have a very large bearing on the market's perceptions of the individual company even if the company is relatively immune to developments in its industry. It is therefore critical to think from the top down before looking at a company from the bottom up. In other words, one should evaluate the macro influences on the company and its industry before looking at the company itself.

Choosing Corporate Bonds from the Top Down

There are many ways to determine a company's intrinsic value, and no two investors follow the same methodology. Nevertheless, value investors, particularly disciples of the economist Benjamin Graham, have settled on a set of exercises for determining intrinsic value. The list is rather long, but I have settled on a few that I believe can be augmented by a top-down investing approach.

Value the Company's Assets
In any analysis of a company's assets, there is plenty of room for top-down principles. For example, if your task is to value the real estate assets on a company's books, wouldn't it be helpful to know a thing or two about the macroeconomic environment for real estate? Drilling down, wouldn't it be helpful to know more about the economic condition of the regions within which the real estate is owned, as well as the vacancy rate in the case of commercial real estate? If it is your task to value the inventory on a company's books, might it not be helpful to know whether the inventories are held in abundance or in short supply economy-wide?

Determine How Liquid the Company Is
Value investors find it very important to know how liquid a company is. Macro variables can help. In the case of financial assets, some knowledge of the climate for those assets can be very valuable. This was certainly the case during the financial crisis. Another important insight is the condition of the money market and the availability of credit, both of which can have an impact on the ability to raise much needed short-term funding.

Determine the Company's Long-Term Financial Health
Obviously some sense of a company's long-term viability must relate to the long-term secular trends affecting the economic and financial climate.

Analyze the Growth Trends in the Company's Revenues and/or Sales
Here's an example to bring the point home: Suppose you are considering investing in a company that sells medical products. In this case, it would be very useful to know the demographics that will influence future sales. This is something the balance sheet can't tell you.

Analyze the Cost of Goods Sold
In the top-down realm, there is always some sense of inflation trends to be had. This is important in analyzing a company's cost of goods sold because it is determined in large part by inflation trends.

Analyze the Company's Net Profit Margin

Value investors believe that by tracking trends in a company's profit margin, which is the percentage of each dollar of revenue received that is turned into a net profit, you will spot important trends that are specific to the company you are analyzing and to the company's industry. Many of these trends are driven by top-down factors. For example, in the toy industry, profit margins have been shrinking for many years, largely because of the influence of China's market share, an influence made more obvious by familiarity with big-picture, top-down trends.

Think Macro

In addition to the preceding strategies, the investment decision-making process for purchasing corporate bonds is in many ways the same as it is for equities, at least in terms of the macro variables that one must consider when considering an investment in a company or industry. In the same way that an equity investor must be mindful of where the economy is with respect to the business cycle, a corporate bond investor must use the same considerations. For example, when the Federal Reserve begins to raise interest rates or when the economy is expected to be weak, equity investors tend to shun economically sensitive stocks.

Corporate bond investors should do the same thing and choose bonds in more defensive industries and higher-quality bonds during such times. Similarly, when the economic outlook is favorable, this is a time to consider purchasing corporate bonds in economically sensitive groups such as consumer cyclicals, basic materials, and capital goods. Moreover, since the yield spread between low-grade corporate bonds and investment-grade bonds tends to narrow when the Fed lowers interest rates, low-grade corporate bonds are often a better investment than both Treasuries and investment-grade bonds. This depends, however, on the severity of the economic weakness that provokes the Fed to lower interest rates. If you worry about buying corporate bonds when the economy is weak because you fear you will not be paid the principal and interest that are due, remember this: in the event of bankruptcy, bondholders are first in line; equity investors are way in the back (see Table 4.2 later in the chapter). The conservative bet is therefore to buy a company's bonds rather than its stock.

How Corporate Bonds Are Collateralized

Corporate bonds are collateralized in many different ways. This is an important aspect of bond investing because if there is a corporate default, bankruptcy, or liquidation, bondholders have legal priority over stockholders in bankruptcy court. It is also important because it will affect the yield-to-maturity on a bond. Generally speaking, bonds that are collateralized yield less than do those that are not. Most corporate bonds are not collateralized with any specific assets but are instead backed by the general credit and capacity of the issuing companies. These bonds are called *debentures.* Although debentures are not secured by specific assets, the overall assets of the issuer protect the bonds, and there are often pledges to secure the bonds in other ways.

Here are the main types of collateralized bonds:

- *Mortgage bonds.* These bonds are secured by a legal claim on real estate or other real property such as a factory or office building, and they are used mostly by utility companies. There are many different types of mortgage bonds, reflecting the priority of claims. A *first-mortgage bond,* for instance, has priority over a second-, third-, or junior-mortgage bond.
- *Collateral trust bonds.* Collateral trust bonds are issued by companies that have very few real assets to pledge. Instead, they collateralize them with financial assets such as stock or bond holdings. The assets are held by a trustee on behalf of bondholders.
- *Equipment trust certificates.* As the name suggests, specific types of equipment back equipment trust certificates. These certificates often are called *rolling stocks* because historically they have been issued by railroad rolling equipment such as the locomotives and cars. They are considered a very safe form of collateral.
- *Guaranteed bonds.* Guaranteed bonds are bonds backed by a company other than the issuer. The guarantee is like the guarantee a co-signer makes on a loan for an individual. In both cases the debt is by no means guaranteed and is dependent on the creditworthiness of the guarantor.

These various forms of collateral can be an important source of security to bond investors, but there is no better security than a strong balance sheet and an abundance of cash flow.

Credit Risk: Key to Corporate Bond Yields

An even more important determinant of a bond's yield-to-maturity and price performance than its collateralization and industry-related considerations is its credit rating. A *credit rating* essentially ranks a company's ability to repay its debts as well as withstand various types of financial and economic stress compared with other companies. Credit ratings are intended to help provide forward-looking opinions on a company's ability and willingness to pay interest and repay principal as scheduled. Credit ratings therefore can help investors assess the likelihood that their money will be returned to them in accordance with the terms on which they invested.

Credit ratings are assigned by three major rating organizations: Moody's Investor Services, Standard & Poor's, and Fitch Ratings. Of the three, Moody's and Standard & Poor's are considered the leading agencies. Each of the three rating agencies follows a very thorough and rigorous methodology for determining a company's creditworthiness. The agencies have been under pressure in recent years for having rated many securities at levels that implied there was much lower credit risk than turned out to be the case, particularly in mortgage-related securities. Nevertheless, investors continue to look to the rating agencies for guidance on the financial health of companies, municipalities, and sovereign nations.

A bond's credit rating has a significant impact on its yield-to-maturity. As one would expect, the lower a bond's credit rating is, the higher its yield. On bonds with sharply different credit ratings, the yield differences can be substantial, often more than several percentage points. A high-grade, or investment-grade, bond (bonds rated BBB or higher), for example, which is a bond considered to have a low probability of default, will tend to yield much less than will a bond rated below investment grade.

As an investor you must strike a careful balance between choosing bonds that are deemed safe but are low yielding and bonds that are deemed risky but are high yielding. This difficult balancing act is a reminder of the benefits of diversification, which can increase your rate of return while spreading the risks. Keep in mind, however, one of the top lessons of Chapter 3, which is that asset diversification does not necessarily equal risk diversification. For many individuals, diversification of a portfolio can be difficult to implement because of limited capital, limited knowledge, high transaction costs, difficulty finding suitable bonds, and the challenges associated with understanding how to assemble a portfolio that considers how the many risk factors will affect a portfolio in its entirety. For those investors, a bond mutual fund is an excellent way to invest.

For more on credit ratings, see Chapter 12.

Lien Position Is Important

Corporate bond investors should pay careful attention as to where they sit in the capital structure, particularly in today's environment where market acci-

TABLE 4.2 Average Corporate Debt Recovery Rates Measured by Postdefault Trading Prices Based on 30-Day Postdefault Market Prices

Lien Position	Issuer Weighted			Value Weighted		
	2008	2007	1982–2008	2008	2007	1982–2008
Bank Loans						
Sr. secured	63.4%	68.6%	69.9%	49.0%	78.3%	62.1%
Second lien	40.4%	65.9%	50.4%	36.6%	65.8%	49.8%
Sr. unsecured*	29.8%	—	52.5%	22.6%	—	41.0%
Bonds						
Sr. secured	58.0%	80.5%	52.3%	45.9%	81.7%	53.0%
Sr. unsecured	33.8%	53.3%	36.4%	26.2%	56.9%	32.4%
Sr. subordinated	23.0%	54.5%	31.7%	10.4%	67.7%	26.4%
Subordinated	23.6%	—	31.0%	7.3%	—	23.5%
Jr. subordinated	—	—	24.0%	—	—	16.8%
Pref. Stock†						
Trust pref.	—	—	11.7%	—	—	13.0%
Nontrust pref.	8.6%	—	21.6%	1.7%	—	13.1%

* 2008's average senior unsecured loan recoveries are based on three observations.
† Only includes defaults on preferred stock that are associated or followed by a broader debt default. Average recovery rates for preferred stock covers only the period of 1983 to 2008.

Source: Moody's.

dents and economic strain remain constant threats. This means that investors should determine what place in line they would have in case the issuing company were to default on its obligations. The higher up in the capital structure, the safer it generally is. In other words, investors highest in the capital structure generally recover more of their money than do those at the lowest end of the capital structure, which generally means the equity investor.

Take a look at Table 4.2. It shows that, from 1982 to 2008, the recovery rate on senior secured corporate bonds was much higher than it was for lower-ranked debt. The lower the lien position, the lower the recovery rate.

Covenants: The Fine Print

When a corporate bond is issued, the issuer agrees to abide by a set of promises set forth in a contract known as an *indenture*. Aside from protecting investors, the indenture also spells out specific rights that protect the issuer in its contract with investors. The issuer's rights can work against investors at times and therefore should be known before investors consider the purchase of a bond. A good example of these rights is the issuer's *right to call*, or redeem, its bonds before maturity. Issuers typically invoke this so-called *call provision* when it is advantageous to them but generally disadvantageous to investors. There are many other provisions in a bond's indenture, and they can vary from one bond to the next. It is therefore critical to read the fine print before you purchase a bond because it can have a significant impact on your investment. You can read more about this topic in Chapter 3.

Government Agency Securities

There are two main types of federal agency securities: securities issued by government-sponsored enterprises (GSEs) and those issued by federally related institutions. Most agency securities are issued by GSEs; federally related institutions only rarely issue debt on their own but instead obtain funding from the Federal Financing Bank (FFB), which was created in 1973 to help meet the funding needs of about 20 separate U.S. agencies, such as the General Services Administration, the Farmers Housing Administration, the U.S. Postal Service, and the Export-Import Bank. (FFB holdings of obligations issued, sold, or guaranteed by other federal agencies totaled $61.3 billion on October 31, 2009.)

Some federal agencies are owned and directed by the federal government, and their debt obligations are backed by the full faith and credit of the U.S. government. Others are federally sponsored but "privately" owned, obviously a misnomer following the September 2008 move by the federal government to put Fannie Mae and Freddie Mac into conservatorship (see Chapter 2). The obligations of federally sponsored agencies presumably have de facto backing from the federal government, as evidenced by the government response to Fannie's and Freddie's woes.

Government-Sponsored Enterprises

When the United States was running budget surpluses in the late 1990s, there were some who believed the agency securities market would overtake the U.S. Treasury market in size and become the benchmark for rates. This made no sense to anyone who understood Washington: budget surpluses were not the norm, and politicians would eventually succumb to temptations and lose their resolve on fiscal prudence. We all know how that movie turned out.

Although the core reason for believing the agency securities market might overtake the Treasury market never took sail, elements of the reasoning had credence. In particular, the size, liquidity, and high credit quality of the GSE market supported the argument. These elements have since lost their momentum, and they remain in place only because of the de facto U.S. backing of the GSEs. Today, the GSE market is shrinking, as is liquidity, and as for credit quality, well, there is none except for Uncle Sam's backing.

Government-sponsored enterprises are publicly chartered, privately owned companies that were created by Congress to provide funding to important sectors of the economy, including housing, farming, and education. GSEs issue debt to raise capital to lend to prospective borrowers, particularly in the housing market. As we showed in Chapter 2, the agency securities market grew rapidly in the 1990s until the housing bubble burst. In the third quarter of 2009, the agency securities market was $2.8 trillion in size.

There are seven government-sponsored enterprises:

1. Federal Farm Credit Bank System
2. Farm Credit Financial Assistance Corporation
3. Farm Credit System
4. Federal Home Loan Bank
5. Federal Home Loan Mortgage Corporation (Freddie Mac)
6. Federal National Mortgage Association (Fannie Mae)
7. Federal Agricultural Mortgage Corporation (Farmer Mac)

Two other entities—the Financing Corporation and the Resolution Funding Corporation—technically speaking are GSEs, but they're not. They're funding shells, not operating companies. These entities were given GSE status to keep their funding off budget; which is to say their funding did not appear as federal borrowing for purposes of the federal budget. Another entity, the Student Loan Marketing Association (Sallie Mae), is often though of as a GSE, and it once was, but in 2004 Sallie Mae became a private company: the SLM Corporation.

Two of the GSEs—the Federal Home Loan Bank and the Farm Credit System—are owned cooperatively by their borrowers. The two largest are Fannie Mae and Freddie Mac, both of which supply funding to borrowers in the housing market. These days Fannie and Freddie fund the vast majority of new mortgages. The Federal Home Loan Bank is the third GSE geared to facilitating activity in the housing market. Let's take a look at how these three entities perform their vital functions.

Fannie and Freddie: Housing's Backstops Now Backstopped by Uncle Sam

In 1938 the federal government established the Federal National Mortgage Association (Fannie Mae) to help counter the funding problems prospective home buyers faced during the Great Depression. Fannie Mae remained a government agency until 1968, when it was divided into a private company and the Government National Mortgage Association (Ginnie Mae), an institution that is still a government agency. Keep in mind that there is a difference between a government-sponsored agency and a government agency. A GSE is federally chartered, and securities issued by a GSE are not backed by the full faith and credit of the U.S. government, whereas debt issued by agencies such as Ginnie Mae is.

In its own words, Fannie Mae's current mission is "to provide liquidity, stability, and affordability to the U.S. housing and mortgage markets." This mission statement differs from 2001 when Fannie stated its mission was "to provide products and services that increase the availability and the affordability of housing for low-, moderate-, and middle-income Americans." The change that has occurred in the statement is interesting, and it fits with the perception that Fannie, as well as Freddie and many other entities involved in mortgage financing, overreached in their mission to expand homeownership.

Since 1968 Fannie Mae has nonetheless helped more than 30 million families purchase their own homes. Fannie Mae accomplishes this mission by lending indirectly rather than directly to prospective home buyers. This means that Fannie Mae operates in the secondary market for home mortgages rather than in the primary market. In other words, instead of lending directly to prospective home buyers, Fannie Mae purchases mortgage loans from mortgage lenders such as savings and loan institutions, mortgage companies, and commercial banks. By purchasing existing mortgages, Fannie Mae enables those institutions to preserve their capital and lend to a greater number of borrowers than they would otherwise. This became particularly important in 2008 when banks significantly tightened their lending standards and cut their lending, leaving the GSEs to carry the load.

To finance its mortgage purchasers, Fannie Mae issues debt securities with a variety of maturities, albeit on a much smaller scale than in the past. Fannie's debt issuance includes bills, notes, medium-term notes, discount notes, subordinated debt, and other somewhat arcane products. Fannie's Benchmark Bills, Benchmark Bonds, and Benchmark Notes are registered trademarks of Fannie Mae. Fannie uses the proceeds of the sale of its debt securities to retire outstanding debt, to add to the proceeds of its working capital, and for general corporate purposes. Fannie's financing needs depends on many factors, including the volume of its maturing debt obligations, the volume of mortgage loan prepayments, the volume and type of mortgage loans Fannie purchases, and general market conditions.

The majority of Fannie Mae's short-term funding needs are met through its Discount Notes and Benchmark Bills programs. Fannie's Discount Notes are unsecured general obligations issued in book-entry form through the 12 Federal Reserve banks. Discount Notes have maturities ranging from overnight to 360 days from the date of issuance, and they are offered each business day through a selling group of securities dealers and brokers. The sale of Discount Notes provides bridge financing to a date when Fannie intends to issue longer-term securities.

Through Fannie's Noncallable Benchmark Securities Program, Fannie sells large-sized, regularly scheduled issues that seek to emulate many of the characteristics that draw investors to U.S. Treasuries, primarily by establishing a full yield curve of liquid noncallable benchmark notes. Fannie is generally expected to price each new issue within three business days of the announcement of its debt sales, and it will generally settle within two days after pricing. Securities are sold with maturities of 2, 3, 5, and 10 years, and they are available in minimum increments of $2,000 and in subsequent increments of $1,000.

Freddie Mac operates much in the same way as Fannie Mae. Since Congress chartered it in 1970, Freddie Mac's stated mission is "to provide liquidity, stability, and affordability to the housing market," the same as Fannie's and is a change from 2001 when the stated mission was to "create a continuous flow of funds to mortgage lenders in support of homeownership and rental housing." As with Fannie Mae, Freddie Mac purchases mortgages from lenders and packages them into securities that are sold to investors. In doing so, it ultimately provides homeowners and renters with lower housing costs and better access to home financing than would otherwise be possible.

An increasing share of agency debt issuance has been from the Federal Home Loan Banks (FHLB). FHLB issuance in the third quarter of 2009 was $141.1 billion, data from SIFMA show, bringing the year's total to $349.1 billion, exceeding the net issuance, which was mostly flat for the year ended September 2009.

Mortgage-Backed Securities

Mortgage-backed securities (MBS) are perceived as one of the more complex segments of the bond market. This is understandable in light of the considerable differences that exist between mortgage-backed securities and conventional bonds. Two of the biggest differences relate to the very different structures of their cash flows and maturity dates. With most bonds these two characteristics are pretty straightforward and predictable, but they are far more uncertain with MBS. For investors this presents both risks and opportunities. For most investors, however, a basic understanding is enough to avoid some of the pitfalls of investing in mortgage-backed securities and to capitalize on the relatively attractive yields and many opportunities the MBS market often presents.

In its simplest form, a mortgage-backed security is a pool of mortgages that have been securitized, or repackaged, so that they can be sold to investors. Investors in mortgage-backed securities have many of the same experiences that banks have when they issue mortgage loans. For example, both receive regular payments of principal and interest on the mortgage loans, both are subject to prepayment risks, and both are subject to effects from defaults on mortgage loans. One of the most basic forms of a mortgage-backed security is a *mortgage pass-through security,* also known as a *participation certificate.* A mortgage pass-through security represents pro rata ownership interest in the principal and interest payments of a pool of mortgage loans. The pools contain varying amounts of loans, from just a few to many thousands. The cash flows are said to "pass through" from homeowners and other property owners to the holders of the pass-through securities. The payments are made regularly, generally on a monthly basis, and include both principal and interest.

Most pass-through securities are issued by government agencies, including the Federal National Mortgage Association, the Federal Home Loan Mortgage Corporation, and the Government National Mortgage Association. Pass-through securities that are issued by nongovernment entities are called *private-label mortgage-backed securities,* a market that froze in the aftermath of the financial crisis. These securities typically are constructed with a pool of large mortgages taken out by individuals with above-average incomes.

The interest paid on the pass-through securities is lower than the interest paid on the underlying mortgages for a couple of reasons. First, when either a government agency or a private-label company creates a mortgage-backed security, it normally pays a service fee to the institutions from which it purchased the mortgages that underlie the mortgage-backed securities. The mortgage lenders that sell their mortgages generally retain servicing of the loans and earn a fee for collecting payments from homeowners and performing other functions. A second factor that reduces the actual interest payment on a pass-through security relates to the fee paid by investors to government agencies for their guarantee of the mortgage loans. Fannie Mae, for example, collects a guaranty fee for its guarantee of the timely payment of principal and interest on the securities. Fannie Mae's guaranty is solely its own, and it does not have the backing of the full faith and credit of the U.S. government. Ginnie Mae's securities, in contrast, have the government's backing.

Agency-backed mortgage-backed securities have high credit quality because they are backed by assets—the homes underlying the loans. Moreover, the securities are guaranteed by the GSEs, and in essence the U.S. government.

Collateralized Mortgage Obligations

A more complex type of mortgage-backed security is known as a collateralized mortgage obligation (CMO) or, since 1986, a real estate mortgage investment conduit (REMIC). A CMO is a mortgage-backed security constructed by repackaging and redirecting the cash flows from other mortgage-backed securities. A typical CMO, often called a *plain vanilla* or *sequential pay CMO*, consists of a few *tranches*, or classes of securities, that are prioritized to distribute the payments made on the underlying mortgages according to a predetermined payment schedule. In other words, both the scheduled and unscheduled principal payments made on the mortgages will be distributed to holders of a CMO on a predetermined prioritized basis. This is different from a pass-through security, where the principal payments are distributed in a pro rata, or proportionate, basis. CMOs were created to offer investors a wide variety of securities from which to choose. With CMOs, investors are more likely to find a mortgage-backed security that fits their needs and their risk profiles.

For example, in a CMO that has four classes of securities, Class A could have first priority on all mortgage prepayments, Class B could have second priority, Class C could be third, and Class D could be last in line to receive prepayments. In this case Class A would be the most likely to be prepaid early, thus making it a relatively short-term security, while Class D would be prepaid last, making it a relatively long-term security. This CMO is structured in a way that gives prospective investors a better sense of when the securities will mature than it would if it were a pass-through security.

Prepayment Risks

One of the biggest risks of holding mortgage-backed securities is the prepayment risk. *Prepayment risk* is the risk that a mortgage security will be prepaid early, exposing the investor to reinvestment risk. Mortgages are prepaid for a variety of reasons, including mortgage refinancing, a home sale, and repossession and liquidation of a home, or simply because a homeowner chooses to prepay the mortgage early incrementally or with blocks of money. When the mortgages that underlie an MBS are prepaid, the investors are also prepaid. Investors are therefore at risk of having to reinvest their money at lower interest rates. Prepayment risks are greatest when interest rates decline enough to prompt homeowners to refinance their existing mortgages. In 2003, for example, nearly 12 million mortgage loans were refinanced after more than 8 million were refinanced in 2002.[2] This amounts to about 25 percent of the total number of mortgages outstanding (at the time, there were about 75 million homes owned, with about 58 percent of those having a mortgage).

During these periods, investors in mortgage-backed securities had much of their invested principal returned to them. Those investors then faced the unpleasant prospect of reinvesting their capital at interest rate levels that at the time were the lowest in about 40 years. The prospect of early prepayments can cause a mortgage-backed security to perform very much as a callable bond does when interest rates decline. In both cases the securities are subject to negative convexity, which is the risk that a bond will perform poorly when a certain interest rate threshold is reached. In the case of an MBS, this threshold kicks in when market interest rates decline below the interest rate on the MBS and accelerates as interest rates continue to decline below the threshold. CMOs can give investors in MBSs a greater degree of certainty with respect to prepayment risks but cannot eliminate this critical risk.

One of the best ways to simplify the very complex realm of investing in mortgage-backed securities is to remember that you are holding a pool of mortgages and are therefore apt to have many of the same experiences that a bank does in different interest rate climates. In today's environment, many additional considerations are necessary, in particular paying very close attention to the credit quality of the mortgage-backed security. This consideration has driven many investors to steer clear of the market for private-label mortgage-backed securities and into the more comfortable realm of *conforming mortgages* (so-named because they are mortgages that conform to purchasing guidelines set by Fannie Mae and Freddie Mac). As with many other types of investments, if you first think of the investment in its simplest form—in this case a home mortgage—you will at least have an understanding of the most critical aspect of the investment.

Municipal Bonds

Municipal bonds are bonds issued by state and local governments as well as other governmental entities to fund a variety of public spending needs, including the construction of new schools, hospitals, utilities, and highways, and to fund a variety of general obligations. Municipal bonds are very popular with individual investors, collectively holding $980 billion worth at the end of the third quarter of 2009. In fact, next to corporate bonds (households held $2.37 trillion worth of corporate bonds at the end of the third quarter of 2009), households own more municipal bonds than any other fixed-income security. When indirect holdings of municipal securities are included (mutual funds), households hold about 67 percent of the $2.7 trillion in municipal bonds outstanding. Expanding this further to closed-end funds boosts the tally to closer to 70 percent.

The reason municipal securities are so popular with individuals is that the interest paid on them is exempt from federal income taxes. U.S. laws are such that the federal government cannot tax the states and vice versa. This is why these securities are tax exempt. For individuals who purchase municipal bonds issued in the state in which they live, the interest paid on those bonds is likely to be exempt from state and local taxes too. Two tax bills passed by Congress helped boost the popularity of municipal bonds. First, the Tax Reform Act of 1986 reduced many tax deductions that previously had limited tax liabilities for individuals. Municipal bonds therefore became a bastion for tax sheltering.

Second, the tax bill of 1993 raised marginal tax rates in the upper income brackets, creating the need for tax shelters. It can be persuasively argued that the Clinton tax increase of 1993 was a leading factor in the rise in the proportion of taxes that individuals paid as a percentage of the gross domestic product (GDP).

In the late 1990s, this key statistic reached its highest level in over 40 years. The prospect of higher federal tax rates expected to be put in place to address the large U.S. budget deficit is expected to support the municipal bond sector in the years ahead, although increased selectively among municipalities is also likely because of the financial strains that many municipalities face in the aftermath of the financial and economic crisis (economic downturns impact state budgets one to two years after the downturn is over as a result of falling revenues and an increase in Medicaid enrollment, which tends to occur very late in an economic downturn).

Calculating the Taxable Equivalent Yield

In considering the purchase of a municipal bond, it is critically important to know how to compare its yield with the yields on taxable securities. This will help an investor judge which of the two investment choices has the highest after-tax yield-to-maturity. For example, if you were considering the purchase of either a municipal bond with a yield-to-maturity of 5 percent or a corporate bond yielding 7 percent, you would want to know which of the two securities actually produced the best after-tax return. The calculation is very simple:

$$\text{Taxable equivalent yield} = \frac{\text{tax-exempt yield}}{1 - \text{marginal tax rate}}$$

The *tax-exempt yield* is the yield-to-maturity on the municipal bond (or municipal bond fund); the *marginal tax rate* is the tax rate that you pay on the last dollar of your income. In this example, assuming the marginal tax rate is 39 percent, the calculation is done as follows:

$$\text{Taxable equivalent yield} = \frac{5 \text{ percent}}{1 - 0.39} = 8.20 \text{ percent}$$

In this example, the municipal bond has a greater after-tax yield-to-maturity than does the corporate bond. Put differently, to achieve an after-tax yield-to-maturity that is higher than that of the municipal bond, you would have to find a taxable security yielding more than 8.2 percent.

Keep in mind that if the municipal security is selling at a deep discount to its par value, the yield-to-maturity used in the calculation could overstate its taxable equivalent yield. This is the case because its yield-to-maturity will be inflated by the capital gain that will be realized when the security matures. Since the capital gain is taxable, you want to use a yield-to-maturity that eliminates the capital gain and focuses on the coupon payment instead. Of course, only the coupon payments are tax exempt.

Types of Municipal Securities

With over 1 million different municipal bonds outstanding and more than 60,000 entities issuing them, there is obviously a wide variety of municipal bonds to choose from. It is therefore very important to look closely at the bond you are considering buying. Although there is an array of municipal bonds outstanding, there are two main types: general obligation bonds and revenue bonds.

General Obligation Bonds

Also known as GO (gee-oh) bonds, *general obligation bonds* are backed by the full faith and credit of the issuer, chiefly the issuer's power to tax the public. This means that only an issuer with the power to tax can issue a GO bond. States, cities, counties, and towns are examples of entities that issue GO bonds.

Some GO bonds are backed by revenue other than taxes, such as fees. These bonds are known as *double-barreled municipal bonds.* Some GO bonds are backed by an assessment on the entities that benefit directly from the borrowing; these bonds are called *special assessment bonds.* Keep in mind that there is a legal limit on the taxing power used to back some GO bonds. These bonds are called *limited-tax general obligation bonds.* When buying GO bonds, investors should inspect both the economy and the strength of the tax base in the municipality.

Revenue Bonds

As the name implies, *revenue bonds* are backed by revenues generated by projects financed with the bonds. Examples include toll bridges, toll roads, airports, hospitals, and utilities. Revenue bonds are issued by agencies, commissions, and authorities created by legislation passed by state or local governments.

Although revenue bonds are backed by specific revenue sources, they can be riskier than GO bonds because the municipality does not back the bonds explicitly. When buying a revenue bond, investors should determine the *debt-service coverage ratio,* which is a measure of the amount of revenue coming in versus the debt payments going out. *Essential-purpose revenue bonds,* which are those backed by revenues for essential services such as water delivery, are viewed as relatively safer than other revenue bonds. Nevertheless, investors in a fragile economic climate must closely inspect the revenue source. For example, a revenue bond that is backed by fees collected for water and sewer use in residential neighborhoods would be affected by the vacancy rate of the neighborhoods where revenues are expected to be collected.

Build America Bonds

A new type of municipal bond known as *Build America Bonds* (BABs) was created in 2008 under the American Recovery and Reinvestment Act of 2009, which was signed into law on February 19, 2009. The Treasury Department announced the implementation of the program on April 3, 2009. BABs are a much different breed of municipal bond because they are taxable. The Build America Bond program enables municipal bond issuers to increase the yield offering on their bonds by an amount equal to the size of the federal subsidy provided for the bonds. The increased yield attracts a wider class of investors, many of whom traditionally avoid municipal bonds because of their low yields and because the tax advantages do not apply to them.

There are two types of Build America Bonds: tax-credit BABs and direct-payment BABs. *Tax-credit BABs* provide a federal subsidy of 35 percent of the total amount of interest paid on the bond to the issuer. *Direct-payment*

BABs provide a subsidy directly to those that hold the bonds. In the fourth quarter of 2009, data from SIFMA indicated that BABs represented 32 percent of all long-term municipal bond issuance during the quarter. From April through December 2009, the total amount of BABs issuance was $64.1 billion, or 15.66 percent of the total long-term municipal bond issuance.

Municipal Bond Insurance

Some municipalities are too weak or too small to attract a large group of investors to buy their bonds. To entice investors, these municipalities enter into agreements to have their bonds insured by insurance companies. Municipal bond insurance guarantees that the insurer will pay the interest and principal on the bonds even if the issuer defaults on its debt obligations. The insurance generally lasts for the life of the bond being insured. Historically, about half of newly issued municipal bonds have been insured. Insured bonds have historically yielded less than those that were not insured because of the lower risk of holding insured bonds, although they typically have yielded more than municipal bonds that are AAA rated in their own right.

This changed beginning in 2007 when the major monoline insurance companies began reporting losses related to activities in the mortgage market, particularly from having insured structured products having mortgage exposure. *Monoline insurance companies* are known as such because their focus is primarily on insuring municipal bonds. When the monoline insurers incurred losses from activities that diverged from their core businesses, it shook the municipal bond market, causing yields on insured bonds to trade higher than those that were not. This showed the distrust that investors had developed toward the monoline insurers.

The major municipal bond insurance companies are American Municipal Bond Assurance Company (AMBAC), Municipal Bond Insurance Association (MBIA), Financial Guaranty Insurance Company (FGIC), and Financial Security Assurance (FSA). The move by large financial companies such as the major multiline property and casualty companies to insure municipal bonds as well as structured products was seen as one of the major mishaps facilitating the financial crisis.

Summary

- The five largest and most active segments of the bond market are the markets for U.S. Treasuries, corporate bonds, government agency securities, mortgage-backed securities, and municipal bonds.

- The U.S. Treasury market is the most active segment of the bond market, although it is surpassed in size by the mortgage-backed securities market. The deep liquidity of the Treasury market and the perception that Treasuries are risk free attract investors to use Treasuries as the benchmarks for quoting and pricing of other fixed-income securities.
- The Treasury's inflation-indexed securities provide a means of protecting investors against inflation risks and tracking the market's inflation expectations.
- As with corporate equities, the investment performance of corporate bonds can depend greatly on the group or subgroup of which they are a part. Investors should approach purchases of corporate bonds with the same philosophies that work well in investing in stocks. Chiefly, one must be aware of the importance of picking bonds in industries that have the best prospects for economic growth. Attention to a bond's place in the capital structure and recovery rates are important elements of successful investing in the corporate bond market.
- There are two main types of federal agency securities: securities issued by government-sponsored enterprises (GSEs) and those issued by federally related institutions. To finance its mortgage purchasers, Fannie Mae issues debt securities with a variety of maturities, albeit on a much smaller scale than in the past.
- Mortgage-backed securities are complex securities with characteristics that are relatively unconventional in the bond market. The complexities are a key reason for their relatively attractive yields. Investors can choose from different types of mortgage-backed securities, including the so-called plain vanilla pass-through securities and the more complex but tailor-made collateralized mortgage obligations.
- Municipal bonds are very popular with individual investors because of their tax benefits. The interest paid on the vast majority of municipal bonds is exempt from federal taxes. Investors should compute the after-tax equivalent yield on municipal securities when comparing yields on municipal securities to those on taxable securities such as corporate bonds. A new type of municipal bond was introduced in 2009 called Build America Bonds, which are taxable bonds subsidized by the federal government.

5

RISKS FACING TODAY'S BOND INVESTORS
Asset Diversification Does Not Equal Risk Diversification

True or false? Unlike stocks, bonds are risk free. Answer: Not what you would expect.

When some people think about bond investing, they conjure up visions of senior citizens comfortably sitting on their nest eggs and bristling with prosperity after years of eschewing risk taking. However, this is a very dusty image that is decades removed from reality. Bonds are far from risk free. True, they are less risky than many other types of investments, but bond investors must be aware of a number of risks that could significantly affect their fixed-income investments. This was a major lesson learned during the financial crisis, as virtually no segment of the bond market was spared from losses, except for the Treasury market, which benefited from a flight to quality from nearly every asset class. The value of the more exotic types of bonds—in particular those with exposure to the housing market—were particularly hard hit, with many collapsing in value.

Bond investors learned during the crisis that asset diversification did not equal risk diversification. In other words, just because they had put together a mix of stocks, bonds, and other assets in their portfolios, they were not necessarily shielded from the chief investment risk: equity losses. To be successful, bond investors must neutralize the equity risk factor such that the correlation between their stocks and bonds will be low during periods when equity prices are falling. Remember this idea: there is equity risk in a bond, just as there is interest rate risk in a stock. Similarly, there are liquidity risks in most asset classes, as well as volatility risks.

Welcome to the world of investing in the new normal. It behooves to-day's investors to be more cognizant of the commonalities that exist in the risk factors present across the asset classes they own.

It's simplistic to equate bond investing with risk-free investing. The degree of risk facing today's bond investors depends on many factors, including the economic climate, the types of strategies investors employ, and the types of fixed-income securities investors choose. Bond investors can control some of the risks they face, but their degree of control is sometimes minimal. As with most risks, however, awareness of the risks involved in bond investing can help minimize the extent to which these risks may have a deleterious effect on a portfolio's investment performance. The benefits of knowing the risks involved in bond investing are akin to the benefits of knowing the risks involved in crossing a street before the light turns green. The main point is that risks can be managed if one is aware of them.

Bonds are at risk of being affected by a variety of risk factors. There are two main ways in which risk factors can affect a bond. First, some risk factors pose a threat to a bond's current value. In this case the bond's price will fluctuate with the degree to which certain risk factors threaten its value. Second, some risk factors pose a threat to the cash flows on a bond. In this case certain risk factors can affect the timeliness and value of a bond's cash flows.

There are three major risk factors that affect virtually all bonds and many others that affect specific types of bonds and strategies:

- Risks to virtually all bonds:
  ○ Market, or interest rate, risk
  ○ Reinvestment risk
  ○ Event risk
- Risks to specific types of bonds and strategies:
  ○ Sector risk
  ○ Call, or prepayment, risk
  ○ Liquidity risk
  ○ Credit, or default, risk
  ○ Yield curve risk
  ○ Spread risk
  ○ Inflation risk
  ○ Currency risk
  ○ Hedge risk
  ○ Volatility risk
  ○ Odd-lot risk

Let's take a look at each of these risks, starting with the three most important ones.

Market, or Interest Rate, Risk

Ask bond traders on Wall Street whether there is much risk in holding bonds and they will give you an earful. Bond prices can and do move sharply, probably more than most people perceive. Make no mistake: bond investors are by no means immune to market fluctuations and the risk of capital losses. As with most financial assets, bond prices are subject to market risk. As the label implies, *market risk* refers to the risks associated with market fluctuations. In the bond market this risk is also called *interest rate risk*, and generally it is one of the biggest risks a bond investor faces.

Interest rate risk arises from the fact that bond prices move inversely with yields. Put simply, when interest rates rise, bond prices fall, and when interest rates fall, bond prices rise. This is a risk for any investor who may sell a bond before its maturity date because the bond is at risk of fluctuating in price. For investors who hold their bonds to maturity, interest rate risks are basically irrelevant because those bonds will be redeemed at their par value regardless of the interest rate volatility that has occurred between the date when securities were purchased and the maturity date.

All bonds are subject to interest rate risk regardless of whether they are insured against losses (as is the case with many municipal bonds) or the creditworthiness of the bond issuer is strong. The prices on these bonds respond as other bonds do to fluctuations in interest rates.

Interest rate risk is largely out of bond investors' control; investors are powerless against the forces that cause interest rates to fluctuate. This does not mean, however, that bond investors are completely helpless in the face of interest rate risks. Indeed, bond investors can control the degree of interest rate risk to which they are subject by varying the maturity length of the bonds in their portfolios. By selecting shorter maturities over longer maturities, for example, bond investors can reduce their interest rate risk. Interest rate risk is greater on long-term maturities than it is on short-term maturities because a bond's price sensitivity to changes in interest rates increases with maturity length. A bond's price sensitivity to changes in interest rates can be quantified by its duration, which was discussed in greater detail in Chapter 3. Duration is basically a mathematical means of determining the approximate percentage change that will result when a bond's price changes by 100 basis points. Knowing a bond's duration is one of the best ways to control interest rate risk.

Attempting to control interest rate risk by choosing short maturities over long maturities seems simple, but it can introduce new risks. One risk, as discussed below, is a variant of reinvestment risk. *Reinvestment risk* is the risk that the cash flows on a bond will be reinvested at falling interest rate levels. This risk normally applies to a bond's regular interest payments, but it also can apply to an investor who chooses short-term maturities over long-term maturities when that investor engages in the strategy in effort to control interest rate risk. In this case an investor who chooses short-term maturities over long-term maturities will have to reinvest the capital from the maturing bonds more often, increasing the risk that the capital will be invested at a lower interest rate.

A second risk introduced by attempts to control interest rate risk is the possibility that investors will incur opportunity costs by investing in short-term maturities during times when owning long-term maturities would have produced larger capital gains. In this case investors forgo the chance to achieve higher investment returns in order to reduce their interest rate risk. This trade-off is very common in investing; investors recognize that low-risk assets generally have lower investment returns than do riskier assets.

Bond investors that bet correctly on the shape of the yield curve can reduce the interest rate risk of their portfolios by choosing a mix of maturities that, while having the same aggregate duration as other mixes, performs optimally because of the maturity selection. This is done by assessing the portfolio's yield curve risk, discussed below.

Reinvestment Risk

As was just mentioned, *reinvestment risk* is the risk that a bond's cash flows will be reinvested at falling interest rate levels. This risk is of particular concern to investors who invest in short-term maturities and bonds with high coupon rates.

When interest rates decline, bond investors are less likely to be able to invest the interest income they receive on their bonds at the same interest rate level they receive on their bonds. Consider, for example, a bond investor who owns a bond with a par value of $1,000 that pays a 6 percent annual coupon. The investor therefore will receive $60 per year in interest income from that bond. Let's say interest rates decline and the investor can no longer find a bond that both pays a 6 percent annual coupon and meets his or her investment criteria. The investor must instead reinvest the interest income at 5 percent, and the investor's interest on interest will decline and thus have an impact on a key element of the investment returns. Of course, if interest rates rise, the investor will benefit by being able to reinvest the interest payments at a higher interest rate.

The degree of reinvestment risk for a particular bond depends largely on three key factors. First, the longer the maturity on a bond is, the more the bond's total dollar return will depend on prevailing interest rates to achieve the yield-to-maturity calculated at the time of purchase. This is a critical point because for long-term maturities, interest on interest can account for a large percentage of the total dollar return. In fact, when interest rates are high, interest on interest can account for more than half of a bond's total dollar return. This is why it is extremely important for bond investors to be as diligent with their investment choices as they are with the reinvestment of interest.

A second factor that determines a bond's degree of reinvestment risk is its coupon rate. As was shown above, fluctuations in interest rates can have a direct bearing on the interest on interest received on a bond. The higher the coupon rate on a bond, the greater the reinvestment risk. Bonds with low coupon rates have low reinvestment risk. As with maturity length, the higher the bond's coupon rate, the more the bond's total dollar return will depend on prevailing interest rates to achieve the yield-to-maturity that existed at the time of purchase. In light of these risks, bond investors who are concerned about the dollar return on their bond portfolios should consider purchasing bonds with high coupon rates when interest rates are rising. (Another reason for doing so is because when interest rates rise, bonds with higher coupons fall at a slower rate than those with lower coupons because bonds with relatively high coupons have lower convexity than do bonds with relatively low coupons.) Conversely, when interest rates are low, investors should consider investing in low coupon bonds. Zero coupon bonds, for example, have no reinvestment risk except when a bond is sold or matures. This is one reason why insurance companies and pension funds are attracted to zero coupon bonds—they can be surer of their investment returns. However, buying bonds with higher coupons during periods when interest rates are falling could result in opportunity costs since bonds with high coupon rates tend to increase in price more slowly than do bonds with low coupon rates. This is the case because of the relatively lower duration and convexity of high coupon bonds relative to those with lower coupons (assuming other aspects of the bond's characteristics are the same).

A bond's maturity length is the third factor that determines the bond's degree of reinvestment risk. The shorter a bond's maturity is, the more it is subject to reinvestment risk. Investors in bonds that have short-term maturities are therefore at risk of having to reinvest the proceeds received on the bonds when they mature.

One of the best ways to limit the reinvestment risks in a bond portfolio that result from maturity length is to stagger the maturities so that bonds mature on different dates. This way there will be an opportunity to reinvest the proceeds from maturing bonds at prevailing rates that are likely to reflect both the ups and the downs of the interest rate climate. This strategy also provides a steady flow of capital for reinvestment without the need to sell securities to generate it. This allows for more opportunistic investing and can reduce transaction costs.

Interest Rate Risk and Reinvestment Risk Can Offset Each Other

It is important to note that interest rate risk and reinvestment risk can offset each other. Indeed, many fixed-income portfolio managers recognize this and construct their portfolios to create a high degree of immunization against both of these risks. Portfolios constructed in this way benefit when the capital losses that result from rising interest rates (causing prices to fall) are offset by the benefits of higher reinvestment rates on a portfolio's cash flows.

Event Risk

There are a number of ways in which unexpected events can affect a bond. After some events, for instance, the ability of an issuer to pay both interest and principal can be seriously affected. In other cases, unexpected events can cause a bond's price to drop sharply. These risks are known as *event risks.* Event risks affect nearly all financial instruments, but the magnitude of the impact depends on the instrument's risk characteristics. A high-yield bond, for example, is likely to be affected more than a Treasury bond when unexpected events occur.

Event risk is too often seen as improbable by investors, who are accustomed to thinking only in terms of a so-called *normal distribution curve,* which basically depicts the probably of certain events occurring. The financial crisis, as well as numerous other events that occurred in preceding years, illustrated the importance of thinking more in terms of a *fat-tail distribution curve,* which assigns a greater probability to the occurrence of fat-tail, or black swan, events—that is, those that normal distribution models suggest a low probability of occurrence.

Five types of event risk pose the greatest risk to bond investors:

1. Systemic risk
2. Takeovers or restructurings
3. Sudden shifts in market sentiment

4. International financial events
5. International political or military events

Let's take a brief look at each of these event risks.

Systemic Risk

As just mentioned, the improbable seems to happen much more often than people generally expect. Investors therefore need prepare for the possibility of fat-tail events more than they think.

When events occur that investors believe pose systemic risks to either the U.S. or world financial system, they shun riskier assets and flock to the perceived safety of U.S. Treasuries. During the financial crisis and in particular after Lehman Brothers collapsed in September 2008, the underperformance of riskier assets relative to Treasuries was in high gear and far more severe in scope and scale than had ever been seen before. Still, many precepts held intact, and the behavior of markets during the crisis serve as a lesson for what to expect when systemic risks are perceived and how investors should invest when seeking true risk diversification:

- Securities lower in the capital structure incurred more damage than those higher in the capital structure, which is to say that securities that ranked higher from a legal sense in case of default faired better. For example, senior secured bonds faired better than lower-ranked, junior subordinated bonds.
- Securities with the least amount of liquidity faired worse than those that could be bought and sold in relatively larger quantities at prices perceived closest to their fair value.
- Securities with the least amount of price transparency faired worse than those whose price could be determined more readily.
- Price volatility increased across the fixed-income spectrum, and bid-ask spreads widened.
- The price of options, which give investors the right to buy or sell securities at certain prices, increased across asset classes, making it more expensive to purchase hedges to protect against adverse price movements.
- Correlations increased between fixed-income securities and the equity market.
- The interbank market seized up, spurring increases in the federal funds rate and the LIBOR.

- In the foreign exchange market, the U.S. dollar was sought for its perceived safety. Currency performance worldwide was a function of perceived credit risk and investors' perceptions about each country's external foreign exchange debt exposures. In other words, investors shied away from exposures to currencies of countries perceived to have borrowed relatively large sums of money in currencies other than their own.

Recognizing these adverse movements, investors seeking true risk diversification should seek to neutralize them as much as possible. Mostly this means neutralizing the equity risk factor because equity risks tend to be the largest risk factor investors face. Take a look at Figure 5.1. It shows the correlation between two popular styles of portfolios—the 60/40 stocks and bonds split, and the endowment style model, which includes a wide array of asset classes—and the equity market, as measured by the MSCI World Index.

The figure clearly illustrates the idea that asset diversification does not equal risk diversification. The only way to achieve true risk diversification is to neutralize the equity risk factor and to find the commonalities that exist in the risk factors present across the assets the investors own. This means paying close attention to the factors mentioned above and constructing their portfolios accordingly. For example, this means recognizing that be-

FIGURE 5.1 Asset Diversification Has Not Shielded Investors from Risk

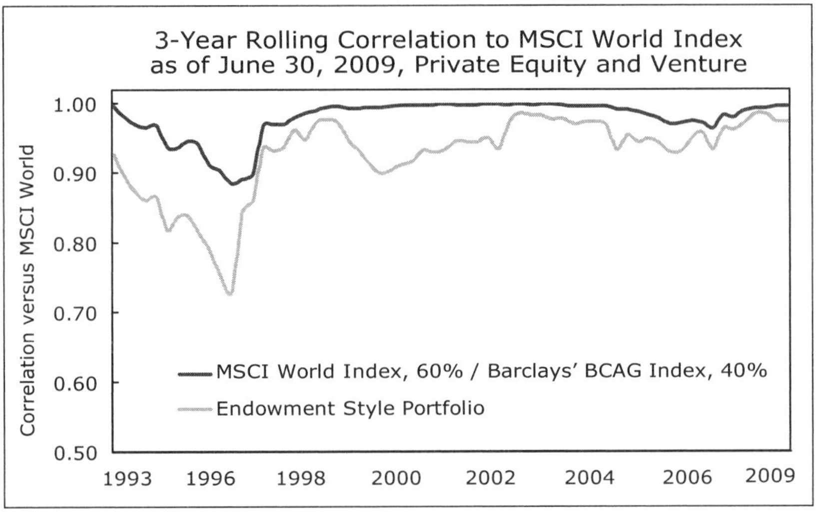

Note: Capital quarterly returns are released approximately 12 to 15 weeks following the close of each quarter.

Source: Morgan Stanley, Bloomberg, Cambridge Associates, and Hedge Fund Research.

cause correlations between fixed-income securities and equities tend to rise, investors wanting to both neutralize the equity risk factor and hedge against fat-tail risks might consider owning put options on equity indexes such as the S&P 500.

Systemic events can't be predicted, but what can be predicted is that they will occur more often than normal distribution models would have you expect. Figure 5.2 shows the very different outcomes to be expected from the normal and fat-tail distribution models. Table 5.1 compares two things, the frequency of occurrence projected by normal distribution models for a 7 percent change in the Dow Jones Industrial Average, and their actual frequency of occurrence between the years 1916 and 2003. The results are stark and speak to the idea of being prepared for fat-tail events rather than ignoring them. Put simply, the unexpected happens more often than expected.

Investors that tailor their portfolios for the possibility of fat-tail events can fair better than those that do not. They can do this by giving up some of their return in exchange for protection against losses. Rather than a sunk cost, it is a way of adding alpha, or incremental returns, because in a market decline investors that are kept whole can play offense while others are playing defense. In other words, when markets fall, investors left whole have the

FIGURE 5.2 Normal and Fat-Tail Distribution Models

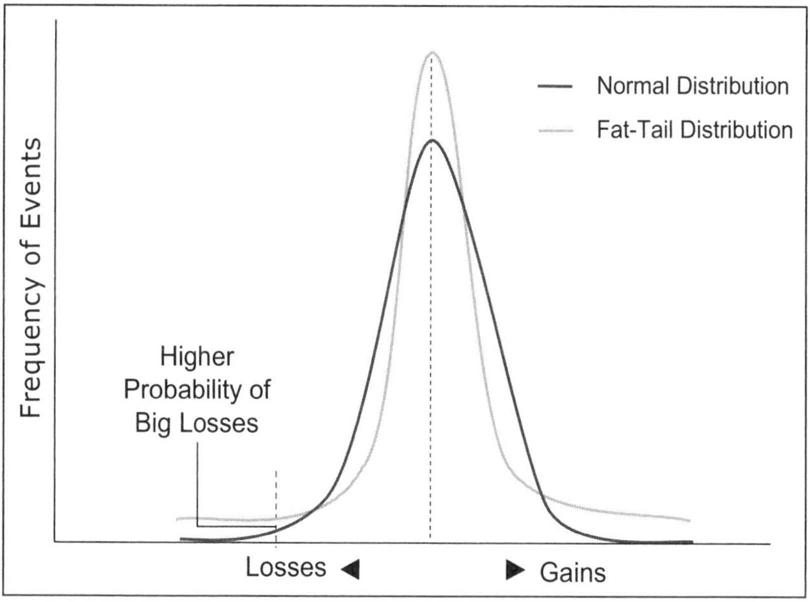

Source: PIMCO. Sample for illustrative purposes only.

TABLE 5.1 Fat-Tail Events Have Occurred More Often Than Models Would Have You Expect

Daily Change in the DJIA from 1916 to 2003 (21,924 Trading Days)			
Daily Change (+/−)	Normal Distribution Approximation	Actual	Ratio of Actual to Normal
> +3.4%	58 days	1,001 days	17×
> +4.5%	6 days	366 days	61×
> +7.0%	1 in 300,000 years	48 days	Very large

Source: PIMCO, Benoit B. Mandelbrôt, *The (Mis)behavior of Markets*, Basic Books, New York, 2004. Sample for illustrative purposes only.

capital to purchase assets at distressed prices. Those battered by the decline can't participate to the same extent that these investors can and in many cases they can't participate at all.

Many of you have probably experienced this, feeling eager to pick up assets at distressed prices but not having the wherewithal (or the stomach!) to do it because of having incurred losses yourself in the market decline. Then, when prices rebounded, you felt that angst of having missed an opportunity. To put a halt to this, just remember the credo, "Asset diversification does not equal risk diversification," and remember to be prepared for fat-tail events. Don't ignore them.

Other Examples of the Market Response to Systemic Risks

A classic example of how markets respond when investors worry about the integrity of the financial system occurred in September 1998, when a hedge fund named Long-Term Capital Management (LTCM) incurred large investment losses on a variety of highly leveraged investments. (*Hedge funds* are investment firms that are structured to avoid certain regulations by limiting their clientele to highly sophisticated, very wealthy individuals who seek high rates of return by investing and trading in a variety of financial instruments.)

LTCM is thought to have amassed investment positions with a notional value of over $1 trillion on just $4.8 billion of capital by using its $200 billion of borrowing capacity. Investors feared that liquidation of LTCM's highly leveraged investment strategies posed risks to the U.S. financial system because it might create panic selling that would be tantamount to a fire sale. The fear was so great that the Federal Reserve helped arrange what Federal Reserve Chairman Alan Greenspan called "an orderly private sector adjustment" by gathering major banks and investment firms to raise $3.5 billion of bailout money in exchange for a substantial dilution of the existing shareholders' stake in LTCM. Greenspan described the risks LTCM's potential failure posed to the financial system just a few weeks after the bail-out:

> *Had the failure of LTCM triggered the seizing up of markets, substantial damage could have been inflicted on many market participants, including some not directly involved with the firm, and could have potentially impaired the economies of many nations, including our own.*

Bond investors had similar thoughts and flocked to Treasuries. The desire for safe liquid assets became so great that older, less actively traded Treasuries were shunned in favor of newer, more actively traded Treasuries, causing yield spreads between the two to widen sharply. Figure 5.3 illustrates this widening. Importantly, the widening occurred despite the fact that all Treasuries have the same risk characteristics since they are backed by the full faith and credit of the U.S. government. Investors who recognized this anomalous response in the Treasury market took advantage of the widening spread by buying the older, less actively traded Treasuries and selling the newer, actively traded Treasuries.

Illustrating the strong proclivity for investors to treat securities within asset classes similarly when an event is viewed as carrying systemic risk for

FIGURE 5.3 Yield Spread between U.S. Treasury of 5.5 on 8/28 and 6.875 on 8/25 (Number of Basis Points)

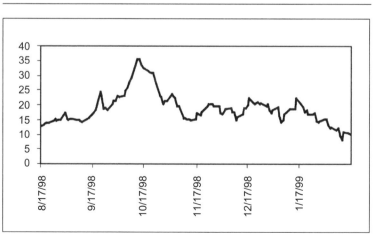

Source: Bloomberg.

the entire asset class is the case of the Orange County, California, bankruptcy in 1994 after the county lost nearly $2 billion on highly leveraged investments. The sudden bankruptcy spurred weakness in other municipal bonds across the nation, particularly in California, owing to fears that there might be other cases like it. Anxieties stretched beyond the municipal bond market to other segments of the bond market, with investors fearing that adverse price movements associated with the unwinding of all sorts of financial assets would self-feed. It is one of the reasons why the bond market in 1994 posted one of its worst declines in decades, with the 10-year Treasury topping 8 percent in November 1994 from 1993's low of 5.17 percent.

Concerns over systemic risks arise much more often than those risks pose actual threats to either the U.S. financial system or the world financial system. Investors therefore can benefit by spotting anomalies that arise in the markets when these events surface and appear unfounded. In today's environment, concerns over sovereign, or government, credit risks could at times cause movement in government securities within regions simply by association when a nation within that region either has difficulties or is perceived as having them. For investors who do their homework, opportunities could arise to gain exposures in countries whose debt securities have been adversely impacted by concerns about credit risks simply by association with countries within its region.

Takeovers or Restructurings

In the 1980s there were a high number of corporate takeovers, restructurings, and leveraged buyouts that significantly affected the value of many corporate bonds. Companies initiating the acquisition of other companies saw their debt burdens increase sharply as a result of the huge costs of the acquisitions. This resulted in rating downgrades that sent the value of the new company's existing debt spiraling downward—particularly for companies whose ratings were downgraded to below investment grade from investment grade.

The flurry of activity that occurred during that period created widespread fears among corporate bond investors who were worried that their bonds might be affected next. In some cases corporate bonds declined in value when companies in related industries were acquired. The reasoning was that there could be further consolidation in the industry. Following the 1980s, takeover or restructuring risk declined, but in the aftermath of the financial crisis, they have again become a formidable threat to bond investors, chiefly because many companies will be forced to restructure in order to remain a going concern. Moreover, increased government involvement in private industry raises the risk of an apparent abrogation of property rights, a change in a bond's position in the capital structure, a dilution of company earnings, or a change in the structure of the way in which a company is run.

Bond investors should pay close attention to developments in the industries in which they invest, track trends in takeover and restructuring activity, and stay atop news of government involvement in the private sector to reduce the risks associated with this type of activity.

Sudden Shifts in Market Sentiment

The financial crisis showed that market sentiment can shift abruptly, affecting the value of all segments of the bond market in the process. Of course, it is rare for market sentiment to shift in a day's time, but there have been plenty of cases in which it shifted in a matter of days or over short spans of time—quickly enough for shifts in market sentiment to qualify as a form of event risk. The abrupt shift in sentiment in the aftermath of Lehman's collapse in September 2008 is the most clear and recent example. Sentiment collapsed so severely that it led to a near complete breakdown of the financial system, both in the United States and abroad. It was months before there was some semblance of normalcy in the financial markets, and the model for many parts of the financial system was broken and remains so to this day.

Figure 5.4 shows the abrupt move higher that occurred in yields on high-yield bonds in the aftermath of Lehman's collapse. The important takeaway from the figure is that the bonds of a wide variety of companies performed poorly even though they had no direct association with Lehman whatsoever, showing the large role that confidence and investor sentiment play in the behavior of the financial markets.

Another example of a rapid change in market sentiment occurred in the early part of 2000 when the financial bubble burst. In a very short span of time, investors turned sour on the outlook for long-term corporate assets, including both stocks and corporate bonds. There was no particular catalyst to prompt the sudden reversal except perhaps the Federal Reserve, which was in the middle of raising interest rates. However, the Fed had started raising interest rates many months earlier, and so it would be incorrect to say that the Fed prompted the sudden shift in sentiment. There have been many other occasions when market sentiment shifted abruptly; the 1987 stock market crash is a good example.

When market sentiment shifts, this generally is manifested in the many ways shown earlier, chiefly through an underperformance of risk assets. Investors caught holding securities affected by shifts in investor sentiment

FIGURE 5.4 Junk Bond Yields Spiked after Lehman Collapsed

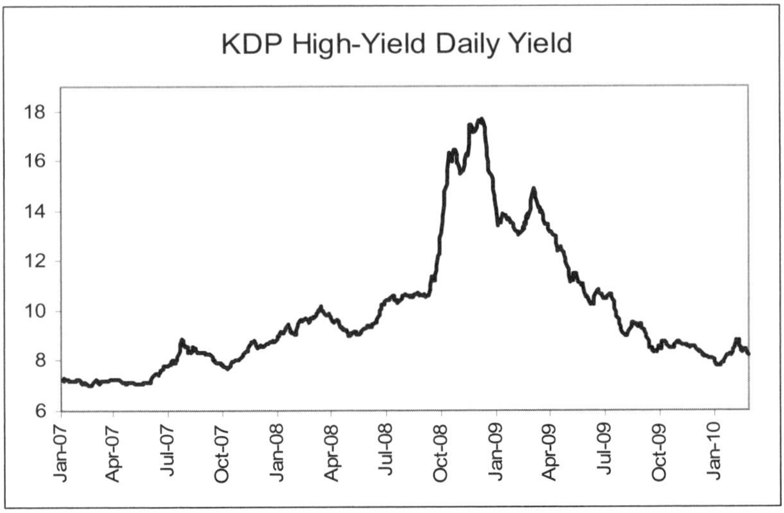

KDP High-Yield Daily Yield

Source: KDP Investment Advisors and Bloomberg.

must focus on the destination and prepare for a bumpy ride. It is of course better to be prepared for such events in ways described earlier. With respect to market sentiment in particular, there are ways of detecting vulnerabilities, as will be described more thoroughly in Chapter 10.

International Financial Events

Bond prices often are affected by financial events abroad. Over the past few decades, the main source of that impact was the emerging markets, particularly countries in Asia and Latin America. *Emerging markets* are markets in countries considered undeveloped relative to industrialized nations such as the United States, Japan, and the countries in western Europe. In these relatively undeveloped countries, severe weakness in emerging market bonds, which are government bonds in emerging economies rated below investment grade, often spilled over into U.S. markets, sparking weakness in various segments of the U.S. bond market and in the equity market. In what has become an upside-down world, the tables have turned, with problems in developed nations now at the epicenter of the world's financial problems and the root of the de-leveraging impetus, and developing nations now the world's creditors and seen in better shape to handle difficulties. The age of decoupling appears to be at hand.

TABLE 5.2 The 10 Largest Holders of the World's Reserve Assets, in Billions of Dollars

Country	Reserve Assets
China	$2,399
Japan	1,001
Russia	434
Saudi Arabia	397
Taiwan	351
South Korea	271
Hong Kong	257
India	254
Brazil	241
Algeria	147

Source: International Monetary Fund (IMF), Banco Central do Brasil, China National Bureau of Statistics, and Central Bank of Russia.

Table 5.2 lists the 10 countries holding the largest amounts of the world's reserve assets. *Reserve assets* are defined by the International Monetary Fund (IMF) as official reserves, which are "external assets that are readily available to and controlled by monetary authorities for direct financing of payments imbalances, for indirectly regulating the magnitudes of such imbalances through intervention in exchange markets to affect the currency exchange rate, and/or for other purposes." Total reserves comprise gold, foreign currency assets, reserve positions in the IMF, and *special drawing rights* (SDRs), and they are earned when a country's balance of payments situation is positive, which is to say that it takes in more money than it pays out. This is why China, which runs a very large trade surplus with the United States, has such a vast amount of foreign exchange reserves.

Figure 5.5 contrasts the debt-to-GDP ratios of developed nations versus those of developing nations, showing clearly which way the trend is moving. This, combined with Table 5.2, hints that going forward, the international financial events that spur seismic moves in the world's financial markets could be rooted in the developed nations, not in the developing nations.

International Political and Military Events

Political and military events can have a direct impact on bond prices. The terrorist attacks that saddened and roiled the United States on September

FIGURE 5.5 The Gross Debt-to-GDP Ratios for G-20 Industrialized versus Emerging Market Nations, as of August 31, 2009

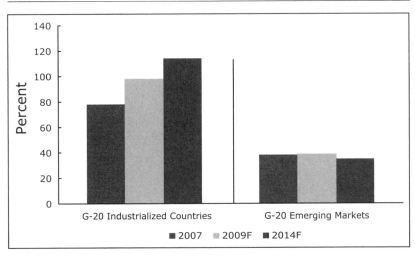

Source: International Monetary Fund (IMF), PIMCO, and Credit Suisse.

11, 2001, are recent examples. The events of that day had a large impact on the bond market, spurring a flight out of riskier assets and into U.S. Treasuries. Figure 5.6 shows the large impact of the September 11 tragedies on speculative-grade bonds. As you can see from the chart, the yield spread between speculative-grade bonds and U.S. Treasuries widened dramati-

FIGURE 5.6 S&P Speculative-Grade Credit Spread, in Basis Points over Treasuries

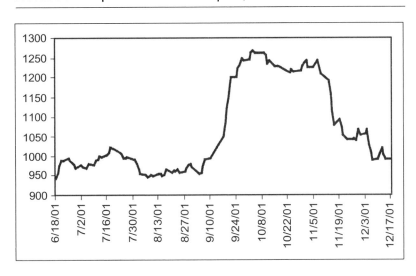

cally and did not begin to narrow until a string of U.S. military victories in Afghanistan gave the investing public a sense that the crisis would not have a lasting impact on the global economy. Yield spreads also widened after Iraq's invasion of Kuwait in August 1990 and narrowed when the United States and its allies won the war in early 1991.

There is obviously very little that investors can do to prepare themselves for events such as the September 11 tragedies. However, investors should take note of the trading pattern throughout U.S. history in both bonds and stocks when unexpected events have occurred so that they can both prepare for and respond accordingly to major events when and if they occur.

Sector Risk

In the stock market choosing stocks in industries that are prospering can be one of the most important determinants of an equity investor's total return. In fact, many studies suggest that industry selection is the most important aspect of stock selecting. In a study conducted by William J. O'Neil, fully 67 percent of the biggest market movers during the period 1953 to 1993 were part of group advances. A good example of the powerful influence group moves can have on individual stocks is the behavior of all housing-related stocks beginning around 2006, near the time when the housing market peaked, and the behavior of bank stocks in the aftermath of the financial crisis.

Another example is the behavior of the dot-com stocks between 1999 and 2001. During that time, shares in individual dot-com companies were bid sharply higher, often without any basis other than the fact that other dot-com companies were being bid sharply higher. Of course, when the dot-com stocks began to implode, they imploded together, showing clearly that group movement is one of the most important influences on the value of a company's stock.

Industry selection is therefore one of the most important elements of investing in stocks as well as corporate bonds. Corporate bond investors therefore should be alert to trends in the industries in which they invest. Failure to be alert will significantly increase the degree of sector risk that investors face.

One of the best things an investor can do to limit sector risk is to be alert to where the economy stands in the business cycle and stay abreast of potential shifts in monetary policy, as well as financial conditions more generally. These factors play a very large role in the behavior of the various sectors of the economy. During the later stages of an economic expansion, for example, bonds in economically sensitive industries such as consumer cyclicals (retailers, automotive companies, home building, and so on), basic materials (paper, chemical, and metals companies), financials (commercial banks, brokerages, insurance companies, and savings and loans companies), and transportation (railroads and trucking companies) tend to perform poorly compared to companies in less economically sensitive industries such as utilities, pipelines, consumer noncyclicals (food, cosmetics, soft drinks, house nondurables), and health care (pharmaceuticals, health-care providers, and medical products).

During such times it is therefore important to consider shifting money from economically sensitive companies to companies that are less economically sensitive. These sectors benefit from companies having hard assets that can be sold in the event of liquidation. The recovery rate for bondholders seeking claims on company assets is higher for defensive industries such as utilities and pipelines than it is for many of the more cyclical companies, particularly those that are service oriented.

Staying abreast of the direction of monetary policy is critical to limiting sector risk. Bonds in economically sensitive companies respond directly to changes in monetary policy. A good time to reduce an investor's exposure to economically sensitive industries is when the Federal Reserve is in the process of raising interest rates. When the Fed is lowering interest rates, increasing an investor's exposure to economically sensitive industries is likely to be the best strategy.

Another way to limit sector risk is to diversify between industries of varying economic sensitivity. This age-old advice can help in the bond market too, by spreading an investor's exposure among the different sectors of the economy because while one sector is faltering, others will be prospering.

Call, or Prepayment, Risk

If it is specified in a bond's indenture, a bond can be *called*, or redeemed, by the issuer at a predetermined price before its maturity date. Bond issuers use this feature to give themselves an opportunity to refinance their debt if market interest rates decline. For example, suppose an issuer sold a $1,000 bond with a yield of 6 percent three years ago, but current interest rates are 2 percentage points lower. In this case, the issuer would have a strong incentive to refinance its existing debt. Suppose the call feature allowed the issuer to call the bond at 102, or $1,020, per bond. The issuer could sell a new bond at $1,000 with a yield of 4 percent and use the proceeds to call its existing bonds at $1,020 and thus benefit from lower borrowing costs.

What may be good news for bond issuers is not necessarily good news for bond investors. When bonds are called early, an investor must reinvest the principal from the redeemed bond at lower interest rate levels, reducing the investor's rate of return. This risk may make you wonder why an investor would consider purchasing bonds with call risks. The reason is that one of the advantages of owning callable bonds is that investors are compensated for the added risk by a higher yield. While the opportunity to achieve enhancements to a portfolio's total return by buying callable bonds may appeal to some investors, the disadvantages are strong enough to make other investors loath to buy them.

The most prominent disadvantage relates to the reinvestment risks posed by the call feature. A second big disadvantage of a callable bond is the limited upside potential in the bond's price. Bond prices rise, of course, when interest rates fall, but the interest rate decline raises the odds that the issuer will call a callable bond, limiting the price appreciation in the callable bond. This occurs because bond investors worry that if they purchase a bond at a price that is above the call price, they could be subject to a capital loss (because the purchase price is higher than the call price). The only time an investor would engage in such a purchase would if there were plenty of time remaining before the bond's call date.

The call feature can affect a variety of bonds, including municipal, corporate, agency, and all mortgage-backed securities. Treasury bonds are no longer issued with call features, but a large number of Treasury bonds that were issued in past years have call features. Thus, call risk is a threat to most segments of the bond market.

Investors can limit call risk in a number of ways. First and foremost, investors should determine whether the bonds they are thinking of purchasing have a provision that allows the issuer to call them before the maturity date. An investor can do this by asking his or her broker or by reading the bond's indenture or prospectus. Keep in mind that mortgage securities do not have provisions that specify a call date. Mortgage bonds are not actually "called." They are refunded when the homeowners in the mortgage pools that underlie the mortgage bonds prepay the principal on their mortgage debt.

A second way to limit call risk is to be wary of buying bonds with high coupons. Those bonds are generally bonds that were issued at some point in the past when interest rates were higher. In this case there is a greater probability of the bonds being called than there is for bonds with low coupons since it is more likely that an issuer will call bonds that were issued at interest rate levels that are higher than prevailing interest rates. This partly depends on whether the issuer swapped out of its fixed-rate debt obligation in exchange for a floating-rate obligation, as many issuers are apt to do in the interest rate swap market when the fixed-rate debt is issued.

Third, an investor should reduce exposure to high coupon mortgage-backed securities when interest rates are falling to limit prepayment risk. Fourth, an investor should avoid buying callable bonds trading at a premium over their par value if the call date is near.

For more on callable bonds, refer back to Chapter 3.

Liquidity Risk

As was shown in Chapter 2, liquidity is an extremely important element of trading fixed-income securities. Low levels of liquidity can create *liquidity risk*, which is the risk that a bondholder will have difficulty selling a bond at or near its fair value—a major dilemma for investors during the financial crisis.

Liquidity can be defined as the ease or difficulty with which buyers and sellers can transact in small and large quantities at prices that are considered representative of the true market value. Liquidity risk is greatest for bond investors who intend to sell their bond holdings before they mature; investors who generally hold their bonds to maturity do not have to worry much about the liquidity of their bonds except as a means of raising capital unexpectedly.

There are two key measures of market liquidity: the bid-ask spread and the market or quote depth. The bid-ask spread is probably the best measure of a bond's liquidity. The narrower a bond's bid-ask spread is, the easier it is to sell the bond. Keep in mind, however, that the bid-ask spread depends a great deal on a bond's market depth. *Market depth* is the quantity of securities that broker-dealers are willing to buy and sell at various prices. This means that bonds that have larger average bids and offers have greater market depth and liquidity than do bonds that have smaller average bids and offers. Thus, a narrow bid-ask spread on a bond does not necessarily mean that the bond's liquidity will be high on all transactions; the bid-ask spread could well be wider for transactions requiring high levels of market depth.

In addition to the many examples that can be drawn from the financial crisis, a dramatic example of the effects of liquidity on bond prices occurred in 1998 during the LTCM, Russian, and Asian financial crises. As was shown in Figure 5.4, liquidity concerns were so heightened that less actively traded Treasuries performed poorly compared with actively traded Treasuries despite a complete lack of difference in their creditworthiness.

Liquidity risk can be reduced either by investing in bonds that are actively traded or by holding bonds to the maturity date. Similarly, by concentrating more of one's fixed-income exposure in securities that are self-liquidating, liquidity risks can be reduced. For example, investors can hold futures or options contracts, both of which have expiration dates, or engage in swaps or swaptions agreements, both of which have end dates.

Transacting with Wall Street's primary dealers, who tend to provide greater quote depth than do nonprimary dealers, also can reduce liquidity risk. Another way to reduce liquidity risk is to transact early in the trading day, when the bond market is the most active. In addition, one should avoid trading just before the release of important economic reports, when broker-dealers sometimes widen their quotes on bid-ask spreads out of concern that the reports will have a big impact on their fixed-income positions. Broker-dealers often want to avoid the added risk that comes with buying and selling securities from customers who buy and sell securities from those broker-dealers. The broker-dealers do not want their positions to change much when the market might be about to move sharply as a result of the release of economic data.

Credit, or Default, Risk

Bond investors loathe few things more than *credit*, or *default*, *risk*. This is the risk that bond issuers will not be able to make timely interest and principal payments on their bonds—in other words, default. Defaults are relatively uncommon except during periods of financial and economic strain. According to a study conducted by Moody's Investor Services, from 1920 to 1997 an average of just 0.17 percent of investment-grade issuers defaulted within one year after the assignment of their investment-grade rating. Speculative-grade credits fared worse, of course, with a default rate of 3.27 percent per year. The study also found that the overall one-year weighted-average default rate for corporate issues during that period was less than 0.01 percent for the highest-rated firms.

Figure 5.7 shows the default rates for speculative bonds between the years 1920 and 2007, based on data from Moody's.

Despite the low level of default rates over the years, bond investors shudder when there is even the slightest hint that a bond issuer is at risk of a rating downgrade or at an increased risk of default. Bonds that are downgraded by the rating agencies often fall sharply in price, pushing their yields upward. Given the low likelihood of default on investment-grade bonds,

FIGURE 5.7 Annual Default Rates for Speculative-Grade Bonds, 1920 to 2007

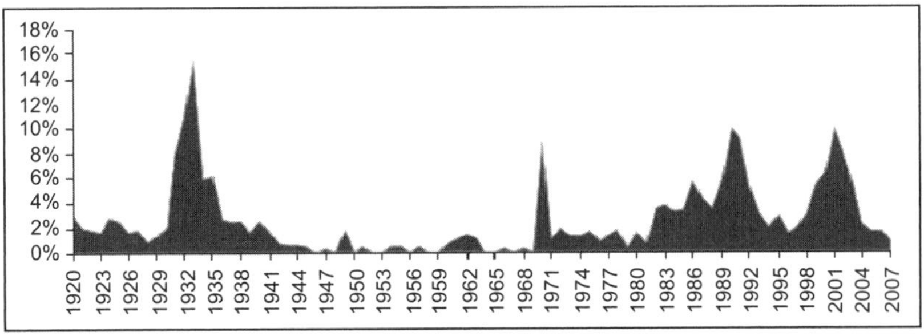

Source: Moody's.

investors have tended to overreact, but the dislocation that occurs in markets presents both risks and opportunities.

Nearly all bonds are subject to some degree of credit risk, and until recently U.S. Treasuries have been kept out of the equation and viewed as risk-free assets, backed as they are by the full faith and credit of the United States. A similar view has been held for the debts of other developed nations. These views might be changing in light of the deterioration of public finances resulting from the battle against the financial and economic crisis. This means that credit risk applies to sovereign debts too.

The degree of credit risk inherent in a particular bond depends on a myriad of factors. Because of this, bond investors typically gauge credit risks primarily by utilizing the credit ratings assigned by the rating agencies. These agencies review the myriad factors that could pose risks to the timely payment of principal and interest on the bonds and assign their ratings accordingly. Therefore, one of the best ways to reduce credit risk in a portfolio is to utilize credit ratings and stay abreast of any potential changes in the ratings.

Any analysis of an entity's creditworthiness can be augmented by looking at the credit default swaps for the issuing entity, which can give added insight into the views that market participants have toward the issuer. For example, if the price that investors pay for default protection against the issuer rises, it could indicate that concerns are rising toward the issuer's creditworthiness.

An obvious way to reduce credit risks is to limit one's purchases of speculative-grade bonds in favor of investment-grade bonds, which are bonds rated BBB or higher (see Chapter 12 for ratings definitions). Doing this, however, could of course reduce total return since the investor will be foregoing an opportunity to achieve a higher yield in favor of greater stability of the total return. Yet another way to reduce credit risks is to either diversify one's bond holdings or invest in mutual funds so that the default of one or more bonds will not substantially impair the investment performance.

Yield Curve Risk

We described in Chapter 3 the concept of curve duration, which relates directly to yield curve risk. *Yield curve risk* is the risk that investors and in particular portfolio managers face when selecting where it is on the yield curve they would like to obtain more or less of their net duration exposure. For example, if a portfolio manager chooses to obtain his or her duration from the short end of the yield curve, it will turn out to be a good choice if the yield curve steepens because short maturities outperform long maturities when the yield curve steepens. The risk in this case is that the curve will flatten, leading to underperformance. When a portfolio manager chooses to obtain his or her duration from the short end of the yield curve, the duration is known as *soft duration*, chiefly because the short end of the yield curve is typically the least volatile portion of the yield curve.

Inflation Risk

Inflation is the bane of the bond market because it erodes the value of a bond's cash flows. That is why inflation risk is one of the biggest risks facing bond investors. Inflation risks that affect the price of a bond pose significant interest rate risks, which was discussed earlier. Inflation risks also pertain to the interest payments on a bond, the value of which can be eroded by inflation. If, for example, a bond paid an annual coupon rate of 5 percent and inflation was also 5 percent, the value of that coupon payment would be completely eroded by inflation.

In recent years inflation risks have been low as a result of a long period of relatively low inflation. Investors therefore have had little reason to guard against inflation risks. Many investors are concerned that the large expansion of the Federal Reserve's balance sheet and the increase in financial liquidity it has caused will provide tinder to spark an eventual increase in inflation. Many subscribe to Milton Friedman's credo that inflation is and always will be a monetary phenomenon, and this is what has some investors worried. One way to neutralize this risk factor is to engage in strategies that benefit from an acceleration of inflation. One strategy is to purchase the Treasury's inflation-protected securities commonly known as TIPS. In Chapter 4, we said that TIPS are securities whose principal value is adjusted upward to compensate investors for inflation (as measured by the U.S. Consumer Price Index). Holders of TIPS therefore can protect themselves against inflation risks, although not completely because the real rate (the amount of yield above the inflation rate) might also increase, spurring price declines in TIPS.

Another strategy is to purchase floating-rate notes or bonds, commonly known as *floaters*. The coupon rate on floaters is reset periodically, usually every six months, utilizing a short-term interest rate as its benchmark. The benchmark might be Treasury bills, the London Interbank Offered Rate (LIBOR), the prime rate, or another short-term interest rate. Although these instruments are not directly tied to the inflation rate, fluctuations in short-term interest rates tend to be tied to market perceptions about inflation risks and the Fed's possible response to those risks. For this reason, floating-rate securities provide a fairly good hedge against possible inflation risks since their yields are likely to mirror either actual or perceived changes in inflation.

If inflation risks are considered to be strong enough to compel the Federal Reserve to change its monetary policy, numerous other investment strategies are called for. For example, investors in this case could consider reducing their curve duration by shifting more of their duration exposure to long-dated maturities.

Currency Risk

Investors have increasingly ventured abroad for investment opportunities in foreign bond markets, and for reasons mentioned earlier they are likely to continue to, chiefly because of the deteriorating public finances of developed nations. When investors invest abroad, they expose themselves to currency risk. Currency risk results from holding bonds denominated in foreign currencies. U.S.-based investors who buy bonds denominated in foreign currencies must convert their dollars into foreign currencies, exposing themselves to the ups and downs of the value of the foreign currencies against the U.S. dollar. This assumes, of course, that an investor in foreign bonds plans to convert the cash flows from the bonds back into U.S. dollars.

Individual investors can limit these risks by investing in mutual funds, which often hedge their currency risks by using *forward contracts*, which are agreements to buy or sell a financial instrument at a specified price on a given date in the future. Institutional investors can limit their currency

FIGURE 5.8 The Federal Reserve's Trade-Weighted Dollar Index

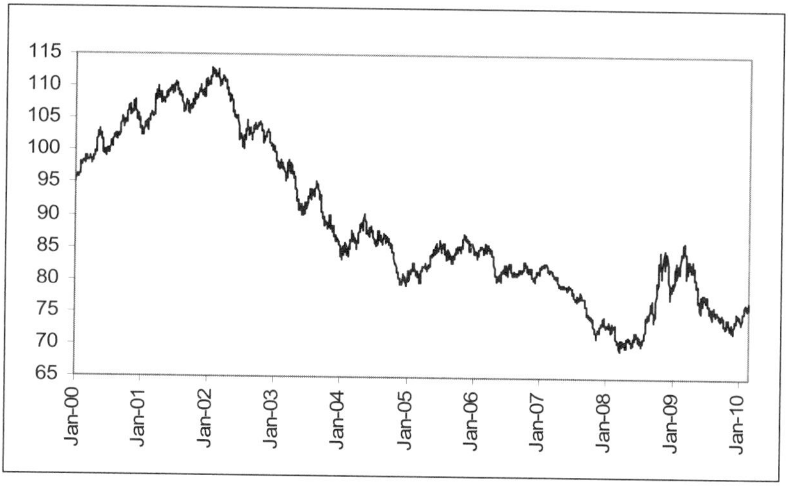

Source: Federal Reserve.

risks by using forward contracts in the foreign exchange market. The decision to hedge, however, is complicated by questions of just how much of the currency exposure should be hedged. A certain degree of currency risk can be desirable in some cases if there appears to be a good chance that one currency will perform better than another. The prevailing bet for the years ahead is that the U.S. dollar will continue to decline in value, as it has for the most of the time since 2002.

Diversification is just one of many factors expected to continue to weigh on the dollar. The world's central banks want to diversify their nearly $8 trillion of international reserve assets, as they have for quite a number of years. In 2002, for example, 70 percent of the world's reserve assets were denominated in U.S. dollars. In January 2010 that figure was down to 63 percent. The euro, on the other hand, ascended to 27 percent of reserve assets from 20 percent in 2002.

Figure 5.8 shows the trend in the trade-weighted value of the U.S. dollar between 2000 and 2010, as measured by the Federal Reserve.

Hedge Risk

Not all hedges are perfect; many simply do not work. A *hedge* is a security position bought or sold with the expectation that gains and losses from the hedge will offset gains and losses in another security position. *Hedge risk* is the risk that the hedge will not offset gains or losses in the hedged position. In the bond market, investors use hedges for a variety of purposes. A common strategy is to use U.S. Treasuries to hedge against potential losses in other types of bonds. This is known as *cross-hedging*. This strategy works well most of the time since yield changes on most bonds generally tend to mirror yield changes on Treasuries; their prices therefore tend to move in the same direction.

This strategy can go awry, however, when the prices of the two securities move in opposite directions, as was the case in 2008, when the prices on corporate bonds fell sharply while Treasuries prices soared. This caused a sharp widening in the yield spread between corporate bonds, including high-yield bonds, and Treasuries, as was shown in Figure 5.5. Investors who were long corporate bonds and simultaneously short Treasuries incurred large losses. The hedge failed to work primarily because corporate bonds and Treasuries have very different risk characteristics. When risk aversion fell, investors sought the safety of Treasuries and shunned riskier assets such as corporate bonds.

In such an environment, investors who needed to hedge against price declines in corporate bonds would have fared better if they had hedged with securities with risk characteristics more like the risk characteristics of corporate bonds. One of the best ways to do this is to establish hedges in the interest rate swaps market. *Swap spreads*, which measure the difference between swap rates and Treasuries, will move directionally with credit spreads, helping investors to recapture some of the increase that occurs in credit spreads when they occur. The lesson here is to beware of circumstances in which a hedge is not really a hedge.

Odd-Lot Risk

Odd-lot risk is the risk that an investor who buys or sells small quantities of bonds will not be able to obtain a fair market price because of the transaction size. In the bond market, which is largely an institutional market, any bond trade under $1 million is considered an odd lot. This is certainly much different from the situation in the stock market, where an odd lot is any stock trade under 100 shares. Odd-lot orders can hurt individual investors because broker-dealers tend to quote wider bid-ask spreads on these small orders and the price is often at a discount (on sales) or a premium (on purchases) compared with prices on orders of $1 million or more. This penalty increases as order size decreases. This puts individual investors at a disadvantage compared with institutional investors.

What can an investor do? For one thing, if you are a buyer of Treasuries, consider buying Treasuries directly from the Treasury over the Internet via the Treasury's widely used system: Treasury Direct. You can buy Treasuries directly from the Treasury Department at the auction prices, and you will pay no commissions or fees. A second measure to take is to buy mutual funds with the lowest possible management fees. This way you will essentially be assured of getting better market prices on the bond holdings and will minimize transaction fees. A third measure to take is to call several brokers for a quote on the bonds you wish to buy or sell before placing your order. This way you will have a better chance of getting a better price. It pays to shop around.

Summary

- While bonds are indeed less risky than many other financial assets, they are far from risk free.
- The biggest risk faced by most bond investors is market risk (or interest rate risk)—that is, the risk that the price of a bond will decrease as a result of an increase in the bond's yield. Market risk can be managed by being aware of a bond's duration, a key measure of a bond's price sensitivity to changes in interest rates.
- Reinvestment risk, or the risk that a bond's cash flows will be reinvested at falling interest rate levels, is a concern for bond investors. A significant portion of the total return on a bond—sometimes more than half—comes from interest on interest. It is therefore critical to be very mindful of the reinvestment rate on the cash flows that an investor receives on a bond.
- Curve risk can be managed through effective duration management, discussed in Chapter 3.
- A major principle illustrated clearly by the financial crisis is that asset diversification is not the same as risk diversification. Investors in today's environment must be mindful of the commonalities that exist in the risk factors present across the assets they own.
- The improbable seems to happen much more often than people generally expect. Investors therefore need prepare for the possibility of fat-tail events more often than they might think.

- There are many other risks that bond investors must contend with and assess before they purchase bonds.
- There is risk in almost everything people do. Whether it's crossing the street, climbing an icy stairway, lifting heavy objects without bending the knees, or buying bonds, risks abound. But these risks need not inhibit investors from taking risks. By being aware of the risks they face, investors can keep them at bay and dance their way between the storms.

6

DON'T FIGHT THE FED
The Powerful Role of the Federal Reserve

Don't fight the Fed! There has been perhaps no better advice to give investors over the years but to heed these words. Time and time again investors have learned that it is dangerous to ignore the powerful influence of the Federal Reserve, yet many investors put little effort into gaining a better understanding of this powerful institution. Amid the financial crisis, many now understand just how powerful the Federal Reserve truly is. Many find it comforting. Many are less sure and want the Fed's powers curtailed. Washington, looking for scapegoats, has looked to the Fed and pointed fingers.

Nevertheless, although legislative reforms will probably change the Fed's role in the U.S. financial system, the Fed is likely to retain its ability to carry out the main responsibilities it was granted under the Federal Reserve Act of 1913 and be able to do so without the interference of political considerations. In truth, the financial crisis adds to bountiful evidence on the need for a central bank, both in the United States and abroad. The Fed's impact on the performance of nearly all financial assets is so unmistakable that it behooves every investor to learn more. This is an endeavor that can have great rewards.

In this chapter, we will look at how the Fed works, with an emphasis on the many ways you can use your knowledge of the Fed to formulate an investment strategy. In addition, I will show you the art of Fed watching so that you can anticipate the Fed's actions with greater precision. We will also look at the many new programs the Fed has put in place to battle the financial and economic crisis.

Before we examine how the Fed affects the markets, let's take a look at how the Fed works, who its members are, and the crux of its raison d'être.

The Fed's Raison d'Être: Financial Stability across the Land

Ever since President Woodrow Wilson signed the Federal Reserve Act of 1913 at 6:02 p.m. on December 23 of that year, the Federal Reserve has been evolving into one of the most powerful institutions in the United States. The act established the Fed with the goal of providing stability to the U.S. financial system, which at that time had no official backstop in the event of financial crises. The act stated that the Fed would "provide for the establishment of Federal reserve banks, to furnish an elastic currency, to afford means of rediscounting commercial paper, to establish a more effective supervision of banking in the United States, and for other purposes." Other purposes, indeed. Ever since that important day in the nation's financial history, the Fed's role has expanded to the point where its influence now stretches around the globe.

Over time new legislation has molded the Fed into the institution we know today. Two particular acts of Congress refined and supplemented the objectives of the Fed as originally stated in the Federal Reserve Act of 1913: the Employment Act of 1946 and the Full Employment and Balanced Growth Act of 1978 (sometimes referred to as the Humphrey-Hawkins Act after its original sponsors). Those two acts restated the Fed's objectives to include economic growth in line with the economy's growth potential, a high level of employment, stable prices (in terms of the purchasing power of the dollar), and moderate long-term interest rates. Other important legislative changes clarifying and supplementing the act of 1913 include the Depository Institutions Deregulation and Monetary Control Act of 1980 and the Gramm-Leach-Bliley Act of 1999.

From the Fed's vantage point, its duties now fall into four general areas:

- Conducting the nation's monetary policies by influencing the money and credit conditions in the economy in the pursuit of full employment and stable prices
- Supervising and regulating banking institutions to ensure the safety and soundness of the nation's banking and financial system and protect the credit rights of consumers
- Maintaining the stability of the financial system and containing the systemic risk that may arise in financial market
- Providing certain financial services to the U.S. government, the public, financial institutions, and foreign official institutions, including playing a major role in operating the nation's payment systems

Of the four duties, the first is the most prominent and the one that gets the most attention in the financial markets by far. It also is the main focus of this chapter. Let's take a look at how the Fed conducts its monetary policies and how those policies affect the economy.

The Structure of the Federal Reserve System

To understand how the Federal Reserve influences the U.S. economic and financial system and forecasts changes in monetary policy accurately, it is important to understand how the Fed is structured and how it formulates its policies. The Federal Reserve System was designed by Congress in a way that helps ensure that the Fed maintains a broad perspective on how the economy is fairing in all parts of the nation. The Federal Reserve System was thus created with 12 regional Federal Reserve banks located in major cities. Figure 6.1 shows a map of the 12 Federal Reserve districts. Reserve banks perform a variety of functions that are similar to the services provided by regular banks and thrift institutions. For example, Federal Reserve banks hold the cash reserves of depository institutions and make loans to them. The banks also move currency in and out of circulation and process checks.

The roles of the Federal Reserve banks go far beyond these relatively mundane tasks, of course, and they range from the actual printing of currency and minting of coins to supervising and examining banks for safety

FIGURE 6.1 The 12 Federal Reserve District Banks

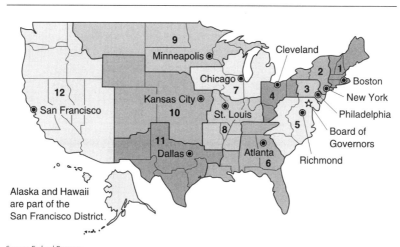

Source: Federal Reserve.

and soundness. (Their bank examiner role was the focus of recent criticism for their failure to detect risky lending and leverage practices among major U.S. banks.) To Wall Street the most prominent role of the Federal Reserve banks is the participation of the bank presidents in the formulation of monetary policy. Wall Street watches the Fed bank presidents closely for clues to the direction of monetary policy. Each president is elected to a five-year term by the board of directors of the respective Federal Reserve banks. The terms of all 12 presidents run concurrently, ending on the last day of February in years ending in 6 and 1. The bank presidents are part of the Federal Open Market Committee (FOMC), the committee that sets interest rates.

A proposal the Fed is attempting to stave off in the aftermath of the financial crisis is the nomination of Federal Reserve bank presidents by the White House to be approved by the U.S. Senate. It is one proposal of many that attempts to reduce the Federal Reserve's autonomy, and it is seen by many as a threat to its independence. In early 2010, the proposals considered the most intrusive were seen as unlikely to become law.

TABLE 6.1 Term Lengths of Federal Reserve Officials

Position	Term Length	Term Begins and Ends	Appointed By
Reserve bank president	5 years	Terms end on the last day of February in years ending in 1 or 6.	Board of directors of each of the respective 12 Reserve banks.
Governor	14 years	Term dates vary, but one ends every 2 years on February 1 of even-numbered years.	The president of the United States appoints; the U.S. Senate confirms.
Vice chair	4 years	Dates vary.	The president of the United States appoints from existing board members or names a new member; the U.S. Senate confirms.
Chair	4 years	Dates vary.	The president of the United States appoints from existing board members or names a new member; the U.S. Senate confirms.

Source: Federal Reserve.

Wall Street also pays close attention to the seven members of the board of governors who are appointed by the president of the United States and confirmed by the Senate for a term of 14 years. A term begins every 2 years on February 1 of even-numbered years. The chair and the vice chair of the board are named by the president from among the members and are confirmed by the Senate.

The FOMC is composed of five presidents of the Federal Reserve banks and the seven members of the board of governors (including the chair). The presidents of the banks serve one-year terms on a rotating basis beginning on January 1 of each year, with the exception of the president of the Federal Reserve Bank of New York, who serves on a continuous basis. All of the Federal Reserve bank presidents, even when they are not voting members, attend the FOMC meetings, participate in the discussions, and contribute to the assessment of the economy and of policy options. In other words, investors should listen to what they have to say too.

Table 6.1 provides a reference of the various term lengths and appointments of members of the Federal Reserve System.

From the Mint to the Grocery Store: How the Fed Implements Monetary Policy

The primary policy tool available to the Fed is its *open market operations*—that is, its ability to create bank reserves in any desired quantity by monetizing some portion of the national debt. The Fed could in theory monetize anything—scrap metal to soybeans—but it has stuck largely to Treasury IOUs because there has never been any shortage of them, as recent times have made abundantly clear. Also, they are highly liquid, so the Fed can sell them with as much ease as it buys them. Today, the implementation of monetary policy has been complicated by the many means by which the Fed has added financial liquidity into the U.S. financial system. In particular, the Fed must decide how it will eventually dispose of or effectively neutralize the impact of the $1.25 trillion of mortgage-backed securities it purchased through March 2010.

In formulating policy, the first question the Fed faces is what macroeconomic *targets* to pursue. There are various possibilities: full employment, price stability, or a "correct" exchange value of the dollar. The achievement of *all* these targets is desirable. However, since the Fed ultimately has only one powerful string on its bow—the ability to control bank reserves and thereby money creation by the private banking system—and given the fact that the Fed now targets interest rates rather than reserve levels, the Fed must conduct its open market operations in a way that strikes the right balance first and foremost via the appropriate target rate. (See Table 6.2.)

Once the Fed has chosen its policy targets, it faces a second difficult question: What policies should it use to achieve these targets? For example, if it wants to pursue a tight money policy to curb inflation, does that mean

TABLE 6.2 The Fed's Changing Definitions of Money Supply

Prior to February 1980

M1	Currency in circulation plus demand deposits.
M2	M1 plus small-denomination savings and time deposits at commercial banks.
M3	M2 plus deposits at nonbank savings institutions.
M4	M2 plus large-denomination CDs.
M5	M3 plus large-denomination CDs.

February 1980

M1A	Currency in circulation plus demand deposits.
M1B	M1A plus other checkable deposits, including NOW accounts.
M2	M1B plus overnight repos and money market funds and savings and small (less than $100,000) time deposits.
M3	M2 plus large time deposits and term repos.
L	M3 plus other liquid assets.

January 1982

M1	Currency in circulation plus demand deposits plus other checkable deposits, including NOW accounts.
M2	M1 plus savings and small (less than $100,000) time deposits at all depository institutions plus balances at money funds (excluding institutions-only funds) plus overnight repos at banks plus overnight euros held by nonbank U.S. depositors in the Caribbean branches of U.S. banks.
M3	M2 plus large (over $100,000) time deposits at all depository institutions plus term repos at banks and S&Ls plus balances at institutions-only money funds.
L	M3 plus other liquid assets such as term Eurodollars held by nonbank U.S. residents, bankers' acceptances, commercial paper, Treasury bills and other liquid governments, and U.S. savings bonds.

December 1982

The Fed included the new money market deposit accounts (MMDAs) that depository institutions were permitted to offer on December 14, 1982, in M2.

May 2006

Fed ceases publication of M3 on March 23, 2006.

it should force up interest rates, or what? If the Fed wants to pursue a loose money policy to battle a liquidity crisis, how low should interest rates be brought and which of the newest of Fed tools is bested suited to the task?

Not surprisingly, the Fed's answers to the questions of what targets it should pursue and of how it should do so changes considerably over time. One reason is that external conditions—the structure of financial markets and the state of the domestic and world economies—are in constant flux. A second reason is that central banking is an art form that's not fully understood, and the Fed's behavior at any time is therefore partly a function of how far it has progressed along its learning curve.

Although the Fed's mandate hasn't changed much over the years, the policies the Fed has chosen to meet its mandate have. This was demonstrated in 2008 and 2009 when the Fed had to devise a crisis response by dusting off many of its old tools and creating some new ones. Over the past 30 years, the Fed has had to choose many different policies to meet its mandate. In October 1979, the Fed switched to monetarism in a last-ditch effort to wring out of the economy a high and obdurate rate of inflation. In 1988 and 1989, when the consumer price index jumped to over 6 percent, the Fed showed a renewed sensitivity to the danger of inflation as indicated by its tightening in 1988 to 1989. Its gradual interest rate cuts beginning in early 1989 reflected a shift to a new style of fine-tuning, or gradualism, which Federal Reserve Chairman Alan Greenspan became widely known for and stayed with until his term ended in January 2006.

Whatever its ultimate macroeconomic goals may be, the Fed currently states its immediate policy objectives in the policy statements that follow its policy meetings. It does so by indicating a target level for the federal funds rate. During the financial crisis, guidance regarding other actions has been included. What's next? Rate targeting is likely here to stay, but it has become complicated by the many other liquidity programs the Fed is using.

In addition to the many new tools in the Fed's toolbox (we discuss these new tools later in this chapter), the Fed typically implements its monetary policies through three main channels:

- Open market operations
- Reserve requirements
- Interest rates

Open market operations are the Fed's daily buying and selling of Treasury securities in the open market. When the Fed buys and sells securities, it affects the amount of money in the banking system. How? When the Fed buys Treasuries, for example, from a bank or a primary dealer, the Fed has to pay for the securities, and when it does that, the purchase adds money to the banking system. This money is known as *reserves*. By increasing the amount of money, or reserves, in the banking system, the Fed's securities purchases have the effect of lowering short-term interest rates, particularly the *federal funds rate*, which is the rate banks charge each other for overnight loans.

Using this example, which is not far removed from the way the Fed actually implements its monetary policies, understanding how the Fed affects short-term interest rates through its open market operations is pretty easy. It's a matter of applying the laws of supply and demand to the relationship between money and interest rates. Basically, the more money there is, the cheaper money will be. In other words, when the supply of reserves increases, the cost of money (interest rates) decreases. The opposite holds true, of course, when the Fed sells securities in the open market and thus decreases the amount of money in the banking system. In this case interest rates will rise. We will get back to these points about the impact of the Fed on short-term interest rates later in this chapter.

The Fed also can affect the economy by altering reserve requirements. Reserve requirements are the amount of money banks are required to keep in reserve against their existing capital. This is done to provide a safety net of sorts. Since the early 1990s banks have been required to maintain reserves only against transactions balances (basically interest-bearing and non-interest-bearing checking accounts). Banks keep their reserves either in vault cash or in an account held by a Federal Reserve bank in a bank's Federal Reserve district. By decreasing reserve requirements, the Fed can expand the money supply and economic growth. The opposite occurs when the Fed raises reserve requirements. This tool is very rarely used as a means of transmitting the Fed's monetary policies; it is employed mostly as a means of regulating the soundness of the banking system.

The most important way in which the Fed influences the economy is through its ability to set interest rates. These days the way the Fed accomplishes this task has become complicated because the Fed has added such a large surplus of reserves into the U.S. banking system as a result of its securities purchases. When the Fed exits its emergency-induced regime, it will likely return to its usual method of implementing policy, simultaneously pulling two of its three most important levers.

FOMC Meetings: The Great Debates

By law the FOMC must meet at least four times a year in Washington, D.C., but since 1980 it has held eight meetings a year at intervals of five to eight weeks. At each meeting, which is closed to the public and generally begins at 9 in the morning eastern time (ET), staff officers of the Federal Reserve System present oral reports on the economy, conditions in the financial markets, and international financial developments. Then the manager of the System Open Market Account (SOMA), who is essentially in charge of seeing to it that the Fed's open market operations are carried out in a way that is consistent with the Fed's directive on interest rates, reports on the SOMA's transactions since the previous meeting.

Following these reports, both the committee members and the other Federal Reserve bank presidents discuss their views on the economy as well as the appropriate course to take on monetary policy. Each voting member then votes on a specific policy recommendation to be carried out during the coming intermeeting period. Once a consensus is reached, the committee issues a directive to the Federal Reserve Bank of New York, which is the bank that handles transactions for the SOMA. The directive provides guidance to the manager of the SOMA for the implementation of the committee's decision on interest rates.

Although the Fed's chair has only one vote in this process, his or her power of persuasion goes far beyond that single vote. Former Federal Reserve Chairman Alan Greenspan, for instance, was well known to seek a consensus around his own personal views on the appropriate policy stance. Fed Chairman Ben Bernanke's style is a bit different and seen as a bit less centric. There is little doubt that the chair wields immense power at the FOMC even though existing laws do not mandate that power. In fact, the FOMC is headed by its own chair, voted on once per year. Traditionally the chair of the board of governors is voted chair of the FOMC. Rifts can develop, of course, and it takes a chair with astute political skills to negotiate them without undermining the credibility of the committee.

The bond market's anticipation of the FOMC meetings and the announcements of the Fed's policy statements are the subjects of intense debate and are at the center of many investment strategies. That is easy to understand when one looks at the relationship between the federal funds rate and bond yields. This point is illustrated clearly in Figure 6.2. The focus on the FOMC meetings can reach the point of obsession, with each piece of economic data spurring a new round of intense debate and market volatility. Public comments from Fed officials intensify the debate and are an important aspect of the way in which investors form their opinions on the likely outcome of FOMC meetings. We'll talk more about this later in the chapter.

The Federal Reserve generally announces its decision on interest rates at about 2:15 in the afternoon ET on the day of an FOMC meeting except

FIGURE 6.2 2-Year Treasuries versus the Fed Funds Rate

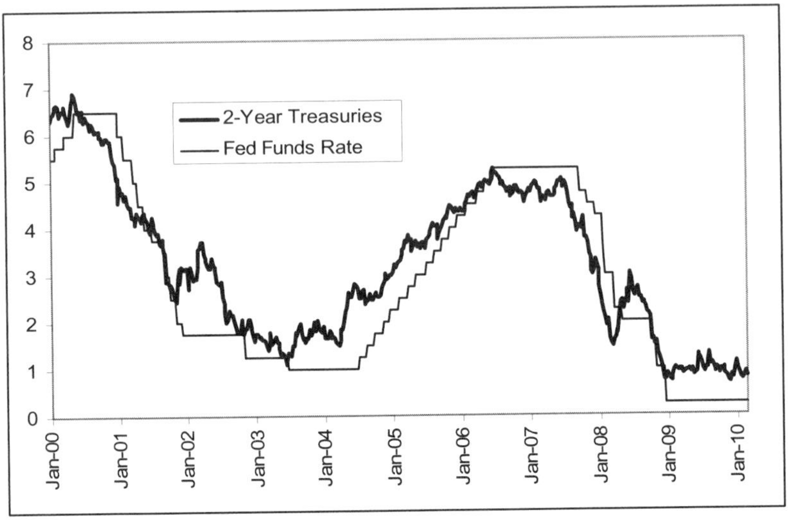

Source: Federal Reserve.

when the FOMC meeting spans two days. (In 2009, all eight scheduled meetings lasted two days; in 2010, four two-day meetings were planned; there were five in 2008; during Greenspan's tenure, two-day meetings occurred only in the two meetings prior to the Fed chairman's semiannual monetary policy report to Congress.) If the meeting lasts two days, the announcement is delivered on the second day at about 2:15 in the afternoon ET. The bond market's reaction to the FOMC's decision is often sharp, particularly on the short end of the yield curve, but sometimes it is tempered by the market's preparedness for the decision. Nevertheless, the reverberations from the Fed's actions can last for months, especially at the onset of a series of rate moves.

Day-to-Day Operations of the Open Market Desk

As noted, the FOMC gives the account manager in New York several sorts of directives: target ranges for monetary growth, a target range for fed funds, and so on. Amid the financial crisis, the directive continued to target a fed funds rate, but it also contained a directive regarding asset purchases "with the aim of providing support to private credit markets and economic activity."[1]

TABLE 6.3 Calculating the Desk's Reserve Target

Reserves needed to support deposits consistent with target
+   Appropriate borrowings at the discount window
−   Estimated excess reserves

=   Reserve target to be supplied by the desk

Having picked its primary operating target, the New York Fed's open market desk, with the aid of staff at the board of governors in Washington and at the New York Fed, estimates what reserves depository institutions will need to support its principal target. The desk then adds to this figure an estimate of the excess reserves that banks will hold and deducts from it an estimate of what appropriate or currently target borrowings from the discount window will be. The net of these figures is the amount of reserves that the desk seeks to supply on average over the week through its open market operations (Table 6.3). This is the way the open market desk operates under normal conditions, and the process would be expected to be utilized again in some form or fashion when the Federal Reserve normalizes interest rate levels.

The desk's task under ordinary circumstances sounds straightforward, but in practice it's tricky to carry out. First, the numbers of which its reserves target are based on estimates. In other words, the Fed itself can't be sure what amount of reserves will bring the federal funds rate closest to the Fed's target. Second, the quantity of reserves actually available on any day to depository institutions is influenced not only by actions taken by the desk but also by unpredictable changes in Treasury balances, float, currency in circulation, and other operating factors.

Take a Closer Look at the Buck

You can remind yourself of the Fed's ability to control the money supply and interest rates by looking closely at a dollar bill or any other denomination of U.S. paper currency. On it you will see that the Federal Reserve is in control of printing money. It says: "Federal Reserve Note." There's also a stamp that describes which of the Fed's 12 district banks printed the note. Although the Fed does not use its power to print money to control the money supply by handing it out to all who would take it (just about everybody), the Fed nonetheless controls the money supply through its open market operations and its liquidity facilities. Put simply, the Fed has enormous resources at its disposal to help regulate interest rates, the economy, and the U.S. financial system.

Transmission Effects of Monetary Policy

When the Fed either pulls on the interest rate lever or injects financial liquidity into the banking system via its new arsenal of programs, it affects more than just interest rates. Indeed, there are numerous ways in which the Fed's policies are either amplified or offset via the capital markets and the banking system. These are known as *transmission effects*. There are five main ways in which the Fed's interest rate adjustments are transmitted into the economy:

- Stock prices
- Government bond yields
- Corporate bond yields
- The value of the dollar
- Lending standards

The role that the Fed has played in affecting asset prices has always been indirect. Its new role, however, has been very direct, with the Fed playing a dual role as both referee and player. Today, as a result of its asset purchases and lending for the purchase of assets, the Federal Reserve is also a price setter.

Even in its new role, the Fed still largely influences asset prices through the interest rate lever. The Fed's interest rate changes are transmitted through the five market forces shown above, each of which can significantly affect whether the Fed's actions have their intended effect. In other words, the greater the transmission effects, the more effective the Fed's rate actions will be and the less work that the Fed will need to do in order to achieve its objectives on economic growth and inflation. If, on the other hand, the transmission effects are either small or run counter to the intended effects of the Fed's actions, then the magnitude of rate adjustments needed to reach the Fed's objectives will likely be greater. In this case, market forces would be cannibalizing the Fed's actions. This is what happened during the financial crisis. The Fed had to do more because the transmission effects were not showing through. For example, lending standards tightened dramatically, as shown in Figure 6.3.

FIGURE 6.3 Net Percentage of Banks That Tightened Lending Standards

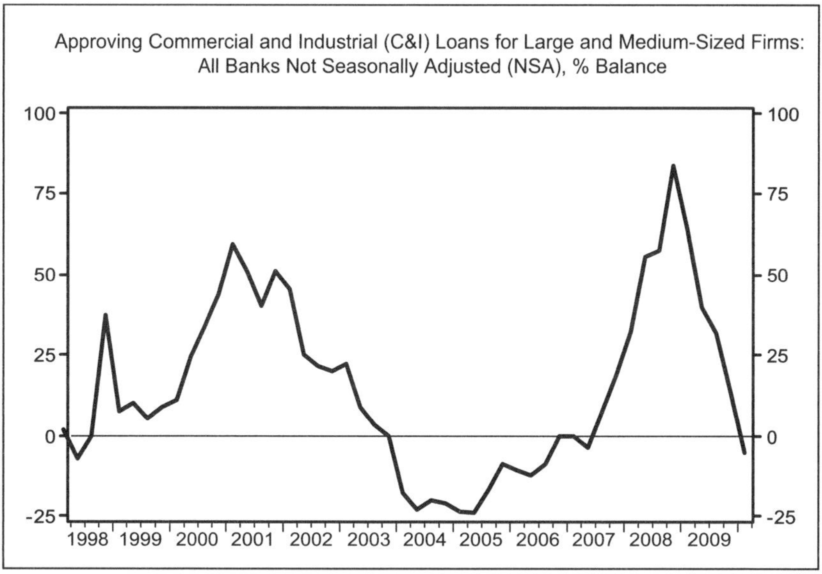

Source: Federal Reserve Board and Haver Analytics.

So the collective impact of the five transmission effects can have a very large bearing on the magnitude of interest rate adjustments needed to solve a particular economic problem.

The conditions that describe the net effect of all the financial variables that affect the economic climate are known as *financial conditions*. Financial conditions are said to be loose, or accommodating, when they are conducive toward a strengthening of economic activity. Financial conditions are said to be tight when they are conducive toward a weakening of economic activity.

A classic example of two completely different ways in which transmission effects can affect the economy and the difficult task the Fed has in shaping the appropriate monetary policies occurred between 1999 and 2001. In June 1999 the Federal Reserve embarked on a campaign to raise interest rates to quell the rapid pace of economic growth and the rampant pace of speculative fervor that was building up in the equity market. The Fed continued to raise interest rates for many months, and in early 2000 its actions began to be transmitted through a number of channels, causing financial conditions to tighten dramatically. Indeed, the technology bubble of 1999 and 2000 burst, sending technology stock prices sharply lower and inducing so-called negative wealth effects, which resulted in a weakening of consumer spending. In addition, the yield spread between corporate bonds and Treasuries began to widen sharply, particularly on low-grade corporate bonds. In response, credit became scarcer as lenders tightened lending standards and investors refrained from investing in all but the best and most creditworthy companies. This crimped growth in credit and thus reduced the level of business investment. The Fed's rate increases also resulted in a strengthening of the U.S. dollar, which eventually reduced U.S. exports.

This episode shows the enormous degree to which the Fed's interest rate changes can be magnified by numerous other financial channels. It also provides evidence of the very difficult task the Fed has in attempting to estimate the full impact of its interest rate adjustments while implementing them and awaiting their impact. One might say that *formulating the appropriate interest rate policy is like trying to walk a dog with a long leash.* In the current situation, the leash has gotten longer as a result of the large amount of financing liquidity the Fed has put in the financial system. The Fed can't as easily know how best to time its moves in order to keep the dog (the economy) under control. In general, the Fed has the unenviable task of providing a remedy to a problem without knowing to what degree the patient will respond to the remedy. As with people, the required remedy and the intended effects can vary greatly. The complications are always difficult to know from the start.

On the opposite end of the spectrum, when the Fed sought to revive economic growth in 2001, it faced a very different set of circumstances when financial conditions tightened while the Fed was easing. As a result, the magnitude of interest rate adjustments needed to cure the economy's ills was far greater than what probably would have been necessary if the transmission effects had been more consistent with historical precedent.

That extraordinary episode began on January 3, 2001, when the Fed delivered the first of an unprecedented 11 interest rate cuts that year. The typical response to such aggressiveness normally would entail a number of positive transmission effects, but the opposite occurred. Stock prices, for example, which normally rise when the Fed lowers interest rates, fell throughout the year, with the decline briefly worsening in the aftermath of the September 11 tragedies. The weakness in stock prices contributed to a dampening of consumer confidence and consumer spending. In addition, the yield spread between low-grade corporate bonds and U.S. Treasuries stayed wide most of the year, reaching the widest point exactly 10 months after the Fed's first rate cut of the year. The widening in credit spreads made borrowing costs prohibitive for many fringe borrowers and thus reduced the aggregate level of borrowing and spending. That was the opposite of what normally occurs when the Fed lowers interest rates.

The exchange value of the U.S. dollar also moved in the opposite direction of the way it normally does when the Fed lowers interest rates. A rise in the value of the dollar hurt U.S. exports and thereby cannibalized the Fed's efforts to boost economic activity.

Lending standards also remained tight through most of the year before easing at the end of the year. Commercial and industrial lending, for example, began to weaken sharply and did not begin to recover until 2003.

As a result of these uncharacteristic responses to the Fed's interest rate reductions, financial conditions were actually tighter following the Fed's rate cuts than they were when the cuts began. The lack of positive transmission effects therefore necessitated a more aggressive series of rate cuts that eventually brought the federal funds rate down to 1 percent in June 2003, its lowest level in 40 years.

The two sharply different ways in which financial conditions evolved after the Fed's interest rate adjustments in 1999 and 2001 clearly illustrate the importance of assessing the impact of the key transmitters discussed above. It is not sufficient to surmise that interest rate adjustments in and of themselves will succeed in bringing about a desired economic outcome. Moreover, the magnitude of the interest rate adjustments needed to reach a desired economic outcome can vary greatly from one economic cycle to the next, depending on a variety of factors and on the net change in financial conditions that follows the onset of the interest rate adjustments. It is therefore critical to think outside the box and assess the net change in financial conditions as well as the potential impact on the economy rather than fixate on the direct impact of the interest rate adjustments alone. This will assist you in determining the degree of rate adjustments that probably will be necessary to reach a certain economic outcome. The answer to this question will help you judge the extent to which the market's expectations on rates and their impact on the economy will be validated. If after analyzing the net transmission effects you sense that the market's assumptions are unreasonable, you will have a very strong basis for betting against market expectations. If you find that you agree with the market's assumptions, you will have a firm conviction about following market trends.

Gauging the Impact of Transmission Effects on the Economy

To gauge the effectiveness of any transmission effects of the Fed's interest rate changes on the U.S. economy, I look to three sectors of the economy in particular:

- Housing
- Automobiles
- Capital spending

These sectors are almost always the first to be affected when the Fed embarks on a course of either raising or lowering interest rates. When these sectors show signs of being affected by changes in interest rates, in due course an additional impact is likely to be seen throughout the economy. Consider the impact of a jump in car sales, for example. When car sales increase, automobile manufacturers raise production schedules, increasing both worker hours and employment. This results in additional income for workers, who spend that income on a variety of goods and services, boosting the incomes of numerous other workers. In this way there is a significant multiplier, or ripple, effect from the increase in car sales, which presumably occurred as a result of the Fed's interest rate actions. An added importance of tracking the automobile sector is the fact that the U.S. economic calendar is dominated by factory-related statistics. This means that the bond market's perception about the U.S. economic outlook can be meaningfully affected by developments in the factory sector, affecting the direction of rates, spreads, the yield curve, and such.

The housing sector can also have very large multiplier effects, as has been obvious in recent times. For example, data from the National Association of Home Builders (NAHB) indicate that an increase of about 100,000 new housing starts can result in an increase of about 250,000 full-time construction jobs. Fluctuations in housing activity are very important not only because of the impact the housing sector can have on construction employment but also because of the impact the housing sector can have on the sales of a variety of goods used to furnish a home. New home buyers often purchase new appliances, for example, and engage in a variety of remodeling projects. This is why the multiplier effects for the housing sector are perhaps greater than in any other sector in the economy. This makes sense when one considers that a home purchase is usually the biggest purchase most people will ever make.

Interest rate levels affect capital spending in two main ways. First, because capital projects are capital intensive (that is, they are more dependent on capital resources than on labor), the cost of money could have a direct bearing on a business's decision to engage in capital spending projects. Building a new plant or purchasing new equipment, for example, could become more feasible or less feasible depending on the level of interest rates. A second way in which interest rate levels affect capital spending is through their effect on the economic outlook and its impact on business confidence. If businesses feel the economic outlook has worsened as a result of interest rate increases by the Federal Reserve, they are less likely to engage in capital spending. Why, for example, would a business want to expand its capacity to produce goods and services if it felt the demand for its products was about to weaken? In most cases it wouldn't except if the business thought it needed to maintain capital spending in order to stay ahead of its competitors.

The Fed's Resounding Impact on the Bond Market

As will be shown in Chapter 9, few factors move the bond market more than the Federal Reserve does. Speaking more broadly, the Fed's ability to both control short-term interest rates and influence the rate of economic activity has an immense impact on a variety of financial assets. The Federal Reserve's monetary policies are manifested in the bond market through four main channels:

- Nominal interest rates
- Real interest rates
- The yield curve
- The performance of spread products relative to Treasuries

Importantly, the Fed's monetary policies tend to work with an uncanny degree of simultaneity. Although no two financial episodes are alike, especially with respect to the magnitude of reactions to the Fed's policies, the direction of change is generally fairly predictable. For example, when the Federal Reserve raises interest rates, both nominal and real interest rates tend to rise, the yield curve tends to flatten, and spread products (corporate bonds, agency securities, mortgage-backed securities, and the like) tend to underperform Treasuries. All these responses aid the Fed's efforts to achieve a particular economic objective, providing transmission effects. Let's take a closer look at how the Fed spurs these responses.

Nominal Interest Rates

It is pretty easy to understand how the Fed's rate changes affect nominal interest rates. *Nominal interest rates*, of course, are the actual levels of interest rates. When the Fed adjusts short-term interest rates, bond yields adjust accordingly, although the degree of adjustment for yields depends on many factors—in particular, the maturity point along the yield curve, the ongoing outlook for monetary policy, and financial conditions in general. There are several reasons why nominal yields move in the direction the Federal Reserve moves interest rates. First, yields on short-term maturities are determined largely by the cost of money, which is determined principally by the federal funds rate—which is the interest rate that the Fed controls. This subject is discussed further in Chapter 10.

Figure 6.4 shows the tight relationship between the federal funds rate and short-term maturities. This tight relationship extends beyond short-term maturities, although to a lesser degree. It is important to note that nominal interest rates on short- and long-term maturities rarely fall below the federal funds rate except in periods that precede imminent rate cuts by the Federal Reserve. Indeed, over the last 20 years the 2-year T-note has dipped below the federal funds rate on only five occasions. On each occasion the Fed lowered interest rates a very short time afterward, generally within just a few months. This pattern alone clearly suggests that the federal funds rate is an important determinant of nominal interest rates.

Real Interest Rates

As will be shown in Chapter 7, the Federal Reserve has a great deal of influence on the level of *real interest rates*, which are nominal interest rates minus inflation. Real interest rates tend to rise when the Fed raises interest rates and fall when the Fed lowers interest rates. There are a few reasons for this. First, when the Fed decides to move interest rates up or down, bond investors begin to anticipate additional interest rate adjustments by pushing nominal interest rates up or down more quickly than changes occur in the inflation rate. For example, when the Fed is in the process of raising interest rates, it presumably is doing so because of an increase in inflation

FIGURE 6.4 Short-Term Interest Rates Track the Federal Funds Rate Very Closely

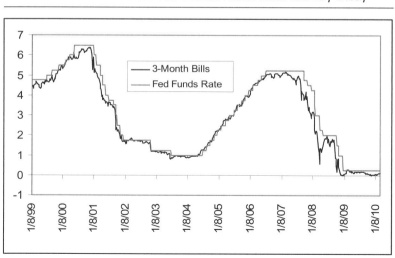

Source: Federal Reserve.

risks. Bond investors recognize this as well as the Fed's historical tendency to push the federal funds rate well above the inflation rate during periods when inflation is accelerating or is at risk of doing so. Bond investors respond by pushing up real interest rates.

Second, the Fed tends to try to engineer low real interest rates when the economy is weak and high real interest rates when the economy is strong. It does this in an attempt to alternately encourage (when the economy is weak) and discourage (when the economy is strong) both consumption and risk taking, doing so by calibrating the incentives to save disposable income and invest in the economy. For sake of this argument, by *savings* I mean actual savings (the difference between disposable personal income and personal consumption) and in particular savings in interest-bearing assets, and cash and cash instruments; by *investments* I mean investments of all sorts, including investments in corporate equities and capital equipment. By varying the real interest rate, the Fed can have an enormous impact on savings and investments. When the rate that can be earned on savings is high (as determined largely by rates affected by the federal funds rate) and the rate of return on investments is low relative to the savings rate (as determined by the inflation rate, the level of economic growth, and hence the return on capital), an investor has a greater incentive to save than to invest. Thus, a high real interest rate tends to dampen economic activity because it dampens investment.

Similarly, when the interest rate paid on savings is low and the rate of return on investments is high relative to the savings rate, investors and businesses have an incentive to invest rather than save, and when they do, this spurs economic activity. This is why during times of economic weakness, it is critical for the Fed to move the federal funds rate down to as close to the inflation rate as possible, in order to spur investment and consumption relative to savings. In other words, the Fed needs to spur risk taking when economic activity is weak. This is what happened in 2008 when the Fed pushed the federal funds rate below the inflation rate. The Fed was attempting to stimulate investment by bringing the interest rate paid on savings so low that it would serve as a powerful motivation to invest.

The Federal Reserve's recognition of the need to bring the savings rate below the investment rate stands in stark contrast to the situation in Japan, where chronic deflation has kept the investment rate below the savings rate for many years, resulting in extremely weak economic conditions. Investors in Japan have had little reason to invest in the economy when deflation is reducing the nominal value of their investments. The deflation in real assets—real estate, for example—has been a powerful disincentive to investment. Investors would rather save their money at interest rate levels that are barely above 0 percent because the return on savings exceeds the return on investments. It therefore behooves Japan's central bank, the Bank of Japan, to make every effort to keep real interest rates as low as possible to reverse the deflationary pressures in Japan. Although this is a difficult task, it seems imperative after nearly 20 years of recession and meager economic growth.

Japan's difficult situation and its policy response may have influenced the actions of the Federal Reserve and other central banks during the financial crisis. The Fed, recognizing the risks of deflation and the so-called zero-bound limit on the federal funds rate, saw that it had to choose another route to spur risk taking—quantitative easing. By purchasing $1.75 trillion of fixed-income securities, the Fed encouraged investors to move out the risk spectrum, producing a behavioral response it tries to encourage when lowering the federal funds rate below the inflation rate.

A third way in which the Fed affects the level of real interest rates is through its credibility as an inflation fighter. When bond investors have confidence in the Fed, real interest rates tend to be low. This is the case because investors tend to demand less of an interest rate premium over and above the inflation rate when they are confident that inflation will stay low. By contrast, when confidence in the Fed's ability to fight inflation is low, bond investors demand a higher real interest rate to compensate them for the risk that inflation will accelerate and erode the value of their bonds.

The Yield Curve

As will be shown in Chapter 7, one of the biggest influences on the yield curve is the Federal Reserve. The Fed affects the yield curve largely through its control of short-term interest rates. When the Federal Reserve raises or lowers the federal funds rate, yields on short-term maturities tend to follow. Figure 6-2 clearly illustrates this. As a result, the yield curve tends to get steeper when the Fed lowers interest rates, as yields on short-term maturities fall faster than do those on long-term maturities. Yields on long-term maturities respond more slowly to the Fed's interest rate moves because they are affected by a wide variety of other factors, including speculative trading activity, technical factors, and inflation expectations. This brings us to the next point.

A second way in which the Fed has an impact on the yield curve is by affecting inflation expectations. Changes in inflation expectations have a large bearing on the behavior of long-term interest rates, particularly compared with short-term interest rates. The Fed affects inflation expectations in two ways. First, when the Fed adjusts interest rates, the market's outlook on economic growth changes, altering inflation expectations. Second, inflation expectations will be higher or lower depending on the Fed's inflation-fighting credibility. If investors are confident that the Fed will be able to contain inflation, this will tend to keep inflation expectations low, resulting in low long-term interest rates and a relatively flat yield curve. By contrast, if the market lacks confidence in the Fed's ability to fight inflation, the yield curve will be steep, reflecting the market's uncertainty about the inflation outlook.

The yield curve also is affected by the bond market's expectations of future Fed policies. In theory, since long-term interest rates are thought to reflect expectations of future short-term interest rates, the yield curve reflects expectations of future Fed interest rate actions. Thus, when the market expects higher or lower interest rates in the future, long-term interest rates tend to reflect those expectations, having an impact on the shape of the yield curve.

There is one important point to remember in this regard. The degree to which the market embeds future Fed interest rate actions in long-term interest rates depends a great deal on the degree to which inflation expectations are well anchored. In other words, if inflation expectations are well anchored, the market will tend to expect a smaller amount of interest rate adjustments. For example, if the Fed begins to raise interest rates at a time when inflation expectations are high or a bit fragile, the rise in long-term interest rates is likely to be larger than it would be if inflation expectations were low. This occurs because the market will assume that a larger magnitude of rate increases will be needed to quash inflation.

This type of response occurred in 1994, as will be discussed later in this chapter. The opposite occurred in 2004 and 2005 when the Federal Reserve's interest rate increases had relatively little impact on long-term interest rates, prompting Federal Reserve Chairman Alan Greenspan to call it a "conundrum," because the muted impact on long-term rates was cannibalizing to some extent the Federal Reserve's increase in short-term interest rates.[2] The "conundrum" occurred in part because inflation in the early 2000s was very benign and the Fed had built up a high amount of inflation-fighting credentials. The impact of the Fed's rate actions on long-term interest rates is therefore very dependent on inflation expectations. Thus, it can be said that the degree of leverage exerted by short-term rates over long-term rates is regime dependent. In other words, the impact depends on the market's perception of the degree of interest rate adjustments needed to fight inflation. This can vary from one interest rate cycle to the next but is largely related to the Fed's inflation-fighting credibility over a period of inflation episodes.

The Performance of Spread Products Relative to Treasuries

The Federal Reserve can have a large influence on the performance of spread products, or fixed-income securities other than Treasuries, including agency securities, corporate bonds, and mortgage-backed securities. These securities are called *spread products* because their yields are priced and quoted in terms of their yield spread over Treasuries and in relation to the LIBOR, or swap rates. Since these spread products are deemed to be riskier than Treasuries, their yield spreads tend to fluctuate as perceptions of the risks of holding them change.

These perceptions generally change when views about economic growth change. For example, during periods of economic weakness, the financial prospects for a wide variety of companies turn sour. Revenues decline, pricing power diminishes, and productivity declines, putting downward pressure on profit margins and in some cases producing outright losses. Bonds in companies with low credit ratings therefore come under pressure as investors worry about the ability of those companies to meet their payment obligations. Investment-grade bonds are not immune to this effect; only the magnitude of the impact differs.

The Fed affects credit spreads when it adjusts the federal funds rate and thus affects the economy. For example, when the Fed raises interest rates, credit spreads tend to widen because investors fear that the rate increases will weaken the economy. Similarly, when the Fed lowers interest rates, credit spreads tend to narrow in anticipation of a strengthening in economic activity. In 2007 and 2008 the Federal Reserve's interest rate cuts were accompanied by a *widening* of credit spreads because investors were concerned about a variety of risk factors, including liquidity and volatility, for example. There were also concerns about the outlook for the U.S. and world economy, which produced a concern about credit that overwhelmed for a time any positive impact of the Fed's rate cuts. The point is that while the Fed's interest rate changes tend to affect the direction of credit spreads similarly from cycle to cycle, the timing of the impact depends a great deal on the broader assessment that investors make on the risk factors they must consider when investing, and in investor perceptions about the economic outlook.

The clear pattern of the Fed's impact on credit spreads is a solid basis on which to formulate investment strategies for buying and selling spread products. Keeping in mind the idea that no two financial episodes are alike, spread products should be expected to outperform Treasuries when the Fed is lowering interest rates and should be expected to underperform Treasuries when the Fed raises interest rates. Acting on these principles, it is possible to tailor a fixed-income strategy around the Fed. One must keep in mind, of course, that there can be sharp differences in the performance of the various spread products relative to each other when interest rates fluctuate. For example, when interest rates fall sharply, mortgage-backed securities tend to underperform other spread products owing to worries that prepayments of the securities will rise as a result of increases in mortgage refinancing and housing turnover.

Don't Fight the Fed: Follow It

As I stated earlier, the adage "Don't fight the Fed" is Wall Street lore. History is strewn with periods when the performance of the stock and bond markets was affected significantly by Fed policy. Along the way many investors either profited from or were hammered by the Fed, depending on the degree to which they respected the Fed's ability to affect the economy and the financial markets.

Despite the unmistakable impact the Fed has had on the markets over the years, investors do not always heed the power of the Fed. Instead, they get caught in bouts of excessive optimism and pessimism, often finding it difficult to see past their emotions. However, investors always seem to come around at some point, eventually recognizing that the Fed's handiwork will have its intended effect. Investors who show confidence in the Fed's actions early on are likely to have better investment returns than those who choose to bet against the Fed.

A great way to see the very large impact the Fed can have on the markets is to look at the bond market's response to policy speeches made by Federal Reserve Chairmen Alan Greenspan and Ben Bernanke. Twice a year the Fed chair delivers testimony to Congress in a report called the *Monetary Policy Report to Congress*, which was known as the "Humphrey-Hawkins testimony" until the Humphrey-Hawkins Act of 1978 was altered in July 2000. These testimonies, which are mandated by law, require the Fed to give its view on both monetary policy and the economy to both houses of Congress.

In the House the chair delivers testimony to the Committee on Financial Services; in the Senate the chair delivers testimony to the Committee on Banking, Housing, and Urban Affairs. The testimonies usually are given in February and July. The reason these testimonies are so revealing is that the detail in which a Fed chair describes the Fed's sentiments almost always pushes the chair into sensitive subject areas, spurring a sharp response in the bond market. Table 6.4 illustrates these reactions by highlighting the sharp

TABLE 6.4 Historical Reactions in the Front-Month T-Bond Contract to the Fed Chair's Semiannual Monetary Policy Report to Congress

Year	February	July
1993	+7	−5
1994	+14	−31
1995	+30	−58
1996	−68	+43
1997	−55	+40
1998	−29	+18
1999	−29	−34
2000	+15	+50
2001	−6	+31
2002	+27	−34
2003	−2	+71
2004	+29	−32
2005	−19	+15
2006	+4	+24
2007	+27	+22
2008	+7	+4
2009	−1	+37
2010	−5	

reactions on the days Greenspan and Bernanke delivered their semiannual reports.

The table shows that the most actively traded Treasury bond futures contract has averaged an absolute change of 28/32 on the first day of the Fed chair's testimony. That is a big move for one day—the average daily change on T-bond futures is about half that. Eurodollar contracts, which are basically a reflection of the federal funds rate, also have moved sharply relative to their daily average.

That there have been sharp reactions should not be surprising. However, what stands out and what is perhaps more important for investors to remember is the follow-through to these reactions. During the periods shown in Table 6.4, in the week that followed the testimonies the cumulative reaction has been usually double that of the initial reaction. And it goes on: One month later the reaction continues further in the same direction as the initial reaction, as the realization of the Fed's policy stance sets in and market participants continue to adjust their positions accordingly. Remember this the next time a Fed chair delivers one of these speeches (investors should read the entire speech; they shouldn't just listen to sound bites). If, for instance, in the aftermath of a semiannual testimony, the market trades sharply higher or lower, investors could consider placing a trade in the same direction of that reaction and wait for there to be follow-through in the market. Investors should give it at least one week and then reassess, but they should keep in mind that the market response to the Fed chair's semiannual policy speeches tends to reverberate at least a few weeks.

Ostensibly, the market reacts so sharply to the Fed chair's semiannual report to Congress because it believes that what it hears from the Fed chair is an unmistakable reflection of Fed policy. And since Fed policy does not change on a dime, the market finds cause to continue the response in the weeks that follow. Indeed, the Fed generally maintains its monetary policies for many months and sometimes years. The lesson here is to identify the Fed's monetary policy stance and formulate one's investment strategies in ways that are consistent with the Fed's stance. Moreover, investors could seize the short- and long-term trading opportunities that arise when the Fed's chair delivers a policy speech by establishing trading positions that anticipate a sustained market response to the speech. Long-term investors can use these principles to time their entries into and exits from their portfolio positions. Investors should use these principles in their consideration of directional bets and bets on the relative performance of the various segments of the bond market. These principles can also be used to assess the outlook for investment returns in bonds compared to other financial assets.

A Classic Case of the Fed's Tough Love

In the same way that parents must discipline their children, the Fed chair's duty is to act as a disciplinarian—of the U.S. economy. It is the Federal Reserve's duty to take the proverbial punch bowl away before the party gets out of hand. There are some who believe the Fed failed to do this in the early 2000s, but the jury is still out on the role that interest rates played in sowing the seeds to the financial crisis, given that many of its roots arguably date back to the 1980s when consumerism was getting into high gear and policy makers were actively encouraging homeownership.

On the interest rate front, a classic example of the Fed's tough love took place in 1994. During that year the economy seemed to be rolling along just fine, but the Fed felt it was growing too strongly and that the growth rate could accelerate inflation. In response, the Fed implemented a series of interest rate increases, raising the federal funds rate six times in 1994 and once more in early 1995. Many investors were dismayed by the interest rate increases, and it looked as if the Fed might derail the nascent expansion. The Fed's tight grip resulted in a subdued year for the stock market and a wretched one for the bond market. In fact, 1994 was the worst year for the bond market in decades. The yield on the 30-year Treasury bond rose from a low of 5.78 percent on October 15, 1993, to a peak of 8.16 percent on November 7, 1994. The poor performance of the bond market spilled over into the stock market, where the S&P 500 fell 1.5 percent in 1994.

As bad as the interest rate increases seemed, the Fed had good intentions: the inflation rate looked set to rise in a way that could undermine the economic expansion. The inflation rate was kept at bay because of the Fed's actions. In 1994, there were many more people worried about inflation than there are today. Late 1990s expressions such as "the new era economy" and the "Goldilocks economy" were themes that very few investors believed in at that time (these themes hold that the economy can grow strongly without inflation because of conditions that are "just right"). In 1994, most investors still believed in the more traditional view that strong economic growth leads to inflation. After all, just a few years earlier in 1990 the consumer price index got as high as 6.3 percent on a year-over-year (YOY) basis. That's why,

FIGURE 6.5 The Year-Over-Year (YOY) Changes in the Consumer Price Index (CPI) versus the Federal Funds Rate

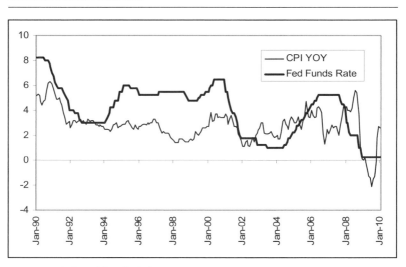

Source: Bureau of Labor Statistics and Federal Reserve.

when economic growth strengthened at the end of 1993 and into early 1994 after several years of sluggish growth, inflation expectations immediately began to rise.

The Fed's challenge in 1994, therefore, was to convince investors that the inflation threat would be quashed. Mind you, given the economic backdrop, the inflation threat that existed was mostly psychological: the unemployment rate was relatively high at 6.6 percent; savings and loan institutions were still recovering from a crisis that had begun several years earlier; worker insecurity was soaring in response to a spate of huge corporate layoffs; businesses were starting to invest heavily in new technology that would dampen inflation pressures by increasing productivity; the budget deficit was falling; and the global economy—led by Japan—was weak. In hindsight, it is striking to think that despite all these factors, inflation fears were strong enough to push the yield on the 30-year bond over 8 percent. It has not come close to that in recent years.

When the Fed began its inflation fight, it was fighting fears that were not its own. Chairman Alan Greenspan once said that price stability exists only when "the expected rate of change of the general level of prices ceases to be a factor in individual and business decision making."[3] Other Fed officials have expressed similar thoughts. Thus, even though the inflation threat in 1994 did not appear to be as great as investors feared, it nonetheless was affecting the way individuals and investors behaved. The Fed therefore had to convince the public that there was no inflation threat and that inflation was a thing of the past.

Because the Fed did not fully know the extent to which inflation fears might grow, it began the battle against inflation worries by raising interest rates slowly, beginning in February 1994 with three consecutive increases of 25 basis points in the federal funds rate. However, as the extent of inflation fears became evident in the behavior of commodity prices and long-term interest rates (both were rising, indicating inflation fears), the Fed knew it had to do more to reassure investors that inflation would not return. It then opted for larger rate increases in increments of 50 basis points in both May and August 1994. But in November 1994, when it appeared that the new strategy was failing to calm inflation-wary investors, the Fed asserted itself with a large rate hike of 75 basis points, pushing the fed funds rate well above the inflation rate, as shown in Figure 6.5. One might think that this would deal the markets a decisive blow and push market interest rates sharply higher, but the opposite occurred. Bond yields peaked that month and began a steady decline that lasted throughout the next year, even though the Fed would deliver another rate hike—of 50 basis points—three months later in February 1995.

The Fed had finally conquered investors' inflation fears and the economic imbalances that created them. The payoff from its efforts quickly followed; in 1995, long-term government bonds returned over 30 percent and the S&P 500 returned 34.1 percent. Inflation rose just 2.6 percent, and there was nary an inflation fear for the next decade. That year marked the beginning of several years of almost unparalleled prosperity that benefited millions of Americans.

The episode of 1994 to 1995 is one of the best illustrations of how the Federal Reserve gave the appearance of being the market's nemesis only to prove it was the market's best friend. The episode is a clear illustration of the importance of trusting the Fed, especially in these times of doubt about both the Fed's intentions and its effectiveness. The Fed's mandate, after all, is to conduct its policies in a way that is consistent with the pursuit of full employment and stable prices.

Therefore, when market participants appear to have little faith that the Fed ultimately will be successful in achieving either of its two main objectives, an investor should look to capitalize on the market's wrongheaded conclusions about the Fed's ability to implement policies that will ultimately prove beneficial for both the economy and the markets. Countertrend trades are likely to be successful in this instance, although caution must always be taken when an investor is betting against the collective opinions of the market.

The Art of Fed Watching

Earlier in this chapter we saw that the bond market reacts very sharply to the semiannual reports to Congress delivered by Fed chairs and that reactions to their testimony have tended to be long-lasting. Predicting the market's behavior during months in which the Fed chair delivers testimony is therefore simpler than it is in other months, thanks to the large extent to which the Fed chair is forced to delve into sensitive topics. During the rest of the year, however, the specificity of the Fed chair's remarks and those of his or her colleagues is not nearly as sharp. It therefore becomes necessary to pick up the Fed's signals through other means, and this requires a bit more, shall we say, inspection. One must become an avid Fed watcher if he or she is to predict what the Fed will do next.

Try to think about Fed watching this way: Let's say that you've been asked to solve a mystery in which all of the principal players are known. They talk in public all the time. You've got a plethora of clues about what they're thinking. They give you verbatim transcripts of what they say in private, and they give you the minutes from all their meetings. I bet you can crack that mystery in a jiffy. This is exactly how it is with the Fed, and so there's absolutely no reason to be intimidated.

As I said earlier, Fed watching begins with recognizing that when the Fed's chair delivers a policy speech, the impact is often long-lasting. With this in mind, an investor should tailor his or her trading strategies accordingly, working on the assumption that the chair's policy speeches are a true reflection of the Fed's current stance on monetary policy and that the markets will behave in a way that is consistent with that policy stance.

While the Fed chair can be relied upon to occasionally give guidance on Fed policy, investors must find ways to decipher policy on a regular basis. The best way to do this is to follow the Fed members regularly and closely. What one needs to do is to get in the Fed's shadow, so to speak, by tracking the verbiage spewed by the Federal Open Market Committee (FOMC), whose 13 members, including the Fed chair, are given the privilege of voting at the FOMC meetings. There are five additional Federal Reserve officials who attend the Fed's meetings, alternating the privilege to vote every other year. Although they do not vote, the alternates are proverbial flies on the wall at FOMC meetings. While their presence at the meetings raises the importance of what they have to say, investors are best advised to focus more on the comments delivered by the 13 voting members.

Useful to investors are the minutes of the FOMC meetings, which are released three weeks following the meetings. Until 2005, minutes were released six weeks following the FOMC meetings, but the Fed changed the release date as part of its efforts to improve its transparency. The minutes give Fed watchers greater details about what the FOMC members discussed behind closed doors. In particular, the degree of support shown by Fed members for the Fed's announced policy decisions helps in uncovering potential shifts in the Fed's policy stance. The minutes are also useful in predicting changes to the Fed's policy statements, which themselves can be big market movers. Policy statements are delivered at the conclusion of the FOMC meetings.

Read the Fed's Speeches

One of the best ways to follow the Fed requires a little bit of homework, but the payoff can be huge, and it actually takes very little time. Specifically, I urge you to read the Fed's speeches. Many top investors do this, and when I talk with them and hear them refer to specific lines in those speeches, it always reminds me how valuable it is to read the speeches. The speeches are readily available on the Fed's Web site at www.federalreserve.gov or on the Web sites for the Federal Reserve banks, particularly for the presidents of the Fed's 12 banks.

It is not all that laborious to do this work because most of the Fed's speeches are generally just a few pages long. The speeches give investors far greater insight into the Fed than can be discerned from newswire headlines, which can often reflect a reporter's subjective view about the speeches and thus are open to misinterpretation. Investors should not rely on reporters alone to tell them what the Fed said; it is up to each investor. Some in the media are new to the business and are simply good reporters or writers, but some of them are, quite frankly, novices when it comes to analyzing the Fed in the way that is required of an investor, particularly an institutional investor. That said, a standout is Steve Liesman at CNBC, whose read on the Fed and the economy I have found to be exemplary. Kathleen Hays at Bloomberg is also excellent.

Watch the Fed's Phraseology

What should you look for when reading the Fed's speeches? Look for key phrases that are repeated in lockstep by several Fed members. When I see a few members collectively repeating a particular phrase either verbatim or nearly so, I always sense that the phrase might be a representation of current Fed policy. When Fed members sing the same tune, I envision them meeting with each other either in person or in a telephone conference and drawing conclusions about where they stand on policy and how they should weave their policy sentiments into their public comments.

Of course, each Fed member has his or her personal view on monetary policy and the economy, and each is free to express such views. Wall Street divides the Fed's members into two main camps: hawks and doves. Hawks are members who are wary about the inflation outlook. They therefore tend to express an inclination to raise interest rates when inflation pressures appear to surface or when economic growth is strong. Doves, on the other hand, tend to be more sanguine about the inflation outlook and generally worry less about the implications of strong economic growth than hawks do. Wall Street often measures the degree to which the members are hawkish or dovish by using a hawk/dove scale like the one shown in Figure 6.6.

One might think that hearing a wide range of views from the Fed would make the task of interpreting where the Fed stands on policy more difficult, but these personal opinions help provide insight on Fed policy. How? Basically, if there's consistency in the use of phraseology by members known to have opposing views on monetary policy (similar to the way in which Democrats and Republicans differ on many issues), their joint use

FIGURE 6.6 The Hawk/Dove Scale

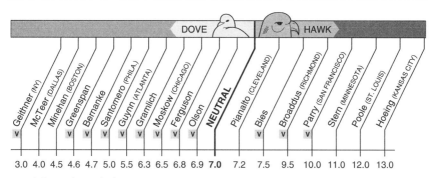

Note: V indicates voting member in 2004.

Source: Bondtalk.com.

of a particular phrase is generally a strong indication of agreement about where the Fed stands on a particular issue. The differing views among the Fed's members can help an investor put the individual views expressed by the members into context, similar to the way in which knowing whether a politician is a Republican or a Democrat helps to put his or her comments in the proper context.

In 1999, for example, just before the Fed began raising interest rates in June of that year, several Fed members repeatedly used the phrase "the balance of risks has shifted [toward higher inflation]." Some of the members who repeated that phrase were not prone to saying so, given their personal views. Their common use of this phrase therefore suggested that the Fed was in the middle of formulating a new policy designed to counter the risks its members were referring to. Indeed, a hike in interest rates soon followed.

Similar phraseology was used at the opposite end of the spectrum at the end of 2000, indicating that interest rate reductions were in the offing, as indeed they were. In 2009, both hawks and doves continued to say that interest rates might stay low "for an extended period," a phrase that New York Fed President William Dudley in early 2010 said meant "at least six months." Hence, the continued use of the phrase was a green light toward bond strategies designed to benefit from a steady hand at the Fed, in particular yield curve strategies, carry trades (whereby leveraged investors earn positive carry—the difference between borrowing costs and the rate of return on an investment), and strategies designed to fair well in a case of low interest rate volatility.

It is always striking to think that by simply following the words of a handful of people at the Fed, an investor can gain insights that give the investor an edge over millions of other investors. That is why I always include the Fed in my required readings and why you should consider it too.

Crisis Tools: The Fed's Credit and Liquidity Programs

The Federal Reserve Act of December 23, 1913, has probably been mentioned more in the past few years than at any time since the act was signed, in particular Section 13(3), which gave the Fed the authority "in unusual and exigent circumstances" to lend money to "any individual, partnership, or corporation" that is "unable to secure adequate credit accommodations from other banking institutions." Here is all of Section 13(3) of the Federal Reserve Act of 1913:

> *In unusual and exigent circumstances, the Board of Governors of the Federal Reserve System, by the affirmative vote of not less than five members, may authorize any Federal reserve bank, during such periods as the said board may determine, at rates established in accordance with the provisions of section 14, subdivision (d), of this Act, to discount for any individual, partnership, or corporation, notes, drafts, and bills of exchange when such notes, drafts, and bills of exchange are indorsed or otherwise secured to the satisfaction of the Federal reserve bank: Provided, that before discounting any such note, draft, or bill of exchange for an individual, partnership, or corporation the Federal reserve bank shall obtain evidence that such individual, partnership, or corporation is unable to secure adequate credit accommodations from other banking institutions. All such discounts for individuals, partnerships, or corporations shall be subject to such limitations, restrictions, and regulations as the Board of Governors of the Federal Reserve System may prescribe.*

These relatively few words grant the Fed enormous powers, which until 2008 it had not exercised since the Great Depression. Six programs were created under Section 13(3) in 2008 in response to the financial crisis, five of which had expired by February 1, 2010. Each has an acronym often cited by members of the Federal Reserve and that is familiar to Wall Street and the financial media.

Primary Dealer Credit Facility (PDCF)

Commenced March 16, 2008, and expired February 1, 2010. The purpose of the PDCF was to provide funding to primary dealers in exchange for a specified range of eligible collateral. Loans from the PDCF peaked at $148 billion in the week ended October 1, 2008.

Term Securities Lending Facility (TSLF)

Commenced March 27, 2008, and expired February 1, 2010. The TSLF promoted liquidity in the Treasury and collateral markets by enabling primary dealers to borrow Treasury securities against program-eligible general collateral. Dealers would then use the Treasury securities as collateral for loans. The peak amount of securities loans was $234 billion in the week ended October 1, 2008.

Asset-Backed Commercial Paper Money Market Mutual Fund Liquidity Facility (AMLF)

Commenced September 19, 2008, and expired February 1, 2010. The purpose of the AMLF was to provide funding to U.S. depository institutions and bank holding companies to finance their purchases of high-quality asset-backed commercial paper from money market mutual funds in times when redemptions by investors might be large. Loans from the AMLF peaked at $146 billion in the week ended October 8, 2008.

Commercial Paper Funding Facility (CPFF)

Commenced October 27, 2008, and expired February 1, 2010. The purpose of the CPFF was to increase the availability of term commercial paper funding to issuers and to provide both issuers and investors assurance that firms would be able to roll over their maturing commercial paper. The CPFF peaked at $350 billion in the week ended January 21, 2009.

Term Asset-Backed Securities Loan Facility (TALF)

Commenced March 17, 2009, and set to expire June 30, 2010. The TALF was designed to make credit available to consumers and businesses at rates lower than could be obtained in the private markets by facilitating the issuance of asset-backed securities.

Money Market Investor Funding Facility (MMIFF)

Commenced November 24, 2008, and expired on October 30, 2009. The MMIFF was provided senior secured funding to a series of special-purpose vehicles to facilitate an industry-supported private sector initiative to finance the purchase of eligible assets from eligible investors. The program facilitated the sale of money market assets in the secondary market in order to give money market mutual funds and other money market investors confidence that they could extend the terms of their investments and still maintain appropriate liquidity positions. No funding was provided through this facility.

Additional programs created under separate existing authority granted by the Federal Reserve Act included the following:

Central Bank Liquidity Swaps

Commenced December 12, 2007, and expired February 1, 2010. The Central Bank Liquidity Swaps consisted of the following programs. Both were authorized under Section 14 of the Federal Reserve Act.

Dollar Liquidity Swap Lines

Commenced December 12, 2007. This swap line provided liquidity in U.S. dollars to overseas markets through many of the world's central banks. The swap lines played a major role in reducing the level of the dollar-based London Interbank Offered Rate (LIBOR) by injecting more dollars into the world financial system. The impact was greatest when on October 13, 2008, the swap lines were increased to "whatever quantity of U.S. dollar funding" was demanded by the Bank of England, the European Central Bank, the Swiss National Bank, and the Bank of Japan, which approved the action a day later. The peak amount of swaps outstanding was $583 billion in the week ended December 10, 2008.

Foreign Currency Liquidity Swap Lines

Commenced April 6, 2009. These swap lines were designed to provide the Federal Reserve with the capacity to offer liquidity to U.S. institutions in foreign currency.

Term Auction Facility (TAF)

Commenced December 17, 2007, and expired March 8, 2010. The purpose of the TAF was to provide loans against eligible collateral to depository institutions through an auction process to augment its discount window program, which depository institutions tended to avoid because of a stigma attached to borrowing from it. Loans from the TAF peaked at $493 billion in the week ended March 4, 2009. Loans outstanding from the facility stood at $15.4 billion in the week ended February 17, 2010.

The Fed's liquidity programs were designed to ensure that financial institutions had access to short-term credit so that they could continue their lending amid a drying up of private sources of liquidity. In doing so, the Federal Reserve performed its vital function as the nation's central bank and helped stabilize a very dysfunctional financial system wrought with fear and panic. Similar credit and liquidity programs were put in place by central banks throughout the world. The combined actions and their positive effects illustrate the vital purpose of central banking.

Summary

- The Fed was created largely to conduct the nation's monetary policies by influencing the money and credit conditions in the pursuit of full employment and stable prices. The Fed's main tool in this regard is the ability to set interest rates.
- Amid the financial crisis, many now understand just how powerful the Federal Reserve truly is. The financial crisis adds to bountiful evidence on the need for a central bank, both in the United States and abroad. The Fed's impact on the performance of nearly all financial assets is so unmistakable that it behooves every investor to learn more.
- The Fed is structured in a way that gives it a broad view of the economy. At the Fed's eight meetings per year, members debate the need for interest rate adjustments, with the Fed's chair having the most sway. The FOMC is composed of five presidents of the Federal Reserve banks and the seven members of the board of governors (including the chair).
- The primary policy tool available to the Fed is open market operations—that is, the ability to create bank reserves in any desired quantity by monetizing some portion of the national debt. Today, the implementation of monetary policy has been complicated by the many means by which the Fed added financial liquidity into the U.S. financial system. In particular, the Fed must decide how it will eventually dispose of or effectively neutralize the impact of the $1.25 trillion of mortgage-backed securities it purchased through March 2010.
- The Fed affects the economy primarily by having an impact on the interest rate–sensitive sectors of the economy, including housing, automobiles, and capital spending. The Fed's impact can be helped

or hindered by transmission effects—the many ways in which the Fed's policies are either amplified or offset via the capital markets and the banking system.

- The Fed's rate decisions have a significant impact on the bond market, affecting nominal rates, real rates, the yield curve, and the performance of spread products relative to Treasuries.
- Authority granted to the Fed via the Federal Reserve Act of 1913 was used during the financial crisis for the first time since the Great Depression. The Fed created numerous credit and liquidity programs aimed at improving the functioning of the financial markets. Most programs had expired by February 1, 2010.
- The adage "Don't fight the Fed" derives from the cumulative experiences of millions of investors over many decades. History has proven that investors who put their faith in the Fed are likely to achieve much higher investment returns than are those who ignore the Fed. You therefore should incorporate an analysis of monetary policy into your investment decision-making process. You can improve your ability to anticipate the Fed's rate actions by becoming an avid Fed watcher. Doing simple things such as reading the Fed's speeches and watching for the repetition of key phrases can go a long way toward putting you ahead of most investors.

7

THE YIELD CURVE
The Bond Market's Crystal Ball

Investors always seem to be looking for a crystal ball to help them predict the future, but for most of them this is an elusive search. Investors often are confused by the myriad of indicators available to them and the wide variety of messages that the indicators send.

In the bond market there is one indicator that many investors put ahead of all the rest: the yield curve. It is the closest thing the bond market has to a crystal ball. For decades it has reliably foreshadowed major events and turning points in both the financial markets and the economy, and it is one of the most closely watched financial indicators. Few indicators are as reliable as the yield curve. More important, there is significant historical evidence that the yield curve is one of the best forecasting tools available. Let's take a closer look.

For simplicity's sake, assume that for our purposes the term *yield curve* refers to the yield curve for U.S. Treasuries (we will discuss why the Treasury yield curve is the most widely used later in this chapter).

The yield curve is a chart that plots the yield on bonds against their maturities. The shape of the yield curve is generally upward-sloping, with yields increasing in ascending order as maturities lengthen. In other words, a *normal yield curve* is one in which the yields on long-term maturities are higher than the yields on short-term maturities. The maturities generally included in yield curve graphs range from 3 months to 30 years. For yield curve graphs on the Treasury market, the most commonly included securities are those that are issued regularly by the U.S. Treasury Department. They include Treasury bills with maturities of 3, 6, and 12 months; notes with maturities of 2, 3, 5, and 10 years; and bonds with maturities of 30 years.

Market observers focus on the shape of the yield curve as a barometer of the U.S. economy. The focus is generally on the yield spreads between various combinations of short- and long-term maturities. The three most commonly watched spreads are the spread between 3-month T-bills and 10-year T-notes; the spread between 2-year T-notes and 10-year T-notes; and the spread between 2-year T-notes and 30-year T-bonds. Each of the spreads has shown a strong historical correlation to the behavior of the economy.

The shape of the yield curve can mean a variety of things to bond investors, but there are two basic ways to look at it. First, if the yield curve is *positively sloped*, or *steep*, this usually is seen as an indication that short-term interest rates are relatively low and are expected to remain low as a result of an accommodating stance on monetary policy by the Federal Reserve. Figure 7.1 shows a normal, or positively sloped, yield curve. In such an environment, short-term interest rates are lower than long-term interest rates because the Fed's interest rate reductions put downward pressure on short-term interest rates, the rates the Fed controls.

Long-term interest rates, however, do not fall in lockstep with the Fed's rate cuts in the same way that short-term interest rates do. Long-term interest rates contain a term premium, and they are influenced by many other factors, such as inflation expectations and expectations about future short-term interest rates. This prevents long-term interest rates from falling as

FIGURE 7.1 A Normal, or Positively Sloped, Yield Curve

Yield-to-Maturity

Maturity

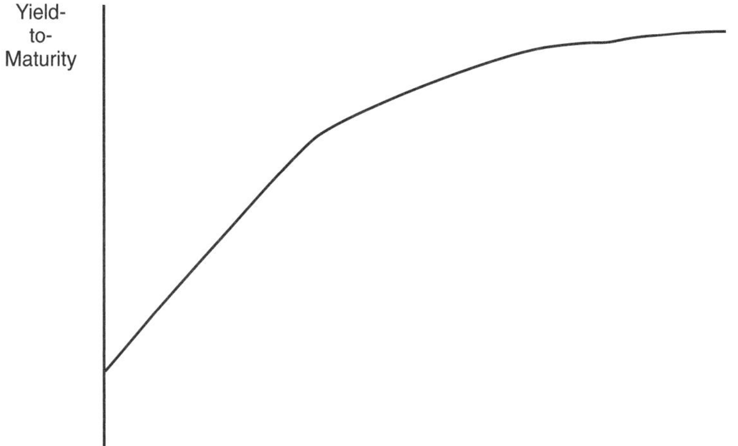

much as short-term interest rates do when short rates fall. (We will discuss the many reasons why long-term interest rates tend to be higher than short-term interest rates later in this chapter.) When the Fed lowers short-term interest rates, its monetary policy is considered good news because it lowers the cost of borrowing and is conducive toward a strengthening of economic activity, which is good news for corporate bonds, stocks, and other risk assets. A steep yield curve therefore generally forebodes good times for investors over a horizon of several quarters.

By contrast, a *negatively sloped*, or *inverted*, *yield curve* usually is seen as an indication that short-term interest rates are relatively high and are expected to remain high, with the Fed engaged in a strategy to slow the growth rate of the economy by raising the cost of borrowing. Figure 7.2 shows an inverted yield curve. In this type of environment, short-term interest rates are higher than long-term interest rates because of interest rate hikes by the Fed. This, of course, generally portends a gloomier set of conditions for bonds, stocks, and the economy because it raises the cost of borrowing. In fact, since 1970 every inverted yield curve has been followed by a period in which the S&P 500 earnings growth was negative, and it has almost always preceded either an economic slowdown or a recession. For example, the

FIGURE 7.2 An Inverted Yield Curve

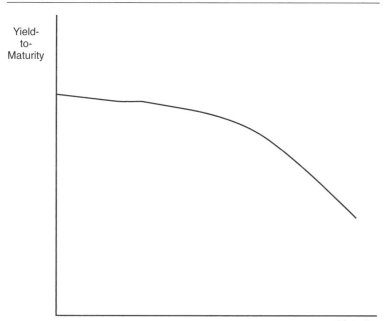

Yield-to-Maturity

Maturity

recession that began at the end of 2007 was preceded by an inversion of the yield curve in 2006.

Three Reasons to Follow the Yield Curve

There are three solid reasons to follow the yield curve as an economic and financial indicator. First, forecasting with the yield curve is relatively quick and simple and does not require a sophisticated analysis. A quick glance at the yield spread between 3-month T-bills and 10-year T-notes is all that is needed to draw a conclusion about the outlook of both the economy and the financial markets. Few indicators with such a stellar forecasting record have the yield curve's simplicity.

Second, the simplicity of the yield curve can be used to double-check conclusions drawn from more sophisticated indicators. If, for example, the conclusion drawn from the yield curve differs from the conclusion drawn from other indicators, the yield curve can serve as a red flag of sorts, perhaps highlighting situations in which the other indicators need rethinking. The yield curve also can be used to help identify potential flaws in other forecasting indicators that otherwise might have gone undetected. If the conclusions drawn from both the yield curve and the other indicators are the same, this can increase an investor's confidence in the conclusions.

Third, the yield curve serves as a useful gauge of market sentiment. The yield curve's shape, after all, results from the combined judgments of millions of investors. Therefore, its shape tells an investor a great deal about what other investors are thinking about the condition of the economy and the financial markets, as well as a variety of other conditions. This is important, of course, because market sentiment is an important indicator in and of itself.

A Crystal Ball Indeed

Throughout the years the yield curve has proved to be one of the best economic indicators among the many that exist. The yield curve is thought to be a better predictor of the economy than the stock market is, for instance, and it can give an investor an edge if the investor follows it. Indeed, studies have shown that the yield curve predicts economic events roughly 12 months or more in advance, while the stock market is thought to foretell events only 6 to 9 months in advance. History has proven that the yield curve can be used to make accurate forecasts of future developments in both the economy and the financial markets.

The yield curve is easily on sounder footing than are many other well-known indicators. It is certainly better than basing predictions on the winner of the Super Bowl or measuring hemlines. Incredibly, these so-called indicators are cited year after year as tools for reading the future.

In various studies the yield curve has been proven to be a superior financial indicator. In a study conducted by Haubrich and Dombrosky of the Federal Reserve, it was found that from 1965 to 1995 the yield curve performed as well as or better than seven professional forecasting services.[1] In a study by Estrella and Mishkin at the Federal Reserve, it was found that the yield curve was superior to the Conference Board's index of leading economic indicators (the Leading Economic Index, or the LEI).[2] That study found that unlike the yield curve, the LEI sent several incorrect signals in the 1982 to 1990 boom period. Estrella and Trubin found that the yield curve spread could be converted into a probability of recession, finding that the estimated probability of recession exceeded 30 percent in the case of each recession since 1968.[3] The findings are shown in Figure 7.3.

There are a number of reasons why the yield curve is one of the best financial indicators. One of my favorite reasons relates to the Federal

FIGURE 7.3 Probability of U.S. Recession 12 Months Ahead, as Predicted by the Treasury Spread, Monthly Average

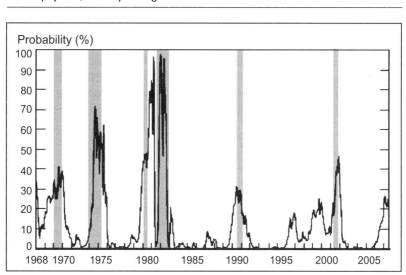

Notes: The probabilities are estimated using data from January 1959 to December 2005. The estimated probability of recession in July 2007 is 27 percent. The shaded areas indicate periods designated national recessions by the National Bureau of Economic Research (NBER).

Source: Author's calculations, based on data from the H.15 statistical release of the Federal Reserve System Board of Governors.

Reserve. Since the yield curve largely reflects actions or expected actions by the Fed, it contains a significant amount of information about monetary policy. This explanation of the yield curve's shape is called the *policy antici-pation hypothesis*. This hypothesis states that the yield curve captures market expectations of future Fed policy. Since market expectations about the Fed tend to be accurate, the yield curve thus is a terrific tool for forecasting the economy. Accurate assessments of the Fed have historically lead to accurate assessments of the economy's performance since the Fed's actions tend to have a large impact on the economy.

In essence, therefore, the yield curve captures a complex intermingling of policy actions, reactions, and real effects. The Federal Reserve's impact is of course smaller at times such as in the early 1990s and in the more recent finan-cial crisis when it has seemed that no amount of liquidity has been enough to boost bank lending. As of this writing, we can't know how far the de-leveraging process will go and for how long, so the signaling obtained from the yield curve could be a bit weaker than in the past, at least until the Federal Reserve's liquidity injections has been converted by banks into new loans.

Another reason the yield curve is such a good financial indicator is that it contains a significant amount of information about the risk premium on longer-term assets. The *risk premium* reflects the risks investors assign to holding various types of assets. For example, for junk bonds the risk pre-mium is considerably higher than it is for U.S. Treasuries. Along the Treasury yield curve, investors do not differentiate between the credit risks of holding various maturities, but they do differentiate between the risks of holding Treasuries with different maturity dates. This is known more commonly as the *term premium on rates*. Holding a 10-year T-note, for example, requires greater tolerance for uncertainties about inflation, economic growth, and other factors than does holding a 3-month T-bill.

The yield curve therefore contains a significant amount of information on the premium investors assign to long-term assets, from the standpoint of both credit and maturity length. The greater the uncertainties are, the less willing people will be to invest in long-term assets. An uncertainty in the cur-rent situation is the outlook for the U.S. budget deficit, the burden of which is shouldered by longer maturities. Conversely, when people are confident about the future, they are far more willing to invest in long-term assets.

There have been many occasions throughout U.S. history when the yield curve accurately foreshadowed events in the economy and the financial markets. Let's take a look at a few of them, starting with recent events.

As I mentioned earlier, the yield curve inverted in 2006, well in ad-vance of the recent recession, which began in December 2007. There were many causes of the inversion, but chief among them were the early actions of the Federal Reserve's campaign to raise interest rates, which began in June 2004 and lasted through June 2006. The rate hikes boosted the fed funds rate to 5.25 percent, up from 1.0 percent at the start of the campaign. The hikes, occurring amid signs of slowing in housing activity, were seen as potent enough to bring about an economic slowdown. This view was reflected in long-term rates, which also reflected the idea that inflation would be stable and that short-term interest rates might eventually fall as a result of a weaker economy. Suffice it to say, the yield curve's inversion was prescient.

While the yield curve was inverted, there were many who questioned the reasons why it was inverting. This is not uncommon when the yield curve inverts. My message to you when such doubts about inversions occur is simple: heed the message of the yield curve, and don't be fooled by detractors. In 2006, a common explanation for the low level of long-term rates relative to short-term rates was the idea that foreign investors—namely, China—were recycling the dollars they were earning through global trade back into dollars. While it is a credible explanation for the relatively low level of rates, ultimately fundamental influences drive long-term rates, not technical ones such as that. History tells us it is risky to doubt the messages inherent in the shape of the yield curve. The financial crisis makes this point abundantly clear.

The yield curve's powerful predictive value was evident in 2000 as well when the events of that year were forecast by the inversion of the yield curve that began in January 2000. Investors who heeded the yield curve's warnings at the start of that year piled a pot of gold. Almost everyone else wound up looking at their stocks like a deer in the headlights.

The inversion that began in January 2000 was the first such inversion since the recession of 1990 and 1991. Similar to 2006, many dismissed the inversion as being related to technical factors such as the U.S. buyback of the national debt (which entailed the purchase of long-dated maturities). Yet there were clearly other reasons for the inversion.

One reason the inversion occurred was that the bond market was beginning to believe that the Fed would have to raise short- term interest rates aggressively to contain the rapid growth in the economy. That is exactly what happened: the Fed raised rates a full percentage point over the next four months. In turn, bond investors began to believe that economic growth would decelerate. It did. Signs of economic weakness began to pile up by the end of 2000, and there were plentiful indications that the economy might enter into a recession in 2001, as it eventually did.

A second message contained in the inversion of the yield curve in 2000 was that stocks might fall. They did. Stock investors initially ignored that message, however, as well as the yield curve's message about what to expect from the Fed. Equity investors finally did get the message, of course, and the stock bubble soon burst. It was no coincidence that the Dow Jones Industrial Average peaked the same month that the yield curve inverted. The S&P 500 and the Nasdaq were not far behind, peaking just a couple of months later in March. Ten years later, the Nasdaq has remained well below its peak.

On the three prior occasions when the yield curve inverted—1980, 1982, and 1989—a recession soon followed. Each of these examples and those above clearly illustrate the powerful predictive value of the yield curve.

Figure 7.4 shows the yield spread between the 10-year T-note and the 3-month T-bill compared to year-over-year growth in real gross domestic product (GDP). The chart clearly shows that inversions in the yield spread almost always precede recessions. One must keep in mind that investors do not always know that a recession is under way until it is partly over. This means that even a short heads-up on a looming recession can be extremely valuable to investors.

While an inversion in and of itself is a powerful indicator of a recession, the probability of a recession increases with the magnitude of the yield curve's inversion. Estrella and Mishkin of the Federal Reserve, whose 1996 study covered the period 1960 to 1995, found values of the yield curve spread that corresponded to estimated probabilities of recession four quarters into the future. They found that the yield curve spread between the 10-year Treasury note and the 3-month T-bill was one of the most successful models

FIGURE 7.4 Yield Spread versus Real GDP Growth

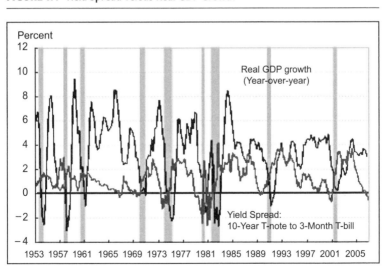

Source: Joseph G. Haubrich and Brent Meyer, "The Yield Curve's Predictive Power," *Economic Trends*, Federal Reserve Bank of Cleveland, December 2006.

TABLE 7.1 Estimated Recession Probabilities for Probit Model Using the Yield Curve Spread, Four Quarters Ahead

Recession Probability (%)	Value of Spread (percentage points)
5	1.21
10	0.76
15	0.46
20	0.22
25	0.02
30	−0.17
40	−0.50
50	−0.82
60	−1.13
70	−1.46
80	−1.85
90	−2.40

Note: The *yield curve spread* is defined as the spread between the interest rates on the 10-year Treasury note and the 3-month Treasury bill.

Source: Federal Reserve.

for predicting recession four quarters into the future. Table 7.1 shows their findings. As the table illustrates, an inverted spread of 2.4 percentage points implies a 90 percent probability of recession four quarters into the future. Remember that Figure 7.3 shows the probability of recession historically, as indicated by the actual yield curve spread. The main message from these findings is that the more inverted the yield curve, the greater the probability of recession in the future.

The previous examples clearly suggest that the yield curve is the bond market's equivalent of a crystal ball. It's a tool that is so simple to use that almost anyone can use it. I keep it in my toolbox at all times; I'm willing to hear out the detractors, but I do so very skeptically.

Three Main Reasons the Treasury Yield Curve Gets the Most Attention

The Treasury yield curve is by far the most closely followed yield curve. It is the first yield curve that market participants and forecasters look to for signals on the economy and the financial markets. There are three main reasons for this. First, because Treasuries are not seen as having little or no risk of default, the Treasury yield curve provides a "clean" look at where market participants believe interest rates should be along the various maturities. Unlike other yield curves, such as the yield curve on corporate bonds, the Treasury yield curve is not distorted by differences in creditworthiness. We know, for example, that market participants view the creditworthiness of 2-year Treasury notes as being equivalent to the creditworthiness of 10-year Treasury notes, putting aside for now the idea that longer maturities contain a term premium. The same cannot be said for other yield curves, which generally include a mix of different securities and therefore different degrees of creditworthiness.

Second, as was shown in Chapter 2, the U.S. Treasury market is by far the most liquid segment of the bond market. Its vast liquidity assures that the yields seen along the Treasury yield curve accurately reflect the value that market participants place on the securities. In other markets illiquidity and infrequent trading often distort yields and thus lead to inaccuracies in the yield curve.

Third, yields on Treasuries are far more accessible than are yields on other fixed-income securities. It is far simpler, for example, to obtain the yield on a 10-year T-note than it is to obtain the yield on a 10-year corporate bond because price information about Treasuries is far more widely disseminated. Moreover, when one is drawing a yield curve for securities other than Treasuries, choosing the specific security to place on the curve is a subjective decision. For example, deciding which corporate bonds to use in a yield curve for corporate bonds requires choosing among numerous different companies. This subjectivity can alter the reliability of the yield curve.

Largely for these three reasons, it is best to stick with the yield curve on Treasury securities to get the most accurate reflection of market sentiment and the most reliable signals on the outlook for both the economy and the financial markets.

Traditional Explanations for the Shape of the Yield Curve

There are many explanations for the different shapes of the yield curve. Ten factors are most prominent. Before we get into them, let's look at a few of the more traditional theories. There are three that are often cited: the expectations theory, the liquidity preference theory, and the market segmentation theory.

The *expectations theory* is based on the notion that the yield curve's shape is purely a function of investors' expectations of future interest rates.

According to this theory, when the yield curve is upward-sloping, it reflects expectations that future short-term interest rates will rise. Similarly, an inverted yield curve reflects expectations that future short-term interest rates will fall. In a flat yield curve environment, short-term interest rates are expected to be mostly constant. To some extent the pure expectations theory is similar to the policy anticipation hypothesis described earlier in this chapter because both theories are strongly influenced by expectations about monetary policy.

The *liquidity preference theory* holds that yields on longer-term maturities are higher than yields on short-term maturities because investors want additional compensation for the increased risks associated with holding longer-term maturities. This is also known as the *term premium* or *liquidity premium*. Investors recognize that maturity and price volatility are directly related. They also recognize that there are many other uncertainties in owning longer-term maturities compared with owning short-term maturities. It is therefore rational to think that investors want compensation for the added risks involved in owning long-term maturities. This is a very good explanation for why the yield curve on corporate bonds is almost always upward-sloping. Unlike Treasuries, credit risks on corporate bonds are subject to considerable uncertainties in the distant future. As a result, investors demand compensation for those risks, pushing long-term interest rates above short-term interest rates. This seems to make sense because today's star company may be a laggard or perhaps not even exist 30 years from now. It stands to reason, then, that the yield curve for corporate bonds is almost always upward-sloping.

The *market segmentation theory* is based on the notion that the yield curve's shape is determined by asset-liability constraints, either regulatory or self-imposed, that confine borrowers and creditors to specific maturity sectors. In other words, the shape of the yield curve is determined by the supply and demand for securities in different maturity sectors. Many banks, for example, are permitted by their charters to invest in maturities of no longer than five years. Restrictions such as this largely benefit short-term maturities, resulting in an upward slope to the yield curve.

The 10 Biggest Factors That Affect the Shape of the Yield Curve

Many factors have an impact on the shape of the yield curve. While the relative importance of each of these factors frequently changes, the following 10 factors that have been and probably will continue to be the most influential for years to come.

By gaining an understanding of the forces that shape the yield curve, you will be better able to spot potential changes in both the economic climate and the financial climate. In addition, you will be able to use your understanding of the yield curve to more deftly select bonds of varying maturities, credit quality, and characteristics that will perform optimally in different yield curve environments. Investors who understand the messages contained in the changing shape of the yield curve are likely to achieve a greater return on their investments than are those who take a more passive approach and ignore it.

Monetary Policy

The Fed is perhaps the single most influential factor in shaping the yield curve. This is the case mainly because the Fed controls short-term interest rates and the Fed's actions have a big bearing on the shape of the rest of the yield curve.

The Fed affects the short end of the yield curve when it raises or lowers the federal funds rate. The Fed controls this rate by adjusting the amount of money available in the banking system. When the Fed wants to raise the fed funds rate, it shrinks the monetary base essentially by selling Treasuries to banks and brokerages (forcing the banks and brokerages to pay for the bonds and hence reducing the amount of cash they hold). When the Fed wants to lower interest rates, it increases the monetary base by purchasing Treasuries from financial institutions. During the financial crisis, the Fed resorted to an extraordinary means of increasing the monetary base by purchasing agency-backed mortgage-backed securities, as well as agency debt, and U.S. Treasuries.

By adjusting the amount of money that exists in the banking system, the Federal Reserve is able to push the fed funds rate up and down. As the fed funds rate fluctuates, the interest rate on other short-term fixed-income securities moves in lockstep. Short-term maturities closely follow the fed funds rate for a couple of reasons. For one thing, changes in the money supply either increase or decrease the cost of money. This is reflected in short-term interest rates, which largely reflect the cost of money. A second key reason is that financial institutions usually operate on borrowed money to hold an inventory of notes and bonds.

For example, if the fed funds rate is 3 percent, it will cost financial institutions about that amount to borrow the money they need to hold an inventory of notes and bonds (they hold the notes and bonds to resell to their customers). Therefore, these institutions generally will be unwilling to hold securities yielding less than 3 percent because they do not want to incur what is called *negative carry*. Negative carry is incurred when the cost of financing to hold a security exceeds the rate of return on that security. Financial institutions are unwilling to engage in transactions with negative carry unless they feel that the cost of borrowing eventually will fall.

Over the years there have been very few times when borrowing costs exceeded the rates of return on fixed-income securities. Indeed, over the last 20 years, the yield on 2-year Treasury notes has dipped below the fed funds rate on only five occasions. On each of those occasions, it went below the fed funds rate within a short time of the Fed cutting interest rates, hence eliminating the negative carry dilemma that financial institutions like to avoid. Those five occasions provided terrific signals about the future course of monetary policy as well as the outlook on the economy. Importantly, the rarity of periods with negative carry illustrates clearly how closely tied the short end of the yield curve is to Fed policy. The consistency in the yield spread between short maturities and the fed funds rate therefore reinforces the notion that the yield curve is influenced directly by changes in Fed policy.

It is easy to see how the Fed has a major impact on short-term interest rates because the Fed controls the fed funds rate, which is an overnight rate. In turn, this affects the yield curve. When market participants expect the Fed to lower the fed funds rate, short-term interest rates fall faster than long-term interest rates, causing the yield curve to steepen. When the Fed raises interest rates, shorter maturities rise faster in yield (mostly because financial institutions fear negative carry situations and because investors feel that they can delay their purchases of short-term securities and get a higher interest rate on their investments if they wait). In this case shorter maturities underperform long-term maturities, and so the yield curve flattens.

While the Fed's adjustments of the fed funds rate are the primary way in which the Fed influences the yield curve, the Fed also has a big influence on long-term interest rates. Long-term interest rates tend to be affected less by the negative carry concerns simply because there is much more time for the negative carry situation to reverse itself. Long-term interest rates behave in a way that reflects expectations about where investors believe short-term interest rates will be in the future. One might say that long-term interest rates are a bet on future short-term interest rates. In this way the Fed affects long-term interest rates. In an inverted yield curve environment, for example, where long-term interest rates are lower than short-term interest rates, long-term interest rates reflect a bet that short-term interest rates eventually will decline.

An even more significant way in which the Fed affects long-term interest rates is through inflation expectations. Inflation expectations are generally the main driver of long-term interest rates. The Fed affects inflation expectations by using monetary policy. The Fed can lower inflation expectations by acting quickly and decisively against any emerging buildup of inflation pressures. Staunch anti-inflation resolve helps keep long-term interest rates relatively low by giving investors confidence that the returns on their bonds will not be diluted by inflation. As a result, investors will demand only a small interest rate premium over and above the inflation rate. However, investors will demand an added premium if they believe that the Fed is too lax and slow to act on inflation. In this environment the market will demand a higher interest rate to be compensated for the risk that inflation will rise and chew away at their investment returns.

As you can see, the Fed has a major influence on both ends of the yield curve.

Economic Growth

The status of the economy affects the yield curve in a number of ways. For starters, it directly affects monetary policy. When the Fed feels that economic growth is too strong (increasing the risk of inflation), it responds by raising short-term interest rates. When economic growth is low relative to the economy's growth potential, the Fed lowers short-term interest rates. Both actions affect the yield curve.

Another way in which economic activity affects the yield curve is through the way that capital is allocated in the economy. For example, when the level of economic activity weakens, banks usually make fewer loans as a result of both a reluctance to lend and weak private demand for capital. As a result, banks have cash that they can invest elsewhere, and they often invest the money in fixed-income securities, including U.S. Treasury securities, although in recent years most of the securities held by banks have been agency mortgage-backed securities. When economic growth strengthens, banks feel they can generate greater returns on their capital by lending their money instead of investing in securities. Banks therefore sell (or just stop buying) their securities holdings, causing the short end of the yield curve to underperform the rest of the curve and flattening the yield curve.

Also, when economic conditions are strong, investors are less drawn to the safety element of short-term securities. They would rather spend and invest their money in equities and the real economy than buy notes and bonds. This tends to flatten the yield curve as investors shy away from short-term maturities. Of course, when the economic environment sours, investors are less driven to spend their free capital and therefore channel more of it into fixed-income securities. Anxieties increase in such times, spurring a flight-to-safety move into shorter maturities and steepening the yield curve. This occurred in dramatic fashion during the financial and economic crisis in 2001.

Fiscal Policy

Around the globe, the experiences of numerous countries throughout the years have illustrated the important role that government finances play in the shape of the yield curve. In countries that have big fiscal deficits, for example, interest rates tend to be higher across the yield curve than they are in countries with relatively smaller deficits. Conversely, in countries with sound balance sheets, interest rates tend to be lower than is the case in countries with larger deficits. Today, with the public sector having had to use its balance sheet to support the private sector, there is increased focus on sovereign credit risk, with investors more intensely scrutinizing the fiscal condition of sovereign nations. The focus is likely to mean that the impact of fiscal policy on the bond market will likely increase in the time ahead as investors give greater consideration to country risk when formulating their investment strategies.

The specific ways in which government finances affect the shape of the yield curve vary, depending on how good or bad a country's fiscal situation is. If a country's fiscal situation is horrendously bad, for example, to the point where the markets are concerned about the possibility that the country will default on its obligations, short-term interest rates tend to be much higher than long-term interest rates. This occurs because investors will demand large compensation for the risk they take in investing in debt that may not be repaid as well as for the risks of currency depreciation. However, longer-term debt does not yield nearly as much in such a situation because investors will bet that the fiscally challenged government will reform itself eventually and create a better overall interest rate environment in the future. But governments in such situations are the exception and not the rule in the industrialized world. How do fiscal issues affect the yield curve in those countries?

Generally speaking, rising budget deficits tend to make the yield curve steeper while falling budget deficits tend to flatten the curve. Here's why.

If investors believe that a government will have big budget deficits as far as the eye can see, they will demand compensation for the risk that an ever-increasing amount of government securities will be sold in the future to finance the deficits. Investors therefore will tend to push up long-term interest rates more than short-term interest rates, reflecting a term premium, because the more time there is, the greater the set of possible outcomes. After all, if an investor bought a 30-year government bond in a country with a shaky fiscal situation, that investor might be able to get a higher interest rate 5 years from now because the supply of 30-year bonds will have increased (as a result of the soaring budget deficit).

Moreover, in 5 years' time the government's finances may be even shakier, putting that 30-year bond at risk. Therefore, the longer the maturity is, the greater the risk is that things could get worse before they get better. Short-term maturities, in contrast, are affected more by short-term considerations, chiefly the government's ability to repay its debt now. These scenarios hold as long as the risk of default is not imminent.

Inflation Expectations

The bond market's perceptions of inflation have a large impact on the shape of the yield curve. That impact is felt in a number of ways. The most important impact is on Fed policy. If the bond market believes that inflation risks are significant enough to prompt the Fed to raise interest rates, short-term interest rates will rise faster than will long-term interest rates and thus flatten the yield curve. Of course, this assumes that the market has confidence that the Fed can quash inflation before it becomes a problem.

In addition to the way inflation expectations affect perceptions of Fed policy and therefore short-term maturities, inflation expectations have a large bearing on the performance of long-term maturities. In fact, inflation expectations are one of the most influential factors affecting long-term interest rates. Here's why.

Suppose an investor were considering whether to invest in a 30-year bond yielding 5 percent when inflation was running at 1.5 percent, for a "real yield" of 3.5 percent. At the outset, the investor probably was assuming that real yields would hold at around 3.5 percent or lower throughout his holding period, which could be for as long as 30 years. The investor has decided that that rate is good enough for him or her. But if the investor began to worry that inflation eventually might rise to 5 percent, he or she would be far less likely to invest in bonds yielding 5 percent and would demand a return of, say, 8.5 percent, in order to maintain the same real interest rate described under the first scenario. In situations such as this, when inflation expectations rise and an investor's real rate of return is threatened, the yield curve would get steeper as longer maturities underperformed shorter maturities because of rising inflation expectations.

Rising inflation expectations also have a bearing on the way that for-eign investors view the value of a country's currency, which in turn affects the way that investors view the outlook for that country's bonds.

The U.S. Dollar

As just mentioned, the value of the dollar significantly influences the shape of the Treasury yield curve largely because of the extent of foreign investment in the United States. Indeed, foreign investors owned about 48 percent of all U.S. Treasuries outstanding in December 2009, and they have been the biggest holders of Treasuries for many years. Since foreign investors are the biggest lenders to Uncle Sam, their level of continued interest in U.S. Trea-suries is closely watched. Bond investors recognize that for foreign inves-tors, the performance of the U.S. dollar is a critical aspect of the investment decision process. They recognize that in many cases foreign investors must sell their own currencies and buy dollars to pay for the Treasuries they pur-chase, thus incurring currency risks. Moreover, foreign investors have many choices in terms of what they can invest in. Fluctuations in and the outlook for the dollar therefore can affect the bond market's perceptions about what foreign investors will do next.

If, for example, the U.S. dollar weakened in a rapid and disorderly way relative to other currencies, bond investors might become concerned that foreign investors eventually would become less willing to finance Uncle Sam's borrowing needs. They would demand greater compensation when buying long-term Treasuries because they would be concerned that reduced foreign demand for Treasuries in the future would push overall interest rates higher. This would result in a steep yield curve.

From 2002 through 2009, the U.S. dollar fell by about 33 percent on a trade-weighted basis (using the Federal Reserve's trade-weighted dollar index as a gauge). Although the nominal amount of Treasuries that foreign investors owned jumped sharply from $1 trillion in 2002 to $3.5 trillion at the end of 2009, the proportion of international reserve assets that foreign investors held in dollars fell from 70 to 63 percent. Furthermore, their hold-ings of the euro increased to 27 percent of the world's reserve assets, up from 20 percent. In other words, although it might seem that the world couldn't get enough Treasuries, the fact is foreign investors have been diversifying their assets out of dollars into other assets. This hasn't been a problem be-cause demand has been more than sufficient relative to the size of Treasury offerings, but if the dollar's decline were to become rapid and disorderly, the equation could change. The "rapid and disorderly rule" is one to stick by whenever you think gradual moves in the dollar will affect markets. They haven't thus far, and it has typically paid to "fade" any moves in the financial markets associated with these gradual moves.

Another way the U.S. dollar affects the yield curve is through its impact on inflation expectations. A strong dollar tends to reduce inflation expectations because it reduces the cost of U.S. imports. This tends to contribute to a flattening of the yield curve. A weak dollar, by contrast, tends to raise inflation expectations because it raises the cost of U.S. imports, contributing to a steepening of the yield curve.

Flight to Quality

In times of political, economic, or financial uncertainty, the United States is a magnet for capital. This was the case even during the financial crisis despite the fact that the United States was at the center of the crisis. In times of uncertainty, both domestic and global investors express a preference for short-term maturities. They do this because short-term maturities carry the least amount of risk to the invested principal. In times of crisis investors shift their focus from the return on capital to the return of capital. The best way for investors to ensure the return of their capital is to invest in securities with the least amount of risk both in terms of liquidity and price. When investors have this mindset, they tend to invest heavily in short-term securities, particularly short-term U.S. Treasuries. As a result, short-term maturities tend to outperform long-term maturities, resulting in a steepening of the yield curve.

Note that during times of uncertainty, investors typically express a preference for short-term maturities not only to protect their capital but in the expectation that the Federal Reserve will respond to the crisis by lowering short-term interest rates. This further increases the tendency of the yield curve to get steeper in times of crisis. Figure 7.5 shows the sharp steepening of the yield curve that took place following the intensification of financial market stresses in the aftermath of Lehman's fall in September 2008.

Credit Quality

Concerns about credit quality develop when investors worry about the ability of bond issuers to repay their debt obligations. The concerns generally develop when the economy weakens, financial conditions tighten, or there is much uncertainty. Any or all of these conditions can be caused by each other. The effects that concerns about credit quality have on the yield curve are similar to the effects that financial crises have on it. In fact, concerns

FIGURE 7.5 Yield Spread between 10-Year Treasury Notes and 3-Month Treasury Bills

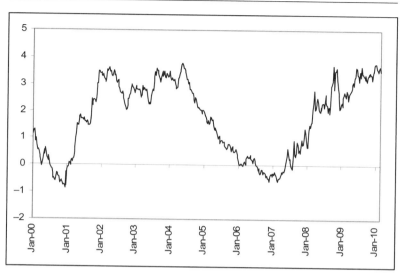

Source: Federal Reserve Bank of New York.

about credit quality often go hand in hand with crises episodes. During such times, the yield curve tends to get steeper.

Views on credit quality are not limited to bouts of worry—there are many situations in which the market's views of the general level of creditworthiness can be quite the opposite. During such times the yield curve tends to flatten. Indeed, the yield curve often flattens when perceptions about credit quality improve, particularly during times of economic prosperity. The reason is simple: When the economy prospers, investors believe that growing corporate coffers and firming household balance sheets reduce the risks of widespread problems in the financial system. As a result, investors become less interested in owning short-term maturities and are more willing to purchase long-term maturities, flattening the yield curve. In times of prosperity, monetary policy is generally tighter than it is in times when the economy is weak, and this contributes to a flatter yield curve.

The timing at which the varying views about credit quality affect the yield curve depends on economic and financial conditions and their degree of entrenchment and intensity when views about credit quality start moving in reverse of their trend. For example, in 2009, even though concerns about credit quality had stabilized from the throes of 2008, financial and economic conditions were so adverse that the yield curve continued to steepen, reflecting the view that any change in monetary policy (toward higher rates) would be delayed for an extended period. Had the stabilization in concerns about credit quality occurred when initial conditions were better, it is more likely that a flatter yield curve would have followed sooner. This is because alleviated concerns about credit quality tend to be associated with improving economic and financial conditions, which increases the odds that the Fed's next move will be to raise interest rates.

Competition for Capital

All financial assets face competition for capital to one degree or another. Fixed-income assets face no less competition than do other asset classes. In fact, it can be argued that fixed-income assets face more competition for capital than do other asset classes because bonds over the very long term have registered a lower rate of return than the equity market, which investors have tended to be enamored with. As a result, when assets such as equities are deemed attractive, it is usually the bond market that's left out in the cold as investors shun bonds in hopes of receiving a higher rate of return elsewhere.

When the bond market faces high levels of competition for capital from other asset classes, the yield curve typically gets steeper. This occurs because the high rates of return investors are receiving elsewhere tend to prompt investors to demand higher-than-normal rates of return in the bond market too. They do this by demanding higher real rates of return. This usually is manifested by higher long-term interest rates where real yields tend to be highest. In turn, the yield curve gets steeper. In contrast, when the competition for capital is low, real yields compress and the yield curve usually flattens. In 2009, despite a rebound in equities prices, real rates of return moved lower, reflecting the idea that the rates of return in equities as well as in other financial assets would likely be restrained by the deep secular forces at the root of the economic and financial crisis.

Treasury Supply

Historically a technical influence, Treasury supply tends to affect the yield curve in a predictable way. For example, when the Treasury is issuing securities on the long end of the yield curve, Wall Street's primary dealers, which are required to bid at the auctions, tend to "set up" the auctions by cheapening the issues to provide a concession to investors to entice them to buy. Dealers do this by either selling longer-dated maturities outright or selling longer-dated maturities against shorter maturities. These actions result in either a steeper yield curve or higher yields, or both. The auction setup generally takes place in the immediate aftermath of auction announcements, and it lasts up until the auctions take place. Thereafter, securities that underperform in advance of supply tend to outperform.

When I say that supply has been a technical influence "historically," I do so in an attempt to draw a distinction between the then and now. Today, investors need to recognize that sovereign credit risk is more in focus than ever before, which means that supply might in the time ahead have a more lasting influence on yields than it has in the past when it was (and still largely is) a short-term influence.

Portfolio Shifts

When bond portfolio managers want to express their bullishness or bearishness on the bond market, they adjust the duration of their portfolios and concentrate their portfolio risk in different areas of the yield curve. When portfolio managers are bullish, they extend their duration because doing so increases a portfolio's price sensitivity to changes in interest rates. Portfolios therefore can benefit when yields decline and prices rise.

While intuitively it would seem that extensions to portfolio duration would flatten the yield curve, the decision to extend usually happens at a time when the yield curve is prone to become steeper. This is because during such times portfolio managers reach their higher duration levels by adding exposure to the short end of the yield curve. Confused? How can a portfolio increase its duration exposure by concentrating its purchases on the short end of the yield curve, where duration levels are lower than those of longer maturities? The explanation is that portfolio managers either purchase securities or add duration exposure via futures or swaps in multiples of what they would purchase if they had purchased securities of higher duration. In this way the yield curve gets steeper. It also shifts, with yields moving lower across the yield curve. Generally, when portfolio managers are bullish in the aggregate, the yield curve gets steeper since yields on short-term maturities typically fall more than do yields on long-term maturities in such an environment.

Summary

- As we have seen, the yield curve has proven to be one of the best financial indicators available. It is a time-tested indicator that continuously shows its predictive value.
- The yield curve is extremely simple to understand and can be used by almost anyone.

- When evaluating the yield curve, remember to stay focused on its shape and evaluate the extent to which the factors listed above may be influencing its shape. This way, you are more likely to pinpoint the message of the market. For example, there will be times when the yield curve's shape changes as a result of technical factors. When it does, you will know to discount any message that the yield curve might seem to signal with respect to fundamentals on the economy and the financial markets.
- The next time you're looking for a crystal ball to peer into the future of the economy and the financial markets, turn to the yield curve.

8

REAL YIELDS
Where Real Messages Can Be Found

One of the best tools bond investors can put in their toolboxes is an understanding of real yields. A bond's *real yield* measures its rate of return minus inflation. In other words, the real yield on a bond is its stated, or quoted, yield-to-maturity minus the current rate of inflation. There is almost always some real yield incorporated into bond yields, largely because investors want compensation for the risks they take in parting with their money. Moreover, in a world where there are many competing investment choices, investors demand compensation to be enticed to purchase bonds instead of other assets.

The amount of compensation investors require in the form of real yields for the risks they take and the opportunity costs they bear varies with a wide variety of factors. It is in these variations in real yields that real messages can be found. Put simply, the fluctuations in real yields contain messages about the condition of the bond market that are not necessarily evident in nominal rates.

Equity investors look at price-to-earnings (P/E) and other ratios, using a historical perspective to draw conclusions about the value of stocks and/or the market on any given day; the same thing is done in the bond market. By looking at where real yields have stood in the past, we can answer the question: Is the market overvalued or undervalued? Real rates can give a fixed-income investor a good perspective on whether bond market yields are too high or too low for a given set of fundamentals. They provide a quick and simple method of valuing a bond. The following are a couple of examples.

Suppose the nominal yield on a 10-year U.S. Treasury note moves from 6 percent to 4 percent over a period of two years. On the surface the yield decline might lead some investors to shy away from investing in the 10-year

T-note because rates optically are less attractive than they were before. After all, the yield decline here is quite substantial. However, investors who approach it this way are making a classic error by not putting their focus where it should be—that is, on real rates. In this example, if the inflation rate over the two-year period fell from 3.0 percent to 1.0 percent, real rates would have held steady at 3 percent (6 percent minus 4 percent and 4 percent minus 1 percent). Thus, while it is true that the nominal yield became less attractive during the period, the real yield did not.

Consider a situation in which nominal rates rise to 6 percent from 5 percent but inflation also rises, moving to 3 percent from 1 percent. In this case some investors might be misled into thinking that just because interest rates increased a full percentage point to 6 percent, the investment is more attractive than it was when nominal rates were at 5 percent. The reality, however, is that it is a less desirable investment than it was before because real rates fell to 3 percent from 4 percent. There is an obvious caveat to this, however. If investors have a firm conviction that inflation eventually will fall and indeed it does fall, investing when nominal rates are at 6 percent is the more attractive investment.

It pays to look beyond nominal rates when making a judgment about yields. One can't judge a book by its cover, and it's no different in the bond market.

Historical Perspective on Real Yields

Forming opinions and judgments about the many messages contained in prevailing levels of real yields is relatively simple, but it is necessary to have a perspective on where real yields have been historically. Once you have this perspective, you will be able to quickly form an opinion not only on the valuation of the bond market but on a wide variety of issues related to the Fed, the economy, inflation, and more.

The best way to gain a perspective on real yields is to focus on U.S. Treasuries. Doing this will help you steer clear of the confusion that can result from having to pinpoint the many possible causes of fluctuations in real yields on other fixed-income securities, particularly the credit component of yields on other types of bonds. This is a must in analyzing real yields because the main objective in this case is to get the big picture and avoid getting bogged down in details. For example, if the real yield on a particular corporate bond increased sharply, the increase could be attributable to many factors, such as company-specific problems, woes in the company's industry, or a change in risk attitudes causing a widening of credit spreads.

Although information like this is important, it will not reveal much about certain other issues such as inflation expectations, and the Fed. Treasuries have the distinct advantage of being free of micro issues such as creditworthiness. They are also simpler to use than other fixed-income securities partly because prices on Treasuries are more widely available than those on other types of bonds and because of the ease with which you can choose specific Treasuries for your analysis. In contrast, deciding which specific security to choose from among the many other types of bonds is a much more difficult task because of the many differences that exist in their creditworthiness, industry type, and other factors.

Now that we've decided that it's best to use Treasuries when tracking real yields, the next step is to get a perspective on the historical behavior of real yields. By doing this, you will be in a much better position to draw conclusions about the messages contained in the level of real yields. It is as simple as knowing the range in which real yields tend to fluctuate and the forces that cause real yields to fluctuate within that range.

The first thing to keep in mind is that real yields are almost always positive except in periods when inflation is much higher than the historical average, such as the 1970s, or on the very long end of the yield curve when the central bank rate is seen as punitive enough that it would be expected to bring the current inflation rate much lower, such that investors would be willing to purchase bonds at yields that are below the inflation rate.

When tracking real yields, an investor has to decide on an inflation gauge to use and a maturity to track. Most choose the consumer price index, but the GDP price deflator is also favored. As for maturity selection, some observers prefer to look at short maturities, while others prefer long maturities. Which is better? It depends on the type of analysis an investor is conducting. An analysis of the behavior of real yields on both maturities, however, probably will lead an investor to draw similar conclusions. Nevertheless, I believe that real yields on long-dated maturities contain the most messages. Intuitively, this makes sense because long-dated maturities contain information about both the short term and the long term; for example, it can be said that long-term rates reflect a string of bets on where short-term rates will be in the future.

I like to examine the real yield on both 10-year T-notes and 30-year T-bonds. Let's take a look at where they've been over the last few decades. We can start by looking at Figure 8.1. It shows that the real yield on the 30-year T-bond generally has been slightly higher than the real yield on the 10-year T-note. This can be attributed to its longer maturity: the longer the maturity on a bond, the more time there is for a wide variety of factors to affect its performance. The extra yield that exists on longer-term maturities

FIGURE 8.1 Real Yield on 10-Year Treasury Notes and 30-Year Treasury Bonds

Source: Federal Reserve and U.S. Bureau of Labor Statistics.

is the so-called *term premium*. Uncertainty about the future is therefore the biggest reason for the historical difference in real yields on 10-year and 30-year Treasuries.

A relatively new way in the U.S. Treasury market to gauge real yields is through the TIPS market, the market for the Treasury's inflation-protected securities. As described in Chapter 4, the yield difference between the stated yield-to-maturity on an inflation-indexed Treasury versus that of a conventional Treasury is a measure of the bond market's inflation expectations. This means that the stated yield-to-maturity on an inflation-indexed Treasury is its real yield. For example, on June 19, 2009, the stated yield-to-maturity on a 10-year inflation-indexed Treasury was 1.849 percent, and the stated yield-to-maturity on a conventional Treasury 3.783 percent. The yield difference of 1.934 percent means that the market was priced for the consumer price index to increase at a 1.934 percent pace over the next 10 years. What remains—the stated yield-to-maturity on the inflation-indexed Treasury—reflects the real yield for 10-year Treasuries. See Chapter 4 for more information about TIPS.

Figure 8.1 shows that with the exception of a few outlying periods, real yields tend to be confined to a relatively narrow range. Importantly, real yields fluctuate much less than do nominal yields. This suggests that bond investors are fairly consistent in their demands for compensation against future risks. Any changes that occur do so over a relatively long period of time.

Figure 8.2 provides an additional perspective on the historical range in real yields. Note that in the 1960s, the real yield on the 10-year U.S. Treasury note, as measured by its average yield minus the average year-over-year change in the consumer price index, averaged 2.26 percent. The decade of the 1960s was similar to the 1990s in terms of trends in both economic growth and inflation, although the timing in which interest rates within each decade were at their lowest and their highest was the opposite. Still, both periods had similar characteristics in terms of growth rates and productivity and the forces that helped to keep interest rates relatively low. In the 1970s, real yields fell sharply, averaging just 0.43 percent, as high levels of inflation cut into nominal yields. In the 1980s the real yield on the 10-year increased sharply to an average of 4.96 percent owing to rising budget deficits and high levels of competition for capital. Also boosting real yields in the 1980s were the extraordinarily high short-term interest rates put in place by the Federal Reserve to combat the double-digit inflation that had developed in the late 1970s and early 1980s. In the 1990s, when both inflation and the budget deficit fell, real yields simmered down. A booming stock market created significant competition for capital as well as demand for credit, and this probably kept real rates from falling as much as they would have otherwise.

FIGURE 8.2 U.S. 10-Year Treasury Notes Yield Minus the Year-Over-Year Change in the Consumer Price Index

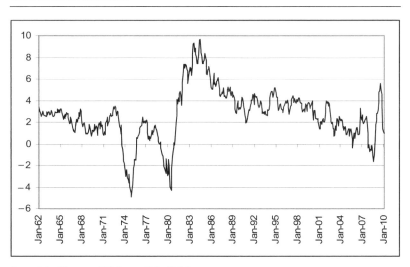

Source: Federal Reserve and U.S. Bureau of Labor Statistics.

The real yield on the 10-year generally spends its time in a range of about 2 to 4 percent except during extraordinary periods. The long-term range on the 30-year T-bond appears to be a bit higher than that.

Real yields can serve as a useful reference for the general behavior of real rates. By remaining cognizant of both the norms and the extremes, an investor can put almost any level of real yields into perspective.

Factors That Cause Real Yields to Fluctuate

Many factors determine the real yield on a bond. For simplicity, I will focus on government bonds rather than corporate bonds and other types. Here's a list of major factors:

- Inflation expectations
- Opportunity costs of investing in bonds versus other assets
- The economy's growth rate
- The U.S. budget situation
- Currency performance
- The Federal Reserve
- Market liquidity and volatility

Inflation Expectations

In the long run the most important influence on real yields is the expected inflation rate. When inflation is falling or low, real yields tend to be low because investors are more willing to accept a low real yield in the expectation that inflation will keep falling or stay low and therefore produce an acceptable return after inflation. Moreover, it is often the case that low-rate environments are the result of slow economic activity, and in such times the rate of return on other assets declines. Investors in this case require less of a real yield when purchasing bonds.

By contrast, investors demand high real yields when they expect inflation to rise to offset the potential erosion of their capital. Bond investors are always cognizant of the possibility that inflation will erode the value of their money and quite possibly take away their returns completely. As a result, when investors are concerned that inflation may accelerate, they demand a higher real rate of return to offset that risk. The extent to which investors demand compensation for inflation risks depends largely on their most recent experience with inflation. In the early 1980s, for example, the double-digit inflation experienced in the 1970s lingered in investors' minds, resulting in very high real yields for several years after inflation peaked.

Similarly, as the U.S. economy gathered momentum in 1994, bond investors drove real yields sharply higher partly out of fear that inflation would accelerate. It was a rational fear because inflation had climbed to over 6 percent at the end of the previous expansion in the late 1980s. However, as that fear of inflation proved to be false, real yields began to fall, and by the late 1990s, inflation seemed only a distant memory. Investors demanded very little compensation for inflation risks despite economic growth rates that in past years would have caused bond investors to shudder with inflation concerns. Investors harbored few worries about inflation because their most recent experience led them to believe that inflation probably would *not* accelerate.

When investors sense that the inflation rate is falling or about to fall, they generally are willing to accept a lower real rate for a while in hopes that the inflation rate will decline.

Opportunity Costs of Investing in Bonds versus Other Assets

A second important factor affecting real yields and one that has had a large impact over the past decade or so is the compensation investors demand for the opportunity cost of investing in bonds compared to assets such as corporate equities, commodities, real estate, and private equity. Most bond investors recognize, for example, that investment returns on corporate equities have, over the very long term, outpaced returns on bonds. This is acceptable to many investors, of course, because they purchase bonds to diversify their portfolios, provide an income stream, and add safety elements to their portfolios. These investors are therefore somewhat indifferent to the idea that the rates of return they earn by owning bonds might lag the return they might earn on other assets.

There is a limit to this indifference, however. When the return on other asset classes far outpaces the return on bonds and when it appears that the returns may be sustained, money almost certainly will be channeled away from the bond market. Bond investors will not pull out en masse, of course, but they will reduce their allocation for bonds for the allure (illusion?) of higher returns elsewhere. This reduced demand for bonds pushes up real yields because bond investors want to be compensated for the opportunity costs they feel they are incurring by shunning other assets. Hence, when the competition for capital is high, bond investors demand higher real yields.

This is precisely what happened in the late 1990s, when a roaring stock market prevented real yields from falling as much as many felt they should have as a result of the elimination of the federal budget deficit, rising productivity rates, and *disinflation*—that is, a slowing in the rate of inflation (*deflation* is defined as an outright decline in prices). When returns on alternative investments sour, as occurred when the financial bubble burst in 2000 and then again in the late 2000s when the housing and financial crisis took hold, bond investors become less choosy. They turn their focus away from the return *on* capital and toward the return *of* capital. In this case real yields fall as investors basically settle for a low rate of return in exchange for the relative safety of bonds.

It is notable that in the aftermath of the financial crisis, real interest fell sharply, doing so despite conditions that were the opposite of the late 1990s in terms of the U.S. budget deficit. The two periods illustrate the large bearing that private demand for credit has on real rates. In other words, during boom times, real rates will tend to be high, reflecting high levels of private demand for credit. During economic downturns, real rates will tend to be low, reflecting weak levels of private demand for credit.

The Economy's Growth Rate

The level of economic activity is also a key determinant of real yields. The economy's effect on real yields is similar to the effects of competition for capital on real yields. The pace of economic activity basically affects the allocation of capital in the economy in the same way that competition for capital affects the allocation of capital in the financial markets. When the economy is growing rapidly, for example, all sorts of financial and corporate entities seek capital: banks seek capital for loans, technology companies seek money for research and development, small businesses seek working capital for inventory investment, and so forth. The more money these and other entities seek for real economic activity, the less money there is available for investment in the bond market, resulting in higher real yields.

Banks, for example, which typically hold a fairly large amount of bonds (during most of 2009, banks held about 25 percent of their assets in fixed-income securities), increase their lending activity when the economy is strong. As a result, banks have less money available to allocate for financial investments and therefore reduce their purchases of bonds accordingly, contributing to a rise in real interest rates. In contrast, when the economy is weak, banks reduce their lending activity and increase their purchases of bonds. This is precisely what happened during the financial crisis, with banks cutting their lending, while at the same time increasing their securities purchases, as shown in Figures 8.3 and 8.4. A very similar pattern occurred

FIGURE 8.3 Loans and Leases at U.S. Commercial Banks, in Billions of Dollars

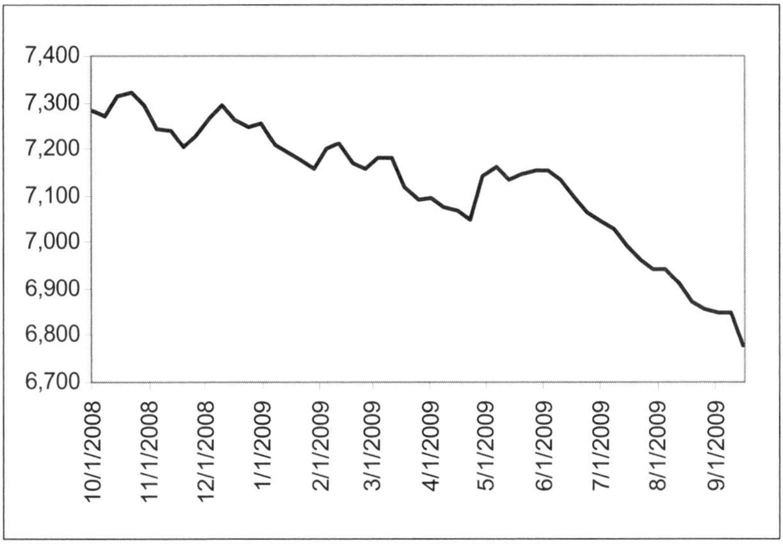

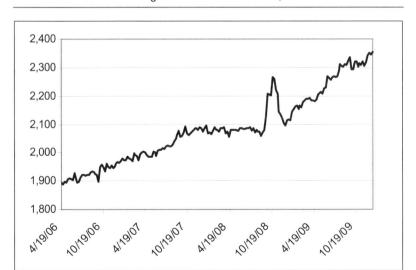

Source: Federal Reserve.

FIGURE 8.4 Securities Holdings at U.S. Commercial Banks, in Billions of Dollars

Source: Federal Reserve.

during the savings and loan crisis of the early 1990s when banks sharply curtailed their lending activities and sharply increased their purchases of bonds, contributing to a decline in real interest rates.

Similar to the behavior of banks, a wide variety of corporate entities shift money in and out of the bond market depending on the economic environment. For example, insurance companies, which are big holders of corporate bonds, will move money between corporate equities and corporate bonds. Pension funds will also vary their allocations, although certainly not with great frequency given their mandate.

The level of economic growth basically affects the aggressiveness with which businesses bid for financing. This affects the price of money: interest rate levels.

The U.S. Budget Situation

Another important factor that affects real yields is the U.S. budget situation, but the impact often is either difficult to decipher or seemingly not present at all. This is because whenever the U.S. budget situation deteriorates, it tends to be when the U.S. economic situation has deteriorated. During such times, the Treasury issues more securities than normal, yet both nominal and real yields tend to be low because of the weak economy and lowered private demand for capital. In other words, supply has very little or no bearing on rates because other more powerful factors are in play. Where then does the impact of the budget deficit show itself? The answer, based on the behavior of real rates over the past few decades, is that it shows itself when concerns about the budget deficit rise above the norm—when investors are unsure about the path of the U.S. budget situation and they are worried that its deterioration may be more structural than cyclical.

This is what happened in the 1980s and into the very early 1990s when both nominal and real rates were higher than in the years that followed. The so-called pay-as-you-go ("pay-go") budget system put in place in 1991 helped break the cycle, and the deficit in fiscal year 1992 reached its 1990s peak at $290.4 billion. During the Clinton years, the U.S. budget situation steadily improved and swung to a surplus of as high as $236.9 billion in fiscal year 2000. Investor confidence in the U.S. budget situation increased along with the improvement, driving down both nominal and real interest rates. The budget situation was so good that the U.S. began buying back its own debt (those were the days!). It is probably not a coincidence that real yields on Treasuries and other fixed-income products began to decline as the government's fiscal situation improved and the supply of both new and existing Treasuries diminished.

In 2008, 2009, and early 2010, real interest rates were behaving as they normally do in times when economic growth and private demand for credit are weak. There were few if any signs that investors were behaving as they did in any parts of the 1980s or before pay-go was instituted in 1991. This probably has to do with the severity of the economic downturn. Still, there are limits, and it is difficult to judge at what point the situation crosses over and investors focus more on the structural nature of the U.S. debt problem. If they do, expect both nominal and real interest rates to increase accordingly.

Currency Performance

Real yields are affected by currency performance in two ways in particular. The first relates to inflation. In countries whose currency tends to appreciate, inflation will be biased lower. In turn, real yields in these countries will be biased lower, reflecting the relatively smaller inflation premium that investors will tend to build into yields relative to countries with higher inflation risks. Second, currency performance will impact cross-border flows. Investors will tend to be more interested in investing in countries whose currencies are appreciating, both because capital gains opportunities will be greater and because appreciating currencies help to preserve a currency's purchasing power. It can be said that real yields can affect currency performance because investors endeavor to earn a high real interest rate, and they will be attracted to countries whose real yields are high, as long as the reasons for the high real yields do not stack against the idea.

The Federal Reserve

Another factor that affects real yields is the Federal Reserve. There are two main ways in which the Fed affects real yields. First, expectations of changes in monetary policy cause interest rates to fluctuate, affecting real yields. If, for example, bond investors expect the Fed to raise interest rates, they will demand higher interest rates as compensation, pushing up both nominal and real yields. The Fed generally raises interest rates when inflation is accelerating or at least about to, yet inflation takes time to accelerate and more time to decelerate—a lag of as much as two years from the trough of the business cycle.

Thus, at the onset of Fed rate increases, real yields may rise, but the rise can be temporary because of the usual lag between growth and inflation, inflation eventually accelerates. In a sense, inflation catches up with the Fed's interest rate increase, and real yields eventually shrink for a while. Then, as the interest rate hikes take hold, economic activity slows a bit. Investors, sensing that the inflation rate will also slow, drive down both nominal and real yields, and when the inflation rate does indeed fall, real yields increase to a level that investors are comfortable with considering the many influences that can affect real yields.

Expected changes in monetary policy affect real yields along the entire yield curve but have a disproportionate effect on the short end of the curve. This is the case because the Fed controls short-term interest rates and because long-term interest rates are affected by a wide variety of factors. Nevertheless, the Fed has a large impact on long-term interest rates too, and this is another way in which the Fed affects real yields. As I just alluded to, when market participants believe that interest rate changes will affect inflation, they adjust interest rates accordingly, affecting real yields. Changes in inflation expectations that are prompted by actions taken by the Federal Reserve are essentially leaps of faith by investors regarding the future inflation rate. The degree to which investors take that leap of faith depends on the amount of goodwill built up by the central bank.

When the Fed has a lot of goodwill, as it did during Alan Greenspan's tenure, real yields tend to be lower, reflecting investors' optimism about the inflation outlook. This occurs because the Fed's accumulation of goodwill translates into confidence in its ability to prevent inflation. The more confidence investors have in the Fed's ability to keep inflation low, the less real yield they will demand as compensation for inflation risks. In this case investors worry less about the risk that inflation will erode the value of their bonds. The decline in real yields that took place in the late 1990s and 2000s no doubt had a great deal to do with the tremendous confidence investors had in the Fed's ability to contain inflation. Confidence in Greenspan's ability to control inflation was particularly high, and market participants during Ben Bernanke's tenure have seemed to believe that the ability to control inflation has been institutionalized at the Fed, helping keep both nominal and real interest rates low.

Whether that confidence will be sustained will be a major challenge for Bernanke. All indications, however, are that Bernanke will battle to preserve the Fed's hard-won gains on inflation, which stretch back to the early 1980s.

Market Liquidity and Volatility

Another factor that affects real yields is market liquidity and volatility. As was discussed in Chapter 2, *market liquidity* is basically the ease with which an investor can buy or sell securities without paying a premium on purchases or taking a haircut (a reduced price) on the price when selling. A *liquid market* is one in which there are many buyers and sellers and the bid and ask prices are generally close together. An *illiquid market* is the opposite: There are few buyers and sellers, and the bid and ask prices are generally far apart. When market liquidity falls, investors flock to the U.S. Treasury market, where liquidity is almost always high. This capital flight reduces real yields on Treasuries, but it increases real yields on the securities from which investors flee.

During the financial crisis, there was a massive flight into Treasuries and out of riskier assets, and as a result, real yields on virtually all fixed-income assets other than Treasuries rose while real yields on Treasuries fell sharply. Liquidity, in other words, had a great deal of impact on real interest rates across the fixed-income spectrum. In 1998 liquidity-related factors stemming from the Asian financial crisis affected Treasuries in an unprecedented way. During that period, risk aversion increased so sharply that investors also shunned older, less active Treasuries (known as *off-the-runs*), causing their real yields to rise too. Certainly, the poor performance of the off-the-runs and their subsequent rise in real yields compared to other Treasuries could not be explained by differences in credit quality: all Treasuries have the backing of the full faith and credit of the U.S. government. Therefore, the only explanation for the variation in performance was liquidity. Recent events and the events of 1998 are two examples of how liquidity can affect real yields.

Three Risks of Using Real Interest Rates as Indicators of Future Economic Performance

Real interest rates historically have been good gauges of future economic performance. As one would expect, high real interest rates resulting from tight monetary policy historically have been correlated with weak economic growth prospects while low real interest rates resulting from loose monetary policy have coincided with strong economic growth. While the historical record of real interest rates as an economic forecasting tool has been solid, there are three risks of using real interest rates as indicators of future economic performance.

First, determining whether real yields are "high" or "low" is a bit subjective. While it may be relatively simple to determine whether current levels of real yields are high or low relative to historical levels, one cannot judge with complete accuracy the market's expectations about future inflation and, hence, the degree to which current levels of real yields reflect expectations about future levels of inflation. Inflation expectations sometimes are difficult to measure. That said, there are many ways to gauge inflation expectations. For example, the University of Michigan includes data on consumers' inflation expectations in its monthly consumer sentiment survey. Also, the Treasury's inflation-protected securities (described in Chapter 4) can be used to track inflation expectations because their performance is directly affected by inflation expectations. Finally, inflation expectations are largely a function of the most recent experiences. If inflation behaves largely in one way over a multiyear period, there is little reason to believe that inflation expectations will change materially over a short period unless there is an exogenous shock that alters the equation.

A second risk in using real yields as an indicator of future economic performance relates to the difficulty of determining the equilibrium real yield that would be consistent with sustainable economic growth. Knowing the equilibrium real interest rate is important because that rate serves as a reference point for the real yield analysis. How, for example, can we say that real yields are "high" or "low" if we do not know what the midpoint of high and low is? That said, the historical range shown in Figure 8.1 provides a good sense of where the equilibrium real rate is.

A third risk in using real yields to forecast the economy is the possibility that the equilibrium real rate will vary over time. It can vary as a result of many different factors, such as changes in the level of risk aversion that investors have, political uncertainties, fiscal policy, inflation, tax rates, competition for capital, and the amount of goodwill investors have toward the Fed. Again, unless one knows what the equilibrium interest rate is, it is difficult to know when interest rates are "high" or "low." However, history provides a good gauge.

When Negative Real Interest Rates Are Necessary

As the figures in this chapter indicate, negative real interest rates are uncommon. This is the case primarily because just as equity investors expect higher returns on riskier stocks, bond investors want compensation for various risks, particularly for the risk of inflation and expected changes in monetary policy. In a sense, this is the demand side of the equation: The Fed plays a role in determining whether real interest rates should be positive or negative. Although history may have proven that negative real interest rates can lead to inflation and the Fed therefore has tended to avoid such a condition, there is at least one predicament in which negative real interest rates are necessary: during a liquidity trap.

A *liquidity trap* is a term used to describe a situation in which reductions in interest rates fail to spur new lending activity either because banks refuse to make new loans or because the demand for new loans is not helped by the low interest rates. A liquidity trap usually occurs when the banking sector is in bad shape or when the economic outlook is poor or uncertain. In such a situation no amount of incentives, including low interest rates, seems to spur lending activity. As a result, when the Federal Reserve cuts short-term interest rates, it is said to be "pushing on a string."

During the financial crisis, the United States entered a liquidity trap. Even after the Federal Reserve cut the federal funds rate effectively to zero in December 2008, lending did not revive, and in early 2010 bank lending was continuing a lengthy period of contraction. If ever there were a period when negative real rates were necessary, the financial crisis was such a time. Still, despite a federal funds rate running about 1.5 percentage points below the inflation rate, it was judged by many to be too *high*. Models attempting to find the optimal federal funds rate—many of which were modeled after the *Taylor rule,* which uses as its central variable the differential between the economy's growth potential and its growth rate—indicated throughout the crisis that in order for the federal funds rate to be stimulative, it would have to run many points below zero. This is why many have considered the Federal Reserve's quantitative easing program justified: the optimal negative real interest rate could not be accomplished with the federal funds rate because of the so-called *zero-bound problem*: the federal funds rate cannot be cut below zero.

A clear example of a liquidity trap has existed in Japan, where lending activity has been weak for more than 15 years despite interest rates near 0 percent. There the equilibrium real interest rate (the rate that equates savings to investment) in the United States also is very likely below zero. How do we know? The fact that lending has either fallen or been miniscule while real interest rates have been in positive territory is evidence that the equilibrium rate is lower than normal. In Japan, zero interest rates have failed to help partly because the inflation rate has actually been negative. This means that real rates remain relatively high in Japan despite the fact that nominal interest rates are near zero.

Businesses and consumers have had no incentive to invest or consume because prices have been falling. If you felt that the price of a good that you were contemplating buying would fall every month, wouldn't you delay the purchase if you could? Doesn't it make sense that a business would curtail its borrowing if it knew that the value of the assets in which it invests would fall but the value of its debt would stay the same? When there is deflation, homeowners, for example, must contend with the fact that the value of their home is falling but their mortgage debt is not. That's certainly not a good environment in which to invest and one of the reasons why the housing market will be slow to rebound. Deflation is worse than inflation in some ways (as long as inflation is low, of course).

To counter a situation such as this, it is imperative for a central bank to endeavor to raise inflation expectations. It can do this by lowering interest rates to low levels and increasing the supply of money. This will result in negative real interest rates, a condition that should spur new lending activity and help restore positive economic growth. With inflation outpacing the rate of return on their investments, consumers will be compelled to spend rather than save and businesses will be compelled to invest rather than save. In this way, the equilibrium between saving and investment is restored.

The challenge in the current situation is that the current de-leveraging process is a structural adjustment, not a cyclical one, and it will therefore be difficult for policy makers to encourage banks to lend. Until bank lending increases, no meaningful increase in money supply growth will occur—only banks can increase the money supply, and this will restrain economic growth and keep the wretched de-leveraging process and its effects in place for a while.

Summary

- Many factors can affect real yields. All those factors are messages that are embedded in the level of real yields every day. An investor need only look closely.
- First determine the level of real yields by taking the nominal, or stated, yield on a benchmark such as the 10-year U.S. Treasury note, and then subtract the current inflation rate (the year-over-year gain in the consumer price index) from that number. Then compare the result—the real yield—against the historical average as well as against more recent levels.
- Make a determination of whether you believe that the level of real yields is justified on the basis of the factors described in this chapter. This will help tell you whether the bond market is overvalued or undervalued.
- But if you are mostly interested in extracting the message of the bond market, simply determine which of these factors most likely explains the prevailing level of real yields. Once you feel you have figured out the market's message, this can be a big help with your investments whether you are invested in fixed-income securities, equities, or other types.

- A better understanding of real yields will help you see the big picture better and hear the messages coming from the bond market loud and clear. The more you know about the factors that affect real yields, the easier it will be for you to understand current interest rate levels and forecast future changes. If, for example, you can explain a particular level of real yields in terms of one of the factors described in the chapter, you can make a judgment about whether you believe the condition will persist or diminish.
- You also can make a judgment about whether you believe the bond market's assessment of where real yields should be is built on a reasonable premise. If you decide that it is not, you have a basis for making a bet against the market. If it appears to you that real yields are being unduly affected by one of the factors described earlier and you sense that there will be a resolution to the factor, think one thing: opportunity.
- Despite the recent deterioration in the U.S. budget situation, real interest rates have been low. This is because of the severity of the U.S. economic and financial crisis, which has lowered inflation expectations and reduced the level of private demand for capital, two factors that suppress real interest rates. Still, we can't know at what point investors might begin to focus more on the structural nature of the U.S. debt problem. If they do, expect both nominal and real interest rates to increase accordingly.

9

THE FIVE TENETS OF SUCCESSFUL INTEREST RATE FORECASTING

On Wall Street, bond traders spend their day in front of their computer screens, watching bond prices gyrate. It would be monotonous and dull work if not for the many interesting reasons behind each movement. Bond prices move for reasons that are rooted in the essence of the dynamics of the economy and the way American citizens live, offering traders a new chance every day to view the world from a unique vantage point. Few areas of the financial markets provide this unique top-down perspective, even though all asset classes are affected by macro influences in one way or another.

Over the years, one of my main endeavors has been to learn as much as possible about what makes the bond market move. I have been exposed to a constant flow of information that has given me a solid understanding of the forces that shape the investment decision-making process. I have focused intensely not only on the big secular moves but also on the small incremental cyclical moves that are part and parcel of the big moves. I am fascinated by every little wiggle in the market, and I believe that there is a message and a lesson to be learned in every move.

For decades investors have spoken of the benefits of watching the tape to glean the message of the markets. Those who have fought the tape may have won a few battles now and then, but in the end most of them probably came to realize that it's a losing battle. An investor cannot wait for the reasons to come to his or her door in a box with instructions on what to do next. Indeed, the real reasons behind a market's move may not be revealed until after the market has moved. Markets anticipate future events, after all.

This is why it is critical to gain an understanding of the major factors that seem most likely to have lasting influence on the markets. This means having an understanding of the major secular forces and overarching themes that will substantially influence the ultimate direction of market prices, while also seeking opportunities and avoiding pitfalls that result from short-term cyclical influences.

The Five Core Elements of Successful Interest Rate Forecasting

In the bond market there are five core reasons behind every move. These are the five elements that I believe are important in developing an accurate interest rate forecast:

- Monetary policy
- Inflation expectations
- The pace of economic growth
- Secular versus cyclical influences
- Technical factors and the market's technical condition

Combined, these factors generally explain the majority of the bond market's moves whether they span 10 years or 10 minutes. Just how much weight the market will give to each of these factors at any point in time depends on a variety of circumstances, and it is one of the most important elements in determining the market's next move.

An accurate interest rate forecast requires the ability to dynamically assess how much weight to give to each of the five core elements and to be as open-minded as possible; things can change quickly in the bond market. It is also very important to be extremely persistent in tracking the key elements of the core factors. It takes tremendous discipline, but this is the best way to achieve the best possible forecasting results. It is especially important to incorporate intangibles into the forecasting equation, including an evaluation of the nation's mood and the cultural forces that shape the way people behave. Data and statistics, after all, reflect what people do, not what machines do. Therefore, it's of the utmost importance to stay connected to the real world. Moreover, an investor must always remember that because people are behind the numbers he or she follows, the full gamut of human emotions is present in every observation he or she makes. Nowhere was this more apparent than in 2008 when emotion had much to do with the direction of market prices.

Let's take a closer look at each of the five core factors that shape the bond market's movements.

Monetary Policy: Ever Present in the Bond Market

Perhaps no measurable factor affects the bond market more than the Federal Reserve's monetary policies do. Indeed, on Wall Street, discussions about the Fed are a daily obsession, and not a trading day passes without ruminations about some reference in the financial media to what the Fed may do next. This obsession can seem excessive at times, but it isn't: Figure 9.1 clearly illustrates the close link between the actions taken by the Federal Reserve and yield changes in the bond market. As the figure shows, the yield on the two-year Treasury note appears to move in virtual lockstep with the federal funds rate—that is, the interest rate the Fed controls and uses as its primary means for transmitting changes in monetary policy.

It is significant that the yield on the 2-year T-note has rarely been below the federal funds rate. In fact, if you look closely, you will see that there have been only five occasions in the last 20 years in which the yield on the 2-year T-note dipped below the fed funds rate. Importantly, on each occasion the Fed eventually lowered interest rates, usually within a few months.

FIGURE 9.1 U.S. 2-Year Notes versus the Federal Funds Rate

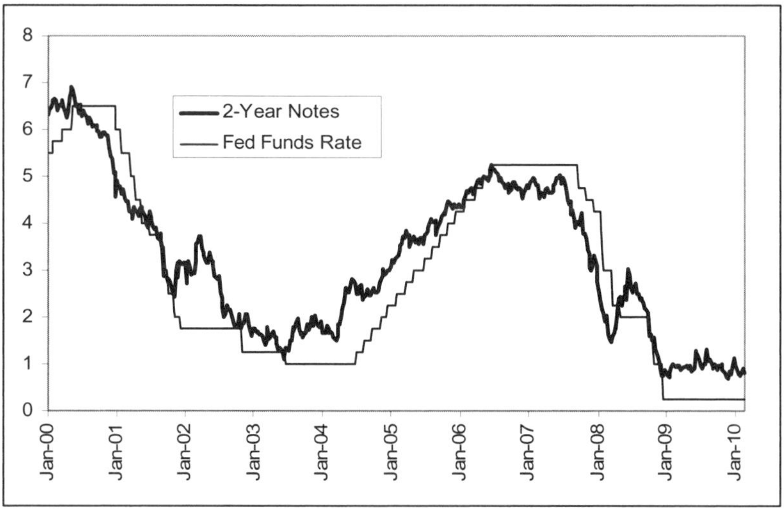

Source: Federal Reserve.

This clearly illustrates that the bond market moves in advance of the Fed, anticipating the Fed's every move.

As will be shown in Chapter 10, the close correlation between the 2-year T-note and the fed funds rate is reason to use the 2-year T-note as a top gauge of the bond market's sentiment toward the Federal Reserve. The correlation is why I use the 2-year note as one of my top gauges for forecasting the overall direction of interest rates. The key to using this excellent indicator is to be mindful of the following general principle: If the yield on the 2-year T-note deviates sharply from its normal yield spread to the fed funds rate, the bond market must be expecting a possible change in monetary policy and, hence, the fed funds rate. With this in mind, the next step is to examine whether the market's view rests on a solid foundation or a house of cards. The weaker the market's rationale is, the more likely it is that the market will reverse course eventually. If the market appears to have a solid fundamental basis for its rationale, it is more likely that the market's trends will be sustained.

During most of the past 20 years, the yield on the 2-year T-note was confined to a range of between 100 basis points above and below it. The average spread was 40 basis points over the fed funds rate. In January 2008, the 2-year traded nearly 200 basis points below the fed funds rate, reflecting expectations for deep cuts in the fed funds rate. On a few occasions—in 2004, 2002, and 1994 to 1995, the 2-year traded 200 basis points above the fed funds rate, reflecting the view that the Fed would increase the fed funds rate, which it did, except in 2002 when the market called it wrong. This conveniently simple range makes it somewhat easy to judge whether the bond market is "cheap" or "rich," both from the standpoint of where the 2-year T-notes and the rest of the market are headed next, and in relation to forward rates.

Forward rates represent yields for particular maturities at a future point in time. For example, a 1-year forward 2-year yield represents the yield expected on a 2-year maturity one year forward. In other words, the forward rate in this case is the yield on the 2-year maturity one year from now. It is calculated by using a combination of maturity points along the yield curve. Nearly all fixed-income strategy attempts to achieve a rate of return that beats implied forwards over a specified period of time. Otherwise, aside from liquidity and structural term premiums, which themselves have forward elements, a portfolio will earn a return equal to the overnight rate.

If this sounds complicated, don't fret. The bottom line is to remember that at all times the 2-year rate reflects where bond investors believe rates will be in the future—investors are at all times betting the rate they receive on the 2-year today and a year from now will exceed today's forward rate.

This means that if the market is romancing the idea of a change in monetary policy, the 2-year rate will reflect it because investors will demand compensation in order to beat the forward rate, which presumably would be higher because of Fed rate increases.

To determine whether the market is either "cheap" or "rich," first get a sense of where the Fed is in its interest rate cycle. Amid this, note that during periods when the Federal Reserve has raised interest rates, the yield on the 2-year T-note has generally traded at the upper end of its spread to fed funds. Conversely, during periods when the Federal Reserve has lowered interest rates, the 2-year generally has traded at the lower end of its spread to fed funds. In both cases the extreme has been 200 basis points. There could well be a new extreme in the time ahead because the Federal Reserve in December 2008 brought the fed funds rate to near zero percent. When the Federal Reserve begins to raise the fed funds rate, markets, having a big imagination, could extrapolate from the first hike a series of additional hikes, pushing the 2-year's yield well above zero percent—by as much as 200 basis points or more.

Whenever the yield on the 2-year T-note moves toward either end of its normal trading range relative to the fed funds rate, savvy investors should question whether it is justified. In other words, operating on the assumption that the 2-year note generally will move to the wide ends of its long-term range only when the Federal Reserve is on the verge of increasing or decreasing the fed funds rate, you must judge whether actual changes in the fed funds rate are truly in the offing. That takes some doing, of course, as it requires numerous other judgments about the economy, the Fed, and so forth, but an analysis of the 2-year note's yield relative to the fed funds rate is absolutely necessary to correctly determine the market's expectations about the Fed. Knowing this makes the task of determining the market's richness or cheapness far easier. The Federal Reserve simplifies the task further because it often signals its interest rate changes in advance, validating or invalidating the market's assumptions about its intentions. To detect the Fed's signals you must be an avid Fed watcher, the art of which was discussed in Chapter 6.

The reason for the tight correlation between the 2-year T-note and the federal funds rate is relatively simple. The correlation exists because yields on short-term maturities are determined largely by the cost of money—which is determined primarily by the federal funds rate—rather than by the factors that dominate the behavior of long-term maturities, including inflation expectations, hedging activity, speculative flows, and new issuance. When the cost of money is higher than the yield on the 2-year T-note, investors who purchase the 2-year note with borrowed money incur what is known as *negative carry* because the interest rate paid on the borrowed money exceeds the yield-to-maturity on the 2-year note. Investors who purchase securities on borrowed money are generally unwilling to engage in investments that incur negative carry unless they believe that borrowing costs eventually will fall and result in positive carry on the investment. Investors recognize that there is very little time for an investment in a short-term maturity to evolve from negative carry to positive carry and therefore avoid negative carry trades, as suggested by the minimal number of occasions over the last 12 years when the 2-year T-note has yielded less than the fed funds rate.

Conversely, when the prospect of cuts in the fed funds rate arises, investors purchase 2-year notes in expectation of collecting positive carry and achieving capital gains when the 2-year "rolls down" the yield curve. A *roll down* reflects the yield decline to be expected on a security solely from its "rolling down" the yield curve, which is to say that through the passage of time the maturity length of a fixed-income security will decline such that when the yield curve is positively sloped, the security will have a lower yield-to-maturity with each passing day. For example, in one year's time, a 2-year note will have a 1-year maturity. If the yield curve is positively sloped and no change in monetary policy is expected, in a year's time that 2-year maturity will have a yield roughly equal to the 1-year maturity. This will result in a price gain because prices rise when yields fall.

As the 2-Year Note Goes, So Goes the Rest of the Market

Importantly, the correlation between the fed funds rate and the bond market does not end with the 2-year T-note. Rather, the forces that shape movement in the 2-year note affect other maturities and other segments of the bond market as well. Take a look at Figure 9.2, which shows the yield on the 5-year T-note closely tracking the yield on the 2-year T-note, which in turn closely tracks the fed funds rate. This clearly suggests that there is a significant correlation between the yield on the 5-year T-note and the fed funds rate. Indeed, the correlation is so strong that it is one reason that I like to think of the 5-year note as the "long bond of the short end" owing to the sharp price changes often seen in the 5-year note when the market adjusts yields for expected or actual changes in the fed funds rate.

The correlation between the federal funds rate and other maturities along the yield curve extends beyond the 2- and 5-year maturities to as far out as the 10-year T-note as well as 30-year bonds. Figure 9.3 shows the clear correlation between the 2-year note and the 10-year note. As with the 5-year notes, the strong correlation between the 2-year and the 10-year maturities

FIGURE 9.2 Yield on U.S. 2-Year Notes versus Yield on U.S. 5-Year Notes

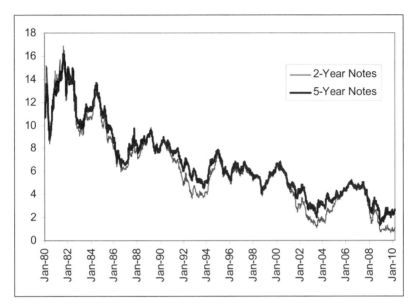

Source: Federal Reserve.

FIGURE 9.3 Yield on U.S. 2-Year Notes versus Yield on U.S. 10-Year Notes

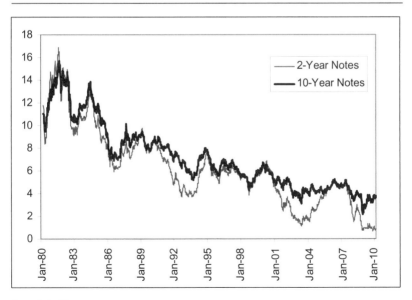

Source: Federal Reserve.

suggests that there is significant correlation between the 10-year note and the fed funds rate. As was mentioned earlier, however, there are many other factors that affect the behavior of long-term interest rates, and so it is important to avoid putting excessive weight on the Fed as a determinant of long-term interest rates. The other factors need to be assigned weights that depend on their relative importance at a given point in time.

Make no mistake, however: the Federal Reserve has an enormous effect on long-term interest rates. Indeed, long-term interest rates are said to be a bet on the future level of short-term interest rates. This is known as the *pure expectations theory*, which postulates that at any given time the yield on all maturities along the yield curve reflects the market's expectations of where short-term interest rates will be in the future.

A great deal of the bond market's time and energy is used to determine the degree to which new news and information may affect the Fed. At times it seems that the market has blinders on and looks at the world only in the context of what it means for the Fed.

This helps explain why there is such a high correlation between the fed funds rate and market interest rates.

The most important point about the connection between the Fed and the bond market as it pertains to forecasting interest rates is twofold. First, keep in mind that the bond market moves in advance of the Fed. You therefore must stay abreast of the forces that can shape the bond market's perceptions of future changes in Fed policy. Second, use the 2-year T-note to gauge the market's assumptions about future changes in Fed policy and as a starting point for assessing whether those assumptions are rational in light of the underlying financial and economic conditions.

The preceding discussion illustrates the idea that the Federal Reserve is one of the biggest determinants of the behavior of the bond market. An accurate interest rate forecast is therefore highly dependent on an accurate assessment of the direction of monetary policy. Chapter 6 discussed ways to stay attuned to the Fed and to become a better Fed watcher. That chapter also discussed the many factors that shape the bond market's perception of the Fed.

Inflation Expectations: A Worry in Constant Flux

Next to the Fed, no topic obsesses the bond market more than inflation. Inflation is the bond market's nemesis because it erodes the value of a bond's cash flows. That is why when inflation accelerates, bond prices fall and yields rise. Inflation is therefore at the root of interest rate risk, the biggest risk facing bond investors. *Interest rate risk*, or *market risk*, is defined as the risk of adverse movement in the price of a bond owing to changes in interest rates. (This topic was discussed more thoroughly in Chapter 5.) Inflation creates interest rate risk because it puts a bond investor at risk of incurring capital losses, which is why the bond market puts so much emphasis on inflation.

In recent times the threat of inflation has been quite low. Indeed, inflation has been on a secular downward trend since the early 1980s, and it has been quite benign since the early 1990s. This relative calm has afforded us the opportunity to observe the extent to which inflation expectations play a role in shaping the ups and downs of the bond market. One might think that inflation worries would be all but gone by now, particularly in light of the substantial amount of asset deflation seen during the financial and economic crisis, and because inflation has been low for more than a generation. To the contrary: Inflation worries remain quite measurable. The only difference now is the magnitude of the way in which the market expresses its inflation worries. Today's interest rate fluctuations may be smaller than those in past years, particularly in the 1970s and 1980s, but the fluctuations probably occur just as frequently. The concern du jour is the idea that the massive expansion of the Federal Reserve's balance sheet will eventually boost inflation. Thus, inflation remains a formidable force in determining the direction of interest rates.

One of the more important aspects of the bond market's fear of inflation is that its fears are not always its own. Bond investors often fear inflation not so much because they are worried about inflation themselves but because they are worried that other investors are worried about it. More important, bond investors worry that perceptible changes in inflation risks and inflation expectations will prompt the Fed to worry about how the public will affect the inflation process and thus prompt a response. Thus, interest rate fluctuations that result from the bond market's concerns about inflation sometimes are related more to fears of the Fed than to fears of inflation. Put this idea in the reflexivity camp, where the market creates its own reality.

Inflation fears are often rooted in the pace of economic growth. Strong economic growth tends to feed inflation fears, while slow economic growth tends to dampen them. When the economy is growing rapidly, bond investors worry that demand for goods and services will exceed supply for long enough to bring the level of economic activity above the economy's ability to produce, thus resulting in a fast rate of inflation. Strong economic growth also tends to result in a tightening of the labor market and thus increased labor costs. This is important because labor costs account for about 70 percent of the cost of producing goods and services, and as labor costs increase, businesses become compelled to raise prices. This is why the bond market pays such close attention to economic data, peering through every report for implications on the pace of economic growth and the inflation outlook. This concept is discussed in greater detail in the section on the economy later in this chapter.

Two Ways to Track the Market's Inflation Expectations

Tracking the bond market's inflation expectations is crucial to interest rate forecasting. Gauging the market's inflation expectations is similar in some ways to gauging its expectations about the Fed in that in both cases one obtains a reference point with which to compare the expectations against reality and then invests accordingly. In other words, you validate or invalidate those expectations on the basis of your own subjective analysis of the underlying fundamentals. From this you can develop an interest rate forecast because you will either agree or disagree with the market's assumptions.

There are two ways to track the bond market's inflation expectations. One method utilizes the Treasury's inflation-indexed bonds, and the other utilizes real interest rates. Let's take a look at both.

An excellent way to track the bond market's assessment of inflation risks is to monitor real interest rates. As was described in Chapter 8, *real interest rates*, or *real yields*, are nominal interest rates minus inflation. Real yields fluctuate as the bond market's views about inflation fluctuate. Chapter 8 described the many other reasons why real yields fluctuate, but this section will focus on how to use real yields to track the bond market's inflation expectations. Figure 8.1 illustrated how real yields are almost always positive, pointing to the important role inflation plays in setting market interest rate levels. That figure suggested that market interest rates tend to track the inflation rate.

Real yields contain a significant amount of information about the bond market's inflation expectations. The information is not so much quantitative as qualitative, however, because while real yields may provide a numeric value with which to gauge inflation expectations, that numeric value is not an exact measure of those expectations; a qualitative judgment is necessary. This is true partly because real interest rates provide information about a variety of other factors that affect interest rate levels, such as competition for capital, sentiments about the Fed, and external factors. In the end, however, real interest rates tend to reflect inflation expectations more than anything else. Here is an example. Suppose the yield on the 10-year Treasury note is 5.0 percent and inflation (as gauged by the consumer price index) is running at about 2.5 percent. In this case the real yield on the 10-year T-note is 2.5 percent. Let's say that over the last five years, the real yield has fluctuated in a range of 2.0 percent to 4.0 percent. With the real yield in this example at 2.5 percent, it is therefore at the lower end of its recent range. This indicates that inflation expectations are low.

How do we know this? If inflation expectations were closer to 4.0 percent and if inflation were running at 2.5 percent, the yield on the 10-year would more likely be 6.5 percent. The bottom line is that real yields contain insight into where the market sees inflation risks. In general, real yields tend to be low when inflation expectations are low and high when inflation expectations are high. In addition, investors demand an increasing amount of compensation for inflation risks when the inflation rate is rising but a decreasing amount of compensation when the inflation rate is falling.

Using the Treasury's Inflation-Indexed Bonds to Gauge Inflation Expectations

A second way to track the bond market's inflation expectations is to follow the yield spread between the Treasury's inflation-protected securities, commonly known as TIPS, and conventional Treasuries. As was described in Chapter 4, TIPS provide compensation for inflation as measured by the Consumer Price Index for all Urban Consumers. The value of these inflation-indexed securities increases at the inflation rate. Holders of these securities therefore are immunized against inflation risks.

The yield spread between the stated yield-to-maturity on TIPS and that on conventional Treasuries is the *breakeven rate*, which is used as a literal interpretation of the market's inflation expectations. Thus, if the breakeven rate on a 10-year TIPS is 2.0 percent, this indicates that bond investors expect inflation to average 2.0 percent per year over the next 10 years. If the breakeven rate on a 5-year TIPS is 1.7 percent, this indicates that bond investors expect inflation to average 1.7 percent over the next 5 years. The formula looks like this:

Breakeven rate = quoted yield-to-maturity on conventional
Treasury security – quoted yield-to-maturity on TIPS

Let's take a brief look at why the breakeven rate is used as an indication of inflation expectations.

The first thing to note is that all the Treasury's inflation-indexed bonds pay a coupon. The coupon rate has declined over the years, reflecting in part the increased acceptance of TIPS as an asset class, but also the interest rate environment itself. In the late 1990s, a coupon rate in the vicinity of 3.75 percent was common. In 2009, the coupon rate averaged closer to 1.75 percent, and in early 2010 it was closer to 1.50 percent. The dollar amount of the cash flows paid on the semiannual coupon rate isn't fixed as it is with conventional bonds because the coupon payment on TIPS will be based on the coupon rate multiplied by the principal value of the bond, which will increase over time as long as the consumer price index increases. (The increase in the principal value of TIPS owing to the indexation of the principal value to the consumer price index is known as *inflation accrual.*) This means that holders of inflation-indexed securities will receive both an incremental return for inflation and a return over and above the inflation accrual. This is the real interest rate, and it is paid via the semiannual coupon payments.

As with conventional Treasuries, the real interest rate on TIPS will vary with the market's view of the economy, the Fed, inflation, and so forth. Both TIPS and conventional Treasuries contain a real interest rate and compensation for inflation. On TIPS the inflation compensation can be readily measured by simply tracking the consumer price index (CPI). On conventional Treasuries, however, inflation expectations must be measured differently. These can be calculated by subtracting real yields from nominal, or quoted, yields, with the difference representing investors' inflation expectations. TIPS provide the information needed to do this simple calculation because their yield-to-maturity is the real yield used in the calculation.

When you look at the yield-to-maturity on a conventional Treasury, keep in mind that you can always gauge the market's inflation expectations by subtracting from it the yield-to-maturity on an equal-maturity inflation-indexed Treasury (the real yield). The yield difference represents the market's inflation expectations (for the consumer price index). This method is widely used and is often cited by the Federal Reserve as a key gauge of inflation expectations. (The Fed of course uses many other gauges such as consumer inflation expectations, data for which are available from consumer confidence surveys.)

Using Real Interest Rates to Gauge Inflation Expectations

Once you have a bead on the market's inflation expectations, you can begin to assess whether you believe that the market's assumptions are rational. This requires a great deal of subjective analysis, of course, but by knowing as accurately as possible how much inflation the market expects, you will have a basis on which to say you agree or disagree. It is far easier to say that you agree or disagree with the market's assumptions when you can assess those assumptions accurately. This makes it easier to judge whether bond prices are "rich" or "cheap." If, for example, owing to a number of factors, inflation expectations fall to abnormally low levels, you may conclude that bond prices are too high relative to the inflation outlook. Of course, you might also say that they remain too high if disinflation or even deflation appears in the cards.

A classic example of what can happen when the market's inflation expectations reach an extreme occurred in 1998 during the Asian financial crisis. During that time, inflation expectations fell sharply, as illustrated by the sharp drop in the breakeven rate on 10-year TIPS. Figure 9.4 shows the sharp drop that occurred in inflation expectations in 1998, with the breakeven rate falling to as low as 0.7 percent. That meant investors believed the consumer price index would increase at an average rate of just 0.7 percent over the next 10 years. While the decline in the breakeven rate also was related to liquidity concerns—TIPS underperformed conventional Treasuries—the bulk of the decline was related to a drop in inflation expectations. A similar move occurred in 2008 when liquidity concerns increased sharply and inflation expectations plunged, as reflected in TIPS, which were priced for the inflation rate to move to zero.

With inflation having averaged 3.4 percent over the previous 10 years, the market's inflation expectations therefore deviated sharply from historical trends. Moreover, the U.S. economic expansion looked likely to hold intact. To me and to many other analysts, the market's inflation expectations therefore seemed unreasonable. This provided a solid basis on which to forecast an eventual rise in market interest rates. Indeed, a bear market in bonds began not long after the plunge in inflation expectations, which were at an extreme because of extreme market sentiment (for more on market sentiment, see Chapter 10).

FIGURE 9.4 Inflation Expectations, as Depicted in the Breakeven Rate for the Treasury's 10-Year Inflation-Protected Securities (TIPS)

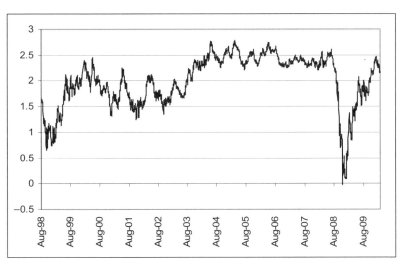

Source: Federal Reserve.

As you can see, inflation expectations play an important role in the behavior of the bond market. Like many key indicators that help in formulating an interest rate forecast, inflation expectations are a moving target. However, once you get a bead on them, you are more likely to derive an accurate interest rate forecast. It is therefore imperative to know the market's expectations when you are formulating investment strategies.

The Pace of Economic Growth: How Much Is Too Much?

Economic data are the grease that makes the bond market move. With each economic report, the bond market moves another stride along its uneven path. In the bond market the economy is at the root of almost every twist and turn because it affects two other dominant influences shown above: the Fed and inflation. These two influences generally explain the majority of the bond market's price movements. Bond investors recognize that the pace of economic growth has a direct bearing on both the Fed and inflation, which is why so much emphasis is placed on economic data.

The Appendix at the end of the book contains a detailed analysis of the importance of each of the major economic reports and its impact on both the bond market and the individual investor. I feel so strongly about the importance of economic data that I placed extra emphasis on this topic in that Appendix.

It is fairly easy to understand how the economy affects the bond market. As was mentioned earlier, when the economy is growing rapidly, bond investors worry that demand for goods and services will exceed available supply and result in faster inflation. Rapid economic growth affects inflation particularly because it tends to lead to fast job growth and faster increases in the cost of labor, which is one of the most important determinants of inflation. In contrast, the cost of parts, raw materials, and the like accounts for only 10 percent of the inflation picture.

Commodity prices are important too, of course, but they merely tend to put an exclamation point on the inflation outlook. Inflation threatens bonds because it erodes the value of a bond's cash flows and creates market risk. However, an even bigger worry for many bond investors is the impact inflation concerns can have on the Federal Reserve, an institution whose mandate is to control inflation. Bond investors recognize that if inflation were to rear its ugly head, the Fed would raise interest rates as much as necessary to swat it down. Few things affect the bond market more than interest rate changes by the Federal Reserve.

Thus, when the bond market looks at economic data, it does so not just through its own eyes but also through the eyes of the Fed, constantly assessing inflation risks and their potential impact on monetary policy.

The focus of the bond market on economic data is almost always intense, but the specific economic reports that get the most attention often vary with shifts in the dominant influences on the economy. Occasionally, data that rarely are given more than a passing glance suddenly become a large force in shaping the bond market's direction. At other times big market movers such as the employment report carry little weight in shaping the market's direction. It is therefore important to be open-minded and flexible when one is weighing the potential impact of a set of economic reports. There are many different situations where the market's focus will change, and the changes can occur frequently. It is therefore important to look several steps ahead at the chain of events that will affect the economy in future months. It's not enough to look at the economy's current problems. The way Wall Street works, that is like looking in the past. Instead, an investor must first identify the economy's key problems or key underpinnings and try to envision the chain of events that could alter the economy's direction.

How to Calculate the Economy's Growth Potential

The bond market can tolerate a certain amount of economic growth without sounding the inflation alarm. Specifically, the bond market is generally comfortable when economic growth is at or below the economy's growth potential. The economy's growth potential is roughly defined as follows:

Economy's annual growth potential = annual labor force growth
+ annual productivity growth

This simple formula is fairly easy to understand and quite intuitive. Its objective is to measure the economy's added capacity to produce goods and services. That capacity can be measured by adding the annual rate of increase in the number of new workers in the labor force to increases in the productivity of the existing labor force.

Labor force growth can be discerned readily because it is largely related to population growth and generally increases at a pace of around 1.1 percent or so annually. The rate of population growth does not change much, of course, and so it is not necessary to worry about finding a value for this part of the equation. That said, keep in mind that because of the aging of the U.S. population associated with the baby boomers, the number of retirees will be accelerating in the years ahead, and this will likely slow the growth rate of the labor force, probably to 1 percent or a bit lower over the next decade, maybe to as low as 0.8 percent. During weak economic times, the labor force often contracts, as people move to the sidelines in discouragement over the lack of job prospects. This is what happened in 2009 when the labor force shrunk about 1 percent.

As the labor force increases, it adds to the economy's ability to produce goods and services because there are more people to produce goods and services. Plain and simple.

Productivity growth is a bit more difficult to estimate than is the labor force because it results from many factors. Productivity gains are rooted largely in advances in technology and in our knowledge about how to produce goods and services more efficiently—something that is difficult to quantify. As businesses deploy new technologies such as computers, software, and equipment, output per worker increases. This makes sense when one considers technology even in its most simple form. Typing and editing documents, for instance, is far simpler today than it was 25 years ago, when carbon paper was still widely used. This is how increases in productivity translate into increases in the economy's ability to produce goods and services.

Productivity since the mid-1990s has advanced at a fairly strong pace compared with the previous 15 years, at a 2.4 percent pace compared to 1.5 percent. Since 1960, productivity has advanced at a 2.0 percent annual rate. In light of these trends, it is reasonable to assume that productivity will generally advance at an annual rate of about 2.0 percent, particularly given the enormous advances in technology and the likelihood of broadened applications of those technologies in the coming years.

Indeed, there is some evidence suggesting that productivity trends move in roughly 20-year cycles, which by this measure means the productivity upswing in place since the mid-1990s has room to run. In the aftermath of the economic and financial crisis, there is risk of a decrease in productivity rates, as many studies show that economic and financial crises tend to reduce the productive capability of a nation. This makes sense because there is a certain amount of supply destruction that takes place during and after a crisis. For example, investment in new factories and equipment weakens, which reduces or slows the growth of productive capacity.

The math for the economy's growth potential therefore goes like this: Add yearly growth of the labor force (about 1.1 percentage points) to yearly growth in productivity (about 2.0 percentage points), and we arrive at an estimate of about 3.0 percent for the economy's growth potential. Postcrisis, the total is probably a bit lower. Let's take this a step further to see what happens when the economy grows more slowly than its growth potential. This example will help explain why businesses lay off workers and cut spending when the economy grows slowly. It also will illustrate why bond yields tend to decline in such an environment.

Think about it like this: Say there is an economy with 100 people in the labor force who have the capacity to produce 100 units of goods to meet current demand of 100 units per year. If one new person enters the labor force, the economy's ability to produce will increase by 1 percent to 101 units. And if the same 100 people producing goods somehow become more productive and are collectively able to produce 2 percent more goods, the economy's overall ability to produce goods will increase by 3 percent to 103 units.

Here is the problem when the economy grows slowly: Since the economy is capable of producing more goods than before, if demand grows at a slower pace, say, by only 2 units to reach 102, the economy will have excess capacity of 1 unit (since it has the capacity to produce 103 units). In this case the economy grew, but so did its excess capacity. The longer that trend continues, the more the excess capacity builds.

The excess capacity is manifested in both excess labor and excess capital stock (plants, equipment, technology equipment, and so on). Businesses can deal with the excess capacity in a few ways: they can shed labor, reduce capital spending, or wait for the economy to grow faster. The route they choose generally depends on the severity of the economic slowdown.

The point is that even when the economy grows, if it grows more slowly than the economy's growth potential, it will result in a buildup of excess capacity owing to increases in the labor force and productivity growth. When this happens, businesses feel compelled to reduce the excess capacity with measures that can cause a great deal of economic pain. Call it a "growth recession." Of course, bad news for the economy is good news for the bond market because excess capacity tends to dampen inflation pressures. When the economy grows faster than its growth potential, the excess demand for goods and services tends to put upward pressure on inflation, which is bad news for the bond market.

Using the Economy's Growth Potential to Forecast Interest Rates

Much of the bond market's price movement evolves from its sense of the extent to which the economy is growing above or below its growth potential. An accurate interest rate forecast therefore requires an estimate of the economy's growth rate relative to its growth potential and an assessment of how the market sees these issues. If your views differ from where you sense the market's views are, you can use this as a basis for forecasting a turn in interest rates. As with the Fed and inflation, your interest rate forecast begins by identifying the market's assumptions about both the economy's growth rate and its growth potential and then comparing the market's assumptions with the underlying fundamentals so that you can validate or invalidate those assumptions. From there you can generate a forecast, relying heavily on the extent to which your assumptions appear to differ from those of the market.

Secular versus Cyclical Influences: Know the Force That Is with You

The reasons bond yields go up and down never cease to amaze me. As Gilda Radner's Roseanne Rosannadanna used to say, "It's always something. If it's not one thing, it's another!" That's how it is in the bond market, or any other market for that matter. Something different is always pushing prices around. It's sometimes as if the proverbial invisible hand were waving its magic wand, telling the market where to go next. In reality, of course, there is a far more substantive explanation of why bond prices sometimes move when there is no tangible explanation. In such cases I believe that either secular or cyclical forces can explain the movement in bond prices.

On Wall Street a *secular trend* is seen as a trend in economic and/or financial conditions that is expected to evolve from a set of factors expected to be influential for long periods of time, even for as long as decades. These sets of factors sometimes are called *deep fundamentals*—that is, or fundamental forces that are so deeply rooted that they are not likely to be uprooted over short spans of time. An example of a secular trend is the decline in interest rates that began in the early 1980s and has continued to this day. Figure 9.5 shows this trend. Another example is the expansion of credit, which was vigorous and sustained for decades until the trend broke in 2008. Figure 9.6 shows this trend.

Cyclical trends are short-term trends that stem from short-term influences such as periodic excesses in supply and demand. In the long run, cyclical forces tend to be dwarfed by secular ones and rarely disrupt long-term trends. Examples of cyclical trends include the numerous short-term bear markets in bonds that have occurred throughout the secular bull market in bonds over the last 20 years. When viewed on a long-term chart such as the one in Figure 9.5, cyclical trends appear as relatively minor blips, suggesting that cyclical forces are indeed dwarfed by secular ones. However, when viewed over shorter periods, cyclical trends appear to have a much larger impact.

FIGURE 9.5 The Secular Decline in Interest Rates in the United States

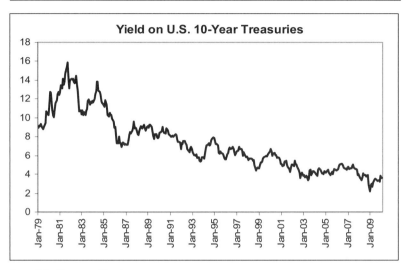

Source: Federal Reserve and Bloomberg.

A good example is the bear market in bonds that occurred between the end of 1998 and the start of 2000, and the one that lasted from around the middle of 2003 through 2006 (more for the short end than the long end for

FIGURE 9.6 The Secular Increase in Bank Credit Accelerated in the Early 2000s Before It Stopped

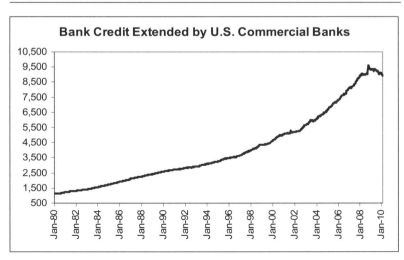

Source: Federal Reserve.

this particular cycle). Figure 9.7 shows the degree to which cyclical trends can spur movements in bond prices that sometimes last for meaningful periods of time. As the figure shows, the bear market of 1998 to 2000 lasted close to 15 months, an eternity to traders and investors, who sometimes are preoccupied with trading patterns for the next 15 minutes! Moreover, as the expression goes, *the market can remain irrational for longer than an investor can remain solvent!*

Although secular forces are the dominant influence on the behavior of bond prices over the long run, cyclical forces can assert a powerful influence for relatively short periods of time lasting days, weeks, or even several years. In a sense, secular and cyclical forces alternately exert their influence like a game of Ping-Pong, with one exerting more influence than the other for variable lengths of time. All the while, however, the secular influences are always present, acting as the larger force and taming the cyclical forces with a sort of gravitational pull that keeps market prices from traveling far from the secular trend.

The constant volley between the changing degrees of influence of secular and cyclical forces can be of tremendous value in formulating an interest rate forecast. For example, awareness of secular forces can help establish an idea of where the limitations are on the degree to which cyclical forces can push interest rates higher or lower over a cyclical horizon. Cyclical forces, for

FIGURE 9.7 A Cyclical Bear Market, Hidden on Secular Charts

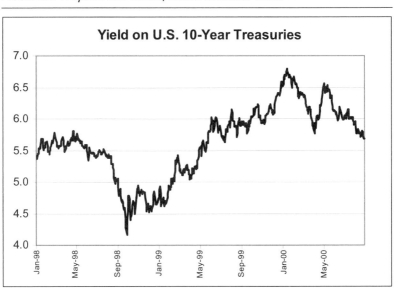

Source: Federal Reserve and Bloomberg.

their part, are by definition almost always destined to be exhausted at some point, and for a forecaster it is merely a matter of identifying the means by which they will run out of gas. Let's take a look at a couple of classic examples.

The bond market entered a cyclical bear market at the end of 1993 that lasted about a year. The yield on the 10-year Treasury note went up sharply, rising roughly 2 percentage points. That yield increase equated to a roughly 20 percent drop in price, which was one of the biggest price declines in a generation. There were a number of reasons for the decline, most of which were related to factors with a relatively short half-life. In other words, cyclical factors were the main force behind the bear market. Specifically, at the end of 1993, after several years of sluggish economic growth, the U.S. economy began to show signs of gaining vigor.

Indeed, in the fourth quarter of 1993, the gross domestic product (GDP) grew at an annualized rate of 6.2 percent (the data have since been revised to a gain of 5.4 percent), the fastest pace in almost 10 years and well above the average growth rate of 2.0 percent seen over the previous five years. The economic performance was led by strength in consumer spending, particularly on new homes and cars, and it was supported by strong job growth and declining unemployment. Bond investors worried that the strong demand for goods and services, along with strong job growth, would put upward pressure on inflation. Indeed, a sharp rise in commodity prices seemed to validate that thesis, and the cyclical forces behind the inflation pressures appeared to be quite strong. In a way, the bond market's worries appeared to be rational.

The bond market might have been missing the forest from the trees, however, choosing to place more emphasis on cyclical forces than on secular ones. Inflation never did accelerate as much as the bond market had feared, owing to powerful secular forces that limited the actual rise in inflation and thus kept interest rates on a downward track. There were a few secular forces that helped keep both inflation and interest rates low.

First, owing to the decline in interest rates in the early 1980s during the Reagan administration, U.S. businesses had a powerful incentive to invest, and therefore they became increasingly competitive in the global economy. This helped make the United States one of the lowest-cost producers in the world for the first time in over 20 years. This encouraged U.S. companies to keep prices low and grab lost market share back from foreign competitors. Second, lower tax rates fostered economic conditions that were conducive to creating strong economic growth. This helped strengthen the U.S. dollar and reduce the cost of U.S. imports and, hence, inflation pressures. Third, cuts in government regulations implemented during the Reagan years reduced business costs, reducing inflation pressures. Fourth, the combination of low tax rates and reduced regulations helped foster an environment that unleashed the so-called animal spirits in the economy, resulting in product innovations that paved the way for a productivity boom by the middle of the decade that would have lasting influence in quelling inflation pressures.

The 1994 bear market in bonds is an excellent illustration of the alternating influences of secular and cyclical forces. In 1994 cyclical forces became immensely important for a while, only to succumb to more powerful secular forces. That episode illustrates the importance of recognizing which of the two forces is likely to be dominant at any given time. This is a difficult task, but it is made easier when the cyclical forces push market prices to levels that begin to go against the secular trend. When this happens, the first step is to question whether there is ample justification for believing that key secular forces have been uprooted. If there is not, and it's generally likely that there will not have been, an investor should consider countertrend investment strategies that take advantage of the apparent dislocation in the market.

However, one must beware of the powerful effects of the cyclical influences because they can last a while, as was seen in 1994. In cases such as that, an investor must have a basis for believing that the cyclical forces are exhausting themselves before deciding to engage in a risky countertrend trade. When there is ample reason to believe that the cyclical forces will be exhausted, it is time to scale into strategies that will benefit from a return to the secular trend. Use the force.

Technical Factors and the Market's Technical Condition as Fundamentally Important in Forecasting Interest Rates

In the bond market, as in other markets, there are all sorts of investors. In the bond market, three types of investors stand out. The first relies almost exclusively on market fundamentals such as the Fed, the economy, and inflation, preferring to base investment strategies on qualitative judgments on fundamentals. The second relies mostly on judgments regarding technical factors, preferring to base investment strategies on charts and quantitative analyses. The third combines fundamental and technical analyses, formulating strategies by utilizing the most important elements and signals from the first two approaches.

I must admit to having been a skeptic about technical analysis early on. After all, it seems irrational to think that one could determine the market's next move by using a chart. Yet after a while I came to recognize that technical analysis is used more than just charts and it includes a wide array of other technical factors related to market sentiment, capital flows, Treasury supply, mutual fund flows, and so forth. Moreover, it also became clear to me that because many other investors were looking at and acting on technical factors, those factors can become a self-fulfilling prophecy. You would be surprised at how many of some of Wall Street's best-known investors incorporate some form of technical analysis into their formulations of investment strategies.

The fact is that even if you had perfect information about the bond market's underlying fundamentals, you still might not be able to predict where it is headed next. There are simply too many other factors that could exert an influence on the market to rely solely on fundamental factors. I say this, however, firmly believing that the best route to an accurate market forecast requires an accurate assessment of market fundamentals above all else. I am a fundamentalist through and through. However, as I just said, even with perfect information on market fundamentals I could still wind up eating crow. Therefore, it is imperative to incorporate some analysis of the major technical factors that can influence the market's behavior. Doing this will augment your fundamental analyses and thereby help you steer clear of wrongheaded forecasts and investment decisions. It also can strengthen or weaken your convictions about particular investment ideas.

Key Technical Factors That Influence the Bond Market

Market Sentiment

From tulips to Treasuries, tracking market sentiment has been one of the most reliable ways to forecast future price changes in stocks, bonds, commodities, tulips—you name it. Extreme bullishness and extreme bearishness have foretold key turning points in asset prices for centuries. The same principles apply to the bond market, and there are a number of ways to track bond market sentiment. Chapter 10 thoroughly outlines the most reliable indicators of market sentiment that for many years have reliably pointed to excesses in bullish and bearish sentiment.

When market sentiment reaches an extreme, the bond market often is poised for a reversal. High levels of bullish sentiment, for example, tend to indicate that a large degree of bullish news already has been factored into prices. This makes it difficult for the market to gain further even if additional bullish news materializes. This is how forecasts that are based exclusively on fundamental analysis can go awry because even with an accurate economic forecast, it is possible to forecast the market's price movements inaccurately. Technical influences are therefore an essential element of an accurate market forecast.

Hedging Activity in the Mortgage-Backed Securities Market

A technical factor that often exerts a great deal of influence on the bond market is the hedging activity tied to the mortgage-backed securities (MBS) market, a market that is larger than the U.S. Treasury market. Treasuries are impacted by the MBS market when portfolio managers buy and sell Treasuries to offset prepayment risks. We described in Chapter 4 that *mortgage-backed securities* are debt instruments backed by a pool of mortgages, generally residential mortgages. These mortgages often are prepaid early as homeowners refinance their homes or move from one home to another.

When a mortgage is prepaid, a percentage of the mortgage-backed securities of which that mortgage is a part are prepaid. This is known as the *constant prepayment rate* (CPR). The prepayment rate generally increases when interest rates fall as more people refinance their homes or buy new ones. This causes more mortgages to be paid off more frequently. These prepayments directly impact portfolios that include mortgage securities because the prepayments inject cash into the portfolios and decrease the amount of securities held. Mortgage portfolios therefore face reinvestment risks associated with having to reinvest the cash from the prepayments at lower and lower interest rates.

In addition, those portfolios subject to increasing amounts of prepayments are at risk of performing poorly compared with other portfolios as well as against the benchmark indexes that are used to judge their performance. This occurs because portfolios with mortgage-backed securities wind up having relatively more cash and fewer securities than do the benchmark indexes they are judged against. This puts a holder of mortgage-backed securities at risk of missing out on profiting from the increases in bond prices that result from the decline in interest rates. To guard against the risks associated with falling interest rates, mortgage-backed portfolio managers therefore buy U.S. Treasuries to hedge against the damages caused by rising prepayments.

This buying can have a substantial impact on the bond market because it can accelerate market trends. Thus, during periods when mortgage origination is high, mortgage-related buying of Treasuries increases, putting additional upward pressure on already rising prices. Similarly, when mortgage origination declines—typically as a result of higher interest rates or, as has been the case in recent years, because of difficulties that homeowners have faced in obtaining mortgage credit, portfolio managers sell Treasuries. This accelerates the downward tract in bond prices. This happens in particular at the end of mortgage refinancing booms, when hedges against rising prepayment risks are unwound.

The best examples of this are the refinancing booms of 1993, 1998, 2001, and 2003. As can be seen in Figure 9.8, refinancing activity during those periods was extraordinary, as measured by mortgage applications for refinancing. In each case, there were numerous occasions when mortgage-related activity put both upward and downward pressure on Treasury prices. Because of the high degree of influence of big shifts in mortgage refinancing activity, it is important to track refinancing activity for potential market impact. An investor can do this by following the data on mortgage applications released every Wednesday by the Mortgage Bankers Association (MBA).

The influence of the MBS market on the Treasury market was altered dramatically in 2008 and 2009 when the Federal Reserve said it would purchase $1.25 trillion of mortgage-backed securities. The program removed a vast amount of the MBS "stock" from the market at a time when new supply was diminishing as a result of factors related to the financial crisis. This drove MBS prices sharply higher relative to Treasuries. Importantly, the Federal Reserve's purchases forced portfolio managers that sold their MBS to the Fed to purchase other securities as replacements because portfolio managers need to maintain a certain risk profile in order to stay close to

FIGURE 9.8 Mortgage Refinancing Index

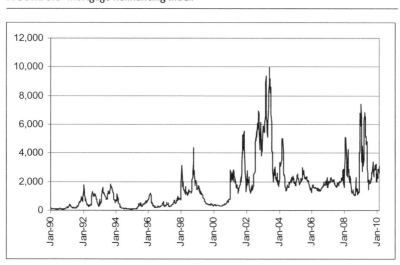

Source: Mortgage Bankers Association (MBA).

their benchmarks. One could say that portfolio managers had to replace the duration they lost with duration from other fixed-income instruments—in many cases Treasuries but also corporate bonds and other segments of the fixed-income universe. In the times ahead, what the Fed does with its large stock of MBS will have an important bearing on the direction of market prices.

New Supply

In Economics 101 students are taught that an increase in supply results in a decrease in price and that a decrease in supply results in an increase in price. Fitting this theory to the bond market, an increase in the supply of bonds should result in a decrease in bond prices (and a rise in yields), while a decrease in the supply of bonds should result in an increase in bond prices (and a decrease in yields). This makes sense because there is a finite amount of capital in the world. Surprisingly, however, increases and decreases in the supply of bonds do not always have the effect that the laws of supply and demand dictate. Indeed, there are times when the bond market seems to defy those laws, and in 2009 it did so in dramatic fashion. It is therefore important to recognize the various ways in which changes in the supply of bonds affect the bond market.

There are many classic examples of the varying ways in which supply-related factors can influence the bond market. In the 1980s and early 1990s, for example, it was felt that the sharp increase in the U.S. budget deficit and the subsequent rise in the new supply of Treasuries would result in lower prices and thus higher interest rates. However, interest rates fell throughout that period. This was due largely to very positive secular forces that helped tame inflation pressures. The fact that bond prices rose even though supply had increased illustrates how fundamental factors, particularly with respect to inflation expectations, are significantly more important than technical factors.

This said, it is important to note that throughout the 1980s and early 1990s there were numerous episodes in which the increase in supply had a large impact on bond prices, although for short periods. Specifically, there were occasions when investors needed to be enticed to buy the ever-increasing supply of Treasuries. On these occasions investors demanded price markdowns known as *concessions*, in which the primary dealers basically knocked prices lower to lure investors. Concessions still occur, but what I am talking about here are concessions of a large magnitude, not the handful of basis points that occur regularly ahead of Treasury auctions.

One of the more important points to make regarding periods when investors seek only trivial concessions for new supply is that they typically do this in periods when market fundamentals are bullish; however, the more bearish fundamentals are, the greater the concessions are likely to be. In other words, supply matters, but only in bear markets—bear markets for Treasuries, that is. No illustration brings this point home better than the absence of concessions required for the large volume of Treasury securities that had to be issued by the United States to fund its battle against the financial and economic crisis. Auctions not only saw sufficient demand but they also saw unusually strong demand.

Why? Because it was a bull market for Treasuries from a fundamental perspective. During such times, private demand for capital diminishes, pushing money toward alternative investments, including Treasuries. In other words, Treasuries do not "crowd out" the private sector. Instead, demand for credit in the private sector diminishes at a time when Treasury supply tends to increase—during recessions for example.

There probably are limits to the amount of Treasuries that can be issued, but it would require a mindset that market participants currently do not have. In particular, for the supply burden to be so great as to cause a failed auction—an auction where demand is less than the amount offered—investors would have to believe that the U.S. debt burden was insurmountable in the near term. With investors these days focused more on sovereign credit risk than ever before, there will be some who can envision such a scenario—the doomsayers. We will talk more about this in the next section of this chapter.

The fact that investors are indifferent toward a concession when they are bullish on bond prices is evidence that the laws of supply and demand do not always apply in the bond market. In other words, increases or decreases in supply do not always result in price changes that fit the changes in supply. In the end, inflation expectations and other key fundamental factors such as the interest rate set by the central bank are much more important.

A classic example of this is Japan, where even though it has had a debt-to-GDP ratio of about 200 percent, there have been enormous increases in the supply of new Japanese bonds. Yet for years Japan has experienced extremely low interest rates. Why? Japan has been experiencing deflation for many years, and the Bank of Japan (BOJ) has kept interest rates low for nearly a decade. Thus, to investors in Japanese bonds, the driving force behind their purchase decisions is not supply but inflation expectations, and the BOJ rate.

Therefore, investors must bear in mind that while supply matters, the extent to which it matters depends on the market's attitude toward fundamental factors, particularly inflation, and the central bank rate. Still, I must admit that the rule I've followed since the 1990s is under threat owing to the enormity of supply issued by developed nations, including the United States.

Read on.

Foreign Investors: Focus on Sovereign Credit Risk Could Prompt the Question of Our Age

Foreign investors hold more U.S. Treasuries than does any other entity, and they hold large amounts of U.S. corporate and agency securities. The nominal amount of U.S. securities bought by foreign investors has increased substantially over the years, largely reflecting a sharp increase in the amount of international reserves held by foreign central banks. The most notable of these is China. At the end of December 2009, China held $2.4 trillion in reserves, up from $400 billion five years earlier and $150 billion in 1999. As with other nations, China built up its reserves by running large current account surpluses with the rest of the world, basically by taking in more money than it sent out. China's trade surplus with the United States has been particularly large, running at around $200 billion in 2009. Worldwide the United States had a $360 billion trade deficit in 2009. The surpluses of dollars China and the rest of the world accumulate need a home. As the world's reserve currency, this means the money is kept in dollars (not converted to any other currency) and housed, typically in U.S. Treasuries, the most liquid fixed-income securities in the world. The safest? Well, that has been viewed as a given for quite a number of years.

As the world's reserve currency, more of the world's transactions are conducted in dollars than any other currency, which by itself gives the U.S. dollar support. Moreover, the United States is a superpower, and hence it is the world's greatest power militarily, economically, and politically. These are reasons to convince any nation to feel safe investing in the United States. As ever present as these conditions have always seemed, the lines between the United States and other nations is blurring largely because of the ascension of other nations—China in particular. The root of this transformation is economic, but it is also political, with the rest of the world seen as having lost confidence in the United States' ability to lead following troubles in Iraq, Afghanistan, and other parts of the world.

On the economic front, the idea that investments in the United States are completely safe has lost some of its luster and is under threat. While the rest of the world is in the midst of a secular upswing, the United States is arguably in the midst of a secular downturn brought on by an unwinding of the excess use of financial leverage. The U.S. government has had to use its balance sheet to repair the balance sheets of the private sector, putting the United States itself at risk. In the past investors did not question actions taken by the fiscal authority to help the private sector. Times are changing. Today, investors have made sovereign credit risk their risk factor du jour. No longer are investors sitting ready with blank checks to underwrite any amount of debt governments wish to offer.

In 2010 the signs of revolt were beginning to appear, with investors pressuring interest rates and the cost of default insurance upward in developed nations in Europe, in particular the PIGS nations—Portugal, Ireland, Greece (especially), and Spain, all of which are part of the European Monetary Union. We are witnessing discriminatory investors as we have never seen them, collectively dropping their bias toward investing in developed nations and letting new criteria dictate their country selection. The focus on sovereign credit risk now means selecting from a shrunken list of developed nations and looking to the emerging markets where debt-to-GDP dynamics for many nations are far better than in the developed world and where economic growth is exceeding that of developed nations.

Like a banker, investors these days are asking themselves, "Would I rather lend money to nations whose debt burden is improving, or to nations where it is worsening?" Increasingly, the focus on sovereign credit risk means that the answer is the former, not the latter.

For the United States, its immense power means that any loss of hegemony will occur over many years. This will help to sustain the U.S. dollar as the world's reserve currency. Moreover, with Europe under duress, there is no alternative to the dollar and there is no other bond market in which the world can house its nearly $8 trillion of reserve assets. Investors can't turn, for example, to China, whose balance sheet is unmatched, because China has no bond market. This all means that the United States can kick the can down the road before it has to worry about whether foreign investors will continue to invest in U.S. Treasuries.

Still, the day of reckoning won't be put off for long if the United States continues to run massive budget deficits and shows no sign that it will tackle the thorniest budget issue: entitlement spending. Estimates are that the U.S. budget deficit, which in fiscal year 2009 was $1.415 trillion, or about 10 percent of the GDP, will stay high for many years, running around 4 or 5 percent of the GDP in 2015 when factors related to the aging of the baby boomers (those born between 1946 and 1964) accelerate the increase in entitlement spending. In addition, the massive accumulation of U.S. debt during the crisis years will boost its interest payments—massively, such that interest payments will exceed all discretionary spending by 2020, as shown in Figure 9.9. This will be the result of the United States' failure to reduce its so-called *primary deficit*, which is the budget deficit minus interest payments.

FIGURE 9.9 Interest Payments on the National Debt Are Set to Soar in the United States

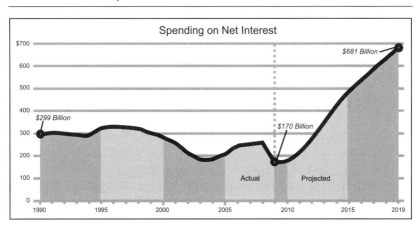

Note: Figures adjusted for inflation into 2009 dollars.

Source: *Heritage Special Report,* July 27, 2009; White House Office of Management and Budget, *Budget of the United States Government, FY 2010,* Historical Table, Table 3.2 (July 15, 2009); and Congressional Budget Office (CBO), *A Preliminary Analysis of the President's Budget and an Update of CBO's Budget and Economic Outlook,* March 2009 (July 15, 2009).

A zero primary balance, which the United States has maintained most years, or at least almost has, is what is needed to stabilize the debt-to-GDP ratio. The problem is that the United States is expected to run a primary deficit of around 2 percent or so into the middle of the decade and possibly beyond, which means that the U.S. debt-to-GDP ratio will continue to rise, as is forecast by many and shown in Figure 9.10.

In the absence of substantive measures to reduce the structural elements of the U.S. budget deficit, the U.S. debt burden will worsen. Investors are smart enough to recognize this, which means the amount of time before investors focus more intensely on the U.S. situation may not be all that far off the horizon. At that time, investors will ask the question of our age: If the United States is backing its financial system, who is backing the United States? For now and in the near future, the answer will be "everyone," including foreign investors. Dream on, though, if you feel that investors have endless tolerance for U.S. fiscal profligacy. The fact is that this is an age in which sovereign credit risk is in focus as never before.

Now that you've got my take on sovereign credit risk, here are a few other factors that normally impact the appetite of foreign investors for U.S. bonds:

- Relative inflation rates
- Relative returns on risk assets such as corporate equities

FIGURE 9.10 Debt Held by the Public as a Percentage of GDP

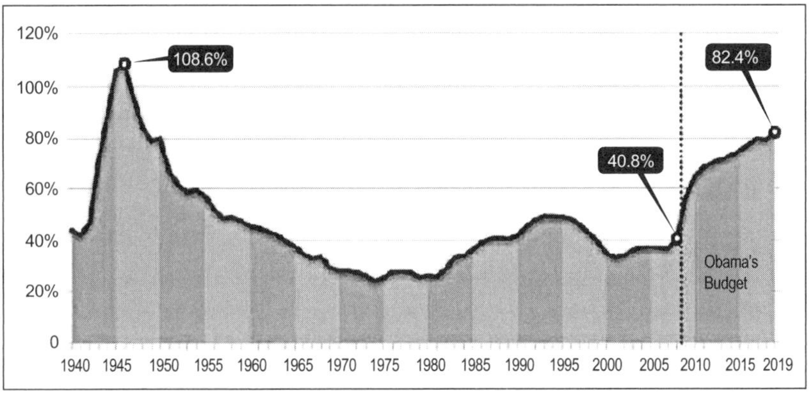

Source: White House Office of Management and Budget and Congressional Budget Office (CBO).

• External events
• International capital flows related to commodity price movements
• Expectations on economic growth
• Liquidity preferences
• Risk attitudes

Technical Analysis

As I mentioned earlier, when it comes to fundamental and technical analysis, investors basically can be divided into three camps: the technicians, the fundamentalists, and the hybrids. While one camp may put more or less emphasis on technical analysis than the others, large numbers of investors use technical analysis in one way or another. Collectively, followers of technical analysis therefore can have a large impact on the behavior of bond prices.

The nature of technical analysis increases its impact on markets. Generally this is an exact science, and followers of technical analysis buy and sell securities at prices dictated by the signals sent by the various forms of technical analysis. Since most of these price points are drawn from the same set of analyses, followers of technical analysis often are prompted to buy and sell at the same prices. Because they act virtually in unison, technical analysis often becomes a self-fulfilling prophecy. This is why it is important to be aware of market levels that may trigger technically driven buying and selling.

It is important to keep in mind that technically driven trading is most prevalent in the futures market. As a result, many technical buy and sell signals are based on futures prices rather than on yields, although at the end of the day yields are by far the more powerful influence. This is because yield levels are dictated by powerful fundamental influences that define the true level of the bond market's fair value. Nevertheless, both prices and yields serve as important support and resistance levels as well as trigger points for purchases and sales.

There are several types of technical analysis I have found to be reliable in terms of conjoining technical analysis with fundamental analysis. I am a fundamentalist at heart, and so I have been very choosy about applying technical analysis to the formulation of investment strategies. Moreover, as a precondition for weaving technical analysis into my fundamental analysis of the market outlook, I first assess whether technical factors may be ascending in importance in the market outlook. This becomes obvious when the market's behavior begins to depart from market fundamentals and/or when market trends accelerate. I have found that the following widely used forms of technical analysis are the important ones in terms of market impact:

- Benchmark yield levels
- Moving averages
- Fibonacci levels
- Previous highs and lows
- Relative strength indexes

The methodology used to compute the prices that correspond to some of these analyses is sometimes a bit complex, so let's take a brief look at each one and focus particularly on how to apply it to the bond market.

Benchmark Yield Levels

Just as occurs when the Dow Jones Industrial Average reaches round numbers such as 10,000, the bond market tends to place a relatively high degree of emphasis on round numbers, in particular for benchmark yield levels. A yield of 4.0 percent, for example, tends to be viewed as a key support and resistance level. Other key support and resistance levels tend to be in increments of 25 basis points—for example, 3.75 percent and 4.25 percent. Widespread recognition of benchmark levels results in technically driven buying and selling.

Once approached, a failure to breach a benchmark yield level tends to push the market in the opposite direction. That is why if you are considering liquidating a security at a benchmark yield level, you should consider placing your price a few basis points short of that level. For example, if yields are falling (prices are rising) and you are considering selling your bond at 4.0 percent, consider selling it at 4.03 percent instead so that you will not run the risk of missing the sell point completely because of the market's failure to breach the benchmark level. An optimist would treat the situation differently, hoping that the yield would break 4.0 percent and draw in new buyers on the notion that the breach will lead to a new, higher trading range for prices.

With respect to what an investor should do in this case, remember the credo: fear losses and hope for gains. You must decide whether, based on fundamental factors, a break will happen and also be sustained. Otherwise, you are just trading—which in some cases is appropriate but it is no substitute for a thorough investment strategy that is based on underlying fundamentals.

Many key yield levels are dependent on where it is that investors believe rates should be relative to inflation, which of course means that investors must have a view on where the inflation rate is headed. Another major influence is the official policy rate, which for the United States is the federal funds rate. It will dictate the yield on short-term maturities in particular, and expectations about the rate will be embedded in maturities across the yield curve.

Moving Averages

Moving averages serve as support and resistance levels. A *moving average* is simply the average price (usually the closing price) of a security for a specified number of trading days. For example, a 40-day moving average is the average closing price of the last 40 trading sessions. Moving averages are useful because they give investors a sense of the midpoint of the most recent trading range. A break above or below the moving average therefore sends a signal about whether the market may be entering a new trend. The most commonly used moving averages are 20-day, 30-day, 40-day, 100-day, and 200-day averages. The best one to use depends on whether an investor is looking at the market's short-term or long-term trends. The 200-day moving average tends to be very important to investors because it is rarely breached and relates to the long-term trend.

Fibonacci Levels

The origin of Fibonacci analysis is quite interesting. Fibonacci is the name of a mathematician who lived in Pisa, Italy, around 1170 to 1240; his first name was Leonardo. To investors, one of Fibonacci's most important theories relates to the so-called *golden mean*, which is basically a ratio that appears to be present in the growth patterns of many things in nature, including the petals on a flower, the spiral formed by a shell, and pinecones. Fibonacci discovered a number series from which the golden mean could be derived. Beginning with the sequence 0, 1, 1, 2, 3, 5, 8, 13, 21, and so on, each number is the sum of the two preceding numbers. Dividing each number in the series by the one that precedes it produces a ratio of about 1.618034, which is equal to the golden mean. The inverse of that number is 61.8 percent. What's fascinating is that so much of human nature seems to relate to the golden mean ratio of 1.618034.

From Pisa to Wall Street, Fibonacci's work has found a home. The financial markets use Fibonacci analysis to determine support and resistance levels. In theory, after a specified move in the market—particularly a significant move—market prices will retrace a certain percentage of the original move. This is intuitive and consistent with the normal patterns of markets. The Fibonacci retracement percentages are 23.6 percent, 38.2 percent, 50.0 percent, and 61.8 percent. Retracements of these percentages are considered normal consolidations of market prices. Retracements beyond these percentages suggest that the previous market move has been invalidated and a full retracement of that move will occur.

There is a bit of fuzziness to this, however. In most cases a retracement greater than 50 percent will invalidate a previous market move and thus suggest that a full retracement is under way. In some cases, however, a market can retrace 61.8 percent of a move yet maintain its trend once the consolidation phase has ended. Many analysts believe that a 61.8 percent retracement is normal. I have found, however, that a retracement of more than 50 percent often portends a full retracement.

Here's an example. If the price of a security rises from 90 to 100, a normal Fibonacci retracement could take the security down to 95 (a 50 percent retracement of the 10-point gain). A 61.8 percent Fibonacci retracement could take the security down to 93.82. If the security holds those support levels, the upward trend remains intact. If the levels are breached, the 10-point gain is invalidated and a reversal back to 90 should be expected.

Thus, to use Fibonacci levels, pick a specific market move and do the math. You can pick almost any price move over any period of time, depending on the market move you believe is ripe for or in the middle of consolidation.

Previous Highs and Lows

When traders look for support and resistance levels, a convenient source is the most recent highs and lows in the futures price or the cash yield. For example, in the futures market the previous day's high and low are looked at as resistance and support levels, respectively. Breaks of these levels often spark an acceleration of the market's price movement. Highs and lows for the previous day, week, month, and so on, frequently are used by bond investors as key levels to track and as a basis for buying and selling securities. Breaks of highs and lows for extended periods of time are likely to have the most potent impact.

Relative Strength Indexes

The math behind the relative strength index (RSI) is quite complex, and so we'll leave it to mathematicians and computers to compute, but RSIs are nonetheless easy to understand and use. *Relative strength indexes* basically measure the degree to which the bond market is overbought or oversold, and they are based on a security's past price behavior. RSIs are expressed on a scale of 0 to 100. In the bond market, as well as other markets, an RSI of 30 or lower indicates that it is oversold while a reading of 70 or higher indicates that the market is overbought. I have found that the 9-day RSI gives one of the best signals of the market's condition, and it is one of the most popular parameters.

The second most frequently used is the 14-day RSI. There is little room for subjective analysis of the RSI, and so when either the 9-day or the 14-day RSI is in overbought or oversold territory, one should look for the market to reverse course and position oneself accordingly. One must keep in mind that the RSI could stay in overbought or oversold territory long enough to cause a trading position to go awry. Therefore, technical indicators such as the RSI should not carry excessive weight in the investment decision.

There are many other forms of technical analysis, but I believe the ones mentioned above are some of the most effective. Chapter 11 describes a number of other indicators in the futures market that can be used to gauge the market's technical condition.

Summary

- Having a deep understanding of the many reasons why bond yields fluctuate is an essential part of interest rate forecasting.
- The five elements of an accurate interest rate forecast are monetary policy, inflation expectations, the pace of economic growth, secular and cyclical influences, and the market's technical condition.
- In assessing each of these major influences, it is important to ask several questions: How much inflation does the bond market expect,

and are its expectations reasonable or do they reflect excesses in market sentiment? How much economic growth is the bond market priced for, and what are the chances that this growth rate will be realized? Are cyclical or secular forces likely to be the more dominant influence in the short run, and have cyclical forces pushed bond yields into territory that conflicts with secular trends that will likely push yields in a different direction? What is the market's technical condition, and what are the technical influences that might upend conclusions drawn about the market outlook from an analysis of market fundamentals?

• Combined, the answers to these questions provide a solid basis on which to build an interest rate forecast. From there, a wealth of investment strategies can be formulated along with the convictions needed to implement them and see them through to profitability.

10

FROM TULIPS TO TREASURIES
Tracking Market Sentiment to Forecast Market Behavior

Tracking market sentiment has been one of the most reliable ways to forecast price changes in stocks, bonds, home prices, commodities, tulips—you name it. Extreme bullishness and extreme bearishness have foretold key turning points in asset prices for centuries. The same principles apply to the bond market, and there are a number of ways to track bond market sentiment. In this chapter you will learn about the six indicators that are most closely correlated with key turning points in the bond market. These indicators can be used not only to forecast the future direction of the bond market but also to forecast the future performance of both the stock market and the economy.

On Wall Street one of the best ways to forecast whether the markets are headed up or down is to assess whether investors are bullish or bearish. The theory is that if everyone is bullish, the market is likely to fall. Conversely, if everyone is bearish, the market is likely to rise. Market history is strewn with periods when this time-tested theory has proven true. The demise of the housing and credit bubbles provide the most recent example of this relationship, and a dramatic one at that. Extreme market sentiment occurs more often than investors generally expect, which is a rationale to track it and to consider tail-risk hedging strategies geared to provide protection against big moves in the markets.

The reason why extremes in market sentiment typically portend market reversals is fairly simple. If the preponderance of investors are either very bullish or very bearish, this most likely means that market prices fully reflect sentiments about the market's underlying fundamentals. In other words, extreme bullishness or bearishness tends to reflect the digestion of and reaction to a set of bullish or bearish news, respectively, in the past, present, and near future. For example, if over a number of months the equity market falls because of widespread pessimism about the state of the economy, the decline probably means that a large amount of bearish corporate and economic news has already been priced in. Therefore, if more bad news on the economy rolls in, few investors are likely to be surprised and stock prices probably will not move much lower on the news.

Here's where smart investors have an opportunity to make money from such a situation: With market pessimism at an extreme and most investors therefore on the lookout for more bad corporate and economic news, even a small degree of good news probably will cause stocks to move sharply higher as investors scramble to get on board. A smart investor buys stocks when pessimism is pervasive and a large amount of bearish news already has been factored into prices. Savvy investors that were buyers of risk assets in late 2008 and early 2009 profited handsomely "buying fear." Similarly, when most investors are bullish on stocks or other assets, they become vulnerable to bad news and can readily fall if the news does not fit with investors' notion of a perfect world. Can you say "housing bubble"? Unfortunately, far too many investors in housing and mortgage-related assets know this word all too well.

Blame it on human nature, perhaps. Generations of investors have gone through unavoidable bouts of extreme emotion where rational thinking has been cast aside. In such cases, emotions, not fundamentals, drive the market. Fear and greed become the dominant influences on prices, driving the markets to extreme levels.

A classic example of this was the great tulip mania that occurred in Holland in the period 1634 to 1637. During those years horticultural experiments created new exotic tulips that the common people of Holland craved not only for their beauty but also as a status symbol. Before long buyers who sought tulip bulbs for their beauty gave way to speculators who merely sought financial gain. Local market exchanges developed from the craze, and bulbs were widely traded.

At the height of the tulip mania in 1635, a single bulb was sold for the following items:

- 4 tons of wheat
- 8 tons of rye
- 1 bed
- 4 oxen
- 1 suit of clothes
- 2 casks of wine
- 4 tons of beer
- 2 tons of butter

- 8 pigs
- 12 sheep

- 1,000 pounds of cheese
- 1 silver drinking cup

The present value of these items is roughly $35,000—for a single bulb! What followed, of course, was a reality check in 1637 that brought prices back down to earth, and prices have never looked back.

Modern times have not been without similar bouts of mania-oriented speculation, and the most recent of course was the rise and fall of the housing market, and before that the dot-com bubble in 2000. Here's an important point: the fact that these bubbles occurred with such magnitude in an era of tremendous sophistication clearly illustrates that no generation can escape the power of its emotions. It's human nature.

Extreme sentiment occurs partly because individuals tend to put excessive weight on their most recent experience and unjustifiably extrapolate from recent trends and what they say about the future. In other words, when prices move sharply in one direction for a sustained period, individuals tend to believe that the trend will continue even though it may not be supported by underlying fundamentals and may be against statistical odds. Individuals therefore have a tendency to become overly optimistic when prices are rising and overly pessimistic when prices are falling.

Compounding investors' tendency to put too much weight on their most recent experience is their tendency to adopt a herd mentality when the herd starts running. The herd mentality that tends to develop in the financial markets is no different from the herd mentality seen in holiday seasons gone by, when people rushed to the stores to buy Cabbage Patch dolls, Tickle-Me-Elmos, Pokemons, and Zhu Zhu Pets. Individuals have a tendency to adopt the attitudes of other individuals when they observe that large numbers of people have the same attitude.

It is fair to say that human behavior is not going to change any time soon, and so there is every reason to incorporate an analysis of market sentiment into one's investment strategies. This is one of the essential elements of investing, and it can be applied to virtually every market.

The Bond Market Goes to Extremes Too

While until recently the type of extreme speculation that has roiled other markets has rarely infected the bond market, bouts of speculative excess and extreme emotions have frequently played a large role in the bond market's behavior. It is easy to see how when one considers that in a market as large as the bond market, there are obviously large numbers of participants who are subject to the same human emotions that create excesses in other markets.

Tracking investor sentiment in the bond market can enhance your investment returns in bonds significantly and help enhance the returns on your other financial investments too, mainly by helping you time investments better. If, for example, market sentiment appears to be at a level that historically has indicated that investors may be excessively bullish, you might consider delaying a purchase of bonds until prices retreat a bit. Similarly, if market sentiment appears to indicate excess bearishness, you might want to hasten purchases of bonds or perhaps be opportunistic and buy bonds for a capital gain if achieving capital gains is one of your investment objectives. It is also a good idea to look for signs of extreme sentiment within the various segments of the bond market in order to help decide on which segments to avoid and or invest in. Tracking sentiment can also assist in spotting risks and opportunities along the yield curve.

Beyond the benefits to bond investors, tracking investor sentiment in the bond market can help an investor forecast changes in stock prices and the economy. The basic premise is this: Because the bond market's behavior tends to be influenced strongly by its expectations about the economy and other macro influences, when bond market sentiment reaches an extreme, that extreme can reflect sentiment about the future direction of the economy as well as about bond prices. In other words, when bond market sentiment is at an extreme, sentiment about the economy must be at an extreme too. You therefore can apply your analysis of bond market sentiment to potential turning points in the economy and/or stock prices.

Here is an example. Say bond market sentiment is extremely bullish because bond investors are very pessimistic about the economy. Keep in mind that bond investors benefit when the economy is weak because inflation and the fed funds rate tend to be low in such an environment. In such a situation the bond market's pessimism about the economy is likely to be reflected in the stock market too. After all, bond investors also buy stocks and vice versa, and both bond and stock investors are exposed to basically the same information about the economy.

Therefore, if bond market sentiment reaches an extreme because of extreme sentiments about the economy, you can assume that sentiments toward the economy in other markets also are likely to be near extremes. Equity investors therefore should track bond market sentiment to help them form judgments about the future direction of stock prices, which are influenced significantly by the economy's performance just as bond prices are.

The tendency of markets to reach extreme valuations will exist as long as humans—not machines—are making the investment decisions. It's human nature for investors to fall victim to fear and greed. Emotions therefore play an important role in the behavior of the markets, and it would be extremely naive to think that this will change any time soon. Assessing market sentiment is therefore a worthy endeavor. I cannot imagine assessing the markets without including an assessment of market sentiment. After all, a forecast of the direction of market prices is essentially a forecast of the behavior of people. Therefore, it is essential to incorporate the human element into the formulation of investment strategies. You'll spot more risks and opportunities in the process.

Is the Market Long or Short? The Answer Could Determine Your Next Trade

In the bond market one of the best ways to gauge investor sentiment is to track the aggregate positions of bond investors. In other words, ask yourself if investors are long or short, and by this we mean with respect to duration exposure, curve positioning, futures exposure, and exposure to riskier types of bonds. The answer will give you a sense of whether market sentiment is at an extreme and is poised for a reversal.

For example, a market that is very long is not likely to gain much when investors are already fully invested and a large amount of bullish news already has been factored into prices. Similarly, a market that is very short is not likely to fall much further when investors already are holding large short positions and a large amount of bearish news already has been factored into prices. Historically, and as one might expect, when key indicators have suggested that the market's aggregate position is either very long or very short, the market has tended to move in the opposite direction soon afterward. We will explain how you can tell whether the market is long or short in this chapter.

For Extreme Market Sentiment to Reverse, Catalysts Often Are Needed

The timing of reversals in extreme market sentiment varies, of course, and knowing when a reversal will occur is one of the more challenging aspects of using market sentiment to forecast market behavior. As the expression goes, the market can remain irrational for longer than you can remain solvent. This is why it is extremely important to consider whether a catalyst may be needed before an extreme market condition is reversed. In most cases a catalyst of some sort is necessary before the reversal begins. The form the catalyst will take is often unknowable and often becomes clear only after the catalyst has sparked the reversal.

This said, when market sentiment is at an extreme, the market is extremely susceptible to a wide variety of information that may be at odds with the entrenched views that are at the root of the extreme sentiment. This is the case because by definition, market sentiment reaches extremes because investors have taken into account only one possible outcome in regard to future events. As a result, the market essentially puts itself into a box, requiring the preponderance of new information to fit its one-sided view. It therefore becomes increasingly likely that new information will surface that conflicts with the market's one-sided views and will upend the market's existing trend. Therefore, while there may be times when it is important to wait for a catalyst before concluding that extreme market sentiment will be reversed, it is often not necessary to wait for one since the very nature of the extreme sentiment increases the likelihood that a catalyst will come along. Confidence in an underlying set of fundamental factors can increase one's fortitude when engaging in strategies that use sentiment as a basis for an investment or trading decision.

Once a catalyst comes along, abrupt reversals often emerge and price movements can be quite sharp. The depth and duration of the reversals depend on the extent to which sentiment is at an extreme and the nature of the catalyst that sparks the reversal. The nature of the decline that occurred during the financial crisis was secular, not cyclical, which is why the decline was so severe. Reversals in market sentiment that occur from an unwinding of extreme sentiment alone are not likely to be severe, yet they can be both abrupt and substantial.

The behavior of the bond market and other markets in the aftermath of periods when market sentiment has reached an extreme has proven time and time again that tracking market sentiment is one of the most important elements of formulating investment strategies. In the bond market there are six key indicators that have been excellent indicators of market sentiment and hence reliable indicators of future market behavior. Combined, they send powerful signals about market sentiment:

- The put/call ratio
- The Commodity Futures Trading Commission's Commitments of Traders report
- Aggregate duration surveys
- The yield spread between 2-year T-notes and the federal funds rate
- The yield spread between the LIBOR and the federal funds rate
- The yield spread between corporate bonds and Treasuries

Let's take a look at each of these indicators. Keep in mind that although each indicator has somewhat different information content, it is best to use the indicators together to get the most reliable signal and to develop the best overall strategy.

The Put/Call Ratio

The *put/call ratio* is a popular gauge of market sentiment that is used by stock and bond investors alike. It is simply a measure of the daily trading volume in put options compared with the daily trading volume in call options. Since puts are a bearish bet on the future direction of the market and calls are a bullish bet, extreme volume in either one is a sign of excess sentiment.

A time-tested indicator in the stock market, the put/call ratio has reliably pointed to excesses in bullish and bearish sentiment and, hence, to turning points in stock prices. In early 2000, for example, the put/call ratio accurately pointed to excess optimism about the outlook for equities. The same thing has held true in the bond market where the put/call ratio has been a great guide to spotting tops and bottoms.

Bond investors in the 1990s looked at the inverse of the put/call ratio because call volume generally exceeded put volume, resulting in a put/call ratio of over 1.0, where 1.0 indicates that one call traded for every put. Investors prefer to quote ratios when they are over 1.0, so whenever market participants discussed or analyzed options activity, the put/call ratio was used. In the stock market put volume typically exceeds call volume; that is, the put/call ratio is generally greater than 1.0. Equity investors therefore prefer to follow the put/call ratio.

Call volume in the bond market has tended to be higher than put volume because investors generally are more concerned about sudden increases in prices than about decreases. This is the case because in general there are many more events that could cause bond prices to suddenly surge than to fall. When bond investors buy call options, they are buying protection against unexpected events. This is different from the way it is in the stock market, where most sudden moves tend to be downward and investors buy puts for protection against sudden market declines. After all, whoever heard of a melt-up in stock prices?

Over the past decade, two shocks to the financial system and two recessions contributed to very low interest rate environments. This caused a shift in options volume, such that the put/call ratio fell below 1.0, reflecting the view that there was more downside for Treasury prices than there was upside, given that rates were historically very low (and prices were historically high). In fact, in the over-the-counter market, the prices of options that investors were buying in 2009 to protect against large moves in interest rates were said to be skewed high relative to calls. Investors were thought to be purchasing protection against interest rate increases that might result from the Federal Reserve's loose monetary policy.

In the bond market, the interest rate option used most widely to track the put/call ratio is trade at the Chicago Board of Trade (CBOT). Trading volume in the CBOT's contracts is quite high, and participation in Treasury options includes a wide variety of investors. The CBOT's options therefore capture investor sentiment well. Trading volume in Eurodollar options actually exceeds by a very large margin the trading in Treasury options. The message embedded in trading volume in Eurodollar options is quite useful, but it is narrowly focused on sentiment toward the short end of the yield curve, and therefore it is not as indicative of the risk-taking mindset of the speculative element of the bond market, which is what we are trying to capture when tracking trading volume.

As an indication of trading volume and open interest, note that on February 13, 2010, there were roughly 21 million options contracts outstanding on all interest rate products traded at the CME Group, where Treasury and Eurodollar options are traded. Of that 21 million, roughly 1.6 million option contracts were outstanding in 10-year notes compared to 13.8 million options contracts outstanding on Eurodollar futures. Interestingly, despite the massive difference in open interest, volume for the 10-year options can be near half or more of the volume seen in Eurodollar options, owing to the large presence of speculative flows in the 10-year notes relative to Eurodollars. This is what we want to focus on.

Historically, the put/call ratio on T-bonds was a better gauge of market sentiment than the put/call ratio on 10-year notes mainly because the T-bond contract was once the more active contract and it was where most of the speculative flow tended to reside. Speculators tend to gravitate toward volatile instruments, and it is the speculative fervor of the market that we are most interested in gauging. The Treasury Department's decision in 1999 to curtail and then suspend its issuance of 30-year bonds in 2002 led to the demise of 30-year bonds as a benchmark for U.S. interest rates, and volume in T-bond contracts declined. The 10-year displaced 30-year bonds as the benchmark for U.S. rates.

Although there is a smaller speculative element in 10-year notes compared to that of the long bonds, the 10-year also can be used as an indicator of sentiment and is a great gauge of the extent to which mortgage-related activity may be causing excesses in market sentiment. (Investors with mortgage-backed portfolios tend to buy call options when interest rates are falling to hedge against rising prepayments of their mortgage securities, which are prepaid at an increasing rate when mortgage rates fall and households either refinance their mortgages or prepay their existing mortgages in favor of a new mortgage for a new dwelling.)

The best way to use the put/call ratio is to compare its 10-day average to its one-year average. The 10-day average works well because it removes a great deal of daily noise from the analysis. When the 10-day average moves sharply above or below the one-year average, it generally indicates that market sentiment is moving toward an extreme. From the middle of 2001 through the middle of 2008, the one-year average of the put/call ratio increased steadily, from about 1.3 to around 1.4. The daily put/call ratio began to fall when in the fourth quarter of 2008 the financial markets became unstable and money drifted toward Treasuries.

Investors at that time were more interested in protecting against declines in the price of risk assets, and they sought long exposure to the Treasury market, doing so also by purchasing call options in case events caused rates to continue falling. Hence, in November 2008 the daily put/call ratio frequently traded at around 0.5 or so, reaching a low of 0.4 on November 28, which was just three days after the Fed announced a program to purchase direct obligations of housing-related government-sponsored enterprises (GSEs) and mortgage-backed securities backed by Fannie Mae and Freddie Mac. At that time, put volume increased sharply, and December's put/call ratio averaged 1.76, an extreme for a 30-day period. The activity was a sign of investors' "fighting the tape," so to speak, and yields fell sharply, with the 10-year yield falling from about 3.75 percent in mid-November to as low as 2.055 percent on December 30—its low for the cycle. On a 30-day moving average basis, the 1.76 reading has been very close to the extreme of the past few years, so it serves as a good reference point on market sentiment.

Importantly, the put/call ratio fell fairly sharply relative to the trend in the first quarter of 2009, a period when market interest rates were on the rise, averaging 0.79 following the first week of the quarter through the end of the quarter. The yield on the 10-year note increased to as high as about 3 percent during the quarter, in part reflecting an unwinding of bullish sentiment evident in the level of call volume. The trend continued in the second quarter, with the 10-year yield moving close to 4 percent.

Figure 10.1 shows the behavior of the put/call ratio in recent years (2006 to the present).

The volatility in financial markets in recent times has made it more difficult to evaluate which level of the put/call ratio best indicates an extreme in market sentiment. Nevertheless, using Figure 10.1 as a gauge, and

FIGURE 10.1 Daily Put/Call Ratio for 10-Year T-Note Futures, 2006 to Present

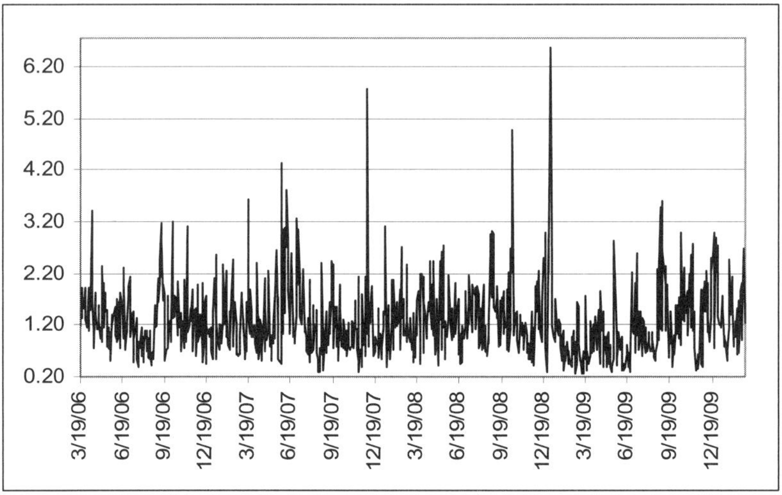

Source: Chicago Board of Trade (CBOT) and Bloomberg.

in particular the 10-day moving average, it is clear that the extremes are roughly a percentage point apart, from about 0.8 to 1.8. For reference, note that in 2009, the put/call averaged 1.18; in 2008, it averaged 1.36; in 2007, it averaged 1.22; and in 2006, it averaged 1.39. Use these ranges and the extremes to form judgments about market sentiment.

When the put/call ratio is at either of the extremes, it is usually not long before the bond market turns. How long? Historically we usually say that it would be a matter of weeks, if not days, before the turn occurs. Today, with major secular forces at the root of much of the bond market's movement, the signal probably won't be as strong or as prescient unless the degree to which the market reaches an extreme is high, as it was in the periods referenced above. Therefore, when the put/call ratio is at either of the two extremes, seek possible catalysts that might send the market in a new direction and formulate your investment strategies accordingly. Typical catalysts include fundamental factors such as economic data and monetary policy. It is important to keep in mind, however, that as with all indicators, it is best to have confirmation from multiple sentiment indicators of the apparent excesses in market sentiment before making final decisions on an investment strategy.

Also keep in mind that when the bond market reverses course, the stock market does not necessarily go in the same direction. This is the case because there are times when the bond market's reversal can be rooted in factors that push the stock market in the opposite direction. For example, if optimism in the bond market is high as a result of pessimism about the economy (interest rates fall and prices rise when the economy is weak), the bond market may be poised to fall, while equities, which are usually weak when the economy is weak, may rise. In this case, a strengthening of the economy would serve as a catalyst for removing the excess bullishness in bonds, but it would be a boon to stocks because a stronger economy will lift corporate profits. Nevertheless, persistent weakness in bond prices is likely to have negative consequences for the equity market eventually because the resultant rise in interest rates probably will have a deleterious effect on the economy and corporate profits.

Tracking the put/call ratio is easy. You can obtain the data on daily volume from the CME Group's Web site (www.cmegroup.com, in the section on "volume and open interest" found within the button for Market Data Services) and take the total volume of puts traded on Treasury options and divide by the total volume of calls. That will give the daily ratio. The 10-day average, of course, is simply the average of the 10 previous trading sessions. You should compute this average yourself since it is not readily available.

The core elements of the put/call analysis can be readily applied to other markets and have proven to be a very useful gauge of investor sentiment in the bond market. When combined with other market sentiment indicators, the put/call ratio has pointed to numerous turning points in the bond market for many years, and it probably will be a useful indicator for years to come.

The Commodity Futures Trading Commission's Commitment of Traders Report

A telling indicator of speculative activity in the bond market can be found in government agency data on the futures market from statistics compiled weekly by the U.S. Commodity Futures Trading Commission (CFTC) in its Commitments of Traders (COT) report. As will be discussed in greater detail in Chapter 11, the COT report basically sums up and categorizes the holders of futures positions in all existing U.S. futures contracts, including futures for U.S. Treasuries. The COT report is useful for determining the extent to which recent activity in Treasury futures has been driven by speculative activity or commercial activity.

The CFTC separates the holders of bond futures into two main groups: commercials and noncommercials. Commercial traders in bond futures are the true end users of the contracts: the hedgers and those who are in the business of buying and selling fixed-income securities. Commercial traders are known as the "smart money." They can be primary dealers, insurance companies, pension funds, and the like. Noncommercials are considered speculators. This is the group to watch.

Market tops and bottoms frequently have been foreshadowed by extreme positions taken by noncommercial traders. This is the case largely because speculators have relatively less information than do commercial players about market fundamentals and the true level of underlying demand for fixed-income securities. In addition, speculators frequently have a herd mentality and are therefore more likely to alter their positions when commercial players ignite a change in the market's direction. Moreover, speculators have a tendency to accumulate relatively large positions toward the end of a market trend, when they let human nature get the best of them by letting greed dictate their actions.

As a group, the noncommercials are most definitely among those people who give too much weight to their most recent experience and extrapolate recent trends that run counter to long-run averages and statistical odds. Their optimism rises when the market rises and falls when the market falls. As speculators profit from their positions, they have an increasing tendency to remember their successes but not their failures or the risk of failure, unjustifiably increasing their confidence and, hence, their risk taking. Therefore, by following the futures positions held by noncommercials, investors can get a solid lead on possible turning points in the market.

Figure 10.2 shows the net positions held by noncommercial traders in 10-year Treasury futures contracts for the period 1998 to 2010. As you can see, the positions can move around a great deal, from long to short and back again. Take note of a few of the extremes, in 1998, 2000, and 2004. (The "extreme" of 1998 is more difficult to see given the expansion of the range over the years but take note that it was an extreme at that time.) In October 1998, just 13 days after noncommercial net long positions reached a record on September 22, bond prices fell over 5 percent in only four days, ushering in a long bear market in bonds that would last until early 2000. By then speculative activity had come full circle when on January 25, 2000, noncommercial traders held a record net short position, hinting at excess pessimism and an impending rally in bond prices.

Indeed, bond prices bottomed a week later, ushering in a long bull run that would last through 2000 and 2001. In 2004, the extreme short position at around midyear was followed by a near 75-basis-point decline in the 10-year's yield following a near 100-basis-point increase in the several months prior. The extreme bearishness reflected concern that the Federal Reserve

FIGURE 10.2 Net Positions Held by Noncommercial Traders in 10-Year Note Futures, in Number of Contracts

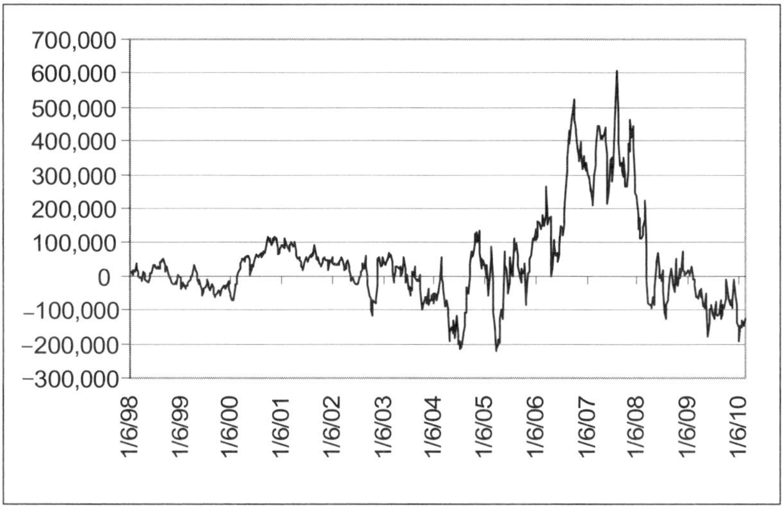

Source: U.S. Commodity Futures Trading Commission (CFTC) and Bloomberg.

might increase interest rates, which it did, delivering its first of seventeen 25-basis-point rate hikes stretching out to June 2006.

These are just a few examples of many similar episodes over many years. The message to take from the COT data is this: Follow the smart money; don't follow the dumb money. Speculators are seldom right about the market's direction.

I've isolated the 10-year note in my examples, when in reality it is necessary to look at trading activity in other Treasury maturities and in Eurodollar contracts. Combined, the positions speak to how traders are positioned along the yield curve, not just the overall market. Yield curve positioning in and of itself says volumes about market sentiment. For example, if traders are positioned heavily long both the Eurodollar and 2-year note contract while at the same time heavily short the 10- and 30-year contract, it would obviously indicate that traders are biased toward a steeper curve.

This says volumes about what investors believe regarding underlying fundamentals—chiefly, that monetary policy will take an accommodative stance. In turn, this says a great deal about how investors expect the evolution of economic data to fair, which is to say, traders would expect economic data to reflect economic growth and inflation to stay low enough to keep the Fed sidelined. If you have a view that is counter to this, it would be a basis for positioning for a flattening of the yield curve. When focusing on the combined activity of noncommercial traders across the yield curve rather than on a single maturity, one can get a better sense as to whether an extreme long or short in a single maturity is indicative of sentiment toward the overall market or toward a segment of the yield curve.

Aggregate Duration Surveys

The put/call ratio and the CFTC's COT report are great tools for gauging speculative excesses in the bond market because both gauges capture trading activity in the futures market, where speculative trading is relatively high. To get a more complete picture of where bond investors stand as a whole, it is important to look outside the futures market. One of the best things to look at is the activity of portfolio managers, the so-called end users of fixed-income securities, who are the main players in the movement of bond prices. Tracking the extent to which portfolio managers are long or short can yield important clues about whether market sentiment is at an extreme.

It is far easier to track the extent to which portfolio managers are long or short in the bond market than it is in other markets partly because the bond market largely consists of institutional investors rather than individual investors. This makes it easier to get data on portfolio positions. The best way to judge the way in which fixed-income portfolio managers are positioned in the market is to follow surveys on aggregate duration.

The rather obtuse term *duration* is less daunting than it seems. As was described in Chapter 3, duration is basically a measure of a bond's price sensitivity to changes in interest rates. It is a bit like a stock's beta. The longer the maturity of a bond, the higher its duration and the greater its price sensitivity to changes in interest rates. When portfolio managers want to increase their level of risk, perhaps to benefit from an impending rally in bond prices, they raise their portfolios' duration levels by increasing the average maturity on their bond holdings. In this way they stand to benefit when prices rise since longer maturities rise faster in price than shorter maturities do when yields fall in equal amounts.

Aggregate duration is basically the average duration of a set of portfolios. Aggregate duration surveys therefore capture the extent to which fixed-income portfolio managers have collectively adjusted their level of risk taking. Since the bond market is largely an institutional business, aggregate duration surveys are a microcosm of the risk profiles of the universe of fixed-income portfolios. Indeed, most duration surveys include portfolios that have a combined total of several hundred billion dollars in assets or more.

In fact, a survey conducted weekly by Ried Thunberg, an economic consulting company based in Connecticut, includes portfolios that in total have over $1 trillion in assets. The best and most reliable aggregate duration survey available that I have found is conducted weekly by Stone & McCarthy Research Associates (www.smra.com). That survey historically has had the best correlation with turning points in the bond market and therefore appears to capture market sentiment accurately.

When portfolio managers are bullish on bond prices, they increase their portfolios' duration to above the duration of their benchmark—the index their performance is judged against—so that if bond prices rise, their portfolios will outperform their benchmark index. A common index for portfolios to be judged against is the Barclays Capital Aggregate Bond Index, formerly the Lehman Aggregate Bond Index. Similarly, when portfolio managers are bearish, they decrease their duration to below that of their benchmark, hoping to outperform the benchmark on the way down.

Figure 10.3 shows that portfolio managers have historically been consistent in maintaining their duration levels between 96 and 106 percent of their target duration except in rare instances, typically when sentiment toward a certain economic condition is at an extreme. One of these periods

FIGURE 10.3 Aggregate Duration Levels of Portfolio Managers, as Percentage of Target, or Benchmark, Duration

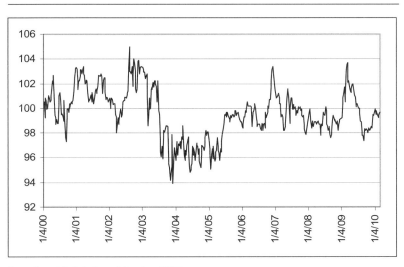

Source: Stone & McCarthy Research Associates (SMRA).

was in early 2009 when portfolio managers increased their duration levels sharply in anticipation of continued weak economic conditions. The situation turned out differently, with the U.S. economy stabilizing in the later half of 2009, compelling portfolio managers to cut their duration levels.

The steadiness of this duration range probably relates to the conservative nature of fixed-income investors as well as the mandate they give to portfolio managers to stay within a fairly strict range of risk parameters. Moreover, if a portfolio manager takes an extreme position and bets wrong, there is a good chance that the manager will disappoint and quite possibly lose investors. Many investors draw comfort from knowing that their investments will not be subject to extreme volatility. A portfolio that sticks to a duration range that is relatively narrow therefore can be a plus because it will tend to translate into lower volatility than it would if the duration level were moved within a wider range. Moreover, it makes the task of judging whether the market is at a bullish or bearish extreme much easier.

Using aggregate duration surveys to spot extreme market sentiment is simple. When aggregate duration falls below 100 percent, this suggests that in the aggregate, portfolios are short. The farther aggregate duration falls below 100 percent, the shorter portfolios are. At 96 percent (think of this as portfolios being 96 percent long relative to their benchmark's duration level), bearishness abounds, and market sentiment should be considered to be at an extreme. In this case the market is likely to be extremely oversold and ripe for a reversal, and you should consider positioning yourself accordingly in both equities and bonds. When aggregate duration is at 105 percent, bullishness abounds, and the market probably is extremely overbought and set to fall.

At 96 and 104 percent, aggregate duration surveys have reliably pointed to turning points in the bond market, but there are other levels that often foreshadow an impending market reversal. Specifically, 97 and 103 percent also can be seen as an extreme at times. This is the case because duration may fluctuate in this range over the short term and the intermediate term simply because conditions that would cause portfolio managers to push their durations to the farthest extremes are less common. Aggregate duration will fluctuate in this more narrow range when few unusual factors are affecting the market. It is therefore important to try to determine whether there may be factors that could push aggregates to their farthest extremes before using the more narrow range as a gauge of whether market sentiment is at an extreme. Keep in mind that even if aggregate duration is at a "neutral" level, you may be able to label the market long or short on the basis of your own subjective analysis of the market's underlying fundamentals.

Aggregate duration can be tracked by following the surveys conducted by several economic and fixed-income services companies, including Ried

Thunberg and Stone & McCarthy. In addition, many major brokerage firms, particularly primary dealers, conduct aggregate duration surveys, and you may be able to get the information from them if you have an account or a relationship of some kind with them. As was mentioned earlier, Stone & McCarthy's survey has been the most reliable and the best at capturing extremes in market sentiment and, hence, at forecasting turning points in the bond market. That is why I strongly recommend tracking Stone & McCarthy's duration survey most. Some of the surveys I mentioned are reported by major new services such as Dow Jones, Bloomberg, and Market News, and they can be tracked that way as well.

In the aftermath of the financial crisis, large increases projected in the amount of U.S. Treasury debt outstanding was expected to increase the average duration of major benchmark indexes such as the Barclays Aggregate index. This is because the Barclays index is market capitalization weighted. In other words, the more Treasuries that exist relative to the fixed-income universe, the more heavily weighted Treasuries will be in the Barclays index, and since the average maturity of Treasury debt outstanding is on the rise (it increased from a 26-year low of 48 months at the end of 2008 to 55 months at the end of 2009), the average maturity of the Barclays index will be on the rise, boosting its average duration.

It is unclear the extent to which portfolio managers will boost their duration to keep pace with the Barclays index (as well as other market-capitalization-weighted indexes). It is possible, for example, that portfolio managers will be reluctant to increase their duration levels by the same amount as is seen in the benchmark indexes that their portfolios are judged against.

The Yield Spread between 2-Year T-Notes and the Federal Funds Rate

Investors often are confused about which U.S. Treasury maturity they should follow as the benchmark for U.S. interest rates. While it is common for most to refer to the 10-year T-note, there is an often overlooked maturity that may be a better benchmark than all the rest and may better capture market sentiment and forecast turning points in the market: the 2-year T-note. The case for this benchmark is compelling.

The reason the 2-year T-note captures market sentiment so well is that it reflects with greater intensity sentiments toward the Federal Reserve better than any other actively traded maturity along the Treasury yield curve. This is the case largely because over time, the 2-year note has had a fairly stable relationship to the federal funds rate, the rate controlled by the Fed.

As you saw in Figure 9.1, the 2-year T-note is tightly linked to fluctuations in the fed funds rate. This is the case chiefly because yields on short-term maturities are determined largely by the cost of money and are not affected nearly as much by factors that dominate the behavior of long-term maturities such as inflation expectations, speculative flows, hedging activity, new issuance, and the budget situation. When the cost of money is higher than the yield on the 2-year T-note, investors who purchase the 2-year note with borrowed money are incurring what is known as *negative carry* because the interest they are paying on the borrowed money exceeds the yield-to-maturity on the 2-year note.

Investors who purchase securities by using borrowed money generally are unwilling to engage in investments that incur negative carry unless they believe that borrowing costs eventually will fall and result in positive carry on the investment. Investors recognize that there is very little time for an investment in a short-term maturity to evolve from negative carry to positive carry, and therefore they engage in negative carry trades very rarely. Investors seek the maximum amount of carry that they can earn, and carry is usually optimal in short-term maturities such as the 2-year note, a very popular instrument during periods when the Fed lowers interest rates. If you're thinking an investor could earn a greater amount of positive carry owning a 10-year note, this is true only on a dollar-for-dollar basis. Adjusted for equal risk, or on a duration-weighted basis, a greater amount of carry can be earned owning shorter maturities.

It is significant that the yield on the 2-year T-note has rarely been below the federal funds rate. In fact, if you look closely, you will see that there have been only five occasions in the last 20 years in which the yield on the 2-year T-note dipped below the fed funds rate. On all five occasions, and most recently in 2007, the Fed lowered interest rates soon afterward, usually within a few months. On each occasion investors tolerated negative carry for short periods because they felt the Fed would lower the fed funds rate, thus reducing borrowing costs and restoring positive carry to their investments.

During periods when the yield on the 2-year T-note has deviated from its historical relationship to the fed funds rate, it has given reliable signals about the bond market's true underlying feelings about the direction of the Fed's policy. The degree to which the yield on the 2-year note gravitates away from the fed funds rate therefore reveals a great deal about market sentiment toward the Fed. This sentiment sometimes reaches extremes owing to either unrealistic hopes for additional interest rate reductions or unrealistic fears of additional interest rate increases.

In many ways the 2-year T-note is therefore a more accurate gauge of the market's sentiment toward the Fed than is any other financial instrument. Longer maturities reflect too many other sentiments toward the market to be used as the optimal proxy for the Fed. This is the case because the longer the maturity on a bond is, the more long-term inflation expectations, speculative flows, and other elements come into play. These reflect the so-called *term premium*, which is the added yield that investors demand in order to compel them to purchase long-dated maturities instead of short-dated maturities. Longer maturities therefore are best used to gauge speculative excesses in the market rather than the excesses surrounding the market's sentiments toward the Fed. The 2-year T-note is best suited for that role.

If there is a maturity other than the 2-year note that is also a good proxy for the market's sentiment toward the Fed, it is the 5-year T-note. The relationship between the 5-year T-note and expectations about the fed funds rate is strong enough that the 5-year note can be called "the long bond of the short end." When sentiment on the Fed shifts, watch out! The 5-year note really moves and will tend to outperform other maturities when prices rise and underperform when prices fall. Nevertheless, the 2-year note historically has had a more stable relationship with the fed funds rate and is therefore a better gauge of market sentiment toward the Federal Reserve.

The 2-year T-note is a terrific benchmark, and I recommend that it be used in concert with the more commonly employed benchmarks on the long end of the yield curve. The other benchmarks do not capture market sentiment toward the Fed nearly as well, and those sentiments are crucial for determining the direction of movements in maturities across the yield curve as well as the direction of prices of other financial assets.

The Yield Spread between the LIBOR and the Federal Funds Rate

In 2008, few gauges provided a better illustration of the deep fear that existed in the financial markets than the yield spread between the London Interbank Offered Rate—the LIBOR—and the federal funds rate. The sharp widening in the spread, which is illustrated in Figure 10.4, indicated that banks were fearful of lending to each other. A widening spread indicates as much because when the LIBOR moves above the cost of money set by the Federal Reserve—the federal funds rate—it means that banks are concerned about both counterparty risk and liquidity, two factors that heavily influenced the behavior of the financial markets during the financial crisis. Such concerns compel banks to demand a higher interest rate from banks that borrow money from them.

FIGURE 10.4 Yield Spread between the Three-Month LIBOR and the Federal Funds Rate, in Percentage Points

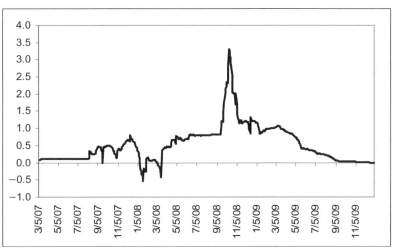

Source: Federal Reserve and British Bankers' Association (BBA).

While some widening of the yield spread between the LIBOR and the fed funds rate is normal when stresses arise, the magnitude of the widening seen in 2008 was unprecedented. The widening may have moved the needle in terms of the level of the spread that can be deemed wide enough to mark an extreme in sentiment. Typically a spread of about 100 basis points would indicate an extreme (see Figure 10.5). The takeaway from the extreme is that it signals fears about counterparty risk and liquidity, which together can cause a large amount of dislocation in prices of many financial assets, including Treasuries, corporate bonds, corporate equities, and much more. A wide spread can at times indicate excessive bearish sentiment toward the Federal Reserve. This happens during periods when the Fed is raising the fed funds rate. Its signaling effect is similar to that of the 2-year T-note.

In 2008, the Federal Reserve along with the world's central banks took actions to fix the interbank problem. For example, on October 13 to 14, 2008, the Federal Reserve announced that it had increased the size of its swap lines with the Bank of England, the European Central Bank, and the Swiss National Bank "to whatever quantity of U.S. dollar funding is demanded." In other words, the Fed said it would lend an unlimited amount of U.S. dollars to the central banks it named. The effort was meant to increase the supply of dollars available in the interbank market in order to increase its price. It worked.

FIGURE 10.5 Yield Spread between the Three-Month LIBOR and the Federal Funds Rate before the Financial Crisis, in Percentage Points

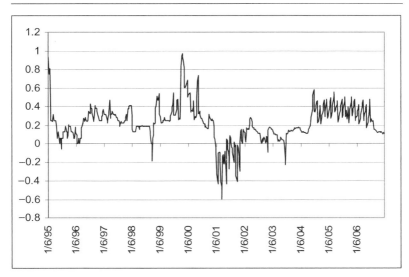

Source: Federal Reserve and British Bankers' Association (BBA).

The Yield Spread between Corporate Bonds and Treasuries

The interest rate spread between corporate bonds and in particular low-grade corporate bonds and Treasuries also sends signals about market sentiment that can be used along with the other sentiment indicators to spot excesses. Figure 5.4 in Chapter 5 illustrates the sharp fluctuations that can occur in the yield spread between low-grade corporate bonds and Treasuries. The yield spread is an effective tool because it can capture a wide variety of sentiments toward major influences such as the Federal Reserve, the economy, liquidity, and external influences such as foreign markets. When the economy weakens, for example, corporate bond investors tend to worry that cash flows will decline and result in an increase in the number of corporate defaults. In turn, corporate bond investors move higher up the capital structure and demand compensation through higher interest rates and a wider spread to Treasuries to be enticed to invest in riskier corporate bonds instead of Treasuries, where there is perceived to be no risk of default. In this way the yield spread between low-grade bonds and Treasuries is a great gauge of market sentiment, particularly with respect to risk aversion.

In a sense, the yield spread between low-grade corporate bonds and Treasuries is a reflection of positions held in Treasuries since it is likely that investors are merely shifting money between low-grade corporate bonds and Treasuries in line with their sentiments toward underlying market fundamentals. This will happen when investors are of the de-risking mindset. Keep in mind that the yield spread between low-grade bonds and Treasuries is probably a better coincident indicator than it is a leading indicator since the spread's behavior often reflects developments in the economy and other markets and therefore generally follows rather than leads those developments. Nevertheless, I recommend that yield spreads between low-grade corporate bonds and Treasuries be included in your toolbox of indicators of market sentiment.

One More Useful Indicator of Sentiment

There is another indicator I like to use to gauge market sentiment: the real yield on Treasury securities. It captures sentiment well and frequently can be used to forecast turning points in the bond market. However, it does not signal excesses as often as the indicators I described above do, and it does not relate as directly to the market's net positions.

As I discussed in Chapter 8, the real yield on a bond is its stated, or quoted, yield minus inflation. Bond investors almost always want some degree of real yield to compensate them for a variety of risks, particularly inflation. The fluctuations in real yields therefore reflect changes in market sentiment toward a variety of market fundamentals. When investors are optimistic about inflation, for example, real yields tend to decline. Real yields also tend to decline when the economy is weak and the Fed is lowering interest rates. With this in mind, real yields can be an excellent gauge of market sentiment. When real yields reach extremes, this should be taken as an indication that investors have strong sentiments toward any number of underlying market fundamentals that may be driving the bond market at that time. Whether the sentiments can be deemed extreme depends on whether the market's assumptions appear realistic; determining this is certainly a difficult task. However, if the extremes in real yields are accompanied by extreme positions, as seen by the indicators above, it is likely that market sentiment is at an extreme and that the risk of a market reversal is higher than normal.

Summary

- From tulips to Treasuries, human behavior has played an immense role in the behavior of markets for centuries. Even in these sophisticated times, however, investors continue to show that no amount of sophistication can release them from the grip of their own emotions, and they clearly remain vulnerable to bouts of fear and greed.

- The six indicators cited in this chapter are just some of the many indicators available for tracking market sentiment, but they are some of the best ones. They cast a wide net on investor sentiment by covering both the cash and futures markets, and it is rare indeed that the collective message of the indicators sends a false signal on the future direction of the bond market.

- Catalysts sometimes are needed before the market's extremes are corrected, but some form of correction is inevitable most of the time. Nevertheless, it is important to be mindful that the depth and duration of market extremes tend to go beyond most investors' expectations. Therefore, it is important to be careful about drawing automatic conclusions about the market outlook when the intelligence you gather from the sentiment indicators points to an impending reversal. Remember the axiom: the market can stay irrational for longer than you can remain solvent!

- Many investors probably have experienced the wide range of emotions that come into play in investing which may have affected their investment decisions. You can put your experiences to work for you by recognizing that there are literally millions of other investors who have the same emotions that you have.

- You also can endeavor to turn these emotions into opportunities to spot market extremes. Once you spot them, you will be able to get off the emotional roller coaster before everyone else does and be first in line for the next ride.

11

USING THE FUTURES
MARKET TO GATHER
MARKET INTELLIGENCE

The ability to trade goods and services freely without burdensome taxes and regulations is one of the most important elements in a capitalist society. Free trade promotes innovation, risk taking, and an efficient allocation of capital. In the United States free markets have been at the core of a wondrous history of economic growth for over two centuries. American citizens have sought prosperity wherever it might present itself. The financial markets have come to epitomize these freedoms and have played an immense role in fostering a climate conducive to the spectacular economic prosperity that the nation has enjoyed over many decades. The financial markets have been diverse for decades, but when most people think about the history of the financial markets, they typically think of only stocks and bonds. Few before the financial crisis ever entertained the thought that more sophisticated financial instruments existed even before people went to the moon. They should think again.

An established market since the early 1800s and a vibrant one since the mid-1800s, the futures market has played an important role in the growth of the U.S. economy and the financial markets. Indeed, since 1848, when 82 merchants formed the Chicago Board of Trade (CBOT)—a centralized market for exchanging agricultural commodities—futures trading has grown concomitantly with the needs of the marketplace. Since the 1970s futures trading has evolved from trading largely agricultural products to today's market where financial products dominate trading. Indeed, in the early 1970s most of the 13 million futures contracts traded were in agricultural products such as corn, wheat, and soybeans. In November 2009, of the 10.7 million futures contracts traded daily in the Chicago Board of Trade, the Chicago Mercantile Exchange (CME), and the New York Mercantile Exchange (NYMEX), less than 10 percent of the volume was related to agricultural products.

The definition of a futures contract hasn't changed much over the years. Today, as it did many decades ago, a *futures contract* represents an agreement between a buyer and a seller in which the buyer (or seller) agrees to take (or make) delivery of a specific amount of either a commodity or a financial security at a specific price at a specific time.

The rapid growth of the futures market that has occurred since the 1970s began in the bond market with trading in futures for the Government National Mortgage Association's (GNMA) mortgage-backed certificates. GNMA contracts paved the way for trading in Treasury bond futures, which were launched in August 1977 and became immensely popular and the hallmark product of the Chicago Board of Trade. The success of Treasury futures contracts paved the way for trading in a variety of other financial instruments in a variety of different asset classes, such as equities and foreign currencies.

Interest rate futures remain extremely active and are at the forefront of the futures market. The most active interest rate futures are Treasury contracts and Eurodollar contracts. We will discuss both shortly. These contracts are used by a wide variety of investors and by market participants who seek an optimal level of information flow to help them formulate investment strategies.

A wealth of benefits can be obtained from tracking activity in the interest rate futures markets. In addition, interest rate futures can be used as investment vehicles in a wide variety of ways. There are two main ways in which you can use futures to help you with your investments:

- Gathering market intelligence
- Managing an investment portfolio

Let's take a closer look at both.

Futures Provide Significant Market Information

One of the most important elements of investing is having an accurate assessment of market expectations. If an investor's assumptions regarding market expectations are wrong, an accurate forecast of market fundamentals will not necessarily translate into successful investment strategies. To be a successful investor, one has to choose investments that do not yet fully capture, or discount, events in the future. It is therefore imperative to estimate as accurately as possible the various assumptions embedded in market prices. It's the best way to compare an investor's assumptions with that of the market so that the investor can decide on an investment strategy.

Interest rate futures can be used to gather market intelligence on three important fronts:

- Market sentiment
- Expectations of future market volatility
- Expectations of future rate actions by the Federal Reserve

Each of these three areas plays an essential role in the direction of bond prices, the shape of the yield curve, the level of real interest rates, and the relative performance of the various segments of the bond market. There are a number of different indicators in the futures market that are excellent sources of market information. These gauges apply to nearly all futures trading, but this discussion pertains to activity in Treasury futures. These indicators are discussed in the sections that follow.

Tracking Market Sentiment

Five main indicators of market sentiment are found in the futures market:

1. Open interest
2. Futures trading volume
3. Options trading volume
4. The Commodity Futures Trading Commission's Commitments of Traders report
5. The bond basis

Open Interest

Open interest is a measure of the total number of futures positions that remain open, or outstanding, at a specific point in time. For each open contract there's a long position and a short position held by two different parties, but it is counted as a single contract in the open interest data. Open interest data can be used to gauge the quality of a move in the market. The main way to use this gauge is to compare the daily changes in open interest with the direction of the futures prices. In general, when open interest increases on a day when prices rally, this is looked at as an indication that new long positions were behind the rally, not short covering. It is looked at as a sign that market participants are confident that prices will continue to rise.

By contrast, when open interest declines on a day when prices rally, this is seen as a sign that the rally may have been spurred by short covering, and it is therefore an indication that the rally may not be sustainable. Prices can increase only so much on short covering alone; new buyers eventually will be needed to sustain higher prices.

Similarly, when prices decline and open interest increases, this is seen as a sign that new short positions spurred the drop in prices, indicating that market participants expect continued price declines. However, when open interest declines as prices fall, this is seen as indicating that existing long positions have been liquidated. Liquidations of long positions cannot continue in perpetuity, of course, and so it is usually only a matter of time before the liquidations are exhausted.

Tracking changes in open interest in the aftermath of important events or the release of economic reports can help investors detect any reversals or changes in the intensity of market sentiment because tracking the open interest isolates the development. For example, if after the release of employment data or in the aftermath of a speech by a member of the Federal Reserve, there is a notable increase in the amount of open interest in an interest rate contract, a clear view on market sentiment could be inferred.

Table 11.1 can be a useful reference on the conventional interpretation of changes in open interest.

Futures Trading Volume

A key gauge in most asset classes, trading volume can be used to judge the degree of investor participation in a price trend. A price move that occurs on strong volume helps validate that move and suggests that it probably will continue, but a price move that occurs on light volume suggests that there is very little sponsorship for the price move and that it probably will not be sustained. It is especially critical to track volume when a price trend is well established. In such a case diminishing volume could be a red flag and could portend a reversal or a consolidation of the trend.

High levels of volume tend to be associated with increases in commercial activity relative to speculative activity, while low volume levels suggest the opposite. Commercial players are considered "smart money," and it is often said that speculative players represent "dumb money." You can track the activity of these two camps more specifically by using the Commodity Futures Trading Commission's (CFTC) Commitments of Traders (COT) report, which is discussed later.

TABLE 11.1 Interpretation of Changes in Open Interest

Price Direction	Open Interest Change	Interpretation	Reason
Rising prices	Increasing	Bullish	Pattern suggests new longs entered the market.
Rising prices	Decreasing	Bearish	Pattern suggests rally due to short covering rather than new long positions.
Falling prices	Increasing	Bearish	Pattern suggests new short positions established.
Falling prices	Decreasing	Bullish	Pattern suggests selloff due to long liquidations that eventually will be exhausted.

Tracking volume in the futures market is especially important in the bond market, where official sources of data on daily volume except for corporate bonds are tracked via the Trade Reporting and Compliance Engine (TRACE) system. The volume captured there is too small to be of meaningful use. In the Treasury market, volume figures are available from the New York Fed but only with a one-week lag and on a daily average basis, which means the volume associated with new data or events can't be pinpointed as is possible in the futures market.

Options Trading Volume
As was shown in Chapter 10, options volume can be used to help in predicting turning points in the Treasury market. Specifically, by comparing the daily volume in calls to the daily volume in puts, an investor can spot excesses in bullish and bearish sentiment in the market. This is an excellent indicator that also is employed in the stock market, using stock options, of course. One of the reasons it is such a good indicator is that it captures speculative activity very well, and it is speculative activity that investors want to capture when tracking market sentiment. This is the activity that results from the collective views of short-term traders, who have a tendency to bet wrong on market direction, especially at turning points.

In the bond market the best way to track market sentiment is to use the options on Treasury futures that trade on the Chicago Board of Trade. The volume in calls is compared to the volume in puts by using a 10-day average of the put/call ratio. This ratio has provided many reliable signals of overbought and oversold conditions in the bond market. Over time the ratio has averaged about 1.25. A ratio of close to 2.0 generally indicates overbought conditions, while a ratio approaching 0.5 generally indicates that conditions are oversold.

In addition to options volume, options volatility is a useful gauge of market sentiment. Option prices that "skew" more for calls than puts or vice versa suggest a certain bias in the market that is worthy of attention. Many investors express their interest rate bias in the interest rate swap market, and these investors use *swaptions*, which enable buyers to enter into a swap agreement to either pay or receive a specified fixed rate at a specific point in time.

The Commodity Futures Trading Commission's Commitments of Traders Report

As was discussed in Chapter 10, the Commodity Futures Trading Commission publishes a very useful report called the Commitment of Traders (COT) report. This weekly report basically divides the holders of the existing open interest in a futures contract into two groups: commercial traders and noncommercial traders. Commercial traders in bond futures are the true end users of Treasuries. That is, they are the entities involved in the business of buying and selling fixed-income securities. Examples of commercial traders are primary dealers, insurance companies, pension funds, and investment management firms. The COT report is used as a gauge of speculative activity in various commodities, including Treasuries, and it has been a very reliable indicator of extremes in market sentiment.

It is relatively simple to use the COT report as a market indicator. An investor need simply track the net positions of commercial and noncommercial traders. Working on the notion that commercial traders represent smart money and noncommercial traders represent the speculative element of the market, one can compare the positions held by the two groups. An investor should pay special attention to the activity of noncommercial traders; they are the ones who tend to get the market wrong and are trading for short-term profits and therefore will be quick to reverse their positions if market trends reverse.

Taking the analysis a step further, market sentiment toward the yield curve can be deciphered. This can be done by aggregating the total amount duration of positions held in the various futures contracts along the yield curve. For example, if noncommercial traders collectively held 100,000 2-year note contracts having a duration of 1.75 years, but they were simultaneously long 5,000 T-bond contracts having a duration of 17 years, the aggregate positioning (based solely on these two contracts) would indicate that non-commercial traders were expecting the yield curve to steepen ($100,000 \times 1.75$ is greater than $5,000 \times 1.75$), indicating more exposure to the short end of the yield curve. Tracking this frequently would give the observer a sense of which way speculators were leaning along the yield curve.

It is truly helpful to know who is long and who is short in the market, and investors are fortunate to have this information at their disposal. The report is especially useful in the bond market, where trading in interest rate futures is much higher than it is in other financial instruments. The data can be obtained at www.cftc.gov.

The Bond Basis

Another way to track the quality of a market move is to track the bond basis. The *bond basis* is defined as the difference between the cash price and the converted futures price. The *cash price* is simply the price of the cash instrument that underlies the future and is eligible for delivery to the buyer of the future. The *converted futures price* is the price of the futures contract multiplied by the conversion factor of the cash instrument. (The *conversion factor* is the factor used to equate the price of T-bond and T-note futures contracts with the various cash T-bonds and T-notes eligible for delivery.) The conversion factor basically converts the price of all eligible cash bonds to bonds with a 6 percent coupon. The cash instrument's maturity date and call date (if any) are taken into account when the Chicago Board of Trade issues conversion factors.

Basis = (bond's cash price − futures price) × conversion factor

The basis can be used to track the performance of cash bonds compared to futures. Divergences in performance that cannot be explained by differences in duration can be used as an indicator of commercial and speculative activity. Market trends that appear to be based largely on commercial trading activity are more likely to be sustained than are those that appear to be rooted in speculative activity. Since most speculative activity in the bond market takes place in the futures market, the performance of the cash market relative to the futures market can be used to track the degree to which commercial players are backing a market trend. Thus, if bond prices rise and the basis narrows because the futures market is outperforming the cash market, this indicates that futures, or speculative, activity led the market higher, not commercial activity. This is a low-quality rally, and it is unlikely to be sustained.

TABLE 11.2 Interpretation of the Behavior of the Bond Basis

Price Direction	Basis Change	Interpretation	Reason
Rising prices	Widening	Bullish	Pattern suggests new commercial buyers behind the rally.
Rising prices	Narrowing	Bearish	Pattern suggests commercial players are not supporting the rally.
Falling prices	Widening	Bullish	Pattern suggests speculative activity causing the weakness.
Falling prices	Narrowing	Bearish	Pattern suggests selloff due to commercial selling.

Similarly, if bond prices decline but the basis widens, this indicates that futures, or speculative activity, drove prices lower, not commercial activity. One must bear in mind that the basis sometimes can shift because of shifts in the yield curve, as the cash instrument may have a maturity date different from the maturity of the security that underlies the future. (This applies to situations in which one compares the performance of the benchmark bond to that of the front-month futures contract.) In addition, large moves in interest rates can cause a shift in the security deemed cheapest to deliver, affecting the basis. Auctions of Treasury securities can also cause the basis to move around, with cash instruments underperforming futures ahead of the auctions and then reversing course once the auction date has arrived.

Table 11.2 is a helpful reference on the various interpretations of the behavior of the bond basis.

Expectations of Future Market Volatility

The market's expectations of future market volatility can be measured by using the implied volatility levels of options on futures prices. Swaptions volatility levels can also be used, as mentioned earlier in the chapter. *Implied volatility* is the market's expectations of the future volatility of a security over a specific period of time. Implied volatility generally is expressed in percentage terms, and it is calculated by using options pricing models such as the widely used Black-Scholes model. A number of benefits result from accurately assessing the market's expectations of future volatility.

First, this can help you judge whether your expectations about near-term price behavior are at odds with the market's expectations. This can help you spot opportunities in options trading as well as temporary dislocations and anomalies in bond prices. For example, if the performance of low-grade bonds deteriorates sharply relative to that of high-grade bonds owing to expectations of sharp increases in market volatility, you might consider purchasing the low-grade bonds if you felt that market volatility probably would diminish and thus stabilize the prices of low-grade bonds (low-grade bonds tend to weaken in times of uncertainty). This opportunity arose at the end of 2008 when a sharp increase in market volatility contributed to a sharp widening of credit spreads. Those who took the view that government action would stabilize markets and purchased spread products such as corporate bonds bet correctly, as yield spreads, particularly on high-yield corporate bonds narrowed very sharply throughout 2009 and in the early part of 2010.

Second, expectations of future volatility have proven to be a reliable indicator of excesses in bullish and bearish sentiment, and therefore they can be used to forecast turning points in the market. For example, high levels of implied volatility tend to coincide with market bottoms, as they indicate that there is a high level of fear in the market about additional price declines. High levels of fear are a sign of excess pessimism, of course, and therefore are a contrary indicator. Similarly, low levels of implied volatility tend to coincide with market tops, as they indicate that there is a high level of complacency in the market, with market participants expressing unrealistic expectations about risk.

Third, by knowing the degree to which the market expects to react to certain events, you can form a judgment about its expectations of those events. This can help you plot strategies that capitalize on what you believe are unrealistic expectations of the potential ramifications of a specific event. For example, if implied volatility is low before the release of an economic report that you believe might have a substantial impact on the market, this could indicate to you that the market reaction may be even more significant owing to the market's lack of preparedness.

Fourth, as noted earlier, by comparing the implied volatility on call options with the implied volatility on put options, you can gauge the market's expectations about the near-term direction of the market. For example if the skew on the options for a particular security leans toward higher call premiums when it normally leans toward higher put premiums, this could be taken as a sign of excess optimism. In Treasury bonds, the skew is generally toward slightly higher call premiums.

In the Treasury market, implied volatility on the benchmark 10-year T-note future tends to trade at around 6 to 8 percent within a broader range of around 5 to 10 percent. You can track implied volatility by calling your broker, using a professional system such as Bloomberg, or purchasing options software. Information also is available on the Web sites of major futures exchanges such as the Chicago Board of Trade and the Chicago Mercantile Exchange (www.cmegroup.com for both).

Gauging Expectations of Future Rate Actions by the Federal Reserve Using Federal Funds Futures

To augment any analysis that utilizes Eurodollar futures and forward rates to estimate market expectations on monetary policy, investors can utilize federal funds futures, which have evolved into an important and reliable gauge on expectations about future rate changes by the Federal Reserve. Understanding how to assess these expectations by using federal funds futures is therefore an essential aspect of investing. Investors who can assess market expectations accurately on a variety of fronts, particularly with respect to the Fed, are more likely to be successful investors than are those who make inaccurate assessments. Tracking federal funds futures is a great way to accurately assess market expectations of the probable outcomes of future Federal Open Market Committee (FOMC) meetings. Indeed, over the last few years, federal funds futures have been accurately priced for the outcome of these meetings about 90 percent of the time.

Using federal funds futures to assess market expectations of the Fed is relatively simple. Here are the steps:

1. Choose a contract month. This step is not as easy as it might seem at first. The contract month that you choose will depend on the date within the month during which the FOMC meeting is scheduled to take place. If the meeting is scheduled for very late in the month and there will be no meeting the next month, it is best to choose the contract in that following month. If you do not choose that month, you will have a lot of math to do. This way, you are getting a clean read on what the market believes the prevailing federal funds rate will be in the month after the meeting. This is the best method for getting a quick, close approximation. One drawback is that the contract of the contract month that follows FOMC meetings could contain expectations about the possibility of an intermeeting rate move. That is why

the most accurate way to gauge market expectations about a specific meeting is to choose the contract of the contract month in which the FOMC meeting takes place.

2. Calculate the implied federal funds rate on the futures contract. The implied federal funds rate is found by subtracting the price of the federal funds futures contract from 100. For example, if the FOMC meeting is being held in early November and you choose the November contract to determine the market's expectations of the outcome of that meeting and the price of that contract is 97.07, the implied rate is 2.93 percent.

3. Calculate the weighted average expected of the actual federal funds rate. The next step is to calculate the weighted average of the effective federal funds rate (the daily weighted average) by using both the current federal funds target determined by the Fed when it last changed it and a level that you believe might be implemented at the next FOMC meeting. For example, if the FOMC is scheduled to meet on the tenth of a month that contains 30 days, the weighted average would be as follows:

$$\text{Weighted average of federal funds rate} = \frac{(n) \text{ effective federal funds rate} + (n2) \text{ effective federal funds rate}}{30}$$

where (n) = number of days during the contract month on which the effective federal funds rate is expected to prevail at a given target rate

$(n2)$ = number of days during the contract month on which the effective federal funds rate is expected to prevail at a target rate set at the meeting scheduled for that contract month

4. Assuming that the federal funds rate was at 3.0 percent during the first 10 days of the month and at 2.75 percent during the final 20 days of the month (it is lower because we are assuming that the Fed lowered interest rates at its meeting on the tenth of the month), the weighted average is 2.83 percent. This means that if the Fed cut rates from 3.0 percent to 2.75 percent at the FOMC meeting on the tenth of the month, the federal funds rate would average 2.83 percent. This is the rate that traders in the federal funds futures contract are betting on or against and the rate that is used to pinpoint the probability assigned to the likelihood of that rate cut. Keep this in mind for step 5.

5. Subtract the weighted average of the federal funds rate from the current federal funds target (set by the FOMC when it last changed it; assume in this case that it was 3.0 percent): 3.0 percent − 2.83 percent = 17 basis points.
6. Now that you know the number of basis points it will take for the federal funds contract to fully price in a rate move made at the FOMC meeting (17 basis points in this example), divide the number of basis points in rate cuts priced into the federal funds contract (7 basis points in this example) into the number of basis points that it would take to fully price in the rate cut: 7 divided by 17 equals 41 percent. Thus, the contract suggests that the market has assigned a 41 percent probability to the odds of a rate cut at the FOMC meeting.

Here's an important qualifier: First, keep in mind that as you enter the contract month used for your calculation, you must use the actual effective federal funds rate rather than the target federal funds rate, which can differ each day. The target rate is simply that: a target. Where it actually trades is unknowable until it actually trades. Therefore, in your calculation you must substitute the actual rate for the target rate as the month progresses. You can obtain this information from the Fed at www.federalreserve.gov under the data section on the navigation bar.

The effective funds rate could be subjected to additional volatility when the Federal Reserve attempts to normalize its balance sheet—in other words, when the Fed removes the vast amount of financial liquidity it injected into the financial system to battle the financial and economic crisis. This will make it a bit more difficult to pinpoint with greater precision the amount of the market's expectations on the funds rate.

The federal funds futures contract is great for assessing the market's expectations over about a six-month time horizon, but it is a poor gauge for longer horizons. The open interest tends to shrink beyond a six-month time horizon, and it is usually very light beyond seven to eight months. What should you do? Turn to Eurodollar contracts.

Using Eurodollars to Track Expectations of Future Short-Term Rates

Eurodollar futures are one of the most liquid futures contracts in the world. They are used by a wide variety of entities to hedge short-term interest rate exposures. The contract represents rates paid on 3-month Eurodollar time deposits, or dollars deposited outside the United States. The final settlement price of Eurodollar futures is determined by the 3-month London Interbank Offered Rate (LIBOR) on the last trading day. Eurodollar rates tend to be tightly correlated to the federal funds rate, and this makes the Eurodollar contract a great gauge of market expectations about future short-term interest rates.

The method used to determine the market's expectations about the federal funds rate using Eurodollar contracts is similar to the steps shown earlier for the federal funds futures contract. There are a couple of twists, however. First, Eurodollar futures contracts trade in series of three-month, quarterly increments (except in the three months immediately forward, but the federal funds futures are more reliable in this case). This means that when you are calculating the federal funds rate out into the future, you will not be making a pinpoint assessment. This is not a big problem, however, since you are concerned primarily with making an accurate general assessment during those months anyway.

Second and more important, the spread between the Eurodollar time deposit rate and the federal funds rate tends to fluctuate with where the Federal Reserve is expected to be in its interest rate cycle. This means that the implied rate on Eurodollar futures contracts is not likely to reflect the market's expectations about the federal funds rate alone; instead, it is likely to

FIGURE 11.1 Yield Spread between the Three-Month LIBOR and the Federal Funds Rate, in Percentage Points

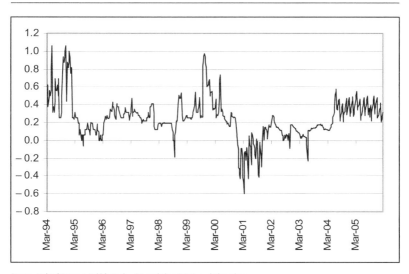

Source: Federal Reserve, British Bankers' Association (BBA), and Bloomberg.

also reflect the market's expectations about both the federal funds rate and the spread between the LIBOR, the rate at which major banks in London lend Eurodollar deposits, and the federal funds rate. This spread tends to widen when the Fed is raising interest rates and tends to be very narrow when the Fed is lowering interest rates, as is evident in Figure 11.1. Take note that the Fed was raising interest rates in 1994 and 1999, and it was cutting rates between 2001 and 2003.

The spread between the LIBOR and the federal funds rate at all times also includes a risk premium, which in 2008 grew to massive proportions when concerns about counterparty risk ballooned (see Figure 11.2). Banks were fearful of lending to each other, and this caused the interbank rate to increase very sharply. The problem began to alleviate in particular when the Federal Reserve on October 13, 2008, said that it was willing to lend an unlimited supply of dollars to the world's central banks in exchange for currencies issued by the central banks. The action brought down the cost of borrowing dollars in the global market for dollars, the Eurodollar market, compressing the yield spread between the LIBOR and the federal funds rate. Here is an excerpt from the Federal Reserve's October 13, 2008, statement, which marked a turning point in the financial crisis:

> In order to provide broad access to liquidity and funding to financial institutions, the Bank of England (BoE), the European Central Bank (ECB), the Federal Reserve, the Bank of Japan, and the Swiss National Bank (SNB) are jointly announcing further measures to improve liquidity in short-term U.S. dollar funding markets.
>
> The BoE, ECB, and SNB will conduct tenders of U.S. dollar funding at 7-day, 28-day, and 84-day maturities at fixed interest rates for full allotment. Funds will be provided at a fixed interest rate, set in advance of each operation. Counterparties in these operations will be able to borrow any amount they wish against the appropriate collateral in each jurisdiction. Accordingly, sizes of the reciprocal currency arrangements (swap lines) between the Federal Reserve and the BoE, the ECB, and the SNB will be increased to accommodate whatever quantity of U.S. dollar funding is demanded. The Bank of Japan will be considering the introduction of similar measures.

The behavior of the spread between the LIBOR and the federal funds rate is therefore an important variable with which an investor must contend when using Eurodollar futures to assess the market's expectations of future changes in monetary policy. Simply assume that the spread will widen when market expectations for interest rate increases grows and that it will narrow

FIGURE 11.2 Post-Lehman, the LIBOR Spiked: Yield Spread between the Three-Month LIBOR and the Federal Funds Rate, in Percentage Points

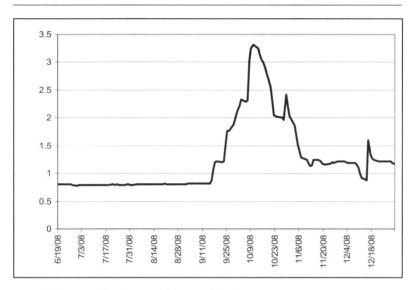

Source: Federal Reserve, British Bankers' Association (BBA), and Bloomberg.

when the market expects rates to be cut. For example, assume that the federal funds rate is currently 2 percent and that the implied rate on the Eurodollar futures contract 12 months hence is at 2.75 percent. This appears to indicate that the market expects the Fed to raise the federal funds rate next year, but to what level?

To find the answer, simply subtract what you think the spread between the LIBOR and the federal funds rate will be next year (as much as 50 basis points is a reasonable assumption when it is early in a Fed campaign to raise interest rates), and that number will represent the market's expectations of the federal funds rate (2.25 percent in this example).

Uses of Interest Rate Futures

There are many ways in which interest rate futures can be used. While the high degree of leverage involved with futures makes them riskier than many other financial instruments, there are a number of ways in which futures can be used to allay risks and to construct portfolios that achieve favorable asset and risk diversification. The most important uses of futures include the following:

- *Hedging.* Wide varieties of entities buy and sell futures to offset the risks they incur in their normal business operations. Primary dealers, pension funds, insurance companies, portfolio managers, banks, and the like all use futures to hedge their various risks. Investors who use futures to hedge their risks must take into account *basis risk*—that is, the risk of unexpected changes between the price of futures and the securities that underlie the futures—particularly when the security being hedged and the hedge security are different.
- *Duration management.* By increasing or decreasing the duration on a portfolio, investors can attempt to capitalize on expected fluctuations in interest rates. In most portfolios, duration can be increased by purchasing long-dated Treasury bond futures; conversely, selling futures can decrease duration. In addition, portfolio managers can choose between futures contracts that reflect different maturity points along the yield curve to adjust their curve duration exposure. Futures hence provide a simple way to alter the risk profile of a portfolio.
- *Asset allocation.* Portfolios that contain a combination of bonds and stocks can use futures to vary their allocations to these asset classes. Insurance companies and pension funds are two examples of users of this strategy. Individuals can use this approach too. The wide variety of futures available in the various asset classes provide investors with a means of achieving broad exposure to multiple assets.
- *Yield enhancement.* Investors can use options on futures to add incremental returns to their portfolios. For example, bond investors can simultaneously sell out-of-the-money calls and puts on Treasury note or bond futures at strike prices that reflect an expected range for the price of the underlying futures, hoping, of course, that the options will expire worthless, adding to a portfolio's return. The decay of option values owing to time is known in the investment community as *theta.* Thus, a portfolio's theta exposure reflects its potential return from selling options short.
- *Speculating.* Speculators actively trade futures to gain a profit by acting on short-term trading opportunities. Speculators play an important role in the futures markets by providing liquidity to those markets, particularly to market participants who use futures for commercial purposes.

As you can see, futures can be used in many different ways and can play a valuable role in an investment portfolio.

Summary

- Futures can be extremely useful to those who use them as well as to bond investors who follow trading activity in the futures market to obtain valuable market intelligence. Much of the information in the futures market is unique and is therefore an invaluable source of market intelligence.
- Futures can be used to gain an edge in forecasting turning points in the bond market.
- The futures market contains significant amounts of information on market sentiment, expectations of future market volatility, perceptions about counterparty risks, and expectations of future rate actions by the Federal Reserve, all of which are extremely important tools for bond investors.
- Futures can be used in a number of investment strategies, including duration management, hedging, and asset allocation, among others.

12

CREDIT RATINGS
An Essential Tool for Bond Investors

Americans love ratings and seem to rate and rank just about everything. This is understandable in light of the plethora of choices consumers and investors face every day.

Ratings help people get a sense of where things stand with respect to each other. They tell people about the quality of the things they buy or plan to buy. They also save busy Americans time by taking a lot of legwork out of the equation. A quick look at a rating or ranking can simplify a purchase decision.

It is no different in the bond market. Bond investors use bond ratings to get a sense of the quality and value on the bonds they buy and to simplify the investment decision-making process. However, bond ratings are not necessarily for bond investors only; equity investors should use them to increase what they know about the companies in which they invest.

The amount of trust that investors should put in credit rating agencies has been called into question in recent years because of fallout from the financial crisis. The rating accuracy of the major credit rating agencies declined relative to the historical average, in part because of a few high-profile defaults by companies rated investment grade, including Lehman Brothers, Washington Mutual, and three Icelandic banks that had over $40 billion of bonds when they were seized by regulators. Investor scrutiny has been even more intense over the rating accuracy that the rating agencies had on more complex financial instruments such as collateralized debt obligations (CDOs) and mortgage-backed securities, particularly those backed by subprime mortgages. In these areas, many believe the rating agencies failed and contributed to the complacent attitudes that kept investors from more accurately assessing the risks inherent in the securities they purchased.

Despite these lingering doubts, investors continue to utilize credit ratings when making judgments about investments. Data regarding the long-term accuracy of the rating agencies are reasons for investors to be confident in the accuracy of credit ratings, although it is prudent to be skeptical and for investors to do their own homework.

In July 2008, the SEC released findings from a 10-month internal examination of three major credit rating agencies and found what it called "significant weaknesses in ratings practices." The SEC's examinations found that rating agencies had struggled significantly with the increase in the number and complexity of subprime residential mortgage-backed securities (RMBS) and CDO deals since 2002. In particular, the SEC found that none of the rating agencies examined had specific written comprehensive procedures for rating RMBS and CDOs. In addition, significant aspects of the rating process were not always disclosed or even documented by the firms, and conflicts of interest were not always managed appropriately, the examination found. The report summarized the remedial actions that credit rating agencies each were expected to take, including these:

- Evaluate whether each has sufficient staff and resources to manage its volume of business and meet its obligations under the Exchange Act and the rules applicable to nationally recognized statistical rating organizations (NRSROs).
- Review disclosure of the rating process and the methodologies used to rate RMBS and CDOs to ensure full compliance with SEC rules.
- Review current policies and practices for documenting the credit rating process and the identities of RMBS and CDO rating analysts and committee members.
- Determine if adequate resources are devoted to surveillance of outstanding RMBS and CDO ratings.
- Review practices, policies, and procedures for mitigating and managing the issuer-pays conflicts of interest.

As you can see, the rating agencies are under greater scrutiny, which hopefully means that they will be better at accomplishing their missions.

Think Like a Consumer

I often think about bond ratings when I see ratings of consumer products. I am reminded how difficult it is to understand why many people are willing to invest thousands of dollars in the bonds and stocks of companies they have never heard of without first looking at the ratings on the securities, yet they will not even consider purchasing consumer products such as washing machines, flat-screen televisions, or digital cameras without first reading rating comparisons produced by companies such as Consumer Reports. This type of behavior clearly suggests that many investors do not have their priorities straight in this regard. It is far more important to be keenly focused when considering financial investments than when making most other types of purchases.

Despite recent events, investors are fortunate to have a comprehensive rating system at their disposal to keep alongside other tools when judging the creditworthiness of debt issuers. I therefore urge you to put ratings in your financial toolbox. If you are primarily an equities investor, remember that the rating system used for bonds is suitable for equity investors too and that the information in this chapter is largely transferable to equities.

Credit Ratings Can Cut an Investor's Risk

As was discussed in greater detail in Chapter 5, investors face a number of risks when investing in bonds, three of which stand out: interest rate risk (the risk that interest rates will rise), purchasing power risk (the risk that inflation will rise and thus erode the value of bonds), and credit risk (the risk that a bond issuer will be unable to meet its debt obligations). While assessing the first two risks requires that individual investors do a significant amount of research on their own, credit risks are arguably the easiest of the risks for investors to assess thanks to credit ratings.

Credit ratings make investing in bonds a little easier by augmenting an investor's analysis of bonds in ways that for many people are not possible because they lack the time or expertise to conduct an analysis as extensive as those conducted by the rating agencies. This is especially important for investing in bonds, which often requires a lot of quantitative and qualitative analysis. Credit ratings can help investors assess the likelihood that their money will be returned to them in accordance with the terms on which they invested.

Credit ratings essentially rank a company's ability to repay its debts and withstand various types of financial and economic stress compared to the ability of other companies. Ratings are intended to provide forward-looking opinions about a company's ability and willingness to pay interest and repay principal as scheduled. (For purposes of simplification, this chapter will discuss ratings mainly as they apply to corporations. However, the same general principles apply to government, municipal, and agency debt as well as to other fixed-income securities.)

Primary concerns for bond investors are whether they will receive the interest payments that are due on their bond holdings and whether they will be repaid at maturity for the principal they invested in the bonds. Credit ratings help investors assess whether bond issuers can meet those debt obligations. Failure to make an interest payment or repay the principal at maturity (usually $1,000 per bond) is considered a default. A default is a bond investor's biggest worry, and it is a risk that exists for almost every bond. The exceptions, of course, are U.S. Treasury securities. Treasuries are considered free of default risks because they are backed by the full faith and credit of the U.S. government.

While there is little doubt that credit ratings can help investors gauge the default risks on a particular bond, it is important to be aware of the limited role credit ratings play in the investment decision-making process. For one thing, credit ratings are not recommendations to buy, sell, or hold a security. In other words, the rating agencies do not assign credit ratings to signal their investment recommendations in regard to the bonds they rate. That is not why these agencies issue credit ratings. Rating agencies are interested primarily in providing indications of the ability of an entity to meet its payment obligations.

Another point to remember is that credit ratings do not contain statements on whether a bond is deemed to be "cheap" or "expensive" relative to other bonds in the market. The price of a bond has no direct connection to the ratings that the rating agencies assign except to the extent that the price and rating of a bond will in many cases reflect the underlying fundamentals of the entity and the credit risk deemed by other investors.

Credit ratings also do not comment on the suitability of a bond for a particular investor. The ratings do not tell an investor, for example, whether a particular bond fits with his or her investment profile. Moreover, credit ratings give no indication of the tax implications of owning a particular bond. That is a job best suited for an accountant.

Despite the limited role that credit ratings play in the investment decision-making process, they are an invaluable tool for investors. Let's take a look at where ratings come from, how they are determined, the definitions of the rating symbols, and the impact they have on the price of a bond.

The Rating Agencies

You probably have heard the names of the three most prominent and nationally recognized private companies that issue credit ratings: Moody's Investor Services, Standard & Poor's, and Fitch Ratings. Of the three, Moody's and Standard & Poor's are considered the leading agencies. In total, 10 companies are registered with the Securities and Exchange Commission as credit rating agencies. Credit rating agencies registered with the SEC are known as *nationally recognized statistical rating organizations,* or NRSROs. As of February 13, 2010, the 10 NRSROs were these:

- Moody's Investor Service
- Standard & Poor's
- Fitch Ratings
- A.M. Best Company
- Dominion Bond Rating Service, Ltd.
- Japan Credit Rating Agency, Ltd.
- R&I, Inc.
- Egan-Jones Rating Company
- LACE Financial
- Realpoint, LLC

The SEC defines a credit rating agency as "a firm that provides its opinion on the creditworthiness of an entity and the financial obligations (such as bonds, preferred stock, and commercial paper) issued by an entity." Under the Credit Rating Agency Reform Act of 2006, an NRSRO may be registered with respect to up to five classes of credit ratings: (1) financial institutions, brokers, or dealers; (2) insurance companies; (3) corporate issuers; (4) issuers of asset-backed securities; and (5) issuers of government securities, municipal securities, or securities issued by a foreign government.

Each of the credit agencies follows a very thorough and rigorous methodology for determining an entity's creditworthiness. The agencies conduct a thorough credit evaluation consisting of a mix of quantitative and qualitative analyses. The agencies' thorough approach, long-term track record, and closer regulatory scrutiny are reasons to be confident in the rating accuracy of the rating agencies.

While the credit rating each of the agencies assigns to a particular bond can vary, the agencies' assessments are not usually far apart. In fact, it is unusual for the agencies' opinions on a particular bond to be sharply divided. Nevertheless, investors can benefit from utilizing the variety of opinions the various agencies have to offer.

The most prominent and oldest rating agency is Moody's Investor Services. The Moody's of today had its genesis back in 1909, when the founder, John Moody, introduced a simple letter grading system for railroad bonds. Moody's had adopted that system from the mercantile and credit rating system used by credit-reporting firms in the late 1800s. Soon Moody's began to apply that methodology to other industries, and the rating system was under way.

Over the years Moody's has extended its reach well beyond its bond ratings. Moody's now provides credit ratings and analyses on tens of trillions of dollars of debt covering 100 sovereign nations, 12,000 corporate issuers, 29,000 public finance issuers, and 96,000 structured finance obligations. Moody's has assigned ratings to the vast majority of public market bonds.

In the 1970s Moody's and the other major rating agencies began charging issuers for their rating services in recognition of the substantial value the issuers were placing on the objective analyses provided by the rating agencies. Issuers increasingly found that objective ratings on the bonds they issued increased the likelihood that investors would participate in their bond offerings, and this tended to lower an issuer's borrowing costs. Charging issuers also became necessary as the financial markets grew in complexity. The increasing size and complexity of the financial markets required many more personnel receiving much higher levels of compensation than could be afforded without the fees.

The growth of Moody's and the other rating agencies thus has been tied directly to the enormous growth in the size and complexity of the financial markets over the last few decades. As the markets have grown, the need for professional services such as those provided by the rating agencies has increased greatly. The challenge for the rating agencies has been keeping up with the rapid pace of financial innovation. Unfortunately, the rating agencies were unable to keep up completely, leading to a decline in rating accuracy.

The Rating System

For anyone who can recite the alphabet, the rating system is simple to learn. One might say that the Moody's rating system is as easy as ABC. I say this because all the rating agencies use the letters A through D to signify a decreasing level of creditworthiness. The highest credit rating, of course, is AAA, while the lowest is D. This simple approach makes it easy for anyone to understand the system. Investors are fortunate that the rating agencies have chosen such a simple system, particularly in light of the complex nature of the work involved in generating the ratings.

There are two main categories of investments within the A through D rating grades: investment grade and below investment grade. *Investment-grade bonds* are believed to have a low probability of default, whereas *below-*

investment-grade bonds are thought to have a relatively greater probability of default. Most people think of the below-investment-grade category as "junk bonds."

Table 12.1 shows the ratings used by the major rating agencies. Note that only Moody's uses lowercase letters in its rating system. In addition, Moody's sometimes attaches a number, or numeric modifier, to its letter ratings. It does this to give its rating assignment greater specificity with regard to rank and to avoid generalizations within rating categories. The modifiers are used to refer to a bond's ranking within the group. Here is how Moody's describes the use of numbers within rating grades: "Moody's applies numerical modifiers 1, 2, and 3 in each generic rating classification from Aa through Caa. The modifier 1 indicates that the obligation ranks in the higher end of its generic rating category; the modifier 2 indicates a midrange ranking; and the modifier 3 indicates a ranking in the lower end of that generic rating

TABLE 12.1 Credit Ratings

Credit Risk	Moody's	Standard & Poor's	Fitch IBCA	Duff & Phelps
Investment Grade				
Highest quality	Aaa	AAA	AAA	AAA
High quality (very strong)	Aa	AA	AA	AA
Upper medium grade (strong)	A	A	A	A
Medium grade	Baa	BBB	BBB	BBB
Below Investment Grade				
Lower medium grade (somewhat speculative)	Ba	BB	BB	BB
Low grade (speculative)	B	B	B	B
Poor quality (may default)	Caa	CCC	CCC	CCC
Most speculative	Ca	CC	CC	CC
No interest being paid or bankruptcy petition filed	C	C	C	C
In default	C	D	D	D

category." Basically, the numerical modifiers Moody's uses increase the number of rating grades it can assign. This gives investors even more information to gauge the creditworthiness of the companies Moody's analyzes.

Thus, if you know the alphabet and can count from 1 to 3, you should have no problem understanding the Moody's rating system.

The Rating Categories

Investment Grade

Investment-grade ratings reflect expectations of timeliness of payment and a low probability of default. As Table 12.1 shows, investment-grade bonds are bonds rated between AAA and BBB. Many investors prefer to invest solely in these bonds to minimize their investment risks. In fact, many financial institutions, such as banks, are not permitted to invest in bonds rated below investment grade. This is a major reason why bond issuers strive to maintain an investment-grade credit rating. They recognize that demand for their bonds would fall if their credit rating fell below investment grade. This would translate into higher borrowing costs and thus lower corporate profits.

An investment-grade credit rating can have a large bearing on the way investors and other entities treat a particular class of bonds. The Federal Reserve Board, for example, will allow members of the Federal Reserve System to invest only in securities with the four highest rating categories. The U.S. Department of Labor will allow pension funds to invest in commercial paper only if it is rated in one of the three highest categories. Similar rules are in place for many other pension funds in both the private and public sectors.

The most familiar investment-grade credit rating is, of course, AAA. As one might expect, AAA-rated bonds are considered to have the highest credit quality. Companies that obtain an AAA rating have the highest capacity to meet their financial commitments. AAA-rated bonds are deemed to be protected by a "large and exceptionally stable margin," and their "principal is secure," according to Moody's. While the outlook for AAA-rated companies is, as with all companies, subject to change, such changes are felt to be "unlikely to impair the fundamentally strong position" of these companies. AAA-rated companies have a superior capacity to weather a variety of economic and financial stresses.

About 30 years ago, there were roughly 25 companies carrying the prestigious AAA rating. Today there are only a handful of AAA-rated companies—just four: ExxonMobil, Johnson & Johnson, Microsoft, and Automatic Data

Processing. All of these companies have very strong balance sheets in industries that are generally not subject to the extremes of the business cycle. Notables that lost their AAA status in 2009 and 2010 include General Electric, Pfizer, and Berkshire Hathaway. American International Group (AIG) is probably the most notable company that was rated AAA just ahead of the financial crisis.

AA-rated bonds "differ from the highest-rated obligations only in small degree," according to Standard & Poor's. Companies with an AA rating are believed to have a very strong capacity to meet their financial obligations. Here is how Moody's characterizes AA bonds: "Bonds which are rated Aa are judged to be of high quality by all standards. Together with the Aaa group, they comprise what are generally known as high-grade bonds. They are rated lower than the best bonds because margins of protection may not be as large as in Aaa securities or fluctuation of protective elements may be of greater amplitude or there may be other elements present which make the long-term risk appear somewhat larger than the Aaa securities."

The AA rating is applied to a diverse group of elite companies in a broad array of industries. Companies that carry an AA rating include Procter & Gamble, Coca-Cola, Walmart, and Berkshire Hathaway. All of these companies have a very strong capacity to meet their debt obligations.

The creditworthiness of companies with lower ratings begins to deteriorate slowly but surely. A-rated bonds, for example, are considered "susceptible" to changing business and economic conditions, and their ability to repay their debts is considered merely "adequate." Thus, investment in A-rated bonds carries a somewhat higher degree of risk than investment in the higher-grade categories. However, this does not mean that these companies are highly risky, and bonds rated A generally are considered to be of good quality with favorable investment attributes; these lower-rated bonds yield more than higher-rated bonds do.

Examples of A-rated bonds include companies with somewhat greater sensitivity to cyclical economic conditions than companies rated AAA and AA. In other words, A-rated bonds are more likely to be affected by the ups and downs of the business cycle than higher-grade bonds are. Included in A-rated category, for example, are consumer cyclical companies such as retailers, chemical companies, and automotive companies. Financial companies often are placed in this category because their profits and potential losses (from loan losses, bankruptcies, trading losses, and the like) can vary sharply as economic growth fluctuates, as recent events have made clear.

The lowest investment-grade rating category is BBB. Bonds in this category are basically on the borderline between investment-grade and speculative-grade debt. As Moody's puts it, they are "neither highly protected nor poorly secured." BBB bonds are felt to have fewer protective elements than higher-rated bonds and are considered vulnerable to potential changes in both an obligor's company business fundamentals and the economic environment. Companies in this category therefore are likely to have a weakened capacity to repay their debts under changed circumstances.

Below Investment Grade

Obligations rated BB, B, CCC, CC, and C are regarded as having significant speculative characteristics. In this rating category, bonds rated BB are considered the least speculative, and bonds rated C are considered the most speculative. Most of the market for below-investment-grade debt consists of bonds rated BB or B, although in recent years a spate of ratings downgrades has sparked an increase in the number of bonds rated CCC or lower. Moreover, a number of bonds previously rated investment grade have been downgraded to below investment grade. This is known as a *crossover*.

Bonds rated below investment grade are commonly called *high-yield* or *junk bonds*. To individuals who invest in high-yield bonds or make a living from them, "high-yield" is the preferred nomenclature. To these individuals, high-yield bonds are anything but junk because of the many benefits they believe high-yield bonds can confer to a portfolio.

Not all companies with below-investment-grade ratings are necessarily outright speculative investments. Indeed, many of them have at least some quality and protective characteristics even if those characteristics are outweighed by many uncertainties and vulnerabilities. This is why it is critical to avoid prejudging a bond by looking only at its rating.

Nevertheless, investing in debt rated below investment grade can be risky unless an investor is very familiar with the company or at least knows how to pick apart its balance sheet and understands the company's business. If you are not very familiar with the company you are considering investing in but are still interested in investing in high-yield bonds, you might consider investing in a bond mutual fund. By investing in a high-yield mutual fund, you get the benefit of having a professional money manager choose bonds for you. In addition, you get the advantage of diversification without having to invest a lot of money in the process. This helps reduce your transaction fees. However, mutual funds incur transactions charges and generally pass on those charges to the investors in their funds. That is why it is important to compare the fees charged by mutual funds companies.

FIGURE 12.1 Annual Speculative-Grade Default Rates for 1920 to 2008

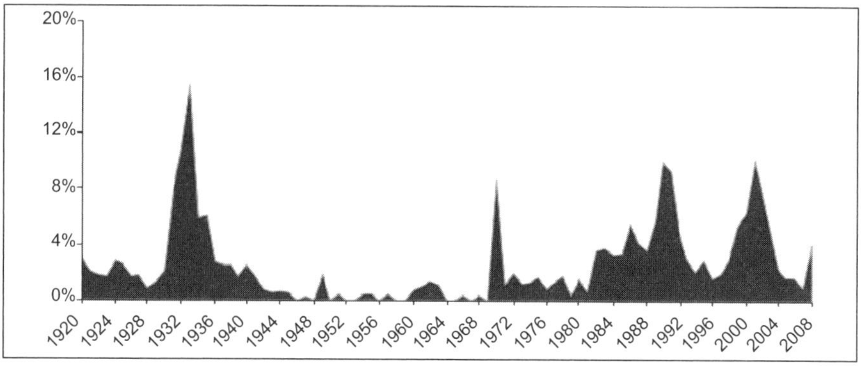

Source: Moody's.

Diversification is especially important when one is investing in high-yield bonds, particularly when the economy weakens. During such times bonds rated below investment-grade tend to underperform investment-grade bonds. For example, in 2009 Moody's forecasted that the global issuer-weighted speculative-grade default rate would climb to as high as 16.4 percent in 2009, up from about 4 percent in 2008 and surpassing the peaks of 11.9 percent and 10.4 percent set in the aftermath of the 1990 and 1991 and 2001 recessions, respectively.[1] If reached, the speculative-grade default rate would surpass the record 15.3 percent rate set in 1933 when the speculative-grade market consisted largely of "fallen angels," or companies previously rated investment grade. Figure 12.1 shows the speculative-grade default rate from 1920 to 2008.

How Credit Ratings Affect a Bond's Yield

The credit rating on a bond has a significant effect on its yield-to-maturity. As one would expect, the lower a bond's credit rating, the higher its yield. This makes sense when one considers that investors deserve to be compensated as they move further out the risk spectrum. A bond's credit rating is not the only factor, however, that determines one bond's yield compared to another. One of the most important factors is a bond's industry classification. For example, bonds in economically sensitive sectors such as retail, finance, gaming, and home building may yield relatively more than do bonds in less economically sensitive industries such as pipelines and utilities, which tend to have both stable revenues and relatively good recovery rates, depending on the economic climate.

Bonds rated below investment grade yield much more than do bonds rated investment grade. Bonds rated BB, for example, yield much more than AAA bonds do. Over the last 10 years BB-rated 10-year industrial bonds have averaged a yield spread of about 333 basis points over 10-year U.S. Treasuries compared with an average yield spread of about 141 basis points for AAA-rated 10-year industrials. Both levels are skewed higher by the financial crisis; for example, AAA-rated industrial bonds averaged a yield spread of about 95 basis points to Treasuries during the latter part of the 1990s. BB-rated industrial bonds traded at an average yield spread of 164 basis points over Treasuries from 1992 through 2000.

Junk bonds historically have yielded much more than investment-grade debt has. The reason for this is simple: junk bonds are more likely to default than other bonds are. Between 1920 and 2008, for example, a study conducted by Moody's found that 2.6 percent of speculative-grade credit issues defaulted compared to zero percent of AAA-rated issues, and 0.27 percent of Baa-rated issuers.

Table 12.2 shows the annual issuer-weighted corporate default rates by letter rating.

The sharp widening in yield spreads on speculative-grade debt in 2008 through early 2009 was far greater than the widening in spreads that occurred in investment-grade debt. AAA-rated debt, for example, widened from an average of 64 basis points over Treasuries in 2006 to an average spread of 97 basis points in 2009. This divergence in performance illustrates the varying degree of impact that the economy has on debt rated investment grade and below investment grade. As the rating definitions describe, AAA-rated bonds are "gilt-edged" and are considered strong enough to withstand various types of financial and economic stress without any meaningful impairment of the issuer's ability to pay obligations on such debt. Bonds rated below investment grade, in contrast, are weak at the core, and their ability to withstand numerous types of stress is not assured.

As was mentioned above, while some bonds may have the same maturity and rating designation, this does not necessarily mean that they will

TABLE 12.2 Mean Issuer-Weighted Corporate Default Rates by Letter Rating, 1920 to 2008

Aaa	Aa	A	Baa	Ba	B	Caa–C	Investment Grade	Speculative Grade	All Rated
0.000	0.063	0.092	0.271	1.063	3.395	13.252	0.149	2.643	1.087

Note: Data are in percents. Includes bond and loan issuers' rates as of January 1 of each year.

Source: Moody's.

have the same yield. Indeed, for a variety of reasons, two companies with identical ratings and maturity dates can have much different yields. Some reasons include the following:

- *Industry fundamentals and characteristics.* These include the extent to which a company's bonds are more or less vulnerable to the ups and downs of the business cycle. For example, a company in the gaming industry is more vulnerable to a weakening of economic activity than is a company in the utility industry because households under economic stress are far more likely to curtail their visits to casinos than cut back on their use of services provided by utility companies. Demand for basic necessities is largely inelastic.
- *Management.* An agency's opinion about a company's management, for example, skepticism about the way a company is managed, will lower that company's credit rating.
- *Cash flows.* Two companies may have similar balance sheets, but the company generating the most cash will tend to have the higher rating because of its ability to generate cash and pay its obligations.
- *Composition of debt.* Two companies could have similar amounts of debt in relation to their business operations and revenues, but the one that has the smaller amount of short-term debt liabilities would be the one considered less vulnerable.
- *Exposure to various risks.* These include regulations and international conditions.

The Impact of Rating Announcements

The importance of the rating assignments issued by rating agencies can be seen in the behavior of bonds in the aftermath of changes to their credit ratings announced by those agencies. Typically, when a rating agency announces a change in the credit rating on a bond, there tends to be what is known as an *announcement effect*. An announcement effect is the price change that occurs in a bond as a result of an announcement by a rating agency that it is changing the bond's rating assignment. Bonds whose rating assignment is upgraded tend to rise in price (lowering their yield), and bonds that are downgraded tend to fall in price (raising their yield).

While the markets generally tend to adjust the price of a bond in advance of announced changes to its credit rating, the actual announcement of the change tends to cause further movement in the bond. The largest degree of movement, however, tends to occur in advance of the announcement. This suggests that the markets are efficient in discounting potential rating changes. This is similar to the stock market, where stock prices move in advance of earnings reports but often respond very little to their actual release, particularly when the reports meet expectations.

With the markets often moving in advance of the rating agencies, some people may feel that the agencies are too slow to recognize changes in the conditions that could undermine the credit ratings they issue for particular bonds. This certainly was the case ahead of the financial crisis, as was discussed earlier. Another glaring example was the financial crisis that gripped Asia in 1997 and 1998. The agencies maintained investment-grade credit ratings on sovereign debt, or government-issued debt, even as investors began to shun those bonds with a vengeance. Many Asian countries experienced enormous outflows of capital that exposed risks which most bond investors could not have imagined existed in light of those countries' credit ratings. Many investors lost significant amounts of money during the crisis—dubbed the Asian financial crisis—on both the government bonds and the currencies they bought to pay for those bonds.

While criticism of the agencies in this case seems appropriate, it is important to be aware that there were many different aspects of the Asian financial crisis that the agencies could not have expected. The large number of events that took place during the crisis were the result of a snowballing of problems that synergistically resulted in problems that were not likely to have surfaced in most circumstances. Thus, while the agencies probably could have done a better job warning investors about some of the potential risks involved in investing in some of the Asian countries, the agencies cannot be faulted for failing to predict events that were so unlikely.

How Credit Ratings Affect Liquidity, Quote Depth, and Bid-Ask Spreads

As was indicated in Chapter 2, many factors can affect a bond's liquidity, quote depth, and bid-ask spread. These three factors, which are a reflection of the marketability of a bond, are important considerations for bond investors, particularly if they feel they may sell their bonds before their maturity. Along with the factors mentioned in Chapter 2, a factor that affects the way a bond trades in the marketplace is its credit rating. Generally speaking, bonds rated investment grade tend to have greater liquidity and quote depth than do bonds rated below investment grade. They also tend to have narrower bid-ask spreads.

To illustrate this point, consider the marketability of bonds rated AAA compared with that of junk bonds. The AAA-rated bonds are more likely to attract a greater number of investors than are junk bonds simply because many investors are barred from investing in bonds rated below investment grade. As a result, at any given point in time the AAA-rated bonds will have more buyers and sellers present in the marketplace than will be present in the junk bond market. This simple fact will translate into far greater marketability for the AAA-rated bonds. In fact, most data show that AAA-rated and AA-rated bonds have significantly lower bid-ask spreads relative to junk bonds.

Keep in mind, however, that some of the bid-ask spread reflects liquidity-related factors rather than credit-related factors. This was a conclusion from a 2008 Federal Reserve study by Han and Zhou.[2]

Methodology Used to Determine Rating Assignments

The rating agencies conduct a thorough review of the companies they rate, saving investors plenty of legwork. Numerous considerations are weighed, the most important of which is a company's cash flow. Basically, if a company is a cash cow and has a plentiful supply of capital flowing in, that company is very likely to have a high credit rating. Conversely, a company that has difficulty generating cash will tend to have a low credit rating. The rating agencies look closely at the sources of a company's cash flows as well as their variety and availability. Companies with high credit ratings have quickly turning, high-quality accounts receivable, meaning that they are getting paid on time and getting all the money they are due. Rating agencies also consider it important that a company have the ability to sustain its profitability.

Rating agencies work meticulously when assigning ratings and have a long checklist of considerations they comb through thoroughly. The agencies are largely interested in reflecting their assessment of an issuer's credit risk as well as the degree of legal protection a bondholder has on a specific security based on that security's indenture provisions. An assessment of these two key risks provides valuable information to investors. The assessment of the credit risks involved in investing in a particular bond helps investors gauge the ability of an issuer to pay its debt obligations. The assessment of the legal protections helps investors understand the level of protection provided to them when they invest in a bond. This is important because securities issued by a single issuer could have different ratings because of different legal protections in each security's indenture provisions.

FIGURE 12.2 Standard & Poor's Debt Rating Process

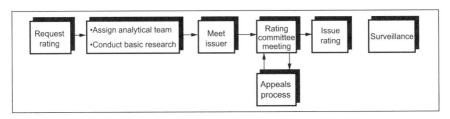

Source: Standard & Poor's.

Rating Methodology

Each rating agency strives to give the best indication it can of the risks of investing in a particular bond. The methodology that each agency uses, however, can vary. The variation in the choice of methodology is a reminder that the ratings those agencies issue are merely opinions.

Take a look at Figure 12.2, which illustrates the debt rating process used by Standard & Poor's (S&P). As you can see, the process it uses is quite thorough, and each step in the process requires an immense amount of work and expertise. What may look like a simple meeting with company management, for example, is anything but that. Standard & Poor's assembles its most experienced staff members to meet a company's management, and when they meet with management, it's not for cake and coffee. The purpose of the meeting is to "review in detail the company's key operating and financial plans, management policies, and other credit factors that have an impact on the rating."

At these meetings the companies are asked to provide significant amounts of information that will help determine the rating assignments. Rating agencies such as S&P scrutinize a company's management for its competence, structure, strategic planning, and composition. It also scrutinizes the company's appetite for risk and often tours a company's facilities, although this is not always a critical factor in the rating process. The many steps carried out in the process quite clearly show that the rating process is quite vigorous, involving many different and intense areas of concentration.

Despite Recent Failings, the Agencies Do Their Homework Thoroughly

As was mentioned earlier, the rating agencies endeavor to base their assessments on two key risks: credit risk and indenture protection. Gauging these risks requires a significant amount of financial and legal review. The legal reviews are complex, but they are less open to interpretation than the financial reviews. The financial reviews therefore must be conducted quite thoroughly. Let's take a look at how the agencies conduct their financial reviews. Table 12.3 details the many factors the agencies consider when conducting their credit analyses.

As the table shows, the two main considerations in a credit analysis are a company's business risk and financial risk. Analysis of a company's business risk mainly involves an assessment of the industry of which the company is a part. The agencies are primarily interested in assessing the industry's growth potential and sensitivity to the ups and downs of the business cycle. An industry's ability to withstand an economic downturn, for example, is an important factor in the assessment of business risk.

The agencies also are interested in assessing the competitive pressures from other companies in the industry as well as the amount of research and development expenses that may be needed for a company to stay competitive. Despite the emphasis on industry considerations, a company's fundamentals always get first consideration and have a far greater bearing on its overall rating. Nevertheless, in recent years rating agencies have increased

Table 12.3 Corporate Credit Analysis Factors

Business Risk

Industry characteristics
Competitive position
Marketing
Technology
Efficiency
Regulation
Management

Financial Risk

Financial characteristics
Financial policy
Profitability
Capital structure
Cash flow protection
Financial flexibility

Source: Standard and Poor's.

their responsiveness to and consideration of factors such as the impact of the economic cycle on various industries.

The assessment of a company's financial risk requires greater use of quantitative analysis than is used to assess a company's business risk. In other words, the rating agencies must do enough homework to make a math teacher proud. Scrutiny of a company's cash flows and overall balance sheet, for example, requires a significant amount of mathematical homework. Rating agencies therefore deploy dozens of mathematical formulas and financial ratios to aid them in their rigorous examinations. The ratios are used to gain an understanding of the financial characteristics of a company.

If you are wondering whether an agency places greater emphasis on the assessment of a company's business or financial risks, the answer is: It depends. The rating agencies take pains to meld both quantitative and qualitative analyses to get the most complete picture of a company. Whether a rating agency will depend more heavily on its assessment of one or the other is essentially a case-by-case issue.

The Four Cs

The various elements of the methodology used by the rating agencies to assign credit ratings sometimes are called the *four Cs*: capacity, character, collateral, and covenants. The four Cs represent a fairly good summary of the rating process. You might want to remember this system to remind you of the rating methodology described above. Let's briefly look at each of the four Cs.

- *Capacity* refers to an issuer's ability to pay its debt obligations, including both principal and interest. The rating agencies assess this mostly by conducting a review of the issuer's financial situation and the various industry considerations that could affect its financial situation in the future.
- *Character* refers to the issuer's management, management policies, operating plans, and reputation in its industry and with its customers. Personal visits with management are an integral part of the review of a company's character.
- *Collateral* refers to the assets that back an issuer's debt. In a sense, a review of an issuer's collateral can be placed under the umbrella of one of the other Cs: capacity. Capacity, however, refers mostly to an analysis of the cash flows needed for a company to pay its debt obligations. A review of a company's collateral, by contrast, can shed light on the amount of assets that would be available to pay an

issuer's debts if the issuer had to liquidate its assets because of a bankruptcy. The review also can indicate the amount of assets available to help fuel a company's expansion.

- *Covenants* refer to the legal protections provided to the bondholder. These legal protections are contained in a bond's indenture. The *indenture* is essentially a contract between a bond issuer and the investors who buy its bonds. Included in the indenture are promises such as the timing and amount of interest payments, the bond's maturity date, and the call provisions. Indentures were discussed in greater detail in Chapter 3.

The significant amount of homework the agencies do should increase your confidence in the rating system.

Credit Ratings Are a Must-Have for Every Fixed-Income Toolbox

As you can see, ratings supply an enormous amount of information to aid in the investment decision-making process. Investors are fortunate to have a few simple rating grades available to summarize the complex and thorough research conducted by the rating agencies. You need only gain an understanding of the various rating grades to include them in your research arsenal. Recent events have shown the wisdom of doing your own homework, but regardless of how much work you do on your own, it is comforting to know that the rating agencies have done a good deal of the homework too.

An interesting exercise to test your understanding of credit ratings would be to make a list of 10 diverse companies and try to guess their credit ratings. Once you have finished, see how you fared by checking the actual credit ratings of those companies. Then take a step back and see how the ratings fit with the companies you chose and try to gain a better understanding of why the rating agencies chose to rate them as they did.

Summary

- Credit ratings are a great tool for gauging a company's ability and willingness to meet its debt obligations.
- The rating system has been in place for decades and historically has been a reliable way to gauge credit risk, a key risk for bond investors.

- Nevertheless, a decline in rating accuracy in 2008, several high-profile rating gaffes, and an inability of the rating agencies to keep up with financial innovation are reasons for caution with respect to putting complete trust in them.
- The methodology used by the major rating agencies is extensive and probably is more rigorous than what can be accomplished by most individuals.
- Although credit ratings are great tools, investors should use them to augment their own investment decision-making tools and consider the many other factors involved in the investment decision.
- Knowledge of credit ratings is very basic yet is essential to investing. The various rating definitions supplied in this chapter can be used to improve your knowledge of credit ratings.

13

BOND STRATEGIES

One of the great things about the bond market is that it is rich with investment choices to fit all sorts of situations, both in terms of one's personal needs and the investment climate. The bond market is also ideally suited to meet the needs of both individual and institutional investors. This is a lot different than other asset classes, where the possibilities are fewer and investors have a relatively narrow ability to manage risk.

Faced with so many choices in the bond market, investors endeavoring to protect their money and optimize their investment returns need gain an understanding of the strategies available to them. The starting point for these strategies is the investment objective. This is analogous to either a construction worker or plumber first knowing what he or she wants to get done and then deciding on the tools that are best for the job.

The format of this chapter is simple. Listed in no particular order are the many objectives investors tend to have and the strategies that can be deployed in the bond market to meet these objectives. All investment strategies contain the possibility of loss as well as gain, and a successful investor needs to understand the potential risks and rewards with each strategy prior to investing.

Preservation of Capital and Liquidity

Investors seeking to preserve their capital and keep their assets liquid have come to the right place: *bonds are higher in capital structure than are equities; as such, bond investors are first in line in case of default.* This characteristic is what makes bonds as an asset class ideally suited for the preservation of capital. While not all bonds are highly liquid, for most investors there are plenty of liquid fixed-income assets to choose from. Here are a few strategies that can help meet the objective of preserving capital and liquidity.

Own U.S. Treasury Securities

In particular, buy *on-the-run Treasuries*, which tend to perform better than older Treasuries in times when liquidity preferences increase. Treasury securities are very actively traded to the tune of about a half trillion dollars per day. Backed by the full faith and credit of the United States, Treasuries continue to be seen as safe, although focus on U.S. budget deficits could become more intense in focus if the U.S. debt problem is not addressed.

Own Money Market Funds

Money market funds tend to be invested in highly liquid securities, including U.S. Treasury and agency securities, repurchase agreements, and high-quality commercial paper and corporate bonds.

Own High-Quality Bonds

These investments have better price transparency than low-quality bonds and thus are better to have in times when liquidity issues rise.

Earn Current Income

Many investors invest in bonds in order to earn current income. This is especially true of older investors. Most bonds pay interest, which makes them suitable for delivering steady cash flows. Cash flow needs and tax situations vary depending on the investor, requiring a high degree of selectivity for strategy. One characteristic to consider is the frequency of cash flows desired or needed. Some bonds generally pay interest every six months, and mutual funds tend to pay interest monthly. Hence, the strategies for this objective are the following.

Own Bonds with Relatively High Coupon Rates

Interest payments will be higher for these bonds than for those with low coupon rates. The duration on a high coupon bond will tend to be lower than the duration on a low coupon bond of the same maturity. This means that for low coupon bonds there is reduced price sensitivity to changes in market interest rates. This is good news when rates are rising, bad news when rates are falling. Pay attention to tax-related issues that surround purchasing *premium* versus *discount bonds*.

Avoid Callable Bonds or Those with Features That Could Result in Unpredictable Cash Flows

For example, mortgage-backed securities have highly uncertain cash flows because of fluctuations in mortgage prepayments. Floating-rate notes also fit into this category. For investors willing to take the risk, however, these instruments provide an opportunity to increase their cash flow if they make the right bets on the direction of interest rates, among other factors.

Gain Exposure to International Markets

It has become increasingly important to consider *country risk* as a risk factor when investing in financial instruments. Investors can no longer take for granted sovereign credit risk given the level of indebtedness that many countries have acquired as a result of their efforts to battle the financial and economic crisis. Moreover, investors that want to participate in the secular upswing of emerging nations need look abroad to do so. The bond market expands this opportunity set, both from the perspective of reducing risk and capitalizing on the improving cash flows of corporations in the corporate sphere. Here are a few strategies for this objective.

Own Sovereign Debt of Countries Abroad

Individual investors can accomplish this through mutual funds, selecting from funds that are dedicated to individual countries, developed nations, emerging markets, and developing local markets and from among funds that are hedged or unhedged against foreign exchange risks. Futures investors can gain exposure through futures whose underlying assets are government securities.

Own Debts Denominated in Local Currencies, U.S. Dollars, or Other Currencies of Choice

One way to speculate (and it is speculating) on the performance of one currency versus another is to purchase a bond denominated in a local currency. For example, an investor wanting to gain exposure to a currency in the emerging markets would purchase a bond denominated in the currency of choice. This entails risk, with an investor's return subject to impact from fluctuations in the foreign exchange market. Investors seeking to avoid this can instead find bonds denominated in the same currency as his or her home country. For example, a dollar-based investor in this case would purchase bonds issued by an entity abroad but denominated in dollars. Local currency bonds can help enhance a portfolio's diversification needs depending upon the mix of securities in the portfolio, among other factors.

Yield Enhancement

Yield enhancement strategies are not for the simple-minded or for those averse to risk, but they are popular among institutional investors. As the label implies, yield enhancement strategies are designed to enhance the return of a portfolio. Sophisticated strategies are often designed to meet this objective, although often they are based on simple themes; for example, investors can speculate on a trading range for Treasury securities or swap rates using options. Keeping in mind that these strategies are not for everyone and entail substantial risks, here are more details on such strategies.

Sell Options on Treasury Futures or Options on Swap Rates

Investors who are confident that rates will hold within a set range for Treasuries and swaps can speculate that the range will hold by selling options struck at either extreme of the range or both. For example, an investor who believes 10-year Treasury yields will neither rise more than 50 basis points nor fall more than 50 basis points from their current levels can sell calls and puts struck at prices that correlate closely to yield levels associated with the strike prices. If the investor bets correctly, the options will expire worthless, providing the investor with an added return to his or her portfolio. This is a way of capturing *theta*, or the time decay associated with options. Incorrect bets will occur when yields move outside of the expected range. The farther the move outside the range, the more a short position will move "in-the-money" and expose investors to losses.

Curve Duration: Bets on the Yield Curve

As was described in Chapter 3, curve duration estimates a portfolio's price sensitivity to changes in the shape of the yield curve. Investors seeking "curve exposure" do so when they expect the yield curve to steepen. A portfolio with positive curve duration will outperform a portfolio that has no curve duration (all else being equal) when the yield curve steepens.

Keep in mind that there is a distinction between moving money dollar for dollar from one maturity to another, and moving money on a duration-weighted basis between maturities. The former provides a means of optimizing a strategy designed to anticipate a particular direction that interest rates will move (for example, investors expecting interest rates to rise would shorten their average maturity); the latter, which requires investors use a ratio of one maturity versus another in order to equate their price sensitivity to changes in interest rates, provides a means of optimizing returns based on changes in the shape of the yield curve. Here are a couple of strategies.

Increase Exposure to Bonds That Mature between 2 and 10 Years

These are the maturities that gain positive curve duration. Longer maturities have negative duration and are best suited for bets on a flattening of the yield curve.

Invest for Carry and Roll-Down

We discussed this concept in Chapter 9. Basically, the objective here is to capture price gains that occur when maturities *roll down* the yield curve. It is a strategy that tends to be best suited for shorter maturities. For example, in environments where the yield curve is steep and no change in official rates is expected over the immediate- or near-term horizon, a 2-year note yielding 1.5 percent will roll down the yield curve to approximate the 1-year maturity in a year's time. If the 1-year maturity yields, say, 0.8 percent, this means that the 2-year note will fall 70 basis points in yield over one year's time, or about 6 basis points per month. Of course, as its yield falls, its price will gain, boosting the total return on the security. Investors can also earn *carry* in this scenario, by earning the yield spread to the cost of financing the issue.

Asset-Liability Management

Asset-liability managers include pension funds and insurance companies. These entities have obligations they expect to pay in the future, and therefore they need to manage their liabilities in order to meet them. Individuals have future obligations as well, including college tuition for their children and retirement, for example. Bonds are well suited to the task because of their fixed maturity dates and predictable cash flows. Here are a few ideas.

Use Laddering

The purchase of several bonds having different maturity dates is one way for an investor to time cash flow needs in future years. For example, an investor could hold a 5-year maturity to meet an expected obligation, as well as 10- and 15-year maturities, or a plethora of other maturity mixes depending on his or her personal situation.

Own Zero Coupon Bonds

Zero coupon bonds pay no interest and are sold at a discount to their face value. Investors anticipating an obligation can purchase zero coupon bonds with a maturity that matches the obligation. Investors having long-term liabilities are typical buyers of long-term zero coupon bonds. In addition to the ability to purchase the securities at a discount to their face value, an advantage of zero coupon bonds is that the stated yield-to-maturity is likely to be earned. They differ from bonds that pay interest because the interest on such bonds needs to be reinvested at a rate equal to the stated yield-to-maturity on the bonds in order to earn that yield. For some investors the lack of cash flow is a negative feature, and for some investors, the fact that the interest accrual is taxable is a negative feature.

Engage in Swaps

The swaps market can be used by a wide variety of investors both to manage interest rate risk and to manage future obligations. For example, a corporation can decide to swap its floating-rate obligations for fixed-rate obligations, and vice versa. The swap market is an institutional market, and it is very large and liquid, with literally hundreds of trillions of dollars of notional amounts outstanding. Participants include corporations, commercial banks, and investment banks.

Tax-Liability Management

Investors can help manage their tax liabilities by owning bonds, generally by owning municipal bonds, as the interest payments received by holders of municipal bonds are often exempt from federal taxation. This is obviously important because income taxes cause a major amount of erosion to the return on some portfolios, chiefly through the erosion of capital gains, dividends, and interest. Investing in tax-exempt bonds can reduce this erosion. See Chapter 4 for a further discussion of municipal bonds and for a discussion of taxable municipal bonds: Build America Bonds (BABs).

Risk Diversification

We discussed in Chapter 5 the idea that asset diversification does not equal risk diversification. By investing in bonds, an investor does not necessarily achieve true risk diversification, which is what is desired when seeking to neutralize the equity risk factor, the biggest risk that investors tend to face. For example, there is equity risk in a bond, just as there is interest rate risk in equities. Attention must be paid to these risk factors in order to effectively neutralize them. Doing so is not an easy task, and it requires careful attention to the many different risk factors that exist, including liquidity, volatility, duration, credit, and equity risk. Nevertheless, bonds can be used to help achieve risk diversification in ways that are not possible in other asset classes. Here are some strategies for risk diversification.

Own Treasuries

When tail events happen, liquidity dries up. Treasury securities tend to remain liquid during such times, making it possible for investors to liquidate their assets more readily.

Stay High in the Capital Structure

We showed in Figure 4.2 the differing recovery rates that have existed historically for securities ranked differently in the capital structure. Put simply, the higher up in the capital structure, the greater the recovery rate on defaulted bonds. Investors therefore seeking to minimize their equity risk can do so by staying high in the capital structure; for example, a senior note is higher in the capital structure than a subordinated one.

Own Bonds in Defensive Industries

Investors who own bonds in industries less prone to the ups and downs of the business cycle can also achieve some degree of risk diversification. Industries considered less sensitive to the business cycle include pipelines, utilities, energy in general, food (not restaurants), and select portions of the health-care sector. The key is to find industries where demand tends to be relatively inelastic. Examples at the opposite end of the spectrum include the retail, manufacturing, hotel, gaming, and restaurant industries.

Own Bonds of Companies in Industries with Hard Assets

When companies default on their obligations, the recovery rates will differ. Much depends upon the type of assets that can be sold. The more hard assets that a company has, the higher the recovery rate is likely to be.

Own Inflation-Protected Securities

We described in Chapter 4 how the Treasury's inflation-protected securities (TIPS) help protect investors against inflation, compensating investors as they do for increases in the consumer price index.

Purchase Credit Default Swaps

Credit default swaps provide buyers with protection against default by an issuer. In a credit default swap (CDS), the buyer of the CDS receives payment from the seller if there is a "credit event," typically a default, or failure to pay interest on a bond, although there can be other triggering events.

Purchase Options to Hedge Adverse Movements

Investors can purchase options to hedge against interest rate risks or equity risks in their bonds. To hedge interest rate risks, investors can purchase options that trade on listed exchanges such as the Chicago Mercantile Exchange, or those that trade over the counter; for example, *options on swaps*, or *swaptions*. The amount to purchase depends on an investor's preferences and objectives. Investors endeavoring to hedge against tail events could spend, say, 5 percent of their expected returns, which for many might mean 25 to 50 basis points per year, as a percentage of the assets they want to hedge.

Summary

- The bond market is rich with investment choices to fit all sorts of situations, both in terms of one's personal needs and the investment climate, probably more so than with other asset classes.

- Investors need to focus on their investment objectives and then tailor their fixed-income strategies accordingly.
- The bond market can help investors meet numerous investment objectives including the preservation of capital and liquidity; yield enhancement; gaining exposure to international markets; asset-liability management; tax-liability management; and risk diversification (asset diversification does not equal risk diversification!).

14

HOW INTEREST RATES HAVE SHAPED THE POLITICAL LANDSCAPE

It is simplistic to think that the vast impact of interest rates ends with the economy; in fact, there are numerous powerful secondary effects. Indeed, while there are many issues that can shape an election and thus the political landscape, I believe that the impact of interest rates is unmistakable. This is relatively new phenomenon can be dated back to the 1976 elections, when President Gerald Ford faced off against Governor Jimmy Carter. In every presidential administration since then, there have been moments when interest rates played a major role in defining the president's place in history. While pundits have noticed that interest rates and politics cross paths now and then, few have noted the clear link that has undoubtedly existed over the last 30 years or so.

Judging the extent to which interest rates have affected politics is quite subjective, but few people argue against the notion that the health of the economy has played a substantial role in shaping the political landscape over the last 200 years. If the economy is known to influence politics, and interest rates are known to influence the economy as well as financial conditions, it stands to reason that interest rates must influence politics. In my view, the only debate should be about the degree of influence.

Economic Issues Have Been Core Political Issues Since the Revolution

Throughout history economic factors have clearly been one of the most influential factors in U.S. politics. As far back as the Revolutionary War economic issues have been at the heart of the nation's political events. The Boston Tea Party in 1773, for instance, was a protest against taxes on tea imports—a tax the colonists felt was unfair. Interestingly, the tax was imposed by Britain to pay interest on its national debt. That debt had doubled during the Seven Years War between Britain and France, and interest payments were consuming more than half of Britain's annual budget. It was not the last time issues related to the economy and the national debt would affect America.

A clear example of the link between the economy and politics occurred during the presidency of Martin Van Buren. Within weeks of his inauguration, the Panic of 1837 thrust Van Buren into a crisis from which he would never fully recover. Van Buren had the unfortunate luck of entering office when the U.S. economy was at the end of a boom period that had been fraught with excesses partly related to speculative demand for lands in the West. The banking system was soon in tatters, and hundreds of banks and businesses failed. The economy sunk into its first depression, and the economic weakness lasted about five years.

During those years the crisis might have been prevented and/or alleviated if the nation had had a means of smoothing the business cycle. Back then, the Federal Reserve did not exist and there was no real equivalent. There was, however, an equivalent in the private sector. Suffolk Bank of Boston served as a clearinghouse for virtually all the bank notes that circulated in New England, and it lent reserves to other banks and kept the payments system working. These functions are essential elements of the operations of today's Federal Reserve. Suffolk Bank's unique role as a "central bank" helps explain why New England and its banks were spared the economic distress that plagued the rest of the country. This episode is evidence of the importance of having a central bank such as the Federal Reserve to provide stability to the U.S. financial system in the way that it did particularly in 2008 when the U.S. faced another panic.

Interest rates, of course, are one of the Fed's most important tools, and there almost certainly would have been a role for the Fed in not only helping to prevent the speculative excesses that led to the Panic of 1837 but also helping the nation recover from them. The Fed could have raised interest rates to reduce the speculative fervor and then lowered them and used more of its available tools to bring stability to the financial system just as it did in the recent financial crisis. (The idea that the Fed can deflate bubbles is nonetheless debatable, and the Fed did not stop the housing bubble from forming in the 2000s.) The Panic of 1837 was a case in which interest rates and the Fed could have played an important role but did not because the mechanism for manipulating rates and stabilizing the economy and financial system did not exist.

As history has proven many times since the Panic of 1837, such a crisis can have major political repercussions. President Van Buren rolled from one crisis to the next and was alienated even in his own party. The economic distress fractured his party and hurt his popularity. In the election of 1840 Van Buren was defeated handily, losing in the Electoral College by a vote of 234 to 60.

The Great Depression Sparked Massive Changes in Politics

The Panic of 1837 was trumped almost 100 years later by an even worse set of economic circumstances during the Great Depression that began in 1929, and the political repercussions would again be dramatic.

On the heels of the booming economy of the 1920s, Herbert Hoover was swept into office as the thirty-first president of the United States, winning in the Electoral College by a vote of 444 to 87—the largest margin recorded up to that time. Hoover's Republican Party was in complete control of the House, the Senate, and the executive branch of the government. That was a condition that would rarely be seen in the rest of the twentieth century, and it was the economy that was at the root of the power shift.

But on October 29, 1929, the stock market crashed, tumbling 11.7 percent and leading to the worst economic depression the country has ever seen. Unemployment skyrocketed to about 25 percent, putting nearly 14 million people out of work. The boom years of the Roaring Twenties were a distant memory. A lot of remedies were proposed at that time, many of which Hoover rejected. For the most part Hoover did not embrace the notion that the government could alleviate economic woes with new programs and fiscal initiatives. Most economists agreed with Hoover, as it was conventional wisdom at that time to expect the economy to right itself. Economists and the Treasury believed that new government spending ultimately would fail to revive the economy because the deficits created by the new spending would result in a decline in private investment. The notion that the economy would be better off if left alone, Hoover would learn, would become politically bankrupt. Laissez-faire was out.

As with the Panic of 1837, the Great Depression might have been less severe if the boom years that preceded it had been fraught with fewer excesses. The Federal Reserve, for instance, could have helped cool the speculative fervor that ran rampant in the 1920s, but the Fed did not fully grasp the powerful role interest rates could have played in cooling the excesses. If the Federal Reserve had raised interest rates during the 1920s, the excesses that built up almost certainly would have been reduced and the bubble would have burst with fewer repercussions. And once the bubble burst, the Fed could have used its interest rate tool again to soften the effects of the economic bust. But with the Federal Reserve having been established not too many years earlier in 1914, the Fed had little experience in handling the ups and downs of the business cycle, and many believe that the Federal Reserve kept monetary policy too tight throughout the 1930s. However, the Fed would be able to draw on its unfortunate experience for decades to come, and in 2008 and 2009 the Federal Reserve's decisive response to the financial crisis has been credited with helping to stabilize the U.S. economic and financial crisis.

To Hoover, however, the invaluable lessons that the Fed learned from the Great Depression could not be redeemed for votes. In the 1930 election Hoover's Republican Party lost the House to a previously weak Democratic Party, and it won a plurality of just one vote in the Senate. In the 1932 election Hoover lost his bid for a second term in a landslide defeat to Franklin D. Roosevelt, losing in the Electoral College by 472 to 59. Roosevelt would go on to implement a series of government programs that ultimately would revive the economy. The failure of Hoover's laissez-faire approach and the success of Roosevelt's support for more proactive government helped define the two parties, particularly in the public's eye. Perceptions about the two major parties and their core beliefs about government involvement in the economy stand to this day. If the Federal Reserve had been more influential during that era and used its powerful interest rate tool, the political landscape might have evolved much differently over the subsequent years.

By the 1950s the Federal Reserve was playing a more active role in regulating the pace of the U.S. economy. Few people probably recognized it at the time, but the Fed's maturity probably had an influence on the stability the nation enjoyed in the 1950s. During that time interest rates were both low and stable. This almost certainly encouraged investment, which helped raise productivity and thus the national standard of living.

As the 1960s unfolded, however, inflation and interest rates began to climb as the effects of the Vietnam War started to affect the economy. The Vietnam War affected the economy in two ways. First, the war was costly. The size of the public debt roughly doubled by the time the war ended, and interest rates rose in response to the increase in debt issuance. Second, the Federal Reserve allowed the money supply to expand through what in hindsight appears to have been an overly accommodating stance on monetary policy. The Fed was essentially monetizing the acceleration in inflation by providing the fuel needed to push up prices. The jumps in interest rates and inflation were arguably contributing factors in the 1969 to 1970 recession.

Interest Rates and Politics in the Modern Era

The political landscape during the 1970s was probably influenced more by the level of interest rates than any other decade of the twentieth century.

Nixon and Ford Were the First to Have to Contend with High Interest Rates as a Political Issue

After the Vietnam War ended, the link between interest rates and politics grew stronger than ever, and for the first time interest rates became a campaign issue. During Ford's term as president, the electorate began to view high interest rates not as a repercussion of the costly Vietnam War but as a symptom of bad economic policies and something it could control with its votes. The electorate came to see high interest rates as something that was detrimental to the national standard of living, as the recession of November 1974 to March 1975 would make clear.

Of course, that recession was precipitated by the first of the two oil shocks in that decade, but the recession also can be attributed to excessive growth in credit and the money supply that was partly fueled by the Federal Reserve. As it did in the late 1960s, the Fed monetized the acceleration of inflation in the mid-1970s by providing the fuel needed to push up prices. In turn, inflation drove interest rates higher and thus weakened demand for homes and other goods and services, resulting in rising unemployment and an economic recession.

Democrats, led by Governor Jimmy Carter of Georgia, pounced on Ford's economic record and made it one of their major campaign issues. Here's how Carter put it during one of the several presidential debates just weeks before the 1976 presidential election:

Seven point nine percent unemployment is a terrible tragedy in this country. He [Ford] says he's learned how to match unemployment with inflation. That's right. We've got the highest inflation we've had in twenty-five years right now, except under this administration, and that was fifty years ago. And we've got the highest unemployment we've had, under Mr. Ford's administration, since the Great Depression.

Carter would repeat that theme many times during his campaign. Ford clearly was on the defensive not only against Carter but also against a weary electorate. The mood of the electorate was captured in these pointed questions posed by the moderator of one of the debates:

> *Mr. President, the country is now in something that your advisors call an economic pause. I think to most Americans that sounds like an antiseptic term for low growth; unemployment standstill at a high, high level; [for a] decline in take-home pay, lower factory earnings, more layoffs. Uh, isn't that a really rotten record and doesn't your administration bear most of the blame for it?*

To which Ford responded, "Well, Mr. Kraft, uh-I violently disagree with your assessment. And I don't think the record justifies the conclusion that you've come to." Ford tried to explain how interest rate levels had not hurt the housing market and how inflation was trending lower. But Carter matched his explanation with a strong response. Here's the exchange:

> **Ford:** *But now let's talk about the pluses that came out this week. We had an 18 percent increase in housing starts. We had a substantial increase in new permits for housing. As a matter of fact, based on the announcement this week, there will be at an annual rate of a million, eight hundred and some thousand new houses built, which is a tremendous increase over last year and a substantial increase over the earlier part of this year. Now in addition, we had a very, some very good news in the reduction in the rate of inflation. And inflation hits everybody: those who are working and those who are on welfare. It means that the American buyer is getting a better bargain today because inflation is less.*
> **Carter:** *With all due respect to President Ford, I think he ought to be ashamed of mentioning that statement, because we have the highest unemployment rate now than we had at any time between the Great Depression caused by Herbert Hoover and the time President Ford took office. Anybody who says that the inflation rate is in good shape now ought to talk to the housewives. One of the overwhelming results that I've seen in the polls is that people feel that you can't plan anymore. There's no way to make a prediction that my family might be able to own a home or to put my kid through college. Savings accounts are losing money instead of gaining money. Inflation is robbing us. And housing starts—he compares the housing starts with last year. I don't blame him, because in 1975 we had fewer housing starts in this country, fewer homes built, than any year since 1940.*

At the root of Carter's assertions about the economy, particularly with regard to his statement on the housing sector—one of the most interest rate–sensitive sectors of the economy—was his view that high interest rates were hurting the economy. Carter's message on the economy undoubtedly contributed to his victory over Ford in the 1976 election. Indeed, Carter won—albeit by slim margins—in many key northeastern states, no doubt helped by the weak economic conditions plaguing those states at that time. While this was not the first time the economy contributed to the outcome of an election, it was the most visible illustration up to that time of the power of interest rates and their subsequent impact on the economy and, hence, politics.

For Carter, High Interest Rates Were a Double-Edged Sword in the 1980 Campaign

While Carter clearly benefited from the high interest rates and weak economic conditions that prevailed in the years leading up to the 1976 election, those forces turned out to be a double-edged sword for him when he sought reelection in 1980. After over a decade of rising interest rates and accelerating inflation, the public was once again poised to show its discontent at the polls. The electorate merely needed a leader to champion its cause, and Ronald Reagan fit that mold.

To many people Reagan represented the best hope of restoring the American dream. The country had entered a slow but dangerous decline that was matched by similar conditions abroad. The economy was mired in an unusual slump consisting of high interest rates, high inflation, and high unemployment. The national standard of living was clearly in decline as a result of those major forces. High interest rates had reduced housing affordability and hurt many other key interest rate–sensitive sectors of the economy, such as business investment. The decline in business investment resulted in a decline in U.S. competitiveness, particularly in the automobile industry, where low-cost producers such as Japan began to make inroads on U.S. automakers, grabbing market share along the way. High inflation was cutting into wages and salaries, eroding the value of disposable income, while high unemployment was making those days even more difficult to bear.

There was a term used back then to define the unusual combination of high inflation and high unemployment that plagued the Carter years: *stagflation.* Stagflation became Carter's nemesis, and the nation looked to Reagan to lead it out of that dilemma.

Reagan saw to it that the public would recall Carter's criticisms of Ford's handling of the economy four years earlier. Carter was basically defenseless. Here's how Reagan, during one of the two presidential debates that took place in 1980, deftly turned an expression Carter had coined and benefited from in 1976 into an issue that he could use against Carter during the 1980 campaign:

> *Now, as to why I should be [President] and he shouldn't be, when he was a candidate in 1976, President Carter invented a thing he called the misery index. He added the rate of unemployment and the rate of inflation, and it came, at that time, to 12.5 percent under President Ford. He said that no man with that size misery index has a right to seek reelection to the presidency. Today, by his own decision, the misery index is in excess of 20 percent, and I think this must suggest something.*

The misery index, which is the sum of inflation and unemployment, could easily be redesigned to include interest rates instead of inflation. Interest rates, after all, typically track inflation and therefore are a good proxy for inflation. Moreover, high interest rate levels relate to the miseries associated with the burdensome cost of borrowing. High mortgage rates, for example, can be disheartening to families hoping to realize the American dream of owning one's own home. Similarly, high interest rates can stymie the dreams of ambitious individuals aspiring to own their own businesses. If the misery index were redefined to include interest rates, a more complete picture of the impact of a set of economic conditions would result.

Throughout the campaign Reagan offered a vision for better economic times. He repeatedly promised to adopt policies that ultimately would bring down both inflation and interest rates and thus restore economic prosperity to the nation. His economic plan would be dubbed "Reaganomics." Reaganomics consisted of four key elements.

First, Reagan supported a restrictive monetary policy designed to purge inflation from the economy and ultimately result in lower interest rates. Lower interest rates, he argued, would spur investment and raise productivity levels, raising the nation's standard of living. Moreover, low interest rates would spur wider homeownership so that more families could realize the American dream. Initially, tight money policies also would help stabilize the value of the dollar and thus reduce the cost of imports and encourage foreign investment in U.S. assets. Second, Reagan proposed a 25 percent across-the-board tax cut to lift consumer buying power, increase savings and investment, and encourage work and worker productivity. (This ultimately became the Economic Recovery Tax Act of 1981.) Third, Reagan promised to reduce discretionary government spending. Fourth, he endeavored to reduce layers of government regulations that he felt were impeding productivity and, hence, economic growth.

With slow economic growth, high interest rates, inflation, and unemployment in mind, Reagan crystallized the 1980 election with these classic closing remarks at the debate on October 28:

> *Next Tuesday is Election Day. Next Tuesday all of you will go to the polls, will stand there in the polling place and make a decision. I think when you make that decision, it might be well if you would ask yourself, are you better off than you were four years ago? Is it easier for you to go and buy things in the stores than it was four years ago? Is there more or less unemployment in the country than there was four years ago? . . . And if you answer all of those questions yes, why then, I think your choice is very obvious as to whom you will vote for. If you don't agree, if you don't think that this course that we've been on for the last four years is what you would like to see us follow for the next four, then I could suggest another choice that you have. This country doesn't have to be in the shape that it is in. We do not have to go on sharing in scarcity with the country getting worse off, with unemployment growing. . . . All of this can be cured and all of it can be solved.*

Reagan knew when he asked people to ask themselves, "Are you better off than you were four years ago?" that the public's discontent with high interest rates, inflation, and unemployment would be voiced at the polls. Reagan offered hope for a departure from the country's economic malaise and ultimately delivered on his promises.

Throughout Reagan's presidency, interest rates, inflation, and unemployment all fell. Reagan's prescriptions for those major ills proved to be the right remedies. During the 1984 election campaign, Vice President George Bush summed up Reagan's accomplishments in regard to the economy, particularly with respect to interest rates, in his debates with vice presidential candidate Geraldine Ferraro:

> *One of the reasons I think we're an effective team is that I believe firmly in his leadership. He's really turned this country around. We agree on the economic program. When we came into office, why, inflation was 21, 12½ percent interest [rates] were wiping out every single American; [interest rates] were 21½ percent if you can believe it. Productivity was down. Savings was down. There was despair. . . . The other day [Ferraro] was in a plant and she said to the workers, Why are you all voting for, why are so many of you voting for the Reagan-Bush ticket? And there was a long, deathly silence, and she said, Come on, we delivered. That's the problem. And I'm not blaming her except for the liberal voting record in the House.*

They delivered. They delivered 21 percent interest rates. They delivered what they called malaise. They delivered interest rates that were right off the charts. They delivered take-home paychecks that were shrinking, and we've delivered optimism. People are going back to work: 6 million of them. And 300,000 jobs a month being created. That's why there was that deathly silence out there in that plant. They delivered the wrong thing. Ronald Reagan is delivering leadership.

Reagan's economic record would catapult him to a landslide victory in the 1984 presidential election.

As well as the economy performed during the Reagan years, the sharp rise in the government's budget deficit has been attributed to his policies. The large increase in defense spending that occurred during Reagan's tenure—the biggest peacetime defense buildup ever—often is cited as one of the main causes of the jump in the deficit. In addition, the massive tax cut implemented in 1981 often is cited as a cause. These assertions fall flat for a few reasons.

First, the tax cuts did not result in a decrease in tax receipts. Tax receipts actually increased in the 1980s. Indeed, tax revenue grew by a whopping 83 percent during his administration. Second, the defense buildup, which pushed defense spending up to 6.2 percent of the gross domestic product (GDP) during the 1980s, arguably helped win the Cold War. Once the Cold War ended in the 1990s, the United States was able to reduce defense spending and enjoy a large peace dividend: defense spending had fallen to just 2.9 percent of the GDP by the year 2000. Thus, in the long run Reagan's defense buildup may have saved the nation hundreds of billions of dollars. Third, perhaps the biggest cause of the increase in the budget deficit was the sharp jump in entitlement spending. An increase in eligibility for entitlement programs and sharply increased costs for medical care contributed to the surge in entitlement spending.

These were forces largely outside Reagan's control.

As large as the budget deficit was, it did not cost Reagan any votes, nor would it hurt the election chances of George H. W. Bush. One of the biggest reasons for this was that the surge in the deficit had little discernible effect on interest rate levels. In economic theory, budget deficits are supposed to result in an increase in interest rates because the government is competing with the private sector for capital. In a world with finite capital, investors would require higher interest rates to be enticed to invest in government bonds rather than in the private sector. In addition, simple economics suggests that if the supply of bonds increased as a result of a budget deficit, the price of those bonds would fall—and yields would rise.

Yet despite the increase in the U.S. budget deficit, interest rates began a long secular decline very early in Reagan's first term. This happened largely because inflation began a secular decline at that time. Moreover, Reagan's low-tax, low-regulation policies sowed the seeds for a sharp rise in business investment and innovation, resulting in a sharp rise in productivity. This is important because rising productivity levels tend to reduce the cost of labor and, hence, inflation and interest rates.

These forces eventually would play a major role in laying the ground-work for the vigorous economic growth that occurred during the 1990s. Investors recognized this well in advance, and that helped to keep interest rates on a downward path during the 1980s. The growing budget deficits therefore had little impact on Reagan and Bush in the 1984 and 1988 elections. Falling interest rates had eased the public's concerns over the budget and therefore played a major role in the outcome of those elections. To most voters, as long as interest rates were falling, they could defer their concerns over the budget.

The Fed's Rate Increases: The Slow Pace of Rate Cuts Hurt George H. W. Bush

While declining interest rate levels undoubtedly played a role in helping George Bush become president in 1988, rising interest rate levels early in his term and their slow pace of decline late in his term probably hurt his reelection bid in 1992. As Bush entered office in 1989, interest rates began to climb. The Federal Reserve had embarked on a course of raising interest rates to combat a steady climb in inflation. Inflation had begun to occur as a result of economic forces that typically emerge when the duration of an economic expansion lengthens. The 1980s expansion, after all, was at the time the longest peacetime expansion since World War II. Nevertheless, Bush would have to contend with the political fallout that higher interest rates would bring.

The Federal Reserve, led by its chair, Alan Greenspan, raised interest rates numerous times just before and soon after Bush took office in 1989. Indeed, the federal funds rate rose from about 6.5 percent in early 1988 to 9.75 percent in March 1989, the highest level since the early 1980s. The rate increases would seal Bush's political fate.

With the usual 12- to 18-month lag, the Fed's interest rate increases eventually slowed the economy. In July 1990 the economy entered into a recession, precipitated partly by Iraq's invasion of Kuwait and the sharp rise in oil prices that resulted from the increased tensions in the Middle East. The interest rate increases dealt a sharp blow to the housing market, where new housing starts fell to an annual level of about 800,000 (recent levels have been closer to 1.5 million). The reduced demand for new homes sparked a decline in home prices, and many individuals were saddled with mortgage debt that exceeded the values of their homes. This prompted a wave of foreclosures and bankruptcies, leading to the savings and loan crisis of the early 1990s. The bank failures were so extensive that the government established an institution, the Resolution Trust Company, to manage the orderly liquidation of failed banks.

The gloomy economy overshadowed Bush's many accomplishments in foreign policy, particularly his handling of the Gulf War and the important role he played in ending the Cold War. After the Gulf War ended, few people would have suspected that Bush might lose his reelection bid, especially in light of his 90 percent approval rating. But the ending of the war turned the public's attention back home, and the public did not like what it saw: The economy remained in recession, and unemployment was still rising.

There was very little Bush could do. The budget agreement he had signed in 1990 did not give him much leeway to stimulate the economy. Bush had agreed to a tax increase that broke his campaign pledge against new taxes (Bush famously had said, "Read my lips: No new taxes"). Just as important was the framework of the budget agreement. It would permit new tax or spending initiatives only on a pay-as-you-go basis. In other words, if Bush wanted to cut taxes, he would have to cut spending to pay for the reduced revenue. The net benefit to the economy thus would be limited. Even without the budget agreement, it might have been politically infeasible to try to stimulate the economy through fiscal initiatives. The budget deficit was already high—approaching $300 billion per year—and so there was basically no money in the till. There would be only one way to stimulate the economy: lower interest rates.

The Federal Reserve also recognized that lower interest rates were needed to stimulate the economy and cut interest rates many times during Bush's presidency. Yet Bush and members of his administration repeatedly voiced their discontent with the pace of the Fed's rate cuts. The administration recognized that owing to the long lag between interest rate cuts and their impact on the economy, the economy might not recover in time to help Bush in the 1992 election campaign. Bush wanted the Fed to move faster, as he stated during the 1992 presidential debates: "Alan Greenspan is respected. [But] I've had some arguments with him about the speed in which we have lowered interest rates."

Bush may have had a point. Despite the recession and the slow economic growth that followed, the Fed lowered rates in baby steps, mostly a quarter of a percentage point at a time. The slow pace of rate cuts was one of the reasons Greenspan became famous for his gradualist approach toward changing interest rates, at least until 2001. Indeed, Greenspan lowered interest rates 23 times during Bush's presidency, and 20 of those cuts were just a quarter of a percentage point.

Baby steps, indeed. In fact, during the 1990 to 1991 recession, Greenspan had lowered interest rates just seven times, a total of only 200 basis points, by the time the recession was over. More was clearly needed, but it would take time for the Fed to recognize that, and it would be too little, too late for Bush. The Fed probed for three and a half years before settling on an interest rate level it felt would help revive the ailing economy. The Fed eventually lowered the federal funds rate to 3 percent. Unfortunately for Bush, that equilibrium level would not be reached until he had left office.

By taking so long to find the equilibrium interest rate level that would revive the economy, the Fed essentially validated the claim that it had moved too slowly. Greenspan must have learned from that experience, judging by the rapid pace of interest rate cuts that he and the Fed implemented in 2001, when the Fed lowered interest rates an unprecedented 11 times in a series of cuts, most of them a half percentage point.

If the Fed had responded as quickly and aggressively as it did in 2001 to the economic slowdown that began in 1990, there is a good chance that the economy might have recovered in time for Bush to be reelected in 1992, but the Fed did not lower interest rates fast enough to pull the economy out the recession that followed its interest rate increases years earlier. Interest rates clearly played a major role in Bush's political destiny.

Clinton Harnessed the Power of the Bond Market as No President before Him

Bill Clinton masterfully used the powerful influence of interest rates as the centerpiece of his economic strategy. Clinton believed that if he adopted a fiscal strategy of reducing the budget deficit and encouraging investment, interest rates would fall and increase economic growth. Clinton's strategy, which was crafted with the help of Robert Rubin, who was Clinton's chair of the Council of Economic Advisors before becoming U.S. Treasury secretary, was a smashing success. During Clinton's administration, deficits turned into surpluses, business investment soared, and interest rates fell in dramatic fashion. His policies helped create a virtuous cycle of economic growth, producing the longest peacetime expansion ever. It would be Clinton's crowning achievement. The remarkable set of economic conditions that prevailed during his presidency helped Clinton weather a number of personal and legal challenges. For Clinton, the dramatic role interest rates played in strengthening the economy helped save his presidency.

Before he entered office, Clinton once said that he would focus on the economy like a laser beam. He clearly had a strategy to help the economy early on. Hints of his strategy were revealed during the presidential debates with President George Bush just weeks before the 1992 election. Note Clinton's apparent awareness of his central bank–like ability to control long-term interest rates:

> We have low interest rates today. At least we have low interest rates that the Fed can control. Our long-term interest rates are still pretty high because of our deficit and because of our economic performance. And there was a terrible reaction internationally to Mr. Bush saying he was going to give us 4 more years of trickle-down economics—another across-the-board tax cut and most of it going to the wealthy, with no real guarantee of investment. But I think the important thing—the important thing—is to use the powers the president does have on the assumption that, given the condition of this economy, we're going to keep interest rates down if we have the discipline to increase investment and reduce the debt at the same time.
>
> That is my commitment. . . . Give me a chance to do that. I don't have to worry in the near term about the Federal Reserve. Their policies so far, it seems to me, are pretty sound.

Clinton was a master of issues and seemed to know them inside and out. His awareness of his ability to affect long-term interest rates is evidence of this.

Clinton's fiscal plan eventually turned deficits into surpluses, spurring a decline in long-term interest rates and freeing up money for investment in the private sector. The result was a sharp increase in capital spending—the so-called good growth that tends to foster increases in productivity and, hence, cuts inflation and increases the national standard of living. Of course, the low-tax, low-regulation policies implemented during the Reagan-Bush years had helped foster an environment conducive to achieving the solid economic growth experienced in the 1990s, but Clinton advanced the cause through his fiscal policies.

In Clinton's nomination speech at the 1996 Democratic convention, he contrasted his record against Republican plans to cut taxes by highlighting the impact interest rates were having on the economy:

> This plan will explode the deficit, which will increase interest rates by 2 percent, according to their own estimates last year. It will require huge cuts in the very investments we need to grow, and to grow together, and at the same time slow down the economy. You know what higher interest rates mean. To you, it

means a higher mortgage payment, a higher car payment, a higher credit card payment. To our economy, it means businesspeople will not borrow as much money, invest as much money, create as many jobs, create as much wealth, raise as many wages.

Time and time again Clinton reminded the American public that his economic plan was working. Clinton illustrated his successes by highlighting the ways in which low interest rates were helping the economy. Clinton often would note the sharp increase in homeownership and business investment, for example, although his successor would have to deal with the fallout from excesses that would build in the housing market in part because of low interest rates.

It is notable that Clinton, a Democrat, achieved economic successes without having to resort to an increase in government spending. Clinton defied the traditional views of his party by adopting an economic plan that depended more on the markets than on the government. Few people would have imagined this before he entered office, particularly people in the bond market. In fact, just before Clinton's election, when there was a sense that he would win, the bond market fell and interest rates jumped. President Bush made note of this: "There was a momentary fear that he might win and the markets went phwee, down like that."

However, despite its initial fears, the bond market eventually recognized that it was at the center of Clinton's strategy. For his plan to work, interest rates had to fall, and the best way for Clinton to accomplish this would be to reduce the budget deficit. As it became clear to bond investors that Clinton was more interested in reducing the deficit than in raising spending, interest rates fell and the economy soared.

The vibrant economy of the Clinton years benefited Clinton immensely, overshadowing his impeachment. In fact, if the economy had been weak at the time of his impeachment, it is conceivable that the political atmosphere might have been venomous enough to result in his removal from office. For Clinton, the economy played a crucial role in maintaining his popularity, which barely wavered through thick and thin. At the center of it all was the bond market. Like a chair of the Federal Reserve, Clinton used his powers to control the interest rates that he could control in order to work wonders for the economy and for himself.

For George W. Bush, Low Interest Rates Were a Double-Edged Sword

To Clinton's successor, interest rates were a double-edged sword. The Federal Reserve's aggressive interest rate cuts in 2001 to 2003 brought the federal funds rate down to 1 percent, its lowest since 1958. The decline contributed to a rebound in economic activity, helping Bush to achieve relatively high marks for his handling of the economy, which for a time helped him to overcome difficulties he faced because of the Iraq War.

The economy was healthy enough to propel Bush to a second term in 2004, but it was largely downhill from there, with Bush eventually having to contend with the severe economic conditions wrought in no small part by the flipside of low interest rates: speculation in the housing market. Debate will rage for many years if not decades over the causes of the Great Recession of 2008 to 2009, but the focus will almost certainly remain on the role that interest rates played in the crisis.

For Obama, Perhaps There Will Be a Paradigm Shift

Low interest rates most times have been tonic for the economy, benefiting the U.S. president. For George W. Bush, the benefit of low interest rates to the economy and to his presidency eroded when low interest rates had un-intended consequences. This was an unusual outcome from a historical per-spective, and it could mark the beginning of a paradigm shift in the way that interest rates affect the political landscape. Today, increased emphasis is likely to be put on the control of excesses, and on tackling the very large structural problems that the United States faces, in particular its very large budget deficit and its current account deficit. This means that the public is likely to deemphasize to some extent short-term cyclical fixes to the economy, which includes accommodative monetary policy. That said, no meaning-ful deemphasis is likely to occur with respect to the employment situation, which means that the popularity of future presidents is likely to continue to be significantly affected by employment conditions. In other words, interest rates will continue to play a role in shaping the political landscape.

The degree to which historically low interest rates impact President Obama's political destiny depends on the extent to which the American public shifts its emphasis toward structural issues. If the public moves away from the consumption-oriented culture of the past few decades, then Obama won't need the sort of economic vibrancy that for past presidents was a nec-essary ingredient for political vibrancy. Still, the public almost certainly will remain focused on employment conditions, which can be impacted to a great extent by the level of interest rates.

The problem for Obama is that much of what ails the U.S. economy is structural, not cyclical. Many industries are impaired and will be for years, and this will prevent any meaningful rebound in economic activity. For ex-ample, U.S. car sales for many years averaged around 16 million units, a level that for many reasons—not the least of which are consumers' de-leveraging and their difficulties in obtaining credit—won't be seen for many years. The problem is that the automobile industry is structurally geared toward a sales rate of about 16 million. This means it is structurally impaired and must shrink. Similar examples can be given about the housing, finance, retail, and commercial real estate sectors. Structural impairments such as these will limit any economic rebound and could hurt Obama and the Democratic Party, simply by association with the economy's woes and because the ruling party is seen as responsible for healing what ails the economy. A problem for Obama is that low interest rates may fail to produce their intended results—a revival of credit growth and economic activity. Low rates may not work this time around because interest rates are a tool geared toward cyclical problems, not structural ones.

Summary

- Throughout history there have been many occasions when interest rates have played an unmistakable role in shaping the political landscape of the United States.
- In the more distant past, when interest rates were not yet ready for use as a policy tool or when their power was not yet fully understood, one can see how interest rates might have had a substantial influence on the economy and, hence, politics.
- In the more recent past, interest rates have played an increasingly visible role in political campaigns and have become an issue in their own right.
- It is unconventional to think about the impact of interest rates on politics, but the evidence clearly suggests that the bond market has played a major role in shaping the political landscape and will continue to do so. The degree of influence in the current situation could diminish because interest rates are a tool geared toward cyclical issues, whereas the United States faces many structural challenges.
- In general, this chapter should remind you of the powerful role interest rates play in people's lives.

15

UTILIZING ECONOMIC DATA TO IMPROVE YOUR INVESTMENT PERFORMANCE

In light of the important role economic data play in the behavior of the bond market, it is crucial for investors to understand the major economic reports that shape the bond market's daily movements. This chapter and the Appendix that follows will help give you that understanding. It is not overly difficult for investors to gain a material understanding of the major economic reports. In fact, you would be surprised at how little many Wall Street professionals know about the various economic reports. With a little work you can bring your knowledge level up to or above the standard that many on Wall Street have taken years to reach.

One of the things that make it easy to gain an understanding of the major economic reports is the frequency of their release: most of these reports are released monthly, and some are released quarterly. That frequency gives you an opportunity to learn more about them. Each month you can take a closer look at how a report is presented and observe its impact on the market. You also can begin to spot patterns in the way the data behave and learn to draw connections between one economic report and the next. Before you know it, it will all come together and you will see clearly how the reports are all intertwined. By simply paying close attention to the monthly economic reports, almost anyone can gain a high level of understanding of how the economy works.

In many ways expert knowledge of economic reports is superior to the benefits of understanding the theoretical work done in college economics classes. In my eyes, there is no substitute for knowledge that can be applied directly to benefiting one's personal life, and I strongly believe that knowledge about economic reports fits this mold. One needn't be an academician to understand the broad macro trends that move markets and are apparent in economic data.

The repetitive nature of economic reports is apparent from a quick glance at the monthly economic calendars. In fact, if you looked closely at economic calendars from one month to the next, you would see that they look almost exactly alike, with most of the economic reports being released at about the same time each month. Figure 15.1 shows a typical

FIGURE 15.1 A Typical Calendar for the Release of Economic Reports

Monday	Tuesday	Wednesday	Thursday	Friday
		1 ISM Index Construction Spending Automobile Sales	2 Jobless Claims Factory Orders	3 Employment Situation ISM Non-manufacturing Index
6	7 Consumer Credit	8	9 Jobless Claims	10
13	14 Producer Price Index Retail Sales	15 Business Inventories Industrial Production	16 Jobless Claims Consumer Price Index Housing Starts Philedelphia Survey	17 International Trade Consumer Sentiment
20 Leading Economic Index (LEI)	21	22	23 Jobless Claims	24 Durable Goods New Home Sales
27 Existing Home Sales	28 Consumer Confidence	29	30 Jobless Claims Chicago Index Personal Income	

economic calendar. One of the more important things to note is the large role manufacturing-related data play in the makeup of the calendar. Manufacturing-related reports include durable goods orders, factory orders, the Chicago Purchasing Managers index, the Philadelphia Fed's Business Outlook Survey, the Institute of Supply Management (ISM) report, industrial production, and capacity utilization.

The heavy concentration of manufacturing-related reports is remarkable because the U.S. economy is largely a service-oriented economy. In fact, the manufacturing sector has been in a secular decline for about 30 years and now accounts for only 9 percent of total U.S. employment compared to about 20 percent in 1980. The service-producing sector is now far greater, accounting for about 86 percent of U.S. employment.

Despite the manufacturing sector's decline and the service sector's rise, the economic calendar is almost completely devoid of economic reports that relate to the service sector. There are a couple of reasons for this. For one thing, the government agencies responsible for tracking the economy have been very slow to respond to the secular decline of the manufacturing sector. Indeed, the economic calendar has hardly changed despite the changed nature of the economy. In fact, the only relatively new service-related economic report is the nonmanufacturing report released monthly by the Institute for Supply Management (ISM), a private organization.

A second reason is the fact that activity in the service sector is much more difficult to measure. It is easy to measure the monthly output of automobiles, but it is another matter to measure the plethora of services performed in the nation each day. It would be difficult, for example, to track the activity of landscapers, cleaning services, repairpersons, lawyers, hair salons, nail salons, and so on. As a result, the government focuses largely on tracking activity in the manufacturing sector.

Most of the time this presents few problems for investors because manufacturing data act as a microcosm of activity in the general economy. After all, if people are buying more cars, they probably are purchasing services more often too. However, there have been plenty of occasions over the years when the manufacturing sector has sent misleading signals on the state of the overall economy. Thus, it would be a good idea for the government to put more focus on measuring activity in the service sector. Budget issues have been an impediment in this regard.

Although the manufacturing sector is a smaller part of the economy than the service sector is, the bond market tends to be swayed more by developments in the manufacturing sector. This is the case largely because of the unusually heavy presence of manufacturing-related reports in the monthly economic calendar. It is therefore important for bond investors to stay abreast of developments in the manufacturing sector most of all. A sustained jump in car production, for example, tends to have a big impact on a wide variety of economic data. As developments in the automobile sector work their way into the monthly economic reports, the bond market will react accordingly. Therefore, it is important to think of the many ways in which developments in the economy may find their way into the monthly reports and spark movement in the bond market.

Forecasting Economic Data: Numbers Do Not Lie

Forecasting trends in the economy is challenging, but the task is made easier when you let both your instincts and the facts guide your forecasts. I believe that many economic forecasters approach forecasting far too conservatively and rarely think outside the box. They tend to avoid making forecasts outside the cluster of forecasts around the mean, or consensus. As a result, they often miss the best calls and are more susceptible to being blindsided by surprises when the economic data are released.

I suppose analysts feel more comfortable making conservative calls. After all, when their forecasts go awry, analysts are likely to be less open to criticism if their peers are also wrong. The investment strategies built around an analyst's forecasts are likely to be conservative too, reducing volatility in investment portfolios. Analysts therefore are shielded against receiving partial blame for any trading and investment losses as well as any bad customer relations that might result from the forecasts.

In some ways the conservatism of most economic forecasters is similar to the reticence shown by equity analysts before the financial bubble burst in 2000. Equity analysts stood by rosy forecasts on stocks that had few realistic growth prospects, and they were extremely reluctant to issue sell recommendations when the environment clearly called for it. In fact, less than 1 percent of analysts' stock recommendations are sells. While there is no doubt that analysts, like many others, were caught in a mania, there was little basis for clustering their forecasts together. Only a few broke away from the pack, delivering more honest and realistic forecasts about the future. The same conservative mindset is what might have kept forecasters from sending cautionary flags regarding the housing market in the mid-2000s, as well as warnings they could have sent about financial institutions but did not even as they were falling in 2008.

I have been known to be willing to make forecasts that are far removed from the consensus. I don't do this only for the sake of being contrary. I let my forecasts be dictated by numbers; numbers do not lie. In doing so, I have been able to deliver many accurate forecasts that few others considered making.

When making an economic forecast, think of yourself as a detective. You are on a mission to collect as many relevant facts as you can. I remember in my early working days taking drives to the local shopping mall just to look at the number of cars in the parking lot to get clues on the pace of consumer spending. Of course, it is best to get as much information on national trends as possible, and there are plenty of data to keep you from having to drive to the shopping mall, but I want to underscore the point that you can never have too much information when you are putting a forecast together. The task has become simpler now that the information age has ushered in new means of obtaining various data. The Internet is particularly helpful, and I recommend utilizing Web sites created by trade associations to obtain information about the various sectors of the economy.

Again, the key is to approach forecasting like a good detective and pull in as many facts as you can before drawing your conclusions. Once you have the facts, it is very important to let them guide your forecasts and avoid being swayed by contradictory information. You must remain open-minded, of course, but there are many situations in which your forecast may seem at odds with some of the more superficial and less important facts that may be guiding the decisions of other forecasters.

I recall that in the middle of 2001, when most of the key indicators I use on the housing sector were pointing down, my forecast for imminent weakening was both counterintuitive and unproven. Mortgage rates had fallen sharply, leading many forecasters to say that the housing market, which had been strong despite the weakening in the economy, would remain strong. But the numbers simply did not point in that direction. Lumber prices were near a nine-year low, mortgage applications for home purchases were slipping, and home builders were saying that their business was softening, as evidenced by a sharp decline in the monthly housing market index released by the National Association of Home Builders.

Those facts, along with a decline in consumer confidence and income growth—the two main pillars of the housing market—suggested that the housing market would slow. It did. New home sales slid 15 percent from their peak by the end of 2001. There was simply no information to suggest any other outcome was likely, and it was only a matter of time before it happened. (The subsequent surge in the housing market years later was equally visible, but that was a new trade, so to speak.) This is a good illustration of why it is important to stand by your numbers, especially if they make a compelling case.

Being Flexible: Investors Change Their Focus Often

The bond market's focus on economic data is almost always intense, but the specific economic reports that get the most attention often vary with the shifts in the dominant influences on the economy. Occasionally, data that rarely are given more than a passing glance suddenly become a large force in shaping the bond market's direction. At other times big market movers such as the employment report carry little weight in shaping its direction. It is therefore important to be open-minded and flexible when weighing the potential impact of a set of economic reports.

Just before a recession, for example, bond investors tend to put a great deal of weight on the employment report because weakness in that report is a necessary prelude to a recession. In fact, it is a key criterion in the designation of the timing of the start of a recession. As a result, the market response to weak employment data released during the period leading up to a recession tends to be quite sharp. And since market prices move in advance of the release of the report as well as afterward, the cumulative response can be large.

Importantly, however, there comes a point when bond investors start to look beyond the weakness and begin to anticipate an eventual recovery. Markets, after all, anticipate and discount events before they occur. Investors therefore begin after a time to treat the employment report as a lagging indicator. They recognize that even if the underlying demand for goods and services has begun to improve, employers will not quickly rehire workers until the pickup in demand is sustained. In this way, employment conditions can be a lagging indicator, or an indicator that lags actual turning points in the economy.

A good example of this is how the markets behaved in 2009. At the start of the year, employment losses were substantial, logging in at over 700,000 people in a single month. Nevertheless, even in the face of these losses, riskier assets rallied. The market sensed that final demand was stabilizing and that stabilization in the labor markets would follow, as it eventually did relative to the horrendous figures seen in the beginning of 2009. Markets treat employment data similarly when the economy begins to show signs of weakening after several years of expansion. Investors recognize that employers generally do not let go of workers just because the employers had a bad month or two. Employers wait to be sure that the trend will be sustained before considering layoffs. Hence, investors focus on the leading signs of economic weakness, not the laggard jobs data.

There are many different situations in which the market's focus will change, and the changes can occur frequently. It is therefore important to look several steps ahead at the chain of events that will affect the economy in future months. It is not enough to look at the economy's current problems. The way Wall Street works, that is like looking in the past. Instead, you must first identify the economy's key problems or key underpinnings and try to envision the chain of events that could alter its direction.

The best way to accomplish this is to recognize that behind each economic event is a series of other events. Once you recognize the large degree of connectivity that exists in the economy, forecasting will be easier. Simply envision the series of events that you expect to occur and simultaneously envision the market response to both the individual events and the series of events. It is especially important to relate developments in the economy to the markets; you cannot put being right in the bank. You cannot trade the consumer price index or the employment report. You must apply your sense of the data to the markets in order to profit from accurate economic forecasts.

Investing from the Top Down

Top-down investing is the investing concept of discovering valuable investment implications in big-picture, macro indicators. It is thematic investing, where an investor buys an idea first and then finds the stocks, bonds, currencies, and other assets that fit the idea.

Top-down investing is an investment approach that has a multitude of advantages over other styles of investing, including its formidable counterpart, *bottom-up investing*, which relies mostly upon value investing, an investment approach that begins with scrutiny of the asset being bought. For example, in the case of corporate bonds, a bottom-up investor would start with the idea that data from the company's financial reports justify the purchase on the basis of an analysis of its balance sheet, cash flow projections, and so forth. The problem with this method is that investors don't always have the expertise to take on such a task, and in many cases they simply do not have the time. For many people, top-down investing is a better place to start, by looking for almost-obvious big-picture themes likely to have lasting influence on the economy and the financial markets.

The 2008 to 2009 financial crisis was a clarion call to embrace top-down investing. When the crisis reared its head in 2007, there emerged a variety of signals that top-down investors caught. Of course, very few could anticipate the magnitude of problems that occurred, but there were many top-down indicators that spoke to the direction of the problem and that investors could utilize to limit damage to their portfolios. One example was the collapse of the commercial paper market beginning in August 2007 (Figure 15.2). Aside from the economic implications of the collapse, which

FIGURE 15.2 U.S. Commercial Paper Outstanding, in Billions of Dollars

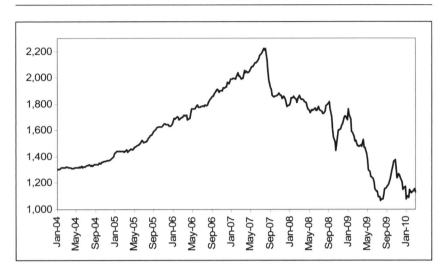

Source: Federal Reserve.

in and of itself had investment implications, the commercial paper market's collapse spoke to the idea that risk attitudes had changed, giving a warning sign for investors to de-risk their portfolios by scaling back their exposures to risk assets.

Economic data are a very important part of top-down investing. The indicators shown in the Appendix are therefore very important to developing profitable top-down views on both the economy and the financial markets.

Learning the Survey Methodologies to Enhance Your Forecasting Abilities

Once you have a good sense of how the economy works and feel comfortable making economic forecasts, you can enhance your forecasting ability by having a better understanding of the methodology used by government agencies and private organizations to produce the major economic reports. By doing this, you will gain an edge on market participants who have scant knowledge about how the monthly reports are put together. The methodology used to produce the major economic reports is described in the Appendix.

A key point is that actual economic data can differ greatly from reported data. Statisticians see to it that the raw data that are captured in monthly surveys and the like are altered in a variety of ways to create consistencies in the data and to smooth seasonal fluctuations. Consider the sale of Christmas trees. Sales increase substantially around the holiday season before nose-diving in January. The statisticians recognize this and therefore attempt to *smooth*, or seasonally adjust, the fluctuations. They do this by adjusting the sales level for the holiday season downward by an amount close to the average percentage increase experienced in past years and by adjusting the sales level in January upward by an amount close to the average decrease seen in past years.

Doing this removes the *noise*, or volatility, from the data so that the data are easy to interpret. After all, if you heard that the sale of Christmas trees jumped 400 percent in December compared to November, you might get a tad confused. The point is that the reported data go through a series of changes before they are delivered in the economic reports. By recognizing the various ways in which the data are altered, you are more likely to spot situations in which those adjustments may have a meaningful impact on the reported data and therefore affect the markets.

It also is important to learn how the data are collected. By doing this you are more likely to spot situations in which the collection methodology could result in unexpected fluctuations in the reported data. Many economic reports, for example, are derived from samples and surveys with specific cutoff dates. This means that when a report is for, say, January, it is not necessarily for the full month of January but for some portion of January. Knowing the cutoff date therefore can help you know whether certain factors influenced the data. In January, for example, a snowstorm that occurs on the twenty-fifth of the month will have an effect on some economic reports for the month of January but not on others. In some cases the effects of the storm will not be captured until the February reports.

If you are familiar with the survey methodology in advance, you are less likely to be fooled by the economic reports and can be opportunistic and use your extra insights to your advantage in trading and investing. We will look at the survey methodologies for each of the major economic reports throughout the Appendix.

Summary

- There is little doubt that economic data are at the root of most of the volatility in the bond market. Recognition of this fact is the first step in using this simple notion to your advantage.
- The next step is to take advantage of the repetitiveness of the monthly data releases to learn them inside and out. If you look closely at the

reports month after month, your understanding of how the economy works will steadily increase, enabling you to forecast the future direction of the economy and the market more accurately.

- Utilize your understanding of the economy to envision the series of events that follows most economic events and weigh the potential market response to each individual event. Remember, however, that it is important to be open-minded. Investors change their focus frequently. What is important to investors today could mean much less to them tomorrow, and vice versa.

- When you have a good handle on how the economy works and feel comfortable making forecasts, enhance your abilities by learning more about how the monthly reports are put together. This will give you a big edge over most market participants.

- Do all these things while remembering that in the economy everything is connected in one way or another. In the economy, for every action, there is a reaction. As an investor, your ability to anticipate these series of reactions will separate you from the pack.

Appendix

HANDBOOK OF ECONOMIC DATA
Power Tools for Investors

The following data are listed alphabetically.

BUSINESS INVENTORIES

Source: U.S. Census Bureau
Web address for report: www.census.gov/mtis/www/mtis_current.html
Release date: Generally around the middle of every month
Time: 10:00 a.m. ET
Report coverage: Inventory levels in retail trade, wholesale trade, and manufacturing for the calendar month two months prior to the report's release
Description of report: The business inventories report provides information about the extent to which businesses are accumulating or reducing their inventories, and whether inventory levels are too high or too low relative to demand. The more out of sync that inventories are with demand, the more likely it is that manufacturers will alter their production schedules to fit

---

Dan Greenhaus contributed to the Appendix. Dan is chief economic strategist at Miller Tabak + Co. and previously worked for Credit Suisse First Boston in its high-yield research department. He also contributed to the book *Investing from the Top Down*, published in 2008. Dan is a frequent guest on CNBC and Bloomberg television and is frequently quoted by the media. He obtained his MBA from Baruch College in 2006 and is currently working on completing the Chartered Financial Analyst examination program.

demand, thereby playing a major role in the virtuous cycle of self-reinforcing increases in production, income, and spending that define economic expansions. Business inventories in the United States totaled approximately $1 trillion toward the end of 2009, and so even small percentage changes in the monthly data can have a large impact on the U.S. economy.

Survey methodology: Aggregate inventory data are derived from three separate monthly surveys: retail trade, wholesale trade, and the survey of manufacturers' shipments, inventories, and orders. For the retail trade survey, which captures about a third of all business inventories, a mail-out/mail-back survey is sent to a few thousand retail businesses that meet minimum size requirements. Those businesses are asked to give information about their month-end inventory levels. The weighting of each response to the survey is dependent on the size of the companies that respond to the survey relative to the size of their respective industries. Inventories on wholesale trade, which account for about 30 percent of all business inventories, are calculated in a similar way, also using a sample of a few thousand wholesale businesses. The same goes for factory inventories, which account for about 38 percent of all business inventories, but there are some important differences: factory inventories are calculated by using data from three different stages of production: finished goods, work in process, and raw materials and supplies.

Key components of the report: The three separate surveys mentioned above are the most important aspects of the report, along with the monthly inventory-to-sales (I/S) ratio. This I/S ratio provides a way to gauge the extent to which businesses may consider their inventory levels too high or too low. In late 2008, data on business inventories took on added importance as companies reduced stockpiles at a record pace. In 2009, inventory data indicated businesses had cut their production levels too low relative to demand, leading businesses to raise output. In 2010, phase 2 of the inventory cycle began, with businesses shifting from a slower pace of liquidation to outright accumulation in anticipation of rising demand—a hopeful sign for any nascent expansion. All the while, data on inventory changes relative to demand—summed up in the I/S ratio, provided investors with important clues as to the likely direction of industrial output and hence, a plethora of economic data that would have a major bearing on the performance of the financial markets.

How it affects the market: Reactions to the release of the business inventories report tend to be muted for a few reasons. First, the report is derived from three separate surveys, two of which are known by the market in advance of the release. Second, while the investment implications of the inventory cycle play a major role in the performance of the financial markets, the individual reports on inventories themselves are not big market movers. Instead, investors respond to data affected by the inventory cycle. Third, inventory data are released well after the survey period, which makes them less timely than other data. Inventory data tend to take on added importance when investors are formulating their views about upcoming data on the gross domestic product (GDP). This is even truer today when data on inventory replenishment will tell forecasters something about the pace of recovery expected by consumers.

What it means to you: From an investment standpoint, inventory data can help you recognize potential turning points in the economy, leaving you better able to shape your investment portfolio. In particular, use the data to form a view about industrial output and the broad swath of factory data that dominate the U.S. economic calendar, all of which have a major bearing on the financial markets. From a consumption standpoint, the inventory data can help you be a smarter buyer. If, for example, retail inventories rise, you could take that as a signal that lower retail prices on everything from cars to clothes may be on the horizon. If, however, inventories fall, this could be taken as a signal that companies are in the driver's seat with respect to prices.

CHICAGO PURCHASING MANAGERS INDEX

Source: National Association of Purchasing Management, Chicago
Web address for report: www.ism-chicago.org/index.cfm
Release date: Typically the final business day of each month
Time: 9:45 a.m. ET; minutes earlier to subscribers
Report coverage: Manufacturing activity in the Chicago region in the month before the release of the survey results
Description of report: The Chicago Purchasing Managers index is a top gauge of the health of the nation's manufacturing sector. This is because the Chicago region contains some of the heaviest concentrations of manufacturers in the country. In addition, because it is released just one or two business days before the national data on manufacturing conditions are released by the Institute of Supply Management (ISM), the Chicago index provides an advance lead on the ISM index, a major market mover. As with the ISM report, the Chicago Purchasing Managers report contains data that relate to important aspects of the manufacturing sector, including new orders, production, order backlogs, employment, delivery time, inventories, and prices.
Survey methodology: Each month the Institute for Supply Management, Chicago, surveys a few hundred purchasing and supply executives, using the

same methodology used to calculate the ISM index. Survey participants are asked whether they experienced an increase or a decrease in important aspects of their business, including new orders, production, employment, delivery time, inventories, and order backlogs. The responses to these questions are compiled into a *diffusion index*, which is basically a number that reflects the percentage of firms that reported an increase in the respective components, minus those that saw a decrease. The diffusion indexes then are adjusted for seasonality and to equate a reading of zero to 100, with 50 representing the dividing line between growth and contraction.

Key components of the report: As with the ISM index, the key component in the Chicago index is new orders, a leading indicator. When new orders rise, many forces are set in motion that lead to increases in the other key components of the survey, such as production and employment. Additionally, the employment component is closely followed.

How it affects the market: The timely release of the Chicago index provides an advance warning on the ISM index. Although it is usually just one or two days, that is enough to enable investors to adjust their positions and boost the total return on their portfolios. As a result, market reaction to the Chicago index is often quite sharp. Moreover, although the Chicago index is a regional survey, because of the heavy concentration of manufacturing industries in the Chicago region, this index is a credible microcosm of national conditions. The Chicago index averaged a spread of about 2 points over the ISM index during the last decade, and during that period the Chicago index was above the ISM about 75 percent of the time. Thus, an investor can roughly estimate the ISM by taking the Chicago index and subtracting 2 points. When the economy is either very weak or in recession, one can expect the Chicago index to be below the ISM index, just as it was in 11 of the 13 months from October 2008 until October 2009, and in other periods of economic weakness.

What it means to you: Use the Chicago index to get an advance lead on the ISM index, and weigh the powerful implications of these indicators. That said, it is important to wait for the ISM data to more accurately gauge national trends and make major changes to one's portfolio. In business, the report can help you navigate a variety of economic climates.

CONSTRUCTION SPENDING

Source: U.S. Census Bureau
Web address for report: www.census.gov/const/c30_curr.html
Release date: Generally the first calendar day of every month

Time: 10:00 a.m. ET

Report coverage: Construction activity in the two calendar months prior to the report's release

Description of report: The construction spending report details construction activity in both the public and private sectors. Construction spending, also known as *construction put in place*, represents approximately 6 to 7 percent of the U.S. economy. Construction spending is especially sensitive to interest rate levels because of the high cost of construction endeavors. The construction spending report tallies construction in a number of areas, including new buildings and structures; additions; renovations; alterations; mechanical and electrical installations; site preparation and outside construction of fixed structures or facilities such as sidewalks, highways, and streets; and parking lots. Excluded from the report are maintenance and repairs to existing structures or service facilities; the drilling of gas and oil wells, including the construction of offshore drilling platforms; and the cost and installation of some production machinery and equipment items. The report is quite volatile and is subject to large revisions.

Survey methodology: The construction data are calculated by combining data from several sources and surveys. The three most important sources of data are the Census Bureau's surveys on new private residential construction, private nonresidential construction, and construction by state and local governments. The data on residential construction are estimated by surveying several hundred permit-issuing places in the country. The Census Bureau contacts those places by using a mail-out/mail-back survey. Where permits have been issued, the Census Bureau contacts the owners and builders to see if construction has been started. Once construction has begun, monthly progress reports are requested from the owner until a project is completed. The Census Bureau measures the "value of construction put in place," or the value of construction installed or erected at construction sites during a specific month. This can include the cost of materials, labor, and architectural or engineering work. Nonresidential data are collected in a similar manner. Some of the data are obtained from McGraw-Hill Construction Dodge for projects valued at $75,000 or more in the United States except Hawaii, where data are obtained from permit-issuing places in that state. About 8,500 projects are in the bureau's survey at any one time. The data on state and local governments are obtained largely from data produced by Dodge and are adjusted by benchmarking the tabulated estimates to annual construction expenditures data collected in the Census Bureau's Annual Survey of Government Finances. All the surveys are combined and adjusted for outliers and for construction projects not reported by Dodge as well as for seasonal fluctuations.

Key components of the report: The two main components are private construction, which accounts for about 65 percent of all construction activity, and public construction, which accounts for the remaining 35 percent. Residential construction activity represents about 45 percent of all private construction activity, and in recent years it has been the main focus of investors. The remaining portion consists of the construction of hotels, nonpublic schools, hospitals, office buildings, and religious buildings. Public construction activity consists largely of educational facilities, highways and streets, and transportation projects. These three areas represent about 63 percent of all public construction activity. Details such as the data on hotel and motel construction can shed light on trends in certain industries. Given the influence that both the housing and commercial real estate sectors have on the health of the overall economy, data on private construction activity are the most important, not just because private construction accounts for such a large percentage of all construction activity but also because it is much more sensitive than public construction to the ups and downs of the business cycle.

How it affects the market: Although construction spending has represented as much as 9 percent of the economy, there has generally been little market response to the construction spending report for several reasons. First and foremost is the timing of its release. The report is almost always released on the same day and time as the ISM report, which is considered one of the most important economic indicators. As a result, the construction report essentially becomes an afterthought. Second, the report's sharp month-to-month volatility limits the significance of any single month's data. In recent years, attention to this report has increased owing to the housing crisis. By the end of 2009, total construction spending had declined by approximately 25 percent from its peak, a $300 billion decline.

What it means to you: I suggest combining this report with the data on housing starts, new and existing home sales, and mortgage applications, as well as the National Association of Home Builders' monthly housing market index, to get the best picture of the construction industry. Also look at the monthly changes in construction jobs for additional clues. Once you have formed an opinion on the construction sector, you can incorporate it into your investment strategies. The construction sector tends to be quite interest rate sensitive, and so its strength or weakness can be used as a barometer of the impact of changing interest rates on the overall economy. For example, during the financial crisis a lack of improvement in construction activity signaled a lack of improvement in both the supply and demand for credit for construction-related activity. An implication of the housing collapse is the potential for subpar construction activity for quite some time owing to the lagging nature of the activity.

CONSUMER CONFIDENCE INDEX

Source: The Conference Board
Web address for report: www.conferenceboard.org/economics/consumer
Confidence.cfm
Release date: Usually the last Tuesday of every month
Time: 10:00 a.m. ET
Report coverage: Generally reflects consumer sentiments in the first half of the month in which the report is released
Description of report: The Conference Board's consumer confidence survey attempts to measure overall consumer confidence and consumer sentiment toward a variety of other issues, including business conditions and buying plans. The index historically has been correlated with consumer spending patterns as well as developments in the labor market. In fact, this survey tends to be more closely correlated with labor market conditions than are most other consumer confidence surveys because two of the survey's five questions relate directly to the labor market.
Survey methodology: At the end of every month, the Conference Board mails its survey to about 5,000 households, of which about 70 percent usually respond. The questionnaires are collected mostly during the first half of the month in which the final results are released. The Conference Board's consumer confidence index has two components: an index of consumers' assessment of the present situation, which is 40 percent of the overall confidence index, and an index of consumers' expectations, which is 60 percent of the overall index. Included in the questionnaire are five questions: two regarding current conditions and three regarding expectations. Consumers also are asked about their plans to buy a home, a new car, and major appliances. The data then are constructed into an index using a base year of 1985 (1985 = 100). A reading of 105 means that confidence is 105 percent of the level in 1985.
Key components of the report: There are a number of important components in the Conference Board's monthly survey, but their level of importance differs, depending on economic developments. My personal experience is that the most important component is the index of the present situation because it can be used in conjunction with other data such as jobless claims and other labor market indicators to derive a view on the job market. This makes sense because the wherewithal to spend matters more than how consumers feel about the future—you can't spend expectations. Confidence about the future, for example, can do little to spur spending by the unemployed. That is why it is important to beware of changes in consumer confidence that are rooted in changes in the expectations component

rather than changes in consumers' assessment of the present. The expectations component often is affected by consumers' emotions rather than by economic realities. With the structural weakness in the labor market, it is particularly important to look at the *labor differential*—that is, the difference between those believing jobs are plentiful and those believing they are hard to get. This measure has dipped into uncharted territory during the financial crisis.

How it affects the market: Investors are very interested in consumer confidence data because they understand that consumer spending accounts for about 70 percent of the U.S. economy. The markets generally take the consumer confidence index at face value and react accordingly; the details of the report usually do not alter the initial reaction to the report. The bond market typically falls when consumer confidence rises on concerns that that rise could portend a strengthening of economic activity. However, investors are far more interested in how consumers behave than in how consumers feel. Therefore, it is important to seek out data on consumer spending that validate any conclusions drawn from the confidence data.

What it means to you: As an investor, consumer confidence data will help shape your judgments about the condition of the labor market, a critical part of any investment strategy. For those in business, consumer confidence data can help in planning for inventory investment, capital spending, and business expansion.

CONSUMER CREDIT

Source: Federal Reserve
Web address for report: www.federalreserve.gov/releases/G19
Release date: Generally on or about the fifth business day of every month
Time: 3:00 p.m. ET
Report coverage: The level of consumer credit in the calendar month two months before the release of the report
Description of report: The consumer credit report provides important information about trends in the level of consumer indebtedness, which will be a critical area of focus in the aftermath of the financial crisis. Consumer credit consists of two main categories: revolving and nonrevolving credit. Revolving credit accounts for roughly 35 percent of all consumer credit and consists largely of credit cards, store charge accounts, and overdraft checking. Nonrevolving credit consists largely of automobile loans and other loans not included in revolving credit, such as loans for mobile homes, trailers, education loans, and vacations. Consumer credit does not include debts

secured by real estate. Consumer credit stood at about $2.48 billion at the end of 2009.

Survey methodology: Each month the Federal Reserve surveys commercial banks, consumer finance companies (including automobile finance companies), and credit unions. The data are tabulated and then adjusted for seasonal variations. In December of each year, for example, consumers sharply increase their use of credit to make holiday purchases. In January, however, consumers sharply curtail their use of credit and begin paying down some of their debts. The Fed smoothes the reporting of these fluctuations by adjusting the December data downward and the January data upward. The Fed's adjustments are derived from patterns observed over prior years.

Key components of the report: In the aftermath of the financial crisis, it will be critical to judge the extent to which the de-leveraging process progresses. Investors should therefore focus on revolving credit. The data will speak not only to consumer demand credit but also to the supply of credit and the health of the asset-backed securities market, which is where financing for credit card issuance is raised. The nonrevolving credit component can be used similarly, given the component's emphasis on consumer loans. The consumer credit report also contains interesting information on the terms of credit at commercial banks and finance companies. This includes the average interest rates charged on new car loans, personal loans, and credit card debt. The Fed also provides information on the average maturity and average dollar amounts financed at automobile finance companies.

How it affects the market: The market response to the consumer credit report tends to be muted because it is open to subjective interpretation. For example, the data speak more to the composition of consumer spending rather than the amount of spending, which is needed to determine the growth rate of consumer spending. Moreover, when consumer credit increases, it can be taken either as a sign that credit remains plentiful or as evidence that consumer finances are strained, requiring the use of credit. Weakness in consumer credit can be seen as either a sign that consumers are being denied credit or as a sign that personal income growth is sufficient to finance consumption. I generally view growth in consumer credit positively as long as the economy is expanding and the savings rate is in the mid-single digits. However, if, as occurred in the early 2000s, consumer credit is expanding when the savings rate is low (south of 5 percent), it signals excessive use of credit and an overleveraged consumer. This is unlikely to occur any time soon because, first, lenders are unlikely to extend credit in the same way they did before the financial crisis and, second, consumers are in a de-leveraging mindset that will likely last many years. Recent events have put increased attention on the consumer credit report. As credit standards have tightened and credit supply and demand has waned, outstanding consumer credit has declined. In December 2009, consumer credit was nearly 4 percent below its high, falling in 14 of 15 months.

What it means to you: The consumer credit report can help you assess progress in the consumers' de-leveraging process and in credit availability. You also can use the report to help with your personal finances. For example, you can utilize the information on the terms of credit at commercial banks and finance companies to assess whether the interest rate you pay on new car loans, personal loans, credit cards, and the like, is consistent with the national averages. This could help you comparison shop when obtaining credit.

CONSUMER PRICE INDEX

Source: U.S. Bureau of Labor Statistics
Web address for report: www.bls.gov/news.release/cpi.toc.htm
Release date: Generally around or slightly after the middle of every month, frequently on a Wednesday
Time: 8:30 a.m. ET
Report coverage: Consumer prices in the previous month (the survey period is the entire month)
Description of report: The consumer price index (CPI) is a measure of changes in the prices of thousands of goods and services, which are grouped into more than 200 categories arranged in eight major groups: food and beverages, housing, apparel, transportation, medical care, recreation, education and communication, and other goods and services. Bond investors are particularly interested in inflation data because inflation erodes the value of money. That is one reason why bond yields tend to be higher than the inflation rate—investors want compensation for the risk of faster inflation. Investors often use the CPI as a reference point on inflation trends when they formulate their investment strategies, although many use the deflator for personal consumption expenditures. The CPI also is used by the U.S. government in its yearly adjustments of payments to the roughly 50 million Social Security benefits recipients, and 4 million military and federal and civil service retirees and survivors, and 35 million food stamps recipients. It is no wonder that the CPI is one of the most closely watched gauges of inflation.
Survey methodology: Starting in the first week of every month, the Bureau of Labor Statistics (BLS) visits or calls 25,000 retail establishments, service establishments, supermarkets, and hospitals to record prices on about 80,000 goods and services in 87 urban areas. Data on rents are collected from about 50,000 landlords or tenants. The BLS compares the prices

recorded each month to the prices recorded in the previous month. In cases where the same item is no longer available, the BLS selects a new item. If the quality of an item changes (for example, if new features are added to an auto-mobile), the BLS records the quality change to measure the effect of the change on the price of that item. Prices are recorded throughout each calendar month. The BLS then takes all the recorded prices and weights them by their impor-tance; then it adjusts the data for fluctuations resulting from seasonality.

Key components of the report: The housing component is tops, account-ing for about 42 percent of the entire CPI. It captures changes in the cost of shelter, rent, and fuel and utilities. This component often is affected by sharp changes in energy prices and the health of the housing market. An-other important component is the index on medical costs. Medical costs not only affect people personally but also affect employment costs, which account for about 70 percent of the cost of producing goods. Given the price gains in oil, gold, copper, and other commodities in recent years, increased attention is being placed on the commodity and service groupings within the CPI report.

How it affects the market: Inflation is the bane of the bond market because it erodes the value of the future cash flows of bonds. The inflation rate is therefore critically important to the bond market—it is a virtual obsession and the common denominator of all that concerns bond investors. To many people the CPI is their top inflation gauge, although others prefer to use the personal consumption deflator, which is released monthly alongside data on personal income and consumption, as well as quarterly with the GDP report. Investors typically discount inflation trends before they occur, and so reactions to the monthly changes in the CPI are not always large. Thus, inflation expectations are first and foremost in the bond investor's mind. Nevertheless, the CPI is one of the bigger market movers.

What it means to you: The markets loathe high inflation rates and are far more stable when there is price stability. Investors worry that high rates of inflation not only will erode the value of their money but could also prompt the Fed to boost interest rates, thereby hurting job and income prospects. Inflation trends are therefore critical not only to the performance of your financial investments but also to your general economic well-being.

CONSUMER SENTIMENT INDEX PUBLISHED BY THE UNIVERSITY OF MICHIGAN

Source: University of Michigan
Web address for report: www.sca.isr.umich.edu

Release date: Preliminary results are generally released to subscribers on or about the second Friday of every month; final results are generally released on or about the last Friday of every month or the first Friday of the subsequent month.

Time: 10:00 a.m. ET, but released to subscribers 15 minutes earlier

Report coverage: Reflects consumer sentiments throughout the month in which the report is released

Description of report: The University of Michigan's (UOM) consumer sentiment survey, which dates back to the 1940s, attempts to measure consumer sentiments about a variety of issues. The index historically has been correlated with consumer spending patterns and developments in the labor market. However, the UOM's consumer sentiment survey is not as tightly correlated with labor market trends as is the Conference Board's consumer confidence survey. Aside from consumer confidence levels, the UOM's consumer sentiment survey captures consumers' sentiments about their personal finances, buying conditions, and inflation expectations. The Federal Reserve is known to track the inflation expectations data within the UOM survey.

Survey methodology: Each month the University of Michigan telephones 500 consumers to ask them about their sentiments toward their personal finances, business conditions, the buying climate, and the inflation outlook. The survey is conducted by using a rotating panel of participants: 60 percent of all participants are first-time participants, while the remaining 40 percent participated once before. The UOM telephones half the 500 consumers in the first half of each month and the remaining consumers in the second half of each month. This index has two components: an index of consumers' assessment of the present situation, which is 40 percent of the overall confidence index, and an index of consumers' expectations, which is 60 percent of the overall index. Included in the questionnaire are five questions: two regarding consumers' assessment of current conditions and three regarding their expectations for future conditions. Regarding the present situation, the UOM asks consumers whether they feel it is a good time to buy a major household item and whether they are better or worse off financially than they were a year earlier. Regarding the future, consumers are asked about how they expect their financial condition to be in a year and how they see business conditions in the country as a whole. The data are constructed into an index using a base year. Thus a reading of 105 means that confidence is 105 percent of the level in the base year.

Key components of the report: Not many details of the UOM survey are released to the public; the survey details are available only to subscribers, and the financial press rarely reveals all the survey results. Nevertheless, there are a few important components in the UOM survey. As with the Conference Board's consumer confidence survey, my experience is that the most important component is the index of the assessment of current conditions, which has higher correlation with the employment situation than the expectations component. This makes sense because the wherewithal to spend matters more than how consumers feel about the future. Confidence about the future, for example, can do little to spur spending by the unemployed.

How it affects the market: Investors are very interested in consumer confidence data because that information helps them assess the likely direction of consumer spending, which accounts for roughly 70 percent of the U.S. economy. The bond market reacts to the preliminary results of the UOM survey as much as or more than it does to the final results, and reactions to the data are sometimes sharp. Equity investors cheer strong consumer sentiment because the economic implications bode well for corporate profits. However, the markets are far more interested in how consumers behave than in how they feel. Therefore, it is important to let spending data be one's primary guide to consumer spending patterns.

What it means to you: As an investor, tracking consumer spending should be a top priority, as an accurate assessment of the consumer can go a long way toward helping you formulate profitable investment decisions. The preliminary results of the survey can help give you an early lead on future spending trends, particularly when they are suggestive of labor market trends.

DURABLE GOODS ORDERS

Source: U.S. Census Bureau
Web address for report: www.census.gov/manufacturing/m3
Release date: Usually the last week of the month
Time: 8:30 a.m. ET
Report coverage: Manufacturers' durable goods orders, shipments, and inventory changes for the previous month
Description of report: The durable goods report is considered an important leading economic indicator because it provides clues about future industrial production: orders lead. Durable goods orders also provide important clues as to the consumers' stomach for purchasing big-ticket items such as automobiles and home appliances. The report also provides important clues on the pace of business spending. Durable goods orders account for about half of all factory orders, and this report's release precedes the factory orders report, providing early clues to factory orders data. The durable goods report is regarded as one of the most volatile indicators.

Survey methodology: Each month the Census Bureau obtains data from a panel of several thousand reporting units, and the data provide an indication of activity in this sector of the economy. The companies surveyed have $500 million or more in annual shipments each. As with most government surveys, responses to the survey are voluntary. Because the companies that respond are generally large, diversified companies, many file separate reports for the different divisions within their companies. The Census Bureau derives its monthly data on durable goods orders not by tallying the respondents' orders data but by looking at the monthly change in shipments and unfilled orders and then estimating the level of new orders through the changes in shipments and unfilled orders. Consider, for example, a month in which shipments of a durable good were 100 units and unfilled orders were 90 units. If during the next month shipments increased to 110 units but unfilled orders remained at 90 units, this would imply an increase of 10 units in total durable goods orders (the increase in shipments should have reduced unfilled orders by 10 units; the fact that they held steady implies an increase in orders).

Key components of the report: The most important component in the durable goods report is the data on nondefense capital goods orders excluding aircraft, a key gauge of capital spending that correlates with the equipment and software component of the quarterly GDP report. Fluctuations in capital spending tend to coincide with changes in business confidence levels. Capital spending, which includes spending on plant and equipment, is critical to the nation's productivity. Another important component is the data on computers and electronics products. This component yields important clues to the pace of economic activity in the technology sector. The shipments data are important because they are used in the computation of the quarterly data on GDP—orders are not counted. Unfilled orders provide clues to the extent to which manufacturers may have to alter their production schedules to meet their orders.

How it affects the market: Because of the sharp month-to-month volatility in the durable goods data, the bond market's reaction to this report varies but can be sharp. Large month-to-month changes that appear to be related to one-time factors often are quickly dismissed, especially if they are due to the report's two most volatile components: transportation (particularly aircraft orders) and defense. The bond market's reaction to the report is greatest when the data are well beyond expectations and lack these one-time influences. The reaction is even greater when the strength or weakness of the report is amplified by the data on nondefense capital goods orders. However, when the report's strength appears to be due largely to strength in capital spending, the bond market, which loathes strong economic activity because of its implications for both inflation and monetary policy, may not react as negatively as it would if the sources of strength were other sectors of the economy because capital spending is perceived to be conducive to productivity growth, which tends to dampen inflation by keeping labor costs in check.

What it means to you: The durable goods report can help you forecast future trends in the economy. Persistent strength in durable goods orders should be taken as a sign that both consumers and businesses are confident. From this you can shape your investments in a way that reflects the likelihood of an economic expansion and increasing corporate profits. Economically sensitive stocks and bonds in industries such as consumer cyclicals, basic materials, technology, and financials will tend to do well during such times. By contrast, when durable goods orders are persistently weak, more defensive sectors such as pipelines, utilities, health care, and consumer products tend to outperform. As a consumer, watch the durable goods data to weigh the climate for the purchasing of big-ticket items. The data will help you know how much bargaining power you may have when making such purchases.

EMPLOYMENT

Source: U.S. Bureau of Labor Statistics
Web address for report: www.bls.gov/news.release/empsit.nr0.htm
Release date: Generally the first Friday of every month
Time: 8:30 a.m. ET
Report coverage: Employment conditions through the early part of the previous month
Description of report: The monthly employment report provides one of the best summaries of current economic conditions, and it is one of the most closely followed economic reports. The employment situation is considered one of the most important determinants of the economy's performance. Employment growth provides the steady flow of fuel needed to keep the economy moving along a sustained growth path by supplying the income growth needed to sustain consumer spending. The employment report provides important insights into both the health of the overall economy and key trends in the economy's major sectors. Trends in employment conditions historically have had a great impact on monetary policy and, hence, the bond market. This is no less true today considering that nearly 8 million jobs were lost during the recession.
Survey methodology: The employment report is produced monthly by using two major surveys: the Current Population Survey and the Current

Employment Statistics Survey, popularly known as the "household survey" and the "establishment survey," respectively. The household survey covers about 60,000 households, and it is used in the production of the monthly data on the unemployment rate, household employment, and the labor force. The establishment survey covers about 160,000 establishments covering just about 400,000 individual worksites, and it is used to produce the monthly data on payroll employment, hours worked, and workers' earnings. The reference period for the household survey is generally the calendar week that contains the twelfth day of the month, and the reference period for the establishment survey is the pay period that includes the twelfth, which may or may not correspond directly to the calendar week. The household survey is conducted by telephone or in person during the week after the reference period. People over age 16 are included in the survey and are selected in a way that the BLS considers representative of the entire population. Information on about 94,000 people is obtained each month. Households remain in the survey for four months, leave the survey for eight months, and return for four months before leaving it for good. People are considered employed if they did any work during the reference period. They are classified as unemployed if they had no employment during the reference period, were available to work, and made specific efforts to find employment during the four-week period ending with the reference week. The establishment survey includes entities that produce goods or services, and the data are collected by electronic means, mostly by touchtone phone, from about two-thirds of the survey participants. The submitted responses are returned to the respondents in mail form for use in the following month. This helps maintain consistency and increases the accuracy of the data. People are counted as employed if they received pay for any part of the reference week even if it was as little as one hour. People are counted in each job they hold. The data in both the household survey and the establishment survey are adjusted for seasonal fluctuations.

Key components of the report: There are many important components in the employment report, but the headline data grab most of the attention: the monthly change in nonfarm payrolls and the unemployment rate. Each of these components provides a quick snapshot of conditions in the labor market, and the jobless rate is perhaps the most frequently cited economic statistic. It is so widely understood that politicians frequently use it as a political tool; few economic statistics can match the political persuasiveness of the jobless rate. Another important area of the report is the breakdown of monthly payroll changes by industry, something that has gained prominence as activity in the construction and manufacturing sectors has turned down. The data on the manufacturing sector are watched particularly closely and are used as a gauge of industrial production. Another important component is the data on average hourly earnings. Expressed in terms of dollars earned per hour, the earnings data are used as a gauge of growth in personal income. The data on the average workweek and overtime hours, for instance, are good gauges of future changes in employment because businesses tend to increase or decrease the length of the workweek before they increase or decrease their payrolls. The index on aggregate hours summarizes the changes in head count and the change in hours worked, providing a proxy for GDP. Other components that go in and out of vogue include the data on the pool of available workers (used when labor shortages develop) and the duration of unemployment. Greater attention is being paid to the average duration of unemployment, which reached nearly 30 weeks at the end of 2009, and the so-called U-6 measure of unemployment, which counts those who are working part-time as a substitute for full-time work and "discouraged" workers who have left the workforce. A very important data point that speaks to the structural nature of unemployment is the tally of the unemployed that are "not on temporary layoff."

How it affects the market: Few economic reports move the bond market more than the employment report does. Investors recognize that labor market trends are one of the most important determinants of the economy's performance, and they respond to jobs data accordingly. There are several reasons why the reaction to the report is often sharp. First, the employment report is one of the first major economic reports released at the start of each month. (The widely followed ISM report almost always is released earlier, but it does not cast as wide a net on the broader economy; manufacturing is just 12 percent of the economy.) The data therefore often set the tone for expectations for the rest of the month. Second, analysts extrapolate data from the employment report to make forecasts on other data, and the data are used directly by several U.S. government agencies in their computations in many other economic reports. Third, investors recognize that the jobs data can influence the way both businesses and consumers perceive the economy. In a sense, the jobs data act as an advertisement for the health of the economy. Fourth, the forecasting record on the monthly jobs data is mediocre. A miss of only 0.1 percent on overall employment levels can translate into a miss of about 140,000 jobs in the headline data. The market response to the data often defies the headlines. The markets recognize that labor market trends sometimes lag other parts of the economy. If, for example, after a long period of economic strength a department store experienced weakness in sales, it would be unlikely to cut workers just because it had a bad month or two. The markets recognize that changes in demand are a better leading indicator of the economy, and that recognition sometimes results in a reduced response to the employment data. A large degree of the bond market's reaction to the jobs report is based on its impact on monetary policy. Keep in mind that Fed rate hikes tend to follow a peak in the jobless rate by about 6 months and that peaks in the jobless rate tend to coincide with peaks in the steepness of the yield curve.

What it means to you: Obviously, employment trends are extremely important to almost everyone. It is essential for an investor to stay abreast of developments in the labor market because labor market trends are at the core of the health of the economy and therefore have an extremely large bearing on the performance of financial assets. Each month you should use the report to prepare yourself for upcoming economic reports and to help you formulate your investment strategies. Strong conditions in the labor market generally translate into strong growth in personal income, and this tends to be associated with strong economic growth, rising corporate profits, and rising bond yields. The opposite is true, of course, when the labor market is weak. In business, the employment data can help you navigate changes in the economic climate by keeping you aware of developments in the economy. Workers can use the report when planning wage and salary negotiations.

EMPLOYMENT COST INDEX

Source: U.S. Bureau of Labor Statistics
Web address for report: www.bls.gov/news.release/eci.nr0.htm
Release date: Generally the final week of the month after the end of the previous calendar quarter
Time: 8:30 a.m. ET
Report coverage: Employment costs in the previous calendar quarter
Description of report: The employment cost index (ECI) is perhaps the most comprehensive measure of changes in the cost of labor. The ECI measures most of the major labor costs incurred by employers, including wages and salaries and employee benefits. The report is a better gauge of employment costs than are the average hourly earning data included in the BLS's monthly employment statistics because it measures straight-time pay and therefore is not distorted by factors such as overtime pay and employment shifts among occupations and industries and because it contains data on benefit costs. The wages and salaries component accounts for roughly 70 percent of the overall ECI, and it includes production bonuses, commissions, tips, room and board, and cost-of-living allowances. Benefit costs covered by the ECI include paid leave such as vacations, holidays, and sick

leave; overtime; nonproduction bonuses; insurance benefits, including life, health, and short- and long-term disability; retirement and savings benefits such as defined-benefit and defined-contribution plans; severance pay; and legally required benefits such as Social Security benefits. Employment costs account for roughly two-thirds of the cost of producing goods and services and therefore have a major influence on inflation and corporate profits. As a result, market participants and policy makers follow the ECI closely.

Survey methodology: During the last month of each calendar quarter, data are collected during the pay period that includes the twelfth of the month from a probability sample of approximately 62,700 occupational observations within about 13,200 establishments in private industry and approximately 11,700 occupations within about 1,900 sample establishments in state and local governments. The occupational observations are placed into about 800 classifications according to the 2000 Standard Occupational Classification system. Individual occupations are then combined to represent 1 of 10 intermediate aggregations, such as professional occupations, or 1 of 5 higher-level aggregations, such as management or professional occupations. The ECI sample is rotated approximately every five years to make it more representative and ensure the best response rate. The individual establishments included in the survey are selected in a way that ensures that larger establishments are more likely to be part of the survey than smaller establishments are. Occupations within the establishments are selected by using a process that gives occupations with higher employment a greater chance of being selected.

Key components of the report: There are two main components in the ECI: wages and salaries, and benefits. The more important of the two, of course, is the wages and salaries component. Wages and salaries are the biggest expense for most businesses, and therefore it is critical to monitor them for clues on inflation pressures and profit margins. The benefits component is unique among economic indicators because it captures trends that are not captured elsewhere. The benefits component can be skewed at the start of each year because a large percentage of insurance companies set their rates at the start of the year. Rate changes that are above or below trend can therefore skew the benefit component. In the early 1990s, for example, as companies migrated to managed-care insurance plans, they experienced a one-time reduction in their benefit costs. This skewed the ECI sharply lower for several years in the first quarter of those years. Large fluctuations in stock prices also can skew the benefit component because they affect the amount of money large corporations must pay into their pension plans. Occasionally, large quarterly changes in commissions in various occupations can skew the wages and salaries component of the ECI.

How it affects the market: The market reaction to the ECI report has tended to be muted, but when trends are evolving, the reaction can be quite sharp for a few reasons. First, since the ECI is a quarterly report, investors get relatively few chances to react to the report, and this sharpens the reaction to its release. Second, much of what is contained in the ECI report is unique. Thus, in a sense, the ECI report provides a first look at previously unknown data. This is unusual for the markets, which generally have a good bead on data before they are released. Third, the ECI is used as a key barometer of inflation, the bond market's nemesis. Hence, the bond market's reaction to the report is generally consistent with the notion that employment costs are the single biggest determinant of inflation. Fourth, investors recognize that the Federal Reserve closely follows the ECI to gauge inflation pressures.

What it means to you: The ECI report should be one of your top economic indicators. Its correlation to inflation is strong enough that you can use it as a key gauge of inflation risks and draw conclusions about the outlook on both interest rates and the economy. There are other ways to utilize the ECI report. For one thing, you can use it to get a better sense of prevailing wage rates, putting yourself in a better position to negotiate your wages. You also can use the benefits data to compare the benefits you receive with the nationwide average. Businesses can use the ECI data to determine compensation rates for pay ranges or annual pay increases. They also can use the data to evaluate and improve their benefits packages to remain competitive in the labor market. Labor organizations can use the report's data on mean and median wages as a reference point for wage negotiations.

EXISTING HOME SALES

Source: National Association of Realtors
Web address for report: www.realtor.org/research/research/ehsdata
Release date: Generally released at the end of the third week in the month
Time: 10:00 a.m. ET
Report coverage: Existing homes sold in the previous calendar month
Description of report: The existing home sales report provides information on the number of existing homes sold, their median and average sales prices, and the amount of inventory currently on hand. This report is considered extremely important given the importance of the housing market to the overall economy in recent years. Existing home sales, however, have a smaller economic impact than do new home sales for obvious reasons. New homes must be built, whereas existing homes already exist. Therefore, the economic activity that results from the sale of an existing home is far less

than that from the sale of a new home. Nevertheless, the sale of an exist-ing home provides meaningful benefits to the economy through brokers' sales commissions, for example. In addition, individuals who move into an existing home tend to purchase new carpeting, appliances, paint, and other home products. The existing home sales data provide important clues to the level of both consumer confidence and income growth, the two main pillars of a strong housing sector.

Survey methodology: Each month the Research Division of the National Association of Realtors (NAR) collects data on existing home sales and prices from a representative sample of approximately 160 of the 700 boards or multiple listing services (MLSs) that regularly participate in its monthly surveys. The 700 boards or MLSs handle approximately 25 percent of all existing home sales that occur in the United States during a given month, and they are situated in every region of the country. The survey participants reflect the regional breakdown of sales reported by the Census Bureau in its American Housing Survey, and they are therefore a microcosm of the existing home sales market. The NAR's monthly data are based on its repre-sentative sample of 160 boards or MLSs. The NAR tallies the data it receives from the 160 boards or MLSs, and it adjusts the data for various outliers and "problematic data" such as erroneous data and missing responses. The NAR divides the home sales data into four census regions: Northeast, South, Midwest, and West. It then weights the aggregated raw volume figures to ac-curately represent sales activity in each region of the country. The data are then adjusted for seasonality, but the data on the median and mean sales prices are not adjusted because their seasonality is difficult to gauge. Exist-ing home sales are reported when a home sale *closes*. This contrasts with new home sales, which are reported when the sales contract is signed. This means that the existing home sales data tend to lag trends in home sales captured in the new home sales report by approximately one or two months.

Key components of the report: Despite being economically less important, existing home sales are a much larger part of the housing market than new home sales. As well, slight variations in the actual sales levels can have a big impact on the annualized number reported each month. Thus, it is important to consider all of the possible ways in which the headline data may have been affected by unusual factors such as extreme weather and sharp fluctuations in interest rates. An important detail that can expose potential flaws in the reported data is the regional data. If one looks at each region, inconsistencies between the regions can be captured. Another important detail is the data on the median sales price, as recent events attest to. The fact is, the bulk of the household sector's net worth consists of the equity in their homes. Par-ticularly important these days are the data on the supply of homes available for sale. Measured in total months of supply remaining on the market, this information provides information about the extent to which the massive overhang of unsold homes is being reduced. Expect it to do so because home construction is running very low relative to household formation. Might there be a shortage of homes in five years? People are born short a roof over their heads, and the more people there are, the more short covering there will be. Population growth can eliminate the inventory dilemma.

How it affects the market: Today's investors know full well the importance of the housing market to the overall economy, the financial system, and the financial markets. Investors have learned firsthand that developments in the housing sector can ripple throughout the economy. It is no wonder that data on the housing sector often spark fairly large reactions in the bond market. While the existing home sales report may not have always provoked a large response in the markets, it most certainly has in the last few years. As the pace of existing home sales began its nearly 40 percent decline from its September 2005 peak, the bond market waited with great anticipation for each release to see if the decline in housing was temporary or perhaps something more. Partially mitigating the market response to the existing home sales report are data on pending home sales, which attempt to gauge future sales by counting contract signings. In addition, the home sales data also are often foreshadowed by the data on mortgage applications released weekly by the Mortgage Bankers Association as well as by the monthly survey of home builders conducted by the National Association of Home Builders.

What it means to you: The importance of the housing market to the economy and bond market cannot be overstated. You therefore should utilize the report when formulating your investment strategies, particularly with respect to economically sensitive sectors of the economy. Beyond your investments, you can use the existing home sales report to get a general idea about the behavior of home prices, which can be useful in assessing the value of your home and, hence, your net worth. Moreover, by tracking the pace of existing home sales, you can improve your sense of the pricing power that exists in areas such as general contracting, appliances, and building materials. If you are in the market to buy a new home, you can improve your bargaining abilities by tracking the level of unsold homes.

FACTORY ORDERS

Source: U.S. Census Bureau
Web address for report: www.census.gov/manufacturing/m3/prel/pdf/
s-i-o.pdf

Release date: Usually the last few days of the month or the very beginning of the subsequent month

Time: 10:00 a.m. ET

Report coverage: Manufacturers' durable and nondurable goods orders, shipments, and inventories for the previous month

Description of report: Factory orders data are considered an important leading economic indicator because they provide advance indications on industrial output. Factory orders data include data on both durable and nondurable goods. These data tend to mirror the trends in the manufacturing sector. Although the factory orders report provides clues to the direction of the manufacturing sector, the report's late release puts it on a lower scale than other manufacturing reports.

Survey methodology: Each month the Census Bureau accumulates data from a panel of 4,300 reporting units to obtain data on durable and nondurable goods orders, shipments, and inventories. The companies surveyed have $500 million or more in annual shipments each. As with the data on durable goods orders, the Census Bureau generates its monthly data on factory orders not by tallying the respondents' orders data but by looking at the monthly changes in shipments and unfilled orders and then estimating the level of new orders through the changes in shipments and unfilled orders. Consider, for example, a month in which shipments of factory goods were 100 units and unfilled orders were 90 units. If during the next month shipments increased to 110 units but unfilled orders remained at 90 units, this would imply an increase of 10 units in total factory orders. (The increase in shipments should have reduced unfilled orders by 10 units; the fact that they held steady implies an increase in orders.)

Key components of the report: Factory orders consist of both durable and nondurable goods. The more important of the two is the durable goods component, which accounts for about 45 percent of all factory orders. Durable goods orders provide clues to the willingness of consumers and businesses to spend on big-ticket items such as automobiles, appliances, and new equipment and structures. The data on capital spending are highlighted in the component called *nondefense capital goods orders*. Data on shipments are also important because this information is used in the computation of the quarterly data on the GDP. The factory report includes data on factory inventories, which account for about 38 percent of all business inventories. Unwanted inventory buildups often foreshadow slowing industrial production, while inventory shortfalls foreshadow increases in production, which are important elements in the business cycle.

How it affects the market: Data on factory orders are very important to the market and are considered leading indicators for the economy. Despite the importance the market places on factory orders, however, the report does not always provoke much of a market response for a couple of reasons. First, durable goods orders, which account for about half of factory orders, are known days in advance of the release of the factory orders report. Second, factory orders data often are foreshadowed by trends in the regional and national purchasing managers' surveys that are released weeks earlier. Nevertheless, the data on nondurable goods orders are never truly completely known until the data on factory orders are released, and so the report always has the potential to move the markets. Moreover, as with the data on durable goods, the market reaction to strong data can vary with the composition of the strength. The bond market, which tends to loathe strong economic activity, may not react as negatively to strong data if the source of the strength is capital spending because capital spending is perceived to be conducive to productivity growth, which tends to dampen inflation.

What it means to you: Because trends in factory orders tend to precede trends in production and, hence, the economy, the factory orders report can help you forecast economic trends. Moreover, because factory orders are driven by demand, the report can reinforce your sense of the underlying strength in the economy. Data on factory orders are best used in concert with other key manufacturing-related economic reports. A broad analysis of the manufacturing sector can be very helpful in assessing where the economy is with respect to the business cycle. That analysis can help you formulate investment strategies that will benefit from fluctuations in the economy.

GROSS DOMESTIC PRODUCT

Source: U.S. Bureau of Economic Analysis
Web address for report: www.bea.gov/newsreleases/national/gdp/gdp-newsrelease.htm
Release date: Generally during the final week of the month after the end of the previous calendar quarter
Time: 8:30 a.m. ET
Report coverage: The gross domestic product for the previous calendar quarter
Description of report: The gross domestic product report is the most comprehensive measure of economic activity available. Comprehensive data on inflation also are included in the report. The GDP measures the total value of the output of goods and services produced by labor and property in the United States. The textbook formula for calculating the GDP is: GDP = C + I + G + $(X - M)$, or GDP = consumption + private investment + govern-

ment + net exports (exports − imports). Personal consumption expenditures (PCE) account for roughly 70 percent of the GDP, and this explains why there is such a sharp focus on consumer spending. About 65 percent of all consumer spending is on services. *Nonresidential fixed investment* accounts for about 9.5 percent of the GDP, but over the past 15 years it has made a disproportionate contribution to overall economic growth, helping to boost productivity. Nonresidential fixed investment, also known as *capital spending*, includes investments in structures (3.2 percent of the GDP) and equipment and software (7.5 percent of the GDP). Over the last 30 years, the GDP has expanded at an annual rate of 2.7 percent. Monetary policy often is shaped by the extent to which economic growth exceeds or falls short of the economy's potential growth rate, the so-called *output gap*. With monetary policy currently quite accommodative, attention has increased regarding this measure.

Survey methodology: As one might expect, tabulating the methodology used to compute the GDP statistics is complex and requires the use of a wide variety of sources and methods. The Bureau of Economic Analysis (BEA) assembles the GDP data by measuring the GDP on both ends of the transaction spectrum. Specifically, the GDP is measured by using estimates of both income and spending. Consider the sale of apples at a grocery store. On the income side, the BEA would measure the labor, capital, and other costs involved in the sale. On the spending side, the BEA would measure the value of the apples sold. Theoretically, the dollar value of the income received and that of the expenditures should be equal, but this is not usually the case. In 2008, for example, the income side exceeded the spending side by about $100 billion. The data sources are independent and are merely estimates; the BEA does not count every apple sold in the country. A fairly large proportion of the PCE data is obtained from the monthly survey of retail trade conducted by the Census Bureau. Many other sources are utilized to obtain data on gasoline sales, home sales, medical spending, and the like. Most of the data are obtained from U.S. government agencies. The inflation data in the GDP report are calculated basically by comparing current prices and quantities with those in a base year (currently 2005). Current prices are "deflated" to equate the current value of the output of goods and services to the past value. The extent to which the price of a good must be deflated is the inflation rate. In calculating quantities and prices of goods and services, the BEA uses a system that incorporates weights used in two adjacent quarters. This helps ensure that the quarterly changes are not affected by the choice of the base year.

Key components of the report: There are a number of important components in the GDP report. First, the PCE component is important because it is the biggest component of the economy. Second, nonresidential fixed investment is a key gauge of overall business spending and of technology spending in particular. Strength in business spending often is called "good growth" by bond investors because it helps lift productivity and thus contain inflation. Third, the final sales component, which is the GDP minus the change in inventories, gives a clean read on the underlying strength in demand. As an example, while the GDP for the fourth quarter of 2009 was initially reported to have increased 5.7 percent, 3.4 percentage points were attributable to inventory investment, leaving the sales rate for final sales at just 2.3 percent, a slow pace of underlying activity. Inventory changes can distort the GDP data because the fluctuations sometimes result from changes in demand. In fact, unwanted inventory buildups, while a net plus for the GDP in the quarter in which they occur, can be looked at as a negative sign on the economy because a buildup can draw from future production. The net exports component is used as an important gauge of the impact of trade on the economy, and that impact can vary widely from quarter to quarter. The data on the government sector are also important and should be watched to gauge the true underlying condition of the private sector. The price index in the GDP report is considered one of the broadest measures of inflation available. The PCE deflator is watched particularly closely and is the preferred consumer inflation gauge among many analysts as well as many members of the Federal Reserve.

How it affects the market: As a quarterly report, the GDP report contains a blend of familiar and unfamiliar news. The familiar news comes from digesting three months of data related to the GDP report during the months covered by the report. In essence the report can be looked at as a summation of previously released data. This lessens the reaction to the report to some extent. However, investors recognize that the GDP report is more comprehensive than the summation of the monthly economic reports. In general, the reaction to the report is often quite sharp. The bond market generally trades lower on strong GDP data, but the magnitude of the reaction depends on the composition of the report. If, for example, the GDP is strong but final sales are weak, the bond market often views the data as weak and trades higher. In addition, if the GDP is strong but appears to have been boosted by capital spending, or so-called good growth, the bond market generally will be quite forgiving.

What it means to you: For those who would rather steer clear of daily ruminations on the constant flow of economic news, the GDP report is the perfect choice because it provides a broad summary of the main macroeconomic themes affecting the economy. However, the monthly data can give you an earlier lead on developments in the economy than the GDP report will, and so it is probably not a good idea to focus mostly on the GDP data. Moreover, the monthly data contain useful details that are not in the GDP report. Nevertheless, the GDP report is a good foundation for formulating your investment plan. The Fed bases its policies largely on the extent to which the GDP is above or below the economy's so-called speed limit, or growth potential. The economy's *growth potential* is computed basically by adding growth in the labor force (about 1 percent per year, but slowly declining) to productivity growth (close to 2 percent over the long term). Thus, as a rough guide, you can shape many of your financial decisions by comparing the economy's growth rate to its growth potential. This will be an important area of focus as a lower-than-normal reading on the GDP has the possibility of restraining potential Fed action while higher-than-expected readings could warrant higher interest rates.

HOUSING STARTS

Source: U.S. Census Bureau
Web address for report: www.census.gov/const/www/newresconstindex. html
Release date: Generally released in the second half of the month
Time: 8:30 a.m. ET
Report coverage: New residential housing construction begun in the previous calendar month
Description of report: The housing starts report provides statistics on the construction of new privately owned residential structures in the United States. The data included in the press release are (1) the number of new housing units authorized by building permits, (2) the number of housing units authorized to be built but not yet started, (3) the number of housing units started, (4) the number of housing units under construction, and (5) the number of housing units completed. The data exclude hotels, motels, and group residential structures such as nursing homes and college dormitories. The housing starts report can provide indications on whether home construction is running above or below the underlying level of demand, something that many lost sight of during the housing boom.
Survey methodology: Each month the Census Bureau attempts to estimate the number of housing starts by surveying approximately 9,000 of the approximately 20,000 permit-issuing places in the country. The Census Bureau utilizes a mail-out/mail-back survey to obtain these monthly statistics. The 9,000 permit-issuing places are selected as a sample of those permit-issuing places that are deemed to be representative of all 20,000 of those places.

The Census Bureau first estimates the number of housing units for which building permits have been issued in all 20,000 permit-issuing places. It then queries the owners and builders through field visits to determine whether construction on the units covered by the permits has started. In places where permits are not required, the Census Bureau visits nonpermit land areas at least every three months to see if there has been any new construction. Units authorized by permits but not yet started in the survey month are reviewed again in successive months to determine if they have actually started. Estimates are made for units started before permit authorization and for late reports. The data collected are used to make an estimate of the total number of housing starts in both permit-issuing and non-permit-issuing areas. All the data are adjusted for seasonal fluctuations.

Key components of the report: The housing starts report is constructed in a manner similar to that of both the new and existing home sale reports. In particular, the details of the report are broken down into four regions: the Northeast, Midwest, South, and West. The regional breakdown provides clues that can expose potential flaws in the headline data caused by inconsistencies between the regions. Data on completions are important because they can be compared against household formation to form judgments about inventory trends. The smaller the increase in the housing stock relative to household formation, the more likely it is that the inventory of unsold homes will decline. This is a process currently in motion and something very important to watch. Another important detail in the report is the breakdown of starts by type of structure. Specifically, the report details the number of starts in single-family structures with two to four units and five units or more. Single-family units typically represent about 80 percent of all starts, and so it is important to focus there. The data on multifamily units tend to be volatile; for example, in November 2009, multifamily starts jumped 67.3 percent following a 29.5 percent decline the previous month. Also important in the report are the data on building permits, a leading economic indicator. Permits are a leading indicator of housing conditions because most state and local governments require that a permit be filed before a new home is built. The permits data are relatively immune to the many factors that can cause starts to fluctuate (the weather, for example). This makes the permits data helpful in weeding out distortions of the true underlying trend. Because some states do not require a permit, starts typically exceed permits, generally by about 30,000 units or more. When the gap is wider, it portends weakness in starts in the months ahead. When the gap narrows, it portends strength.

How it affects the market: Although the housing sector is considered important to the economy, the housing starts report does not always provoke a large market response for a couple of reasons. First, housing starts are largely an offshoot of new home sales activity. This makes the housing starts data of secondary importance compared to the new home sales data. Second, distortions in the data often result from volatility in the multifamily data, regional data, and weather-related factors. Third, the housing starts data often are foreshadowed by data on mortgage applications and the monthly survey of home builders conducted by the National Association of Home Builders. In fact, each month the home builders' survey is released the day before the release of the housing starts report.

What it means to you: On its own the housing starts report provides useful information about current levels of residential construction activity and therefore can be used to form an opinion about the economy. You therefore should utilize the report in formulating your investment strategies. Beyond your investments, you can use this report to get a general idea about the behavior of home prices and in assessing the value of your home and, hence, your net worth.

INDEX OF LEADING ECONOMIC INDICATORS

Source: The Conference Board

Web address for report: www.conference-board.org/economics/bci/press Release_output.cfm?cid=1

Release date: Generally between the seventeenth and twenty-second calendar days of every month

Time: 10:00 a.m. ET

Report coverage: Economic indicators from the previous calendar month

Description of report: The Leading Economic Index (LEI) is meant to act as a barometer of economic activity three to six months in the future. The index is designed to signal peaks and troughs in the business cycle. An increase or decrease in the index over a period of three or more months, generally signals growth or contraction, respectively, in economic activity. The index consists of 10 indicators that are considered top leading economic indicators. Because the index is composed of indicators that are widely followed, the LEI is largely a summation index and therefore provides little value to the markets. Nevertheless, the LEI provides confirmation of the economic trends discerned from its components.

Survey methodology: The LEI is constructed by combining a weighted average of 10 well-regarded economic indicators: the average workweek of production workers in the manufacturing sector; average initial weekly claims for state unemployment benefits; new orders for consumer goods and materials; vendor performance (the speed at which companies make deliveries of goods); new orders for nonmilitary capital goods; new building permits issued; an index of stock prices; money supply data (M2); an index of consumer expectations); and the spread between rates on 10-year Treasury bonds and federal funds. The month-to-month change in each of these components is multiplied by the assigned weighting. This produces the monthly changes in the index, which are expressed in percentage terms and generally average about 0.1 to 0.2 percent per month.

Key components of the report: It is difficult to cite one aspect of the report as the most important. The relative importance of each indicator is largely a subjective matter; the indicators provide few clues to the future direction of the overall index. Predicting the future direction of the index requires close scrutiny of the trends in the individual components. It is important, however, to scan the components to determine if they may be exerting an unusual impact on the overall index. While the details of the LEI report say little about the index itself, the Conference Board releases two additional indexes along with the LEI: the indexes of lagging and coincident indicators. These indexes are meant to give indications of the economy in the past and the present, respectively. The coincident index measures various aspects of production that reflect the current pace of economic activity. The lagging index reflects the cost side of the equation, including production costs, inventories, and debt costs. Many analysts like to look at the ratio of the coincident to the lagging indicators to gauge future economic activity. A rising ratio is considered a positive signal for the economy because it indicates that business costs are falling at the same time that revenues are rising, indicating the likelihood of increases in corporate profits.

How it affects the market: Historically, the LEI report has not affected markets much, but it has reinforced sentiments about the economy. For example, in April 2009, an upturn in the LEI helped reinforce the idea that the economy was turning, helping fuel a rally in risk assets. Hence, to the extent that the LEI report reinforces convictions about the future direction of the economy, its value is greater than might be surmised from the market reaction that follows the report's release. Moreover, media coverage of the report puts the LEI report in the public's eye, thus affecting consumer confidence.

What it means to you: The LEI is best used as a barometer of the future direction of the economy. You can use it as the equivalent of an executive briefing on some of the best time-tested indicators for the economy. The index can be especially helpful if you find it difficult to put much time into following the economy or would rather steer clear of the daily ruminations on economic data. However, it is best to use as many indicators as possible when formulating a view on the economic outlook. The LEI provides an easy and concise way to follow several important indicators.

INDUSTRIAL PRODUCTION AND CAPACITY UTILIZATION

Source: The Federal Reserve
Web address for report: www.federalreserve.gov/releases/g17/Current/default.htm
Release date: Around the fifteenth calendar day of every month
Time: 9:15 a.m. ET
Report coverage: Manufacturing output and utilization rates for the previous month
Description of report: The industrial production and capacity utilization report measures the monthly change in output in U.S. manufacturing, mining, and electricity, gas, and utilities. The changes in output are measured in physical terms rather than by multiplying the output by prices. This makes the data reliable in terms of reflecting actual changes in physical output. The industrial production report does not include production in a variety of industries, including agriculture, construction, trade, finance, and the service industries. The industrial production report is used as a key gauge of the health of the economy; increases and decreases in production tend to reflect changes in the underlying demand for goods and services.
Survey methodology: Each month the Federal Reserve constructs indexes on industrial production by using two main sources: (1) output measured in physical units and (2) output inferred from data on inputs to the production process. The Fed attempts to obtain as much of the data as possible from output measured in physical units by obtaining data from private trade associations and government agencies. In cases in which obtaining data on physical output is not possible, the Fed estimates the physical output by using data on hours worked by production workers. This information is collected monthly by the Bureau of Labor Statistics when it conducts its monthly payroll survey. The Fed weights the components in the industrial production index by their relative importance and then adjusts the data for seasonality. The weights are updated monthly to eliminate distortions in the contributions of several high-technology industries, where weights shift a great deal. Capacity utilization rates are designed to be consistent with the production data, and the Fed utilizes its own estimates on productive capacity in its calculations.
Key components of the report: An important component is the data on manufacturing production and in particular the production of automobiles because of its volatility. The data on automobile assembly rates are particularly useful as a microcosm of the extent to which businesses might be either over- or undershooting their sales figures, a precursor to future changes in output and changes in the inventory cycle. The report also provides data

on the percent of the nation's manufacturing capacity that is being utilized. These data are closely watched for two main reasons. First, they tell us something about the potential for business investment in future quarters: large amounts of unused capacity discourage investment. Second, capacity utilization correlates with inflation, with figures under 80 percent consistent with low inflation pressures.

How it affects the market: The industrial production report provides important information about the level of national output and therefore is an important gauge of the state of the economy. Investors thus put a great deal of weight on these data. The market reaction, however, sometimes is muted by a few factors. First, as was mentioned above, some of the industrial production data are assembled using data from the monthly jobs report, which is released about a week or so before the industrial production report. Second, while the industrial production report indicates plenty about current production levels, it does not provide much guidance on future trends. The market prefers to get that guidance from data on manufacturing orders, a key leading economic indicator.

What it means to you: Changes in the level of industrial production can directly affect both your income and your investments. For example, if you work in the production sector of the economy, your workweek and overtime hours could fluctuate with production levels. You also should watch the capacity utilization rate, which has averaged about 80 percent since 1980, keeping in mind the 80 percent threshold. In today's environment, the Federal Reserve is keenly aware that capacity utilization is well below normal, which is one reason it adopted a zero interest rate policy.

INITIAL JOBLESS CLAIMS

Source: U.S. Department of Labor
Web address for report: www.dol.gov/opa/media/press/eta/ui/current.htm
Release date: Every Thursday
Time: 8:30 a.m. ET
Report coverage: Initial filings for state unemployment insurance filed in the week ended five days before the release of the report
Description of report: The weekly jobless claims report is an important gauge of employment trends and one of the most important gauges of the economy. It is one of those reports about which one might say that if he or she had to choose just one indicator to watch, this would be it. The jobless claims report measures the number of new persons who file for state unemployment benefits, providing an early lead on the closely watched monthly employment

report. Included in the report are a four-week moving average, a state-by-state breakdown of the claims filed along with comments by states where new claims increased or decreased by more than 1,000 people, the total number of people continuing to receive initial unemployment benefits, the unemployment rate for insured workers, and the total number of people on some form of "extended" benefits. Initial jobless claims have averaged about 380,000 per week during the 2000s while continuing claims have averaged about 3.2 million; however, both figures strayed quite far from their averages in 2009.

Survey methodology: Unlike most economic data, the data on jobless claims are derived using very little estimation, and therefore they accurately reflect actual conditions in the labor market. To obtain the weekly data, the Department of Labor (DOL) essentially tallies all the data provided to it by the nation's state unemployment offices. The data provided to the DOL are based on actual filings, and the states do not seasonally adjust the data they submit to the DOL. The seasonal adjustments are made by the DOL before the data are released to the public. An unemployment rate for insured workers is calculated by dividing the number of people receiving jobless benefits by the number of people eligible to receive them. The unemployment rate for insured workers tends to be lower than the national unemployment rate because not all workers are eligible to receive unemployment benefits. Self-employed people, for example, are ineligible. The rate had been declining in recent years as a result of an increase in the number of ineligible workers. This has been caused by a decline in unionization, tighter eligibility requirements, and other factors.

Key components of the report: Most of the components of the initial claims report contain useful information. The data on continuing claims, for example, track the cumulative number of people receiving unemployment benefits rather than only new recipients. This component can help an investor assess the extent to which people who filed for unemployment benefits in the last few weeks are having difficulty finding a new job. I like to use the continuing claims data to predict changes in the monthly employment data. Because state and federal governments now provide extended benefits to qualifying individuals, additional analysis is necessary. The four-week average of claims is also important since it weeds out the weekly variability and provides greater clarity on developments in the labor market. However, the weekly data provide the best insight into emerging developments in this important data series. The unemployment rate for insured workers serves as a good proxy for trends in the national unemployment rate.

How it affects the market: Market participants keenly watch the jobless claims statistics. In 2009 and early 2010, initial jobless claims were closely watched as an indicator with respect to the end of the recession. Historically, a decline in claims has correlated strongly with the official end dates of recessions. The market response to the claims data is often quite palpable because of its correlation to the monthly jobs report. The reaction can be especially sharp if the claims data are compelling enough to alter or reinforce forecasts for the jobs data. Today, as the U.S. economy emerges from recession, attention on weekly jobless claims data has intensified.

What it means to you: For an investor it is essential to stay abreast of developments in the labor market because those trends are at the core of the health of the economy and therefore have an extremely large bearing on the performance of financial assets. The claims data provide insight that few economic indicators shed.

INSTITUTE FOR SUPPLY MANAGEMENT NONMANUFACTURING INDEX

Source: Institute for Supply Management
Web address for report: www.ism.ws
Release date: The third business day of every month
Time: 10:00 a.m. ET
Report coverage: Nonmanufacturing activity in the month before the release of the survey results
Description of report: The nonmanufacturing report issued by the Institute for Supply Management (ISM) is a relatively new indicator that is meant to mirror the construct of the ISM's widely followed manufacturing index, a top leading economic indicator. Over the years the manufacturing sector's share of the U.S. economy has been declining steadily, currently representing about 12 percent of the GDP. In recognition of this, in 1997 the ISM created a nonmanufacturing index. The index captures trends in key service industries that represent nearly 90 percent of all jobs in the United States. The index has been gaining recognition as a key gauge of economic activity in the service sector, where economic data are not readily available. The ISM's nonmanufacturing report contains indexes for new orders, production, employment, delivery time, inventories, and order backlogs. A reading above 50 is consistent with expansion; a reading below 50 is consistent with contraction.
Survey methodology: Each month the ISM surveys purchasing and supply executives in approximately 370 nonmanufacturing companies. Over 62 diverse industries from various geographic areas of the nation are represented in the survey. The 62 industries are weighted according to their contribution to the economy. The ISM asks the purchasing and supply executives whether they experienced an increase or a decrease in nine important aspects of their

businesses, including the six mentioned above. The responses are compiled into separate *diffusion indexes*, which are basically numbers that reflect the percentage of firms that reported an increase in the respective components minus those that saw a decrease. The diffusion indexes are adjusted for seasonality and to equate a reading of zero to 50. The ISM recently introduced a headline figure that is a composite index of four equally weighted subindexes: business activity, new orders, employment, and supplier deliveries.

Key components of the report: The two most important components to watch in the ISM's nonmanufacturing report are new orders and employment. As the service sector accounts for the vast majority of jobs in the economy, the employment component of this index is closely watched. The inventory component is also very important because it indicates whether inventory levels are becoming too high or too low. It is unclear, however, how useful the inventory component is in the ISM's nonmanufacturing survey. When inventories increase in the legal sector, for example, the economic implications are not nearly as important as they are when inventories increase in the manufacturing sector.

How it affects the market: As a leading indicator on the economy, the ISM's manufacturing report is one of the most respected economic reports, and its release often sparks very large market moves. Its nonmanufacturing index has increasingly gained prominence and currently ranks as one of the most watched economic indicators. In the summer of 2007, declines in the employment component were cited by many market analysts as a worrisome sign for the labor market and the economy more broadly.

What it means to you: Unlike the manufacturing sector, there is not all that much information that provides an insight into the service sector, which makes this release from the ISM very important for the markets. Because the U.S. economy is largely service oriented, keeping tabs on the health of the service sector is an important endeavor for both your investments and your personal finances. As the economy emerges from recession, a disparity has emerged between the ISM manufacturing and nonmanufacturing indexes. How this disparity resolves itself will be closely watched by forecasters and investors for signs that the strength in the manufacturing sector of the economy is spreading to other sectors.

INSTITUTE FOR SUPPLY MANAGEMENT REPORT ON BUSINESS

Source: Institute for Supply Management
Web address for report: www.ism.ws

Release date: First business day of every month
Time: 10:00 a.m. ET
Report coverage: Manufacturing activity for the month before the release of the survey results
Description of report: The ISM report is one of the most closely followed economic reports, and it is a top leading economic indicator. The report contains meaningful indications of the pace of economic activity in the manufacturing sector, and therefore it provides extremely valuable information on the health of the overall economy. The ISM releases its composite business index on the findings of its survey of purchasing managers, consisting of five components: new orders, production, employment, inventories, and supplier deliveries. The new orders component is the most heavily weighted component at 30 percent. As a diffusion index, readings above 50 are consistent with expansion in the manufacturing sector; readings below 50 are consistent with contraction. A reading around or below 42 is consistent with contraction in the overall economy.
Survey methodology: Each month the ISM surveys purchasing and supply executives in approximately 400 industrial companies. The companies are selected from a group of 20 diverse industries—including primary metals, transportation equipment, rubber and plastics, food and kindred products, and printing and publishing—from various geographic areas of the nation. The 20 industries are weighted according to their contributions to the economy. The ISM asks the purchasing and supply executives whether they experienced an increase, a decrease, or no change in nine important aspects of their businesses, including the five listed above. Separate questions are posed on prices paid, order backlogs, export orders, and import orders. The responses are compiled into a *diffusion index*, which is basically a number that reflects the percentage of firms that reported an increase in the respective components plus half the firms that reported no change. The diffusion indexes are adjusted for seasonality.
Key components of the report: The most important component in the ISM report is new orders. New orders are the lifeline of the manufacturing sector. When new orders rise, many forces are set in motion that lead to increases in the other key components of the survey, such as production and employment. Thus, as new orders go, so goes the ISM index. The inventory component is also very important because it indicates whether inventory levels are becoming too high or too low. Inventory levels can indicate whether an increase or a decrease in manufacturing output may be in the offing. Given the record pace at which business inventories were depleted in the most recent recession, the inventory component has been closely watched.

How it affects the market: As a leading indicator for the economy with more than 50 years of strong correlation to other widely followed data, the ISM report is one of the most respected economic reports, and its release often sparks very large market moves. The bond market generally receives a strong report poorly because it fears that strong economic growth will stoke inflation and perhaps cause the Federal Reserve to raise interest rates. A weak report, in contrast, usually receives a positive response in the bond market, as it could indicate economic weakness and, hence, low inflation and perhaps interest rate cuts by the Federal Reserve. The market tends to shift its focus on the details of the report, but it basically stays focused on the new orders component. Nevertheless, mood shifts in the market can shift the market's attention from month to month. When this happens, it is usually the employment component or the price index that grabs attention, especially since the national employment report usually follows the ISM release by a matter of days. Other times, the price index can be in focus. The indexes on order backlogs and supplier deliveries (delivery speeds) are important gauges of resource utilization.

What it means to you: Investors recognize that the ISM is a top leading indicator for the economy. You should pay close attention to trends in this important indicator because it provides clues on a wide variety of factory data, which dominate the economic calendar and thus have a substantial influence on the behavior of the financial markets. Moreover, you should follow the report closely to make assessments about the economy. In business, the report can help you navigate a variety of economic climates.

NEW HOME SALES

Source: U.S. Census Bureau
Web address for report: www.census.gov/const/www/newressalesindex.html
Release date: Generally the last calendar week of every month
Time: 10:00 a.m. ET
Report coverage: New homes sold in the previous calendar month
Description of report: The new home sales report provides information on the number of new homes sold, their median and average sales prices, and the number of unsold homes. For obvious reasons, reports related to the strength, or lack thereof, in the housing market are closely watched. The multiplier effects of the housing sector are bigger than those of any other sector in the economy, as recent events attest to. A new home sale affects the economy in many ways. First, the building of new homes creates jobs; data

from the National Association of Home Builders indicate that the construction of a single-family home generates 2.5 full-time jobs in construction and construction-related industries. Another boost to the economy comes when new home buyers furnish their homes with new appliances, tools, carpeting, outdoor equipment, and the like. The new home sales data provide important clues to the level of consumer confidence and income growth, the two main pillars of a strong housing market. The data also can be used to gauge the impact of recent government programs aimed at stimulating this sector of the economy.

Survey methodology: Each month the Census Bureau attempts to estimate the number of building permits issued by the approximately 20,000 permit-issuing places in the country by sampling about 900 permit-issuing places that are considered representative of all permit-issuing places. The Census Bureau's field representatives obtain the data they need for their estimates by visiting a sample of about 900 permit-issuing places. In places where permits are not required, the Census Bureau visits non-permit-issuing land areas at least once every three months to see if there is any new construction. For each permit issued in the 900 permit-issuing places, the Census Bureau asks the owner or the builder whether the house has been sold or is for sale. If it has been sold, the date of sale is recorded. Unsold homes are reviewed again in successive months to determine if they have been sold. The data collected are used to make an estimate of the total number of home sales in both permit-issuing and non-permit-issuing areas. Since the 1960s, the data have been adjusted upward by 3.3 percent to account for homes that would not normally be captured in the survey.

Key components of the report: The new home sales report contains just a few details. Nevertheless, the details shed light on the condition of the housing market, the household sector, and the overall economy. Inventory data have been at the center of attention, providing important insights into the extent to which home prices might fall as a result of excessive inventory levels, both in terms of the outright number of unsold new homes and relative to sales. In 2009, to the surprise of those focused too heavily on credit availability, home foreclosures, and a decline in the homeownership rate, inventory levels fell to their lowest in over 30 years. The decline illustrated the importance of focusing on housing starts relative to household formation. In 2009, housing starts were running substantially below household formation, suggesting the supply of unsold homes would diminish. This looks likely to continue for quite some time and will likely eventually eliminate the supply of unsold existing homes for sale. The destruction of household wealth is one factor expected to weight upon consumer spending in the time ahead.

How it affects the market: Investors are keenly aware of the importance of the housing sector to the U.S. economy. They recognize that the effects of the housing sector can ripple throughout the economy. They also recognize that the condition of the housing sector speaks volumes about consumer confidence and income growth. It is no wonder that the new home sales report often sparks fairly large reactions in the bond market. Large revisions to the report often magnify the market impact. Importantly, the new home sales data have been watched closely in 2009 and 2010 as this area of the housing market has appeared to benefit to a smaller degree from government stimulus programs than the existing home market. While existing home sales skyrocketed in 2009, new home sales tended to move horizontally, averaging around 375,000 for the year, a far cry from the peak of nearly 1.4 million.

What it means to you: As a leading economic indicator, the new home sales report provides important clues about the economic outlook. You therefore should use the new home sales report when formulating your investment strategies, particularly with respect to forming opinions about the economically sensitive sectors of the economy. Beyond your investments, you can use the new home sales report to get a general idea about the behavior of home prices. This information could be useful in assessing the value of your home and, hence, your net worth.

PERSONAL INCOME AND CONSUMPTION

Source: U.S. Census Bureau
Web address for report: www.bea.gov/newsreleases/national/pi/pinewsrelease.htm
Release date: Generally the last week of each month
Time: 8:30 a.m. ET
Report coverage: Personal income and consumption in the previous calendar month, except when the release is delayed until early in a subsequent month
Description of report: The report on personal income (PI) and personal consumption expenditures (PCE) provides important information about the household sector, which accounts for about 70 percent of the U.S. economy. Trends in personal income growth are particularly important since income is at the root of all spending. Personal income consists of more than wages and salaries. In fact, only about 50 percent of total personal income is from wages and salaries. Other categories include rental income, dividends and interest, proprietor's income, disability and health insurance benefits, and Social Security benefits. The data on personal consumption, however,

are less comprehensive, breaking the data down into three major categories: durable goods, nondurable goods, and services. The data on both PI and PCE are used in the quarterly computations of the GDP.

Survey methodology: Obtaining the data necessary to produce the report on personal income and consumption is a comprehensive task. Data must be collected from numerous sources, including the housing stock, insurance premiums, mortgage debt, interest rates, unit sales, receipts, and tax collections. The data for most categories of personal consumption are generated by using what the U.S. Bureau of Economic Analysis (BEA) calls the *retail-control method.* This method is used to estimate over one-third of the PCE data, and it basically captures spending on a wide variety of goods. Consumption data in many areas are estimated by using data obtained elsewhere: motor vehicles, food produced and consumed on farms, and clothing issued to military personnel are all separate. Additionally, spending on dental and other medical services, for example, is estimated by using data on wages and salaries derived from the monthly employment data collected by the U.S. Bureau of Labor statistics (BLS). The data on personal income are estimated by using many of the sources described above.

Key components of the report: The details of the personal income and consumption report provide insight into whether the trends in each of these two key areas are as strong or weak as the headlines suggest. The data on personal income, for example, occasionally are skewed by transfer payments, which include Social Security benefit payments. A delay of just a few days can push these payments out of one month and into the next, distorting the data on personal income. Similarly, the timing of payments of farm subsidies often skews the data. During expansions, growth in PI tends to be strong. PI grew at an annual rate of about 4.25 percent during the last decade, although it fell in 2009. The details of the data on personal consumption help in assessing trends in spending on durable and nondurable goods, and this can shed light on consumer confidence levels. Strong growth in spending on durable goods, for example, suggests that consumers are confident about their personal finances. A key detail now in vogue is the information on the savings rate. The savings rate was in a secular decline for many years, falling below 1 percent on several occasions in recent years (it had been as high as nearly 15 percent in the 1970s, and tended to run between 5 and 10 percent before the secular decline). The savings rate has since increased to around 5 percent, and it looks likely to stay within its 5 to 10 percent range in the long term, reflecting the destruction in wealth, which occurred in the context of an aging population moving closer to retirement, as well as a lack of credit availability.

How it affects the market: Market reaction to the release of the report on personal income and consumption tends to be relatively muted, but there are times when that response is quite palpable. The reaction tends to be muted because it is derived from data to which the markets have already reacted. Personal income data, for example, often are foreshadowed by the monthly data on average hourly earnings reported each month in the employment report. Similarly, the data on personal consumption are foreshadowed by the monthly retail sales report. The reaction to the report on personal income and consumption tends to be greatest when the release occurs just before the release of the quarterly GDP statistics. Market participants recognize that the PCE data are directly plugged into the GDP statistics, and this increases the market's focus on the PCE data when the GDP release is around the corner. Garnering the most attention at times is the PCE deflator.

What it means to you: You should consider using the data on the personal savings rate as a key indicator. A sharp decline in the savings rate, characterized by a break from the secular trend, indicates that consumption is exceeding income; this we learned recently is an unsustainable trend. If the savings rate increases while consumption holds up, it suggests that consumers have the wherewithal to spend, boding well for the long-run health of the economy.

PHILADELPHIA FED'S BUSINESS OUTLOOK SURVEY

Source: Federal Reserve Bank of Philadelphia
Web address for report: www.phil.frb.org/research-and-data/regional economy/business-outlook-survey
Release date: The third Thursday of every month
Time: 10:00 a.m. ET
Report coverage: Manufacturing conditions through the first week of the month in which the report is released
Description of report: The Philadelphia Survey, which has been in existence since 1968, provides an early glimpse of manufacturing conditions every month. Included in the survey are manufacturers in the Fed's Third District: eastern Pennsylvania, southern New Jersey, and the entire state of Delaware. The survey contains important information about business conditions in the manufacturing sector. In a questionnaire, the Philadelphia Fed asks manufacturers about their overall business activity including new orders, shipments, backlogs, the average length of their employees' workweeks, employment conditions, inventories, the prices they pay and receive for goods and services, and delivery times. Market participants use the report to assess economic conditions in the manufacturing sector and to predict the monthly ISM index.

Survey methodology: Near the end of every month, the Philadelphia Fed mails its survey questionnaire to about 145 large manufacturing firms in the Fed's Third District, and about 90 to 100 firms respond to each survey. Firms usually respond by mail or, increasingly, the Internet, by the close of business on the third Tuesday prior to the third Thursday of the month. The survey asks the manufacturers whether they experienced an increase or a decrease in the important aspects of their businesses. The responses are compiled into a *diffusion index,* which is basically a number that reflects the percentage of firms that reported an increase in the respective components minus those which saw a decrease. Thus, a reading of over zero in the survey and its components indicates expansion, while a reading below zero indicates contraction.

Key components of the report: The Philadelphia Survey consists of the various indicators mentioned above, the most important of which is new orders. When new orders rise, many forces are set in motion that lead to increases in the other key aspects of a manufacturer's business, resulting in a rise in many of the other components of the Philadelphia Survey. An increase in new orders means that future production levels are likely to rise, which could mean an increase in employee hours worked.

How it affects the market: Because this index provides one of the earliest indications of manufacturing activity in any given month, the financial markets ascribe a fair amount of importance to the survey. The report generally is released fully two weeks before the release of the ISM data as well as other regional manufacturing surveys, and therefore it can provide an early indication of national conditions in the manufacturing sector. Thus, at times market reaction to the Philadelphia Survey is often sharp. However, because the survey is merely a regional survey, one of many that are released over the course of a given month, the market tends to treat the survey as a second-tier indicator.

What it means to you: Keeping in mind the factory-laden nature of the U.S. economic calendar, manufacturing data such as the Philadelphia Survey can have a large bearing on the financial markets and thus your investments. Generally, the stronger the manufacturing sector is, the more likely it is that the stock market will be rising and the bond market will be falling (with the yield curve flattening). Businesses can use the data to gauge the health of the economy.

PRODUCER PRICE INDEX

Source: U.S. Bureau of Labor Statistics
Web address for report: www.bls.gov/pPI

Release date: Generally slightly before the middle of every month
Time: 8:30 a.m. ET
Report coverage: The previous month's data, mostly for prices on the Tuesday of the week containing the thirteenth of the month
Description of report: The producer price index (PPI) measures price changes in the prices received by domestic producers on the goods they produce. It basically tracks the prices manufacturers pay on the commodities, parts, and raw materials they use to manufacture their products. The PPI therefore tends to be a good gauge of the manufacturing sector and fluctuations in commodities prices. In addition to the headline figure that shows monthly changes in prices for finished goods, the U.S. Bureau of Labor Statistics (BLS) provides data on the prices of goods at different states of production, specifically intermediate and crude goods. More than 9,000 PPIs for products are released each month.
Survey methodology: Each month the BLS collects data from approximately 500 manufacturing and mining industries on over 10,000 specific products and product categories at three stages of the production process: crude, intermediate, and finished. To grasp what happens at these three stages, one can think about the production of a shirt. In this example the crude good would be cotton from the field, the intermediate good would be cotton yarn, and the finished good would be the shirt. The prices on goods at the crude and intermediate stages of production are called *pipeline numbers* since they hint at price changes in finished goods in future months. For most items in the PPI, establishments report their selling prices for the Tuesday of the week containing the thirteenth of the month. This means that the PPI report can be slow to capture the most current developments. That is why it is important for market observers to follow commodities futures prices closely to stay abreast of the most recent developments. As with the consumer price index (CPI), the BLS assigns weights to the surveyed products and adjusts its findings for quality changes and seasonality.
Key components of the report: Because of their predictive value, the indexes for crude and intermediate goods are important to watch. *Core intermediate prices*, which are intermediate prices excluding food and energy, have a very good correlation to the data on finished goods, the headline number that is so widely followed. An investor should look at the details of the report for indications on how various sectors of the economy are performing. For example, sharp declines in the price of copper, a metal widely used for industrial purposes, indicate that the manufacturing sector is weak. It is also important to track prescription drug costs. This component has a high correlation with trends in overall health-care costs, which are key factors in the cost of labor and, hence, economy-wide inflation pressures. One

component that has historically had a large bearing on the PPI report is the automobile component, owing to difficulties the BLS has in adjusting for the introduction of new models and for different-timed incentive programs. The Cash-for-Clunkers program was a big influence in 2009. Tobacco products have also had a large impact on time, as have the prices of various commodities including energy prices.

How it affects the market: The PPI report is important, but it has not always grabbed the market's attention. First, much greater attention is paid to the government's report on consumer prices. While a company's prices going up is not something to ignore, the ability of that company to pass the prices on to the consumer is of far more interest to the markets. When the PPI release date follows the CPI release date, attention paid to the PPI is muted even further. However, the credit crisis and associated government response has heightened inflationary concerns, which has increased attention paid to all measures of inflation. Thus, the PPI has recently seen a resurgence of popularity. As a result, the PPI does not have a large impact on the market, but the report is important nonetheless, particularly in light of the bond market's sensitivity to any and all data that speak to inflation trends.

What it means to you: Keeping in mind that inflation trends tend to lag the economy, the PPI should be used in tandem with other inflation indicators to assess the likely direction of interest rates. With interest rates at historically low levels, any emergence of inflationary pressures in the economy is likely to garner increased attention as the Federal Reserve normalizes its monetary policy. For consumers, tracking the PPI can provide insights on price trends for many goods frequently purchased.

PRODUCTIVITY AND COSTS

Source: U.S. Bureau of Labor Statistics
Web address for report: www.bls.gov/news.release/prod2.toc.htm
Release date: Usually within 40 days of the close of the reference period
Time: 8:30 a.m. ET
Report coverage: Labor productivity and costs in the calendar quarter before the report's release
Description of report: The productivity report measures the productivity of the American workforce. In technical terms, labor productivity is the ratio of the output of goods and services to the labor hours devoted to the production of that output. The U.S. Bureau of Labor Statistics (BLS) has been studying output per hour in individual industries since the 1800s: in 1898 a study titled "Hand and Machine Labor" provided compelling evidence of

the savings in labor resulting from mechanization in the latter part of the nineteenth century. Advances in productivity are extremely important to the economy. The more productive workers are, the more their earnings are likely to increase. Advances in productivity increase the national standard of living because they enable workers to produce more goods and services without having to increase labor time. Advances in productivity keep inflation low by keeping a lid on the labor costs required to produce goods and services. The productivity report provides data on the productivity of workers in the major sectors of business, nonfarm business, and nonfinancial corporations, along with the subsectors of durable and nondurable goods manufacturing. Investors and policy makers closely follow productivity trends to gauge the long-term health of the economy. Annual growth in productivity has averaged roughly 2.3 percent over the last 20 years, but it has grown more rapidly in recent years, at a 2.7 percent pace in the 10 years ended December 2009.

Survey methodology: The quarterly data on productivity and costs are estimated by using data on output, hours worked, and compensation costs compiled by a variety of sources. Output data are provided by the U.S. Bureau of Economic Analysis (BEA) and the Census Bureau of the Department of Commerce, the U.S. Bureau of Labor Statistics (BLS), and the Federal Reserve Board. Data on compensation and hours are provided by the Bureau of Labor Statistics and the Bureau of Economic Analysis. Productivity is calculated by comparing labor output to labor input, measured as hours at work. The primary source for data on output is the data on the real gross domestic product prepared by the BEA. The primary source for the data on labor input is the BLS Current Employment Statistics (CES) program. Unit labor costs are calculated by relating hourly compensation to output per hour. To assure reliability, the BLS revises the data as more complete information becomes available. Data on average weekly hours at work for several workers is obtained from the Current Population Survey (conducted and issued by the BLS and the Census Bureau); the CES; and the BLS National Compensation Survey (NCS).

Key components of the report: The details of the productivity report take a backseat to the headlines. The headline data, which include the quarterly change in nonfarm business productivity and unit labor costs, are essentially the crux of the report. This is a bit different from what happens with most other economic reports, where the headlines often are distorted by the details. One key detail in the productivity report is the breakdown by industry of quarterly changes in productivity and costs. It is helpful, for instance, to observe the data on the manufacturing sector, where details on the durable and nondurable goods sectors are included. Also included in the report are details for each of the covered industries on quarterly changes in productivity, output, hours, hourly compensation, real hourly compensation, and unit labor costs. All quarterly changes are expressed as percentage changes at a seasonally adjusted annual rate.

How it affects the market: As a quarterly release, investors have scant chances to react to productivity data. One might think this would sharpen the reaction to the data, yet the reaction is difficult to discern for a few reasons. First, the markets are interested mostly in long-term trends in productivity, and therefore they do not react much to the quarterly changes unless they feel that there has been a trend change. Second, productivity trends tend to last many years, rendering short-term trends less meaningful to investors. In fact, some studies suggest that productivity cycles last about 20 years in duration. These long productivity cycles have been sparked by innovations such as the automobile, air travel, and the computer. The most recent productivity cycle is believed to have started in 1995, when more widespread use of technology began to significantly lift productivity. It is easy to understand how innovations can raise productivity levels for many years, especially since it usually takes years for enhanced applications of these innovations to develop. The bond market benefits when productivity advances because such advances help keep unit labor costs in check, reducing pressures on businesses to raise prices.

What it means to you: Most people endeavor to be more productive in everything they do and therefore can relate to the concept of productivity as it pertains to the business world. Like individuals, businesses want to produce more in the same or a shorter amount of time. A good sense of productivity trends is an essential element in the formulation of long-term investment strategies. An accelerating productivity trend normally is associated with sustained economic growth, rising corporate profits, low inflation, and low bond yields.

RETAIL SALES

Source: U.S. Census Bureau of the Department of Commerce
Web address for report: www.census.gov/retail
Release date: Usually nine working days after the end of the previous month
Time: 8:30 a.m. ET
Report coverage: Sales through the end of the previous month
Description of report: The retail sales report, one of the most watched data points released each month, provides an indication of sales by retail companies such as department stores, automobile dealers, clothing stores, and

drugstores. Retail sales data contain important information about the pace of consumer spending. Data from the retail sales report, with some adjustments, are used in the computation of quarterly data on the GDP. Retail sales, which were $356 billion in January 2010, are considered a leading indicator for the economy because sales tend to lead production.

Survey methodology: Each month, the Census Bureau mails out questionnaires to about 5,000 firms with survey respondents accounting for about 65 percent of the national sales estimate. Not every firm is surveyed, but several hundred firms, owing to their large size, are sent surveys every month. The report compensates by evaluating only those companies that complete the questionnaire in two successive months while making no adjustments to previous data if a company responded, for example, in January and February but not March. The data then are adjusted to account for seasonal fluctuations. Revisions to the data at the next release date account for information received since the release of the prior report. Revisions tend to be large owing to the fact that only about 25 percent of responses are received and processed in time for the advance estimate.

Key components of the report: The automobile component is important but also is volatile; that is why the Commerce Department also releases data on retail sales excluding automobiles. Nevertheless, one should not overlook this key component, which accounts for almost 20 percent of all retail sales. Strength or weakness in automobile sales can provide evidence of consumers' willingness to spend on big-ticket items and therefore hints at consumer confidence levels. Also important is the general merchandise component, which accounts for about 15 percent of all retail sales. This component is a gauge of consumer spending at department stores and warehouse clubs. One should look closely at sales at grocery stores given heightened concerns regarding food price inflation. Additionally, electronics stores have been gaining importance. Data on restaurant sales and the like speak to trends in discretionary spending.

How it affects the market: The retail sales report can have a large impact on the financial markets. Investors understand the broad implications of trends in consumer spending. The market response often is dictated by the large revisions that often are seen for the previous two months of data. An investor therefore should look closely at the revisions to the report before drawing conclusions based solely on the headline data.

What it means to you: You should use the retail sales report as a leading indicator of the economy. A strong pace of retail sales, for instance, should indicate to you that the economy is likely to grow strongly, helping risk assets to outperform other assets. It is especially important to watch the pace of retail sales during the holiday season, as it often sets the tone for the economy at the start of the new year. Moreover, if sales exceed or fall short of expectations, this tends to affect the manufacturing sector because of the impact of the sales pace on retail inventories.

U.S. TRADE BALANCE

Source: U.S. Census Bureau and U.S. Bureau of Economic Analysis
Web address for report: www.bea.doc.gov/bea/rels.htm
Release date: Generally around the third week of every month
Time: 8:30 a.m. ET
Report coverage: U.S. trade in goods and services two calendar months before the release of the report
Description of report: The trade report provides information on U.S. international trade in goods and services. The report contains details on the dollar value of the goods and services exchanged between the United States and its trading partners and a breakdown of that trade by expenditure category. The report is a useful barometer of the health of the global economy and its impact on the U.S. economy and potential impact on foreign exchange rates. The report is also a useful gauge of the impact of changes in U.S. trade policy, and therefore it can be used in the political arena to galvanize opinion for or against various trade policies. The details of the trade data can be used to assess the outlook for various sectors of the economy, particularly the manufacturing sector. U.S. exports represent about 8 percent of the GDP, while imports total around 12 percent.
Survey methodology: The trade report requires data from many sources. This partly explains why the U.S. Bureau of Economic Analysis (BEA) and the U.S. Census Bureau jointly produce the report. The BEA estimates the merchandise trade balance by using data compiled by the Census Bureau and the Department of Commerce. The data recorded include the movement of goods across U.S. customs boundaries but not always the change in ownership: the BEA assumes that goods moving across boundaries change ownership; in other words, it assumes that physical possession indicates actual ownership. This applies even if goods are shipped between U.S. firms and their affiliates abroad. Examples of sources of data are the Commerce Department's shippers' declaration forms filed at the point of export, surveys conducted by the U.S. Travel and Tourism Administration, and the Treasury Department's International Capital Reporting system. Services are recorded when performed. Investment income is recorded on an accrual basis regardless of when the income is paid or received. Transactions denominated in foreign currencies are reported in their dollar equiva-

lents, generally converted at the exchange rates prevailing at the time of the transaction.

Key components of the report: The details on the monthly percentage changes in exports and imports are followed closely. The data on U.S. exports are a helpful gauge of the extent of U.S. integration into the growth of the world economy, and the data on U.S. imports provide clues as to the strength of domestic demand. Other important details include the country-by-country breakdown of activity. There tends to be a great deal of focus on trading activity with Japan, China, and Mexico. Roughly 45 percent of all U.S. exports are capital goods. *Capital goods* include many of the goods in which the United States is highly competitive, including semiconductors, computer accessories, medicinal equipment, and industrial engines. The fact that so many U.S. goods are capital goods is good news for the U.S. economy since those goods are likely to remain in demand even when the global economy slows. In the times ahead, investors will be watching the U.S. trade data to see if global imbalances in savings and consumption are resolved in a way that creates balance in the world's economic and financial situation.

How it affects the market: As with the Census Bureau's report on business inventories, the trade report has the greatest impact when investors are formulating their views about upcoming data on the GDP because the trade data are often one of the last pieces of information forecasters need to finish their number crunching on the GDP report. The market reaction to the trade report often is muted by the market's informed sense of the many messages contained in the report. For example, trends in exports are manifested in U.S. manufacturing data. Only on rare occasion does the trade report serve as a catalyst for volatility in the foreign exchange market. There is potential for impact in future years if the U.S. trade balance continues to shrink at a time when (if?) the United States puts its fiscal house in order. In recent years, investors have recognized that currency values are dictated by a variety of factors, including capital flows, fiscal policy, and foreign direct investment.

What it means to you: Investors can use the trade report to assess global imbalances and to gauge the competitiveness of U.S. businesses. An accurate assessment of where the U.S. stands in the global economy can help investors make more informed investment decisions.

ENDNOTES

Chapter 1

1. John Duca, Danielle DiMartino, and Jessica Renier, "Fed Confronts Financial Crisis by Expanding Its Role as Lender of Last Resort," *Economic Letter—Insights from the Federal Reserve Bank of Dallas*, February/March 2009.
2. Taylor Nadauld and Shane Sherlund, "The Role of the Securitization Process in the Expansion of Subprime Credit," Finance and Economics Discussion Series, Federal Reserve Board, April 2009.

Chapter 2

1. Securities Industry and Financial Markets Association (SIFMA) and the Federal Reserve's Flow of Funds Statistics.
2. Federal Reserve. See testimony by David Wilcox, the deputy director of the Federal Reserve's Division of Research and Statistics, before the Committee on Financial Services, House of Representatives, May 20, 2009.
3. Securities Industry and Financial Markets Association (SIFMA).
4. Treasury Department, "Treasury Issues Update on Status of Support for Housing Programs," press release, December 24, 2009.
5. Michael Fleming and Bruce Mizrach, *The Microstructure of a U.S. Treasury ECN: The BrokerTec Platform*, Federal Reserve Bank of New York Staff Reports, July 2009.

Chapter 4

1. Kenneth Garbade, "The Emergence of 'Regular and Predictable' as a Treasury Debt Management Strategy," Federal Reserve Bank of New York *Economic Policy Review*, vol. 13, no. 1, March 2007.

2. Margaret McConnell, Richard Peach, and Alex Al-Haschimi, "After the Refinancing Boom: Will Consumers Scale Back Their Spending?" Federal Reserve Bank of New York *Current Issues in Economics and Finance*, vol. 9, no. 12, December 2003.

Chapter 6

1. Excerpt taken from the Minutes to the Federal Open Market Committee's (FOMC) December 15–16, 2009, meeting.

2. Alan Greenspan, testimony before the Committee on Banking, Housing, and Urban Affairs, U.S. Senate, February 16, 2005.

3. Alan Greenspan, statement before the Subcommittee on Economic Growth and Credit Formulation of the Committee on Banking, Finance, and Urban Affairs, U.S. House of Representatives, February 22, 1994.

Chapter 7

1. Joseph G. Haubrich and Ann M. Dombrosky, "Predicting Real Growth Using the Yield Curve," Federal Reserve Bank of Cleveland *Economic Review*, vol. 32, no. 1, March 1996.

2. Arturo Estrella and Frederic S. Mishkin, "The Yield Curve as a Predictor of U.S. Recessions," Federal Reserve Bank of New York *Current Issues in Economics and Finance*, vol. 2, no. 7, June 1996.

3. Arturo Estrella and Mary Trubin, "The Yield Curve as a Leading Indicator: Some Practical Issues," Federal Reserve Bank of New York *Current Issues in Economics and Finance*, vol. 12, no. 5, July/August 2006.

Chapter 12

1. Moody's, "Corporate Default and Recovery Rates, 1920–2008," Moody's Global Credit Policy, February 2009.

2. Song Han and Hao Zhou, "Effects of Liquidity on the Nondefault Component of Corporate Yield Spreads: Evidence from Intraday Transactions Data," Finance and Economics Discussion Series, Federal Reserve Board, March 2008.

INDEX

Note: Page numbers followed by *f* refer to figures and those followed by *t* refer to tables.

A bonds, 301
AA bonds, 299*f,* 301, 307
AAA bonds, 58, 108, 298–300, 299*f,* 304, 307
Academicians, 38
Accrued interest, 73
Afghanistan, 127
Agency discount notes, 66
Agency securities (*see* Government agency securities)
Aggregate duration surveys, 264–267, 265*f*
Aggregate positions, 255
Aggregate price sensitivity, 77
Agricultural products, 275
AIG (American Insurance Group), 301
American Municipal Bond Assurance Company (AMBAC), 108
American Recovery and Reinvestment Act of 2009, 107
AMLF (Asset-Backed Commercial Paper Money Market Mutual Fund Liquidity Facility), 171
Announcement effect, 305–306
Asia, 12–13
(*See also* China; Japan)
Asian financial crisis, 130, 209, 227, 306
Asset allocation, 290
Asset diversification, 15–17, 16*f,* 96, 111, 118*f*
Asset-Backed Commercial Paper Money Market Mutual Fund Liquidity Facility (AMLF), 171
Asset-backed securities, 35, 171
Asset-liability management, 317–318
Assets:
prices of, 150
reserve, 125, 125*f*
risk, 24

Auctions:
coupon securities, 85–87, 86*t*
discount securities, 84
of Treasuries, 282
and Treasury supply, 194–195
Automobile industry, 18–19, 153–154, 329

B bonds, 299*f,* 302
BABs (*see* Build America Bonds)
Bank of Japan (BOJ), 158, 241
Banking institutions, 140
(*See also* Banks)
Bankruptcy, 95, 122, 334
Banks:
commercial, 51, 205*f*
credit issued by, 233*f*
and economic growth, 188, 204
interbank market, 117
investment by, 185
lending by, 212
loans and leases at, 205*f*
securities holdings at, 205*f*
and yield spreads, 269, 270
(*See also* Federal Reserve)
Barclays Capital Aggregate Bond Index, 265, 267–268
Basel Capital Accord, 32
Basis point value (BPV), 73–74
Basis points, 73–75, 84
Basis risk, 290
BB bonds, 299*f,* 302
BBB bonds, 299*f,* 302, 304
BEA (*see* U.S. Bureau of Economic Analysis)
Bear markets, 227, 232–236, 241
Bear Stearns, 31
Bearer bonds, 68

Below-investment-grade bonds, 122, 298, 299*t*, 302–303
  (*See also* Junk bonds)
Benchmark(s):
  bond market as, 4
  short-term interest rates as, 134
  Treasury securities as, 39, 87, 98, 100, 267–269
Benchmark Bills, 100
Benchmark Bonds, 100
Benchmark Notes, 100
Benchmark yield levels, 246–247
Benefits (employment), 368–370, 383, 390
Bernanke, Ben, 147, 161, 208
Bid-ask spread, 56–58, 57*t*, 61, 130, 136
Bid/cover ratios, 24
Black-Scholes model, 283
Bloomberg, 283
BLS (*see* U.S. Bureau of Labor Statistics)
BOJ (*see* Bank of Japan)
Bond basis, 281–282, 282*t*
Bond market:
  complexities of, 63
  corporate bonds in, 45–48
  and credit cards, 8–9
  and crises, 10–15
  in current economy, 28–29
  and equity risks, 15–17
  government agency securities in, 48–53
  historical influence of, 28
  impact of, on economy, 1–3, 17–22
  and interest rate–sensitive sectors, 18–22
  liquidity in, 55–61
  mortgage-backed securities in, 53–55
  municipal securities in, 43–45
  and politics, 21, 23–24
  primary dealers in, 30–33
  role of entrepreneurs in, 27
  role of U.S. government in, 24–25
  size of, 34–36
  specialization in, 29–30
  types of securities in, 36–39
  U.S. Treasury securities in, 39–42
Bonds, 63–79
  accrued interest, 73
  basis points, 73–75
  callable, 68–69
  coupon rate, 68
  current yield, 70
  defining, 65–67
  duration, 75–78
  indenture, 67
  investing in, 64

par value, 72–73
put provisions, 70
yield-to-call and yield-to-worst, 69–70
yield-to-maturity, 71–72
(*See also specific headings*)
Boston Tea Party, 324
Bottom-up investing, 347
BPV (basis point value), 73–74
Breakeven rate, 90, 225, 227
Brokerage firms, 267
Broker-dealers, 29, 67, 131, 136
Brokers, 48
Build America Bonds (BABs), 43, 107–108
Bull markets, 2, 23, 232, 241
Bush, George H. W., 23, 331–335
Bush, George W., 23, 337–338
Business inventories report, 351–353
Business outlook survey, 391–392
Buyouts, 122

C bonds, 299*f*, 302
Calculators, 72
Call options, 257–261, 260*f*, 280, 283
Call premium, 68
Call provision, 97
Call risk, 68–69, 128–130
  (*See also* Prepayment risk)
Callable bonds, 68–70, 77, 129, 130, 315
Capacity (credit ratings), 310
Capital:
  competition for, 194
  and corporate bonds, 92
  formation of, 20–21
  preservation of, 313–314
  and primary dealer requirements, 32
Capital gain, 106
Capital goods, 399
Capital spending:
  and Basel Capital Accord, 32
  in durable goods orders report, 364
  and Fed's interest rate changes, 153–154
  in gross domestic product report, 375
  impact of bond market on, 19
Carter, Jimmy, 21, 327–330
Cash flow, 88, 89*f*, 134, 305, 307, 315
Cash management bills, 83–84
Cash price, 281
Cash-for-Clunkers program, 394
Catalysts (market change), 255–257, 260
CBOT (*see* Chicago Board of Trade)
CC bonds, 299*f*, 302
CCC bonds, 299*f*, 302
CDOs (*see* Collateralized debt obligations)

CDS (*see* Credit default swaps)
Central Bank Liquidity Swaps, 171
Central banks, 324
  (*See also* Federal Reserve)
CFTC (*see* Commodity Futures Trading Commission)
Character (credit ratings), 310
Chicago Board of Trade (CBOT), 258, 275, 276, 279, 281, 283
Chicago Mercantile Exchange (CME), 276, 283
Chicago Purchasing Managers index, 353–354
China, 25, 125, 242, 243
Clinton, Bill, 23, 206, 335–337
CME (*see* Chicago Mercantile Exchange)
CME Group, 258
CMOs (collateralized mortgage obligations), 103
Cold War, 332
Collateral (credit ratings), 310–311
Collateral trust bonds, 95
Collateralized corporate bonds, 94–95
Collateralized debt obligations (CDOs), 293, 294
Collateralized mortgage obligations (CMOs), 103
Commercial banks, 51, 205*f*
Commercial Paper Funding Facility (CPFF), 171
Commercial paper market, 347, 348*f*
Commercial traders, 261–262, 280
Commitments of Traders (COT) report, 261–264, 278, 280–281
Commodity Futures Trading Commission (CFTC), 261, 278, 280–281
Commodity prices, 228
Competition, 309
Competitive bids, 85, 87
Concessions, 240–241
Conference Board, 357, 379, 380
Conforming mortgages, 104
Conservatorship, 49, 51, 98
Constant prepayment rate (CPR), 238
Construction spending report, 354–356
Consumer confidence index, 357–358
Consumer credit report, 358–360
Consumer debt, 5
Consumer price index (CPI), 145, 164*f*, 199, 201, 226, 360–361
Consumer price index for all urban consumers (CPI-U), 88, 91, 225
Consumer sentiment index, 361–363
Consumer spending patterns, 357

Consumption, 5, 6*f*
Contracts:
  enforcing terms of, 66
  Eurodollar, 162, 276
  forward, 134–135
  futures, 131, 276, 286
  options, 131
  Treasury, 276
Conversion factor, 281
Converted futures price, 281
Convertible bonds, 48
Convexity, 76, 115
Core intermediate prices, 393
Corporate bonds, 92–98, 136
  in bond market, 35, 45–48, 46*f*
  collateralized, 94–95
  credit risk with, 95–96, 185
  defined, 92
  gains in prices of, 10
  indentures for, 97, 98
  and insurance, 206
  lien position of, 96–97, 97*t*
  process for purchase of, 94
  sector risk with, 127
  selection of, 93
  yield spread between Treasuries and, 271–272
Corporate default rates, 304*t*
Corporate takeovers, 122–123
Corporations, 21, 45, 65
Cost of goods sold, 93
COT report (*see* Commitments of Traders report)
Counterparty risk, 269, 270, 288, 289*f*
Countertrend trades, 165
Country risk, 315
Countrywide Securities, 31
Coupon bonds, 68
Coupon rate(s):
  defined, 68
  and duration, 76
  on floaters, 134
  high, owning bonds with, 314
  and reinvestment risk, 114, 115
  on Treasury inflation-protected securities, 225
Coupon securities, 84–87
Covenants, 97, 98, 311
  (*See also* Indentures)
CPFF (Commercial Paper Funding Facility), 171
CPI (*see* Consumer price index)
CPI-U (*see* Consumer price index for all urban consumers)
CPR (constant prepayment rate), 238

Credit:
availability of, 3
bank, 233*f*
and bond market opportunities, 3
consumer credit report, 358–360
and corporate bonds, 93
demand for, 34
and state of economy, 18
Credit analyses, 309
Credit cards, 8–9, 9*f*, 11
Credit crisis, 2
Credit default swaps (CDS), 66, 320
Credit programs (Federal Reserve), 170–173
Credit quality, 192–194
Credit rating agencies, 296–298
defined, 297
and financial crisis, 306
methodology of, 307–311, 308*f*, 309*t*
SEC report on, 294
trust in, 293
Credit Rating Agency Reform Act of 2006, 297
Credit ratings, 293–312
accuracy of, 293–294
of below-investment-grade bonds, 298,
299*t*, 302–303
and corporate bond yields, 95–96
determining, 307–311
effects of, 306–307
of investment-grade bonds, 298, 299*t*,
300–302
rating agencies, 296–298
and rating announcements, 305–306
risk with, 132, 295–296
system for, 298–300
and yield on bonds, 303–305
Credit risk, 131–133
with corporate bonds, 95–96
and credit ratings, 295, 296, 307–309
with government-sponsored enterprises, 49
and risk premium, 180
sovereign, 242–245, 244*f*, 245*f*
Credit spreads, 126*f*, 136, 152, 160, 198, 283
Creditworthiness, 184, 193
Cross-hedging, 136
Currency performance, and real yields, 207
Currency risk, 17, 134–135, 315–316
Current Employment Statistics Survey (*see*
"Establishment survey")
Current Population Survey (*see* "Household
survey")
Current yield, 70
Curve duration, 77–78, 316–317
Cyclical trends, 232–236, 234*f*

Data, economic (*see* Economic data)
Dealers, 48
(*See also* Broker-dealers)
Debentures, 95
Debt:
composition of, 305
corporate, 38
credit card, 8
and financial crisis, 10, 11*f*
and fiscal policy, 189
fixed-rate debt obligation, 129–130
household, 5, 6*f*
mortgage, 53
nonfinancial sector, 11, 12*f*
sovereign, 315
U.S. Treasury, 40, 41, 41*f*, 84, 85*f*
Debt securities, 3
Debt-service coverage ratio, 107
Debt-to-gross domestic product ratio:
of industrialized vs. emerging market nations, 126*f*
of Japan, 241
and sovereign credit risk, 244
of United States, 24, 25*f*
Deep fundamentals, 232
(*See also* Secular trends)
Default risk (*see* Credit risk)
Defaults, 66, 296
Defense spending, 332, 364
Deflation, 88, 157, 158, 204, 211–212, 223
De-leveraging:
and consumer credit report, 359
and primary dealers, 33
as structural adjustment, 212
and yield curve, 180
Demographics, 50, 51
Depository Institutions Deregulation and
Monetary Control Act of 1980, 140
Developed nations, 124–125, 126*f*, 243
Developing nations, 124–125, 126*f*
Diffusion indexes, 354, 385, 386, 392
Direct-payment Build America Bonds,
107–108
Discount bonds, 314
Discount Notes program, 101
Discount securities, 83–84
Disinflation, 204
Diversification:
asset (*see* Asset diversification)
benefits of, 96
with junk bonds, 303
for reducing credit risks, 133
risk (*see* Risk diversification)

Dollar value of a 01 (DV01), 73–74
Dombrosky, Ann M., 179
Dot-com bubble, 14, 127, 253
Double-barreled municipal bonds, 107
Dow Jones Industrial Average, 13, 119, 120, 182
Dudley, William, 169
Durable goods orders report, 363–365
Duration, 75–78
    and aggregate duration surveys, 264–267, 265f
    and Federal Reserve, 41
    of high coupon bonds, 115
    and interest rate forecasting, 240
    and market risk, 113
    soft, 133
Duration dollars, 74–75
Duration management, 290
Duration-neutral transactions, 74
Dutch auctions, 86
DV01 (dollar value of a 01), 73–74

Early redemption, 69, 70
Earnings data, 366–369
ECI (employment cost index), 368–370
Economic crises (*see Financial crises*)
Economic data, 341–350
    and economic growth, 228–229
    and flexibility, 346–347
    forecasting, 344–345
    frequency of economic reports, 341–343
    and survey methodologies, 348–349
    and top-down investing, 347–348
    (*See also specific economic data*)
Economic growth:
    as factor in yield curve, 188–189
    impact of bond market on, 19
    and inflation, 223
    in interest rate forecasting, 228–232
    and real yields, 204–206, 205f
    and spread products, 160
Economic Recovery Tax Act of 1981, 330
Economic reports, 341–343, 342f
    (*See also specific reports*)
Economic trends, 374, 379
    (*See also* Cyclical trends; Secular trends)
Economy:
    impact of bond market on, 1–3, 17–22
    pessimism about, 252, 261
    and trading volume in Treasuries, 42
Effective duration, 75
Election campaign of 1980, 329–333
Electronic systems, 30, 60
Emerging markets, 124–125, 126f

Emotions, 253–255
Employment Act of 1946, 140
Employment cost index (ECI), 368–370
Employment report, 229, 346, 365–368
Endowment style portfolios, 118
Entrepreneurs, 27
Equilibrium real yields, 210
Equipment, 20
Equipment trust certificates, 95
Equity indexes, 119
Equity investors, 181
Equity market:
    and financial crises, 14
    and fixed-income securities, 117
    and issuance of corporate bonds, 47
    odd lots in, 59
    ratings systems for, 295
Equity portfolios, 9
Equity risks, 15–17, 111
Essential-purpose revenue bonds, 107
"Establishment survey" (Current Employ-ment Statistics Survey), 365–366, 395
Estrella, Arturo, 179, 182
Euro, 191
Eurodollar contracts, 162, 276
Eurodollar futures, 284, 286–289
Eurodollar options, 258
Event risk, 116–127
    defined, 116
    and international financial events, 124–126
    and international political/military events, 125–127
    and shifts in market sentiment, 123–124
    systemic risk, 117–122
    takeover risk, 122–123
Excess capacity, 231
Existing home sales report, 370–372
Expectations:
    of future rate actions, 284–286
    of future volatility, 282–284
    inflation (*see* Inflation expectations)
    market, 284–285
Expectations theory, 184–185
Extreme market sentiment, 251–252, 255–257, 266

Factory orders report, 372–374
Fair market price, 57–59
Fannie Mae (Federal National Mortgage Association):
    debt obligations of, 98
    establishment of, 100
    and financial crisis, 49

Fannie Mae (Federal National Mortgage
    Association) (*Continued*):
    mortgage-backed securities issued by, 54
    operations of, 100–101
    and pass-through securities, 102
    and put/call ratio, 259
Farm Credit Financial Assistance Corpora-
    tion, 99
Farm Credit System, 99
Farmer Mac (Federal Agricultural Mortgage),
    99
Fat-tail distribution curve, 116
Fat-tail events, 119*f*, 120*t*
Fear, 283
Federal Agricultural Mortgage, 99
Federal Farm Credit Bank System, 99
Federal Financing Bank (FFB), 98
Federal funds futures, 284–286
Federal funds rate:
    expectations of future rate actions, 285
    and Federal Reserve, 155–157
    lowering of, 146
    in technical analysis, 247
    yield spread between LIBOR and, 269–271,
        270*f*, 271*f*
    yield spread between T-notes and, 267–269
    zero-bound problem with, 211
Federal Home Loan Bank (FHLB), 99, 101
Federal Home Loan Mortgage Corporation
    (*see* Freddie Mac)
Federal Housing Finance Agency (FHFA),
    48, 49
Federal National Mortgage Association (*see*
    Fannie Mae)
Federal Open Market Committee (FOMC),
    142, 143, 146–149, 167, 284, 285
Federal Reserve, 139–174, 207–208, 219
    collection of data by, 48
    confidence in actions of, 161–166
    consumer credit report by, 358, 359
    and corporate bonds, 46
    credit and liquidity programs of, 170–173
    duties of, 140–141
    federal funds futures, 284–286
    and financial crises, 9–10, 12–14, 139
    FOMC, 142–143, 146–149, 167, 284, 285
    and Great Depression, 325–326
    Hawk/Dove voting scale in, 168, 169*f*
    industrial production and capacity utiliza-
        tion report, 381–382
    and inflation expectations, 190
    and interest rates, 3, 4, 6–8, 17, 73, 123, 128,
        145, 152–153, 159, 160, 181

and ISM report on business, 387
    key phrases of, 168–170
    and liquidity, 56
    and long-term interest rates, 222
    and market sentiment, 262, 263, 269
    monetary policy of, 140, 143–146, 161–163,
        217–222
    and money supply, 144*t*, 146, 149–150
    and nominal interest rates, 155–156
    officials in, 142–143, 142*t*, 167
    and performance of spread products,
        160–161
    and politics, 23, 324, 333–335
    primary dealer designation requirements, 31
    and primary dealers, 30, 32
    reading speeches given by, 167–168
    and real interest rates, 156–158, 210
    and real yields, 207–208
    role of, 139
    and September 11th terrorist attacks, 14–15
    structure of, 141–143
    tracking flow of funds by, 38–39
    and trading volume in Treasuries, 42
    transmission effects of, 150–155
    and yield curve, 158–159, 179, 180, 186, 187
    (*See also* Federal funds rate)
Federal Reserve Act of 1913, 139, 140, 170
Federal Reserve Bank of New York, 30, 147
Federal Reserve Bank of Philadelphia, 391,
    392
Federal Reserve banks, 141, 141*f*, 143, 168
Federal Reserve Board, 300, 395
Federal taxes, 105
FFB (Federal Financing Bank), 98
FGIC (Financial Guaranty Insurance Com-
    pany), 108
FHFA (*see* Federal Housing Finance Agency)
FHLB (*see* Federal Home Loan Bank)
Fibonacci analysis, 247–248
Financial calculators, 72
Financial conditions, 151
Financial crisis(-es):
    of 1998, 60–61
    of 2007, 12–14, 42, 116, 208, 326
    Asian, 130, 209, 227, 306
    and bond market, 10–15
    and credit ratings, 306
    Federal Reserve's role in, 9–10, 12–14, 139
    and government agency securities, 48
    increasing monetary base in, 186
    and primary dealers, 32
    and risk, 111
    (*See also* specific financial crises)

Financial Guaranty Insurance Company (FGIC), 108
Financial Industry Regulatory Authority (FINRA), 45, 48, 58
Financial information providers, 72
Financial products, 35, 275
Financial Security Assurance (FSA), 108
Financing Corporation, 99
FINRA (*see* Financial Industry Regulatory Authority)
First-mortgage bonds, 95
Fiscal policy, 189–190
Fitch Ratings, 96, 296
Fixed-income securities, 33, 66, 117, 194, 218
Fixed-rate debt obligation, 129–130
Fleming, Michael, 57
Flexibility, 346–347
Flight to quality, 192, 193*f*
Floaters, 134
Floating-rate debt obligation, 130
FOMC (*see* Federal Open Market Committee)
Ford, Gerald, 323, 327, 328, 330
Forecasters, 38
Forecasting, 178–180, 344–345
  (*See also* Interest rate forecasting)
Foreclosures, 5*f*, 334, 355
Foreign currency, 134–135, 172
Foreign exchange market, 118, 135
Foreign investors, 51, 191, 242–245, 244*f*, 245*f*
Foreign purchases, 35, 35*f*
Forward contracts, 134, 135
Forward rates, 218, 284
Freddie Mac (Federal Home Loan Mortgage Corporation):
  debt obligations of, 98
  and financial crisis, 49
  as government-sponsored enterprise, 100
  mortgage-backed securities issued by, 54
  operations of, 101
  and put/call ratio, 259
Free trade, 275
Friedman, Milton, 133
FSA (Financial Security Assurance), 108
Full Employment and Balanced Growth Act of 1978, 140
Fundamental analysis, 236, 237, 245
Future rate actions, 284–286
Future volatility, 282–284
Futures contracts, 131, 276, 286
Futures market, 275–291
  Eurodollar, 286–289
  and expectations of future rate actions, 284–286
  and expectations of future volatility, 282–284
  futures contracts in, 276
  role of, 275
  and sovereign debt, 315
  tracking market sentiment using, 277–282
  and use of interest rate futures, 289–291
  use of technical analysis in, 246
Futures trading volume, 278, 279

Garbade, Kenneth, 82
GDP (*see* Gross domestic product)
GDP report (*see* Gross domestic product report)
General Motors, 82
General obligation (GO) bonds, 106–107
Ginnie Mae (Government National Mortgage Association), 11, 54, 100, 276
Globalization, 34–35
GNMA (*see* Ginnie Mae)
GO (general obligation) bonds, 106–107
Golden mean, 248
Government agency securities, 98–101
  in bond market, 48–53
  issued by government-sponsored enterprises, 98–99
  volume in, 51, 52*t*–53*t*
Government National Mortgage Association (*see* Ginnie Mae)
Government-sponsored enterprises (GSEs), 49–51, 98–99, 259
  (*See also specific enterprises*)
Gradualism, 145
Gramm-Leach-Bliley Act of 1999, 140
Great Depression, 100, 325–327
Greenspan, Alan, 14, 120–121, 145, 147, 159, 161, 165, 208, 333–335
Gross domestic product (GDP), 25*f*, 182*f*, 243, 332, 353
  (*See also* Debt-to-gross domestic product ratio)
Gross domestic product (GDP) report, 374–377, 399
Growth potential, 377
Growth trends, 93
GSEs (*see* Government-sponsored enterprises)
Guaranteed bonds, 95
Gulf War, 333, 334

Haubrich, Joseph G., 179
Hawk/Dove voting scale, 168, 169*f*
Hedge funds, 76, 120

Hedge risk, 135, 136
Hedging, 135, 136, 238–240, 290, 320
High-grade bonds, 96, 301
High-yield bonds (*see* Junk bonds)
Historical perspective, on real yields, 198–202, 201*f*
Homeownership:
    and deflation, 211
    and Federal Reserve, 163
    increases in, 50, 51*f*
Hoover, Herbert, 325, 326
Household debt, 5, 6*f*
"Household survey" (Current Population Survey), 365, 366
Housing market:
    and construction spending, 356
    existing home sales report, 370–372
    and Fed's interest rate changes, 153–154
    forecasting in, 345
    government agency securities' role in, 49–50, 99
    housing starts report, 377–379
    impact of bond market on, 19
    and market sentiment, 253
    and municipal bonds, 44
    new home sales report, 387–389
    and politics, 328–329
    and sector risk, 127
    (*See also* Mortgages)
Housing starts report, 377–379
Humphrey, Hubert, 82
Humphrey-Hawkins Act, 140, 161
Hygienes (bond trading), 64–65

Illiquid markets, 209
Illiquidity, 56
IMF (International Monetary Fund), 125
Implied volatility, 282, 283
Income, 314–315
Income growth, 20
Indentures:
    for corporate bonds, 97, 98
    and credit ratings, 308, 309, 311
    defined, 67
Indexation lag, 91
Industrial production and capacity utilization report, 381–382
Industries, 127, 319–320
Inflation:
    and consumer price index, 361
    and economic growth, 228, 231
    and employment cost index, 370
    fear of, 223

and Federal Reserve, 165
and gross domestic product report, 374
and politics, 326, 328–331, 333
and real yields, 201–203
(*See also* Deflation; Disinflation; Treasury inflation-protected securities)
Inflation accrual, 226
Inflation expectations:
    in interest rate forecasting, 222–228
    and long-term interest rates, 188
    real yields influenced by, 202–203
    tracking, 209–210
    and Treasury inflation-protected securities, 90
    and yield curve, 158–159, 190–192
Inflation risk, 133–134
Inflation-indexed bonds (*see* Treasury inflation-protected securities)
Inflation-linked securities (*see* Treasury inflation-protected securities)
Initial jobless claims report, 382–384
Innovation, 27
Institute for Supply Management (ISM):
    Chicago Purchasing Managers index, 353–354
    nonmanufacturing report, 343, 384–385
    report on business, 385–387
Institutional investors, 59
Insurance:
    and corporate bonds, 206
    for municipal bonds, 108
Intangibles, 216
Interbank market, 117
Interest:
    accrued, 73
    on pass-through securities, 102
    and yield-to-maturity, 71–72
Interest rate forecasting, 215–250
    and changes in market, 215
    economic growth in, 228–232
    incorporating intangibles in, 216
    inflation expectations in, 222–228
    monetary policy in, 217–222
    with real interest rates, 210
    secular vs. cyclical influences in, 232–236
    technical factors in, 236–249
Interest rate futures, 276–277, 289–291
Interest rate risk (*see* Market risk)
Interest rates:
    and construction spending, 355
    on credit cards, 8–9
    and duration, 75–76
    effects of changes in, 4–8

and Federal Reserve, 73, 123, 128, 145,
    152–153, 159, 160
on municipal bonds, 44
nominal, 155–156
and politics, 21, 23–24, 324, 327–339
and prepayment risk, 103–104
and put provision, 69
real, 156–158
and reinvestment risk, 114–115
setting of, 3–4
and state of economy, 17
and stock market, 9–15
on U.S. Treasury securities, 39
volatility of, 169
Interest rate-sensitive sectors, 18–22
Intermediate maturities, 66
International markets:
    and capital goods, 399
    financial events in, 124–126
    gaining exposure to, 315–316
    (*See also* Foreign exchange market)
International Monetary Fund (IMF), 125
International political/military events,
    125–127
Internet, 30, 345
Inventories, 351–353, 376
Inventory-to-sales (I/S) ratio, 352
Inverted yield curve, 177, 177*f*, 180–182, 185
Investment-grade bonds, 96, 122, 131, 298,
    299*t*, 300–302
Investors:
    equity, 181
    foreign, 51, 191, 242–245, 244*f*, 245*f*
    institutional, 59
    stock, 181
    types of, 236
Iraq, 127
I/S (inventory-to-sales) ratio, 352
ISM (*see* Institute for Supply Management)
Issuance:
    of bearer bonds, 68
    of corporate bonds, 46–47
    Treasury, 82–91

Japan, 158, 211, 241
Job creation, 20
Job growth, 23
Junk bonds:
    bid-ask spread of, 57
    credit ratings of, 302–303
    gains in prices of, 10
    and Lehman Brothers collapse, 124*f*
    marketability of, 307

and ratings, 299
risk premiums on, 180
yield of, 304

Labor differential, 358
Labor force growth, 229
Labor market, 357, 362, 365–370
Laddering, 318
Laissez-faire economics, 325, 326
Leading Economic Index (LEI), 179,
    379–380
Legal actions (contracts), 66
Legal reviews, 309
Legislative reforms, 139
Lehman Brothers, 31, 45, 117, 123, 124*f*
LEI (*see* Leading Economic Index)
Lending standards, 150, 151*f*
LIBOR (*see* London Interbank Offered Rate)
Lien position, 96–97, 97*t*
Liesman, Steve, 168
Limited-tax general obligation bonds, 107
Liquid market, 209
Liquidation preference theory, 185
Liquidity, 55–61
    in bond market, 38, 55–61
    and corporate bonds, 93
    defined, 130
    and financial crises, 13, 60–61
    as influence on real yields, 208–209
    and market sentiment, 269, 270
    measuring, 56–60
    preservation of, 313–314
    and primary dealers, 33
    and systemic risk, 117
    of Treasury market, 82
Liquidity events, 87
Liquidity premium, 87, 185
Liquidity programs (Federal Reserve),
    170–173
Liquidity risk, 17, 130–131
Liquidity trap, 210
Loans:
    in bond market, 3, 11
    and Federal Reserve, 141, 146
    repackaging of, 35
    subprime, 12
    (*See also* Mortgages)
London Interbank Offered Rate (LIBOR), 78
    and Federal Reserve, 172
    and futures market, 269–271, 270*f*, 271*f*,
        287–289, 287*f*, 289*f*
Long-Term Capital Management (LTCM),
    120–122, 130

Long-term interest rates:
  in bond market, 17
  and Federal Reserve, 140, 158, 159, 222
  and inflation expectations, 188
  and yield curve, 176–177, 187
Long-term maturities, 66, 115
LTCM (see Long-Term Capital Management)

Macaulay, Frederick, 76
Macaulay's duration, 76–77
Macro variables, 93–94
Management, and company's credit rating,
  306, 308
Manufacturing industry, 343, 366–367
Marginal tax rate, 106
Market (quote) depth:
  in bond market, 38, 58–59
  defined, 130
  and liquidity risk, 131
Market liquidity (see Liquidity)
Market risk, 113–114, 223, 295
Market segmentation theory, 185
Market sentiment, 251–273
  and aggregate duration surveys, 264–267
  and aggregate position tracking, 255
  as bond market factor, 237–238
  catalysts for reversal of, 255–257
  and Commitments of Traders report,
    261–264
  and event risk, 123–124
  extremes in, 251–255
  and futures market, 277–282
  put/call ratio for tracking, 257–261
  reliability of tracking, 251
  yield curve as gauge of, 178
  yield spreads for tracking, 267–272
Maturities:
  and curve duration, 317
  and real yield, 199
  and risk, 115–116, 130
  types of, 66
  of U.S. Treasury securities, 40–41, 41f
MBA (see Mortgage Bankers Association)
MBIA (Municipal Bond Insurance Association), 108
MBS (see Mortgage-backed securities)
Medical costs, 361
Merrill Lynch, 31
Military events, 125–127, 333, 334
Misery index, 330
Mishkin, Frederic S., 179, 182
Mizrach, Bruce, 57
MLS (multiple listing service), 371

MMIFF (Money Market Investor Funding
  Facility), 171–172
Modified duration, 77
Monetarism, 145
Monetary policy:
  as factor in yield curve, 186–188, 207
  Fed's implementation of, 140, 143–146,
    161–163
  in interest rate forecasting, 217–222, 217f
  and investment strategies, 134
  and issuance of corporate bonds, 46
  and market sentiment, 258, 263
  and politics, 338
  primary dealers and implementation of, 31
  and short-term interest rates, 177
  in weak economies, 193
Monetary Policy Report to Congress, 161, 162t
Money market, 93
Money market funds, 314
Money Market Investor Funding Facility
  (MMIFF), 171–172
Money supply, 144t, 146, 149–150
Monoline insurance companies, 108
Moody's Investor Services, 96, 131, 296–304
Mortgage Bankers Association (MBA), 239,
  372
Mortgage bonds, 95, 129
Mortgage pass-through securities, 102
Mortgage portfolios, 238
Mortgage refinancing index, 239f
Mortgage-backed securities (MBS), 101–104
  in bond market, 53–55
  collateralized mortgage obligations, 103
  conventional bonds vs., 102
  and credit ratings, 293
  hedging activity in, 238–240
  held by Fannie Mae and Freddie Mac, 49
  prepayment risks with, 78, 103–104
  and spread products, 161
  uncertain cash flows with, 315
  volume in, 54, 55
Mortgages:
  conforming, 104
  and Fannie Mae, 100
  and homeownership growth, 50
  interest rates on, 3, 4f
  market for, 42
  private-label, 54, 55f
  securitization of, 11
Moving averages, 247
Multiple listing service (MLS), 371
Municipal Bond Insurance Association
  (MBIA), 108

Municipal bonds, 104–108
  in bond market, 43–45
  Build America Bonds, 107–108
  defined, 104
  insurance for, 108
  issuance of, 65
  taxable equivalent yield on, 105–106
  types of, 106–107
Mutual funds, 133, 134, 137, 302

Nadauld, Taylor, 11
NAHB (*see* National Association of Home
  Builders)
NAR (*see* National Association of Realtors)
NASD (National Association of Securities
  Dealers), 48
Nasdaq, 182
National Association of Home Builders
  (NAHB), 19, 154, 356, 372, 388
National Association of Purchasing Manage-
  ment, 353
National Association of Realtors (NAR), 370,
  371
National Association of Securities Dealers
  (NASD), 48
National Governors Association, 44
Nationally recognized statistical rating orga-
  nization (NRSRO), 294, 297
Negative carry, 187, 220
Negative real interest rates, 210–212
Negative wealth effects, 151
Negatively sloped yield curve, 177–178
  (*See also* Inverted yield curve)
Net profit margin, 94
New home sales report, 387–389
New York Mercantile Exchange (NYMEX),
  276
New York Stock Exchange (NYSE)
  Euronext, 48
Noise (economic data), 349
Nominal interest rates, 155–156
Noncallable Benchmark Securities Program
  (Fannie Mae), 101
Noncommercial traders, 261–264, 263*f*,
  280–281
Noncompetitive bids, 85, 86
Nondefense capital good orders, 373
Nonfinancial sector debt, 11, 12*f*
Nonmanufacturing report, 384–385
Nonresidential fixed investment, 375, 376
Normal distribution curve, 116, 119*f*
Notes, 66, 100–101
  (*See also* Treasury notes)

NRSRO (*see* Nationally recognized statistical
  rating organization)
NYMEX (New York Mercantile Exchange),
  276
NYSE (New York Stock Exchange)
  Euronext, 48

OAS (option-adjusted spread), 78
Obama, Barack, 23, 338–339
Odd lots, 59
Oddball bills, 83
Odd-lot risk, 136–137
Off-the-run issues, 87
Off-the-run maturities, 13
Off-the-run Treasuries, 60–61, 209
O'Neil, William, 127
On-the-run issues, 87
On-the-run Treasuries, 60–61, 314
Open interest, 277, 278, 279*t*
Open market operations, 143–146, 149
Opportunistic issuance, 47
Opportunity costs:
  compensation for, 197
  of investing in bonds, 203–204
  and reinvestment risk, 115
Option-adjusted spread (OAS), 78
Options contracts, 131
  (*See also specific types of options*)
Options trading volume, 279–280
Output gap, 375

Panic of 1837, 324, 325
Par value, 68, 72–73, 83
Participation certificate (mortgage pass-
  through securities), 102
Pass-through securities, 102
Pay-as-you-go budget system, 206
PCE (personal consumption expenditures),
  375
PCE (personal consumption expenditures)
  report, 389–391
PDCF (Primary Dealer Credit Facility), 170
P/E (price-to-earnings) ratio, 197
Personal consumption expenditures (PCE),
  375
Personal consumption expenditures (PCE)
  report, 389–391
Personal income (PI) report, 389–391
Philadelphia Survey, 391–392
PI (personal income) report, 389–391
Plain vanilla collateralized mortgage
  obligations, 103
Policy anticipation hypothesis, 180

Politics, 323–339
    1980 election campaign, 329–333
    and bond market, 21, 23–24
    G. H. W. Bush administration, 333–335
    G. W. Bush administration, 337–338
    Clinton administration, 335–337
    and Federal Reserve, 23
    Ford administration, 327–328
    and Great Depression, 325–327
    history of economic factors in, 323–325
    international, 125–127
    Obama administration, 338–339
Portfolio managers:
    and aggregate duration surveys, 264–267,
        265f
    and duration, 74, 77, 78, 195
    fixed-income, 116
    and interest rate forecasting, 239, 240
    and maturity of portfolios, 41
    of mortgage-backed portfolios, 238
    use of interest rate futures by, 289, 290
    and yield curve risk, 133
Portfolio shifts, 195
Portfolios:
    diversification of, 15, 16f
    and duration, 77–78, 290
    equity, 9
    mortgage, 238
    and systemic risk, 119
Positive carry, 268
Positively sloped yield curve, 175–177
PPI (producer price index), 392–394
Premium bonds, 314
Prepayment, 238
Prepayment risk, 78, 103–104
Present value, 72
Price transparency, 59–60
Price value of a basis point (PVBP), 73–74
Price volatility, 117, 185
Price-to-earnings (P/E) ratio, 197
Primary Dealer Credit Facility (PDCF),
    170
Primary dealers:
    aggregate duration surveys by, 267
    in bond market, 30–33, 33f
    and concessions, 240
    defined, 30
Primary deficit, 243
Private construction, 356
Private sector, 242
Private-label mortgages, 54, 55f, 102
Producer price index (PPI), 392–394
Productivity growth, 230

Productivity report, 394–396
Prospectus, 67
Public construction, 356
Public sector, 36, 189
Purchasing power risk, 295
Pure expectations theory, 222
Put options:
    implied volatility on, 283
    put/call ratio, 257–261, 260f, 280
Put provision, 70
Put/call ratio:
    and options trading volume, 280
    recent behavior of, 260f
    for tracking market sentiment, 257–261
Puttable bonds, 77
PVBP (price value of a basis point), 73–74

Quote depth (*see* Market depth)

Rating announcements, 305–306
Reagan, Ronald, 21, 23, 235, 329–333
Reaganomics, 330
Real estate bubble, 7
Real estate mortgage investment conduit
    (REMIC), 103
Real interest rates:
    defined, 224
    gauging inflation expectations with,
        226–228, 227f
    influence of Federal Reserve on, 156–158
    negative, 210–212
Real yield(s), 197–213
    and currency perfomance, 207
    defined, 197, 224
    and economy's growth rate, 204–206
    and Federal Reserve, 207–208
    historical perspective on, 198–202
    and inflation expectations, 202–203
    and liquidity, 208–209
    and negative real interest rates, 210–212
    and opportunity costs of investing,
        203–204
    risks with forecasting based on, 209–210
    on Treasuries, 90, 272
    and U.S. budget, 206–207
Recession:
    and politics, 327, 333, 338
    and yield curve, 177–179, 179f, 182, 183,
        183t
Recovery rate, 97, 97t, 319, 320
Refinancing booms, 239
Refunded bonds, 45
Regularization (Treasury issuance), 82

Reinvesting, 69
Reinvestment risk, 114–116
  with call feature, 129
  with collateralized mortgage obligations, 103
  defined, 68–69, 114
  with mortgage portfolios, 238
Relative strength index (RSI), 249
REMIC (real estate mortgage investment conduit), 103
Reserve assets, 125, 125*f*
Reserves, 146
Residential mortgage-backed securities (RMBS), 294
Resolution Funding Corporation, 99
Resolution Trust Company, 334
Retail sales report, 396–398
Retail-control method, 390
Retirees, 229–230
Revenue, 93
Revenue bonds, 107
Ried Thunberg, 265, 267–268
Right to call, 98
Risk(s), 111–138
  basis, 290
  call, 68–69, 128–130
  counterparty, 269, 270, 288, 289*f*
  country, 315
  credit (*see* Credit risk)
  and credit ratings, 295–296, 305
  currency, 17, 134–135, 315–316
  default (*see* Credit risk)
  effects of, 112
  equity, 15, 111
  event, 116–127
  and financial crises, 111
  with forecasting based on real yields, 209–210
  hedge, 135, 136
  inflation, 133–134
  liquidity, 17, 130–131
  market, 113–114, 223, 295
  odd-lot, 136–137
  prepayment, 78, 103–104
  purchasing power, 295
  reinvestment (*see* Reinvestment risk)
  sector, 127–128
  sovereign, 24
  systemic, 117–122, 140
  and transparency, 60
  yield curve, 133
Risk assets, 24
Risk aversion, 209

Risk diversification:
  asset diversification vs., 15–17, 16*f,* 96, 111
  and bond market opportunities, 3
  and equity risks, 15
  strategies for, 319–320
  and systemic risk, 118
Risk premium, 180
RMBS (residential mortgage-backed securities), 294
Roll down, 220
Roosevelt, Franklin D., 28, 326
Round lots, 59
RSI (relative strength index), 249
Rubin, Robert, 335
Russian financial crisis, 130

Salaries, 368–370
Sales, 93
Sallie Mae (Student Loan Marketing Association), 99
Saving rates, 6*f,* 10, 157
Savings, 157
Savings bonds, 28
SDR (special drawing right), 125
SEC (*see* Securities and Exchange Commission)
Sector risk, 127–128
Secular trends, 232–236, 233*f,* 240, 256
Securities, 36–39
  (*See also specific types of securities*)
Securities and Exchange Commission (SEC), 31, 32, 48, 294, 297
Securities Industry and Financial Markets Association (SIFMA), 45, 54, 108
Securitization, 11
Segments (bond market), 36, 37*t,* 81
September 11 terrorist attacks, 14–15, 125–127
Sequential pay collateralized mortgage obligations, 103
Service sector, 343, 384–385
Sherlund, Shane, 11
Short-term financing, 47
Short-term interest rates:
  and Federal Reserve, 17, 156*f,* 176, 177
  lowering of, 146
  and yield curve, 181, 185
Short-term maturities:
  defined, 66
  effects of fiscal policy on, 190
  preference for, 192
  reinvestment risk with, 114
SIFMA (*see* Securities Industry and Financial Markets Association)

Single-price auctions, 86
Six-month bills, 83
60/40 stocks and bonds split, 118
Social Security program, 39–40
Soft duration, 133
Solvency, 56
SOMA (System Open Market Account), 147
Sovereign debt, 315
Sovereign risk, 24
Special assessment bonds, 107
Special drawing right (SDR), 125
Specialization, 29–30
Speculating, 290
Speculative trading activity, 158
Speculative-grade bonds:
    default rates for, 131, 132*f*, 303*f*
    and diversification, 126, 126*f*
Spending levels, 1
Spread duration, 78
Spread products, 160–161
Stagflation, 329
Standard & Poor's, 10, 96, 165, 182, 296, 297, 308, 308*f*
Standard of living, 20, 27–28
State budgets, 105
Statisticians, 348–349
Steep, 176
    (*See also* Positively sloped yield curve)
Stock investors, 181
Stock market, 9–15
    bond market vs., 34
    and financial crises, 13–14
    and market sentiment, 254
Stock market crash (1987), 123
Stock prices, 152
Stone & McCarthy Research Associates, 265, 267
Stop-out yield, 87
Student Loan Marketing Association (Sallie Mae), 99
Subprime loans, 12
Suffolk Bank, 324
Supply, 240–242
Survey methodologies, 348–349
Swap spreads, 136, 318
Swaps market, 42, 318
Swaptions, 280
System Open Market Account (SOMA), 147
Systemic risk, 117–122, 140

TAF (Term Auction Facility), 172
Tail, 87, 251
Tail events, 76, 319
Takeover risk, 122–123

TALF (Term Asset-Backed Securities Loan Facility), 171
Tax cuts, 332
Tax Reform Act of 1986, 105
Taxable equivalent yield, 105–106
Tax-credit Build America Bonds, 107–108
Taxes:
    and economic growth, 235–236
    federal, 105
    limited-tax general obligation bonds, 107
    and municipal bonds, 43, 105, 106
Tax-exempt yield, 106
Tax-liability management, 318–319
Taylor rule, 211
T-bills (*see* Treasury bills)
T-bonds (*see* Treasury bonds)
Teaser rates, 6
Technical analysis, 245–249
    benchmark yield levels in, 246–247
    Fibonacci analysis, 247–248
    and market fundamentals, 236
    moving averages in, 247
    previous highs and lows in, 248–249
    relative strength index in, 249
Technical factors (interest rate forecasting), 236–249
Technology:
    and bond market growth, 34
    and Internet, 30, 345
    and productivity growth, 230
Technology stocks, 151
10-year Treasury bonds, 85
Term Asset-Backed Securities Loan Facility (TALF), 171
Term Auction Facility (TAF), 172
Term premium, 90, 185, 200, 269
Term premium on rates, 180
Term Securities Lending Facility (TSLF), 171
Theta, 290, 316
30-year Treasury bonds, 85, 87
Three-month bills, 83
Tier I capital, 32
Tier II capital, 32
TIPS (*see* Treasury inflation-protected securities)
T-notes (*see* Treasury notes)
Top-down investing:
    with corporate bonds, 93
    and economic data, 347–348
TRACE (*see* Trade Reporting and Compliance Engine)
Trade barriers, 34–35

Trade report, 398–399
Trade Reporting and Compliance Engine
    (TRACE), 48, 58, 60, 279
Tranches, 103
Transmission effects, 150–155
Transparency:
    in corporate bond market, 48
    price, 59–60
Transportation, 364
Treasury bills (T-bills):
    defined, 66
    issuance of, 83–84
    and yield curve, 175, 178, 182
    yield spread between T-notes and, 193f
Treasury bonds (T-bonds):
    call features on, 129
    and futures market, 284
    and mortgages, 3, 4f
    put/call ratio on, 258
    real yield on, 199–200, 200f
    and yield curve, 176, 182
Treasury contracts, 276
Treasury Direct, 84, 137
Treasury inflation-protected securities
    (TIPS), 72, 88–91
    gauging inflation expectations with,
        225–226, 227f
    and inflation risk, 134
    ownership of, 320
    real yield on, 200
    tracking inflation expectations with, 210
Treasury notes (T-notes):
    creditworthiness of, 184
    federal funds rate vs., 217
    and futures market, 284
    real yield on, 199–200, 200f
    and yield curve, 176
    yield spread between federal funds rate
        and, 267–269
    yield spread between T-bills and, 193f
Treasury securities (see U.S. Treasuries)
Treasury yield curve, 183, 184, 191
Trust funds, 39
TSLF (Term Securities Lending Facility),
    171
Tulip mania, 252–253
2-year Treasury notes, 267–269

Unemployment, 327, 328, 330, 331, 366, 367,
    382–384
University of Michigan, 361, 362–364
Urban sprawl, 44
U.S. bond markets, 21, 22t

U.S. budget:
    deficit in, 82, 83f, 84, 180, 332, 333
    and real yields, 206–207
U.S. Bureau of Economic Analysis (BEA),
    374, 375, 390, 395, 398
U.S. Bureau of Labor Statistics (BLS), 360,
    365, 368, 392–395
U.S. Bureau of the Public Debt, 84
U.S. Census Bureau:
    business inventories report, 349
    construction spending report, 354–356
    data on productivity, 395
    durable goods orders report, 363, 364
    factory orders report, 372, 373
    housing starts report, 377–378
    new home sales report, 387, 388
    personal income and consumption reports,
        389
    retail sales report, 396, 397
    trade balance report, 398
U.S. Commodity Futures Trading Commis-
    sion, 261, 278, 280–281
U.S. Department of Commerce, 396–398
U.S. Department of Labor, 300, 382, 383
U.S. dollar:
    exchange value of, 152–153
    trade-weighed value of, 135f
    as world's reserve currency, 243
    and yield curve, 191–192
U.S. Federal Reserve Bank, 31
U.S. government, 24–25, 65, 242
U.S. government agency securities (see Gov-
    ernment agency securities)
U.S. trade balance report, 398–399
U.S. Treasuries:
    auctions of, 282
    in bond market, 35, 39–42
    and callable bonds, 69
    coupon securities, 84–87
    credit risk with, 132
    and default risk, 296
    discount securities, 83–84
    federal funds rate vs., 148f
    and financial crisis of 1998, 60
    and hedge risk, 136
    historical perspective on, 198–202, 200f
    issuance credo for, 82–83
    and market liquidity, 208
    ownership of, 314
    performance of spread products vs., 160–161
    and primary dealers, 32
    real yield on, 272
    and risk diversification, 319

U.S. Treasuries (*Continued*):
    and supply, 240–241
    and systemic risk, 117, 121, 121*f*
    Treasury yield curve, 183, 184
    and value of U.S. dollar, 191
    yield spread between corporate bonds and,
        271–272
    yield spread between speculative-grade
        bonds and, 126, 127
    (*See also specific types, e.g.:* Treasury bills)
U.S. Treasury:
    debt of, 40, 41, 41*f*, 84, 85*f*
    and primary dealers, 32
    and setting interest rates, 3
    and U.S. government, 24
    and yield curve, 194–195
Utility costs, 361

Van Buren, Martin, 324, 325
Victory bonds, 28
Vietnam War, 326
Volatility:
    determination of, 74, 75
    and duration, 77
    and economic data, 349, 356, 364, 379, 381
    expectations of, 282–284
    interest rate, 169
    and market sentiment, 286
    price, 117, 185
    and real yields, 208–209
    reduction of, 344
Volatility risks, 17, 111
Volume:
    in corporate bonds, 45, 47–48
    futures trading, 278, 279
    government agency securities, 51, 52*t*–53*t*
    in mortgage-backed securities, 54, 55
    in municipal bonds, 44–45
    options trading, 279–280
    in Treasury securities, 41–42, 42*f*

Wages, 368–370
War bonds, 28
Web sites:
    for bond calculations, 72
    of futures exchanges, 284
    trade association, 345
Weekly jobless claims report, 382–384
Wilson, Woodrow, 140
World War II, 28

Year bills, 83
Yield(s):
    and auctions, 87
    and credit ratings, 303–305
    current, 70
    and duration, 77
    taxable equivalent, 105–106
    on U.S. Treasuries, 220, 221*f*
    (*See also specific headings*)
Yield curve, 175–196
    advantages of following, 178–180
    bets on, 316–317
    and competition for capital, 194
    and credit quality, 192–194
    and economic growth, 188–189
    explanations for shape of, 184–185
    Federal Reserve's influence on,
        158–159
    and financial crises, 14
    fiscal policy as factor in, 189–190
    and flight to quality, 192, 193
    and inflation expectations, 190–191
    inversion of, 180–183
    monetary policy as factor in, 186–188,
        207
    negatively sloped, 177–178
    and policy anticipation hypothesis, 180
    and portfolio shifts, 195
    positively sloped, 175–177
    reliability of, 175, 183, 184
    and risk premium information, 180
    studies on usefulness of, 178, 179
    and Treasury bonds, 87
    Treasury supply as factor in, 194–195
    U.S. Dollar's influence on, 191–192
Yield curve risk, 133
Yield enhancement, 290, 316
Yield spreads:
    with corporate bond issuance, 47
    between corporate bonds, 136
    real GDP growth vs., 182*f*
    of short- and long-term maturities, 176
    between speculative-grade bonds and U.S.
        Treasuries, 126, 127
    for tracking market sentiment, 267–272
    U.S. Treasury, 121*f*
Yield-to-call, 69–70
Yield-to-maturity:
    defined, 71–72
    effect of credit ratings on, 303
    on TIPS, 89, 91
Yield-to-worst, 69–70

Zero-bound problem, 211
Zero coupon bonds:
    duration on, 76
    ownership of, 318
    reinvestment risk with, 115
Zero interest rates, 211

ABOUT THE AUTHOR

Anthony Crescenzi is senior vice president, market strategist, and portfolio manager for PIMCO in its Newport Beach, California, office. Prior to joining PIMCO in 2009, he was chief bond market strategist at Miller Tabak, where he worked for 23 years. Crescenzi has written three other books, including a 1,200-page revision of Marcia Stigum's classic, *The Money Market*, and *Investing from the Top Down*, published in 2008. He taught in the executive MBA program at Baruch College from 1999 to 2009. Crescenzi frequently appears on business and finance television stations, including CNBC and Bloomberg, and he is frequently quoted in the news media. He has 27 years of investment experience and holds an MBA from St. John's University and an undergraduate degree from the City University of New York.